*critical essays in modern literature*

# Entrances to Dylan Thomas' Poetry

## BY RALPH MAUD

# CRITICAL ESSAYS IN MODERN LITERATURE

OTHER CRITICAL ESSAYS

*William Faulkner: An Estimate of His Contribution
to the Modern American Novel*
by MARY COOPER ROBB........................ **$1.80**

*The Fiction and Criticism of Katherine Anne Porter
(Revised)*
by HARRY JOHN MOONEY, JR. ................... **$1.85**

*The Fiction of J. D. Salinger*
by FREDERICK L. GWYNN and JOSEPH L. BLOTNER **$1.50**

*Henry Miller: Expatriate*
by ANNETTE KAR BAXTER....................... **$2.50**

*The Fiction of John O'Hara*
by E. RUSSELL CARSON......................... **$1.25**

*James Gould Cozzens: Novelist of Intellect*
by HARRY JOHN MOONEY, JR. ................... **$2.00**

*The Hero in Hemingway's Short Stories*
by JOSEPH DeFALCO........................... **$2.00**

*Entrances to Dylan Thomas' Poetry*
by RALPH MAUD............................... **$2.00**

*The Short Stories of Ambrose Bierce: A Study in Polarity*
by STUART C. WOODRUFF ...................... **$2.25**

*Joyce Cary: The Comedy of Freedom*
by CHARLES G. HOFFMANN ................... **$2.25**

# ENTRANCES TO DYLAN THOMAS' POETRY

# ENTRANCES
## TO
### DYLAN THOMAS'
## POETRY

By RALPH MAUD

University of Pittsburgh Press

Copyright© 1963 by University of Pittsburgh Press
Library of Congress Catalog Card Number: 63:13490

*Second Printing 1966*

Manufactured in the United States of America

# Acknowledgment

PARTS OF THIS BOOK have appeared in different form in *Essays in Criticism*, *Audience*, *The Explicator*, *Explorations*, *Modern Language Notes*, *Western Humanities Review*, *English Studies*, *PMLA*, and *Poesia e Critica*.

I am indebted to the Estate of Dylan Thomas and David Higham Associates Ltd. for permission to quote from Dylan Thomas' writings; to J. M. Dent and Sons, and to New Directions, for permission to use copyrighted poems; to the late Charles D. Abbott of the Lockwood Library and to Oscar A. Silverman, Director of Libraries, State University of New York at Buffalo, for permission to use and quote from Dylan Thomas' notebooks; to Oscar Williams and to William A. Jackson for like permission with respect to holdings in the Houghton Library of Harvard University; to Professor Harry Levin and to Professor Reuben Brower, for their interest over a long period; to the American Council of Learned Societies for a Grant-in-Aid, and to the Committee on Allocation of Research Funds, State University of New York at Buffalo, for several awards; for specific help in research to Ralph Abercrombie,

Julian Abercrombie, Luigi Berti, John Malcolm Brinnin, Edith Capon, Eric Capon, A. C. Cawley, Douglas Cleverdon, J. Howell Daniels, John Davenport, Aneirin Talfan Davies, John Selwyn Davies, Pennar Davies, W. Emlyn Davies, S. W. Dawson, Bonamy Dobrée, William Empson, Meredydd Evans, Doris Fulleylove, Randolph Fulleylove, William Griffiths, Geoffrey Grigson, T. E. Hanley, Rayner Heppenstall, Trevor Hughes, Richard Hughes, Edmund Ions, M. E. James, Alfred Janes, Glyn Jones, Mervyn Levy, Robert MacGregor, Richard Ohmann, Cecil Price, Keidrych Rhys, John Rolph, Ethel Ross, Roberto Sanesi, Pamela Snow, Thomas Taig, Wynford Vaughan Thomas, A. E. Trick, Donald Tritschler, Vernon Watkins, Shirley Whyte, Oscar Williams, Ralph Wishart; and to S. B. and M. P. Jones, first parents of this book.

Ralph Maud
Buffalo, New York

# Contents

ACKNOWLEDGMENT                                      VII

I. Introduction ........................   *1*

II. Explications and Explanations ..........  *17*

III. Process Poems ........................  *57*

IV. Distancing the Intimate ...............  *81*

V. Last Poems ........................... *103*

Abbreviations ........................ *119*

*Appendix*

I. Chronology of Composition ........... *121*

II. Textual Cruxes ..................... *149*

NOTES ..................................... *157*

INDEX OF THOMAS' POEMS ................... *173*

# Chapter 1

# *Introduction*

*"The wisest of the Ancients consider'd what is not too Explicit as the fittest for Instruction, because it rouzes the faculties to act."*

William Blake to the
Rev. Dr. Trusler (1799)

THERE IS A PHOTOGRAPH OF DYLAN THOMAS in his Chelsea flat in 1945, his thirtieth year and the poems of *Deaths and Entrances* behind him. The photographer caught him in a brooding mood, his coat and waistcoat unbuttoned, his left hand deep in his coat pocket.[1] He is set amidst the icons of his life. The glass in his hand is almost empty; a quart Guinness bottle stands on the table. Caitlin Thomas is there. In the background are a couple of hundred books in bookshelves (one can make out Whitman and Coleridge in the Nonesuch editions). And pinned to the wall are cuttings of landscapes — Welsh landscapes, who can doubt it? Looking at this scene now, through glass darkened by almost twenty years, we see a surrealist picture, certain of these symbols grotesquely swollen. The beer bottle, which the young hero of *Adventures in the Skin Trade* stuck on his finger, is now huge out of all proportion. Caitlin Thomas has made her own large gesture in *Leftover Life to Kill*, proving that Dylan was worth ten other men. (One has to endure the disappointment of finding in

1

Thomas' own work no divan or bedroom scene: sex is always too close to birth and death to be salacious.) As for the Welsh landscapes, we can safely say that Thomas had never the Welshness in life that has been granted him in death. These three symbols — Drink, Sex, and Wales — are magnified now to the extent that Thomas is disappearing behind them. The Welsh furor of mourning, for instance, has permanently alienated several younger critics in England. But Dylan Thomas was not a "Welsh bard"; he was an English poet. And most of his poetry was written when the three icons were not monstrous, when they comfortably had their place, as in the reassuring Chelsea photograph.

Thomas' bookshelves are still to be mentioned. Unlike the other icons, the poet's books had no part in his fatal celebrity. No one has suggested that he read himself to death. But he did read, and must have read rapidly in early youth to achieve his precocious vocabulary. The opportunity was there in his father's study. In a radio interview the poet's mother has explained how embarrassing it was to his father, the Senior English teacher at the school, that young Dylan was brilliant in English but inattentive in every other class. By the age of ten he had decided to become a poet. Answering some questions in 1951, Thomas recalled what first led him to "love language and want to work *in* it and *for* it": "nursery rhymes and folk tales, the Scottish Ballads, a few lines of hymns, the most famous Bible stories and the rhythms of the Bible, Blake's Songs of Innocence, and the quite incomprehensible magical majesty and nonsense of Shakespeare heard, read, and near-murdered in the first forms of my school."[2] His reading immediately patterned his apprentice efforts; and he imitated (according to his own listing) Sir Thomas Browne, de Quincey, Henry Newbolt, the Ballads, Blake, Baroness Orczy, Marlowe, Chums, the Imagists, the Bible, Poe, Keats, Lawrence, Anon., and Shakespeare.[3] His friend Daniel Jones remembers Yeats, Richard Aldington, Sacheverell Sitwell, D. H. Lawrence, and Hopkins as active influences on Thomas' early development.[4] When Thomas arrived in London in 1934 and met Geoffrey Grigson, he publicly "preferred" Rosetti, Francis Thompson, James Thomson (B.V.), and Stephen Spender.[5] At twenty-one he reviewed with great aplomb the new two-volume John Clare for the *Adelphi*.[6] In the three years after the war Thomas did about a hundred broadcasts, mainly readings of, and talks on, other writers. This work culminated in the flawless public reading performances of a wide variety of poetry.[7]

T. S. Eliot (with his notes to *The Waste Land*) and Yeats (with *A Vision*) have made clear how much of their poetry was written within reach of their books. Thomas has not; and this default tempts us to picture him writing, for example, the *Ballad of the Long-legged Bait* with Rimbaud's *Bateau ivre* in one hand and Donne's *The Baite* in the other. Thomas, however, has made a few facts clear: "I do wish I had learned some other languages apart from English, BBC Third Programme, and saloon. Then perhaps I could understand what some people mean when they say I have been influenced by Rimbaud."[8] And it seems rather odd to think of Donne's short love poem — or any poem, for that matter — as a source for a *Ballad* whose composition took over a hundred arduously worked sheets of paper.[9] If Thomas was really depending on Rimbaud or Donne for any aspect of form or content, he certainly made a very convincing show of the opposite. Again, *On the Marriage of a Virgin* has been said to echo Marvell's *The Gallery* on the ground that a series of images, "dawn," "thighs," "dove," etc., have the same order of appearance in both poems.[10] However, for this poem too we have Thomas' draft, which shows no such given patterning. Finally, the suggestion that *We lying by seasand* has a source in Rilke's Second Duino Elegy[11] fails, if for no other reason, because the poem is dated 1933 and Thomas had not read much Rilke until 1941.[12]

The question of specific sources is worth taking up because the negative answer supports what we instinctively feel about Thomas' poems: that they are new and unique, that no one ever wrote poems like these before, and that readers of Thomas have to begin without preconceptions. How convenient it would be if what we learned in reading Hopkins, the favorite candidate for general influence on the poet, could really be applied to Thomas. But the similarity between Hopkins and Thomas is only superficial. When Hopkins writes "Miracle-in-Mary-of-flame" he has dislocated normal English usage for special effects of both alliteration and meaning. When Thomas writes "Christ-cross-row of death," Hopkensian though it may seem, our reaction must be geared to entirely new principles. There is no dislocation of syntax here, no deliberate straining for effects of sound. Anyone interested in the antiquity of Thomas' compound noun should refer to the Oxford English Dictionary; it is as old, and as simple, as ABC.[13]

Again, how convenient if the key to Thomas were in Welsh poetry. But Welsh poetry is more difficult to write than to read, and Thomas had no incentive to do either. Those who would like to have Thomas be a "bard" and yet acknowledge that he did not know or study Welsh see Hopkins as the germ-carrier.[14] But a poet cannot be smickled with Welsh by casual contact; the restrictive Welsh forms by their very nature require labored, self-conscious application. Hopkins wrote a couple of poems in Welsh and comes as close as anyone to utilizing *cynghanedd* in English; but if there are one or two lines in Thomas that fit the Welsh patterns it is purely accidental.[15] The particular hoops that Thomas set himself to jump through were quite different.

There must be hoops of a kind. A poet sometimes besets himself with the most excessive obstacles to producing a poem, instinctively knowing that the energy generated in overcoming them vitalizes the final result. Count the number of syllables per line in the seven stanzas of *Poem in October* and one set of Thomas' hoops becomes apparent:

| | | | | | | | | | |
|---|---|---|---|---|---|---|---|---|---|
| 1. | 9 | 12 | 9 | 3 | 5 | 12 | 12 | 5 | 3 | 9 |
| 2. | 9 | 12 | 9 | 3 | 5 | 12 | 12 | 5 | 3 | 9 |
| 3. | 9 | 12 | 9 | 3 | 5 | 12 | 12 | 5 | 3 | 9 |
| 4. | 9 | 12 | 9 | 3 | 5 | 12 | 12 | 5 | 3 | 9 |
| 5. | 9 | 12 | 9 | 3 | 5 | 12 | 12 | 5 | 3 | 9 |
| 6. | 9 | 12 | 9 | 3 | 5 | 13 | 12 | 5 | 3 | 9 |
| 7. | 9 | 12 | 9 | 3 | 5 | 12 | 12 | 5 | 3 | 9 |

If this regularity should strike anyone as fortuitous,

he may refer to Daniel Jones on Thomas' concern for syllable counting[16] and to the poet's work sheets for *Over Sir John's hill*, where syllable totals are put against the lines in a few of the trials with, in one place, an urgent note to his muse: "3 more syllables."[17] Actually, as Thomas approached the end of his work on *Over Sir John's hill* and felt the rightness of certain lines that unfortunately had the wrong number of syllables, it was the syllabic pattern that suffered. The final poem is not absolutely regular, but one would hardly call it unfinished.[18] The inexplicable thirteen syllable line in the sixth stanza of *Poem in October* is another case in point. The self-imposed discipline is strange, the truancy from it stranger; yet both are understandable. A poet has to lever himself into action, knowing the terribly hard work it is to fill a page with original and important utterance. Thomas put the problem well, with customary understatement:

> Sometimes it feels very good to have a blank piece of paper in front of you, and you put down the first line. Then you look at all the paper and think, Now I've got to rhyme this. And it's work. Oh God, it's awful![19]

The intricate syllable and rhyme schemes are tricks the poet uses on himself in order to get the next line written.

But the situation is not adequately described as donkey following carrot, for Thomas was a beast of burden with somewhere to go each time he set out. The carrot, the incidental reward in meeting strict verse forms, is only used in the face of a momentary paralysis at having too much to say, of knowing full well what agony the journey to the final poem involves. The main hurdle Thomas puts before himself is his devotion to a personal and perhaps fleeting truth and to finding the image that can express the truth so that it stays true for the duration of the poem. Thomas' truths are such that it is sheer flippancy to list them as birth, copulation, and death. It is best to approach them as closely as we can in the poems themselves, where we as readers can, as much as possible, find them true.

In any case, Thomas' bookshelves, along with the other icons in the photograph, have to be placed well into the background. Thomas obviously had access to a good dictionary from an early age (or perhaps words like *parhelion* and *hyleg* were commonplace in Swansea Grammar School in 1931?). But his reading was probably very haphazard, done — if according to his own prescription — while hanging by his ears from the chandeliers.[20] Though the reading is not to be slighted on that account, it is of little use in illuminating any particular poem. With Thomas there is no prerequisite reading list. Thomas' obscurity is not aristocratic; it can be tackled with general knowledge and a good dictionary, tools democratic enough.

[2]

Since his poems have this kind of availability, it is surprising that Thomas' reputation should rest on so few poems that are well understood. His *Collected*

*Poems* moves rather like an iceberg; nine-tenths of
its power and weight is under the surface, sensed by
us but not clearly visible. In this situation our main
concern will be the precise nature of Thomas' obscurity — or, to put it a better way, the precise nature
of our difficulty with Thomas' poetic idiom, for
Thomas will undoubtedly become easier to read and
understand as time goes on.

Most poets are aware of the pitfalls of their particular mode of communication, the danger of purely
personal imagery; and they recognize that in the final
analysis the words must be objectively meaningful.
They may postulate for themselves a most persistent
and ingenious reader, but they know they must treat
him right. They cannot pretend that he will follow
their secret thoughts. They must in the long run
make their intention plain in one way or another.
Granted that Dylan Thomas writes about common
things in a most uncommon way, he always (or
almost always) gives the necessary clues to the
reader. The extraordinary is subject to ordinary interpretation.

Let us take a look at one of his favorite techniques. Thomas' instinct to create an original vision
from the everyday event leads him to use clichés
and common phrases, just altered to the extent that
we have to think them out afresh, but within the
aura of their familiarity. He brings to the front of
the mind what was always at the back of it. One
main source of difficulty in Thomas is the ingenuity
of this kind of dislocation. For instance, in the following passage, the opening of *A Child's Christmas*

*in Wales*, Thomas plays very innocently, as befits a children's story, on the common phrases "around the corner" and "out of sound." The epithet "two-tongued sea" later in the paragraph is deceptively simple, however, and worth looking into:

> One Christmas was so much like another, in those years around the sea-town corner now and out of all sound except the distant speaking voices I sometimes hear a moment before sleep, that I can never remember whether it snowed for six days and six nights when I was twelve or whether it snowed for twelve days and twelve nights when I was six. All the Christmases roll down toward the two-tongued sea, like a cold and head-long moon bundling down the sky that was our street; and they stop at the rim of the ice-edged, fish-freezing waves, and I plunge my hands in the snow and bring out whatever I can find. In goes my hand into that wool-white bell - tongued ball of holidays resting at the rim of the carol-singing sea, and out comes Mrs. Prothero and the firemen.[21]

End of paragraph. What the poet is saying is familiar enough: he dips into his rather jumbled memories of Christmases he has known as a child, and one particular incident occurs to him. But, even in this prose piece, Thomas' strange imagination is at work, and he pictures his memories as a cumulative snowball rolling to the edge of the sea of oblivion. His act of recalling the past is like putting his hand (literally dipping) into that snowball, "that wool-white bell-

tongued ball of holidays." "Wool-white" is easy. The
ball is "bell-tongued" and "of holidays" because the
memories are all associated with holidays from school
and Christmas bells. Bells, of course, have tongues,
literally, and metaphorically since they call out to us.
Seas, however, have tongues only in imagination, and
there is certainly no imaginable reason for the sea's
mouth to have more than one tongue in order to
receive the rolling snowball. Yet there is an easeful-
ness about the phrase "two-tongued"; and if one
substitutes "two-faced" one recognizes the familiar
ring. The "distant speaking voices" heard just before
sleep come out of the sea of forgetfulness *defectively*
— it's as though the sea were deceiving him. He can't
recall whether it snowed six days and nights when
he was twelve or twelve days and nights when he
was six. The confusing voices give him two versions;
the sea has thus two tongues. "Two-tongued," we
conclude, is simply a summary phrase for his humor-
ously defective memory. The logic of the image is
both naive and circuitous, extraordinary in effect but
of quite ordinary ingredients. Image is connected to
image by perverse logic, uninhibited leaps of childlike cunning involving word-plays. For instance,
when the sea is mentioned again toward the end of
the paragraph, it is the "carol-singing" sea. Having
tongues, it can obviously sing. But the idea of deceit
has been dropped; there is no deep connection between the two ways of describing the sea. In the
poetry, images are often connected in an equally
spurious and fanciful manner, but a deeper connection is found in the underlying, serious themes shared
by the several disparate images.

We have tried to be precise about Thomas' "two-tongued sea." Can the image be pinned down in this way? Isn't there room for doubt? Of course, there always is room; but reasonable certainty is a legitimate goal. Obscurity does not necessarily imply ambiguity. Unless Thomas was as two-faced as his sea, he had some definite idea in mind when he wrote the image, and was not interested in giving scope for loose guess-work. Consider a possible alternative: a serpent traditionally has two tongues and is a symbol of deceit. The objections to seeing the serpent in the image are, first, the general rule in explication (as in scientific common sense) that the simpler explanation for any phenomenon, other things being equal, must be correct; and, second, the equally basic rule that nothing can be said to exist unless its presence makes a difference to the environment. Had Thomas really meant us to see this intermediary symbolic presence he would have been bound to use the serpent again in context. He doesn't do so. Thus there is no reason to see the serpent there at all. A word or phrase may have two or more meanings, but only those definite meanings that work successfully in context.

Such principles are more easily stated than applied. The two-tongued sea-serpent doesn't work; but there is a more nagging possibility to consider. In the earlier version, "Memories of Christmas" (1945), the sentence in question read:

> All the Christmases roll down the hill toward the Welsh-speaking sea. . . .

"Welsh-speaking" is an incidental adjective, informing us that the setting is Wales. One should note that, in this early version, the sentence is in a new paragraph, a dozen lines away from "the speaking of the voices." Revision (for *Harper's Bazaar* 1950) cut out the intervening lines, and the adjective "Welsh - speaking" must have become unbearably gratuitous (it was gratuitous in the first place). Thomas had used "the bilingual sea" in "Quite Early One Morning" (1945), so that "two-tongued" was a product of a natural piece of wordplay.

With this Anglo-Welsh sea around, were we too hasty in seeing "two-tongued" as describing the two messages of the sea voices? The answer, I think, must be no. The slightly self-mocking notion of defective memory is well summed up in "two-tongued." Our first interpretation is very effective — the "bilingual" interpretation less so. We should not deny Thomas credit for the best legitimate meaning we can find. Is the idea of "Welsh-speaking" retained in the image at all now? The answer here is difficult. One might wish to say no; but, once thought of (and, quite possibly, thought of without the textual variants), this meaning is impossible to shake off altogether. I rather think that the words "two-tongued" recommended themselves to Thomas because in the new and worthier conceit he could still be reminded of his former thought.

This sort of poetic licence suits some readers better than others. One has good reason to be wary; unlimited "extra" meanings become available as targets once licence is given to shoot at random. I am sure it was not the poet's intention to give such licence. In each case we should try our best to obey the poet's precise intention.[22] The idea of a "Welsh-speaking" sea is not *necessary* in the final phrasing of the passage above; it is *permissible*, I think, as an extra meaning subsidiary to the meaning that does the main work in context. The validity of secondary meanings is the stickiest of all questions in Dylan Thomas studies. In the final analysis, whether or not a meaning works successfully in context is a matter of opinion; but one trusts that common sense *is* common, and that agreement on such points can generally be reached.

Again, this implies that Thomas has as much regard for common sense as his readers. A plea for trust in Thomas' good faith and ultimate intelligibility is not unwarranted. Anyone who has heard the poet's recordings will know the insistence and reassurance in his voice, perhaps his most compelling weapon against oblivion. But, turning from the recordings to the printed page, the reader might have his confidence in the poet severely shaken when he tries the opening lines of the *Collected Poems*:

> I see the boys of summer in their ruin
> Lay the gold tithings barren,
> Setting no store by harvest, freeze the soils;
> There in their heat the winter floods
> Of frozen loves they fetch their girls,
> And drown the cargoed apples in their tides.

This, and much more of Thomas, is so uncompromising that the recordings take on great importance. Thomas' vitality and seriousness in those performances are his pledge with the reader. After *hearing* Thomas we are much less likely to assume that such lines as the above are merely self-willed and chaotic.

Faith in Thomas' meaningfulness is not, of course, a prerequisite, merely a useful way to begin. The proof of the poetry's coherence is in the finding of it. The greater part of this book is the seeking of that proof. The first lines of Thomas' first volume have been raised as a challenge; one cannot do better than begin there:

I see the boys of summer in their ruin.

Who are the "boys of summer"? If there were a specific answer, if they were fisher princes in the Grail legend or a Swansea boys' club, say, we would have no need to hesitate.[23] But the boys are apparently Thomas' original conception. Their significance is both universal and important; we do not realize the extent of it until we have absorbed all that they do in the poem, which is a great deal by the end. In this first stanza alone, their actions have such variety and range that they are bewildering at first. They "lay gold tithings barren." "Tithings" are sheaves of wheat, ripe and golden. The boys are ruining the harvest, setting no store by it, actively countering it by freezing the soils. The boys bring cold love to their girls; they negate warm affection and prevent the harvest of sexual fulfilment. They drown ripe apples — another expression of the ruin of harvest.

As before with the "two-tongued sea" (i.e. a sea with two tongues), we begin by taking the words as literally as possible. "Gold tithings," for instance, is not merely a code phrase for something else. Wheat sheaves are to be seen as laid down and left barren. Thomas often demands that we take as perceivable what is usually considered non-material. An abstraction such as "loves" becomes part of a winter flood. The "winter floods of frozen loves" is a way of describing affection at its coldest; but it is the nature of Thomas' metaphor that the two strands be distinctly intertwined: the glimpse of ice floes and the notion of coldness in love. Further, in reiterating the phrase "ruin of harvest" in the above discussion, we are discovering a common ground for all these actions; each can be seen as symbolizing in its own way the same single concept. In the end, some abstract term such as "nullification" or "the negative principle" is necessary to summarize the significance of the boys so that no part of their behavior contradicts or stands outside the summary. But even this will not suffice; as we go into parts II and III of the poem we begin to realize that the boys are constructive in their destructiveness. We need a concept that incorporates both growth and decay, because the boys cause both. Biology provides a convenient term in *metabolism*, with its constituent processes, anabolism (building up of cells) and catabolism (breaking down of cells). Thomas is very conscious of the precarious balance that nature sustains every day in the human body and in the cosmos. A notable expression of this balance comes at the end of *Fern Hill:* "Time held me green and dying." In his green growing youth the poet felt the pull of death. The boys of summer personify these two forces; they too are green (part II, l. 14), but in their ruin. *I see the boys of summer* is an all-embracing poem. Thomas chose it to head his first book, *18 Poems;* it retains its pride of place in the *Collected Poems.* The chronology of composition shows that, far from being the earliest of the *18 Poems*, it was written at the height of the poetic fervor that produced the volume. It is, perhaps, first in importance. We shall use it to take the brunt of analysis in Chapter II.

# Chapter II

# Explications and Explanations

> "*Contraries are positives*"
>
> William Blake, title page
> of *Milton*, Book the Second

## I SEE THE BOYS OF SUMMER

### I

I see the boys of summer in their ruin
Lay the gold tithings barren,
Setting no store by harvest, freeze the soils;
There in their heat the winter floods
Of frozen loves they fetch their girls,
And drown the cargoed apples in their tides.

These boys of light are curdlers in their folly,
Sour the boiling honey;
The jacks of frost they finger in the hives;
There in the sun the frigid threads
Of doubt and dark they feed their nerves;
The signal moon is zero in their voids.

I see the summer children in their mothers
Split up the brawned womb's weathers,
Divide the night and day with fairy thumbs;
There in the deep with quartered shades
Of sun and moon they paint their dams
As sunlight paints the shelling of their heads.

17

I see that from these boys shall men of nothing
Stature by seedy shifting,
Or lame the air with leaping from its heats;
There from their hearts the dogdayed pulse
Of love and light bursts in their throats.
O see the pulse of summer in the ice.

## II

But seasons must be challenged or they totter
Into a chiming quarter
Where, punctual as death, we ring the stars;
There, in his night, the black-tongued bells
The sleepy man of winter pulls,
Nor blows back moon-and-midnight as she
    blows.

We are the dark deniers, let us summon
Death from a summer woman,
A muscling life from lovers in their cramp,
From the fair dead who flush the sea
The bright-eyed worm on Davy's lamp,
And from the planted womb the man of straw.

We summer boys in this four-winded spinning,
Green of the seaweeds' iron,
Hold up the noisy sea and drop her birds,
Pick the world's ball of wave and froth
To choke the deserts with her tides,
And comb the county gardens for a wreath.

In spring we cross our foreheads with the holly,
Heigh ho the blood and berry,
And nail the merry squires to the trees;
Here love's damp muscle dries and dies,
Here break a kiss in no love's quarry.
O see the poles of promise in the boys.

III

I see you boys of summer in your ruin.
Man in his maggot's barren.
And boys are full and foreign in the pouch.
I am the man your father was.
We are the sons of flint and pitch.
O see the poles are kissing as they cross.

Any attempt to justify the ways of God to man, even one by so young a poet as Thomas at the time this poem was written, is interesting. What Milton wanted to justify, and what Thomas here faces, is, in its simplest terms, the existence of death. Thomas does not draw on theology. His frame of reference is not the after-life but the present cosmos; and he values death because it makes possible the miraculous renewal of life. We suggested in the last chapter that the boys of summer personify the basic forces of growth and decay seen by Thomas operating everywhere in the universe. We used the term metabolism, a concept that would have been congenial to Thomas. Biology shows that the breaking down process is essential to growth. It is this interdependence between life and death forces that Thomas is portraying in *I see the boys of summer.*

In the Mutability Cantos of the *Faerie Queene* Spenser allows the Goddess Mutability to have her full say before he finally asserts her ravages to be part of a higher order of nature. Thomas follows a similar plan, for only in part II of the poem is the positive role of the boys of summer brought out. In part I they act like enthusiastic agents of Mutability, showing

How MUTABILITY in them doth play
Her cruell sports, to many mens decay
(VII.vi.1).

"Cruel sports" describes well the actions of the boys
in these first stanzas. They have an air of gaiety about
them in the midst of utmost cruelty. Their paradox-
ical nature is in the first line: they are "of summer"
and "in ruin" at the same time. One might picture
bare-foot, ill-clad urchins; but "summer" and "ruin"
are only casually effective as description. They are
symbolic: "summer" sums up a series of qualities
associated with the season of warmth and well-being,
growth and harvest-time; "ruin" finds an echo in all
the destructive acts against the qualities of summer.
Once the larger themes are established—as here by
the two key words "summer" and "ruin" in the first
line—the symbolic images of the rest of the poem
fall into place. The boys take "gold tithings" (*summer*) and "lay them barren" (*ruin*). They "set no
store" (*ruin*) "by harvest" (*summer*). They "freeze"
(*ruin*) the "soils" (*summer*). "In their heat" (*summer*) they "fetch their girls" (*summer*) "the winter
floods of frozen loves" (*ruin*). They "drown in their
tides" (*ruin*) "cargoed apples" (*summer*). Since *summer* is positive (+) and *ruin* negative (—), the second
stanza can be put:

These boys of light (+) are curdlers in their
    folly (—),
Sour (—) the boiling honey (+);
The jacks of frost (—) they finger in the
    hives (+);
There in the sun (+) the frigid threads
Of doubt and dark (—) they feed their nerves;

The signal moon (+) is zero in their voids (−).

An expectation is set up, and we sometimes grasp the significance of an action before the details of it. This short cut to the symbolic level (along with the hypnotic rhythms) makes it possible to enjoy Thomas' poetry without understanding very much of it. But Thomas meant the poems to be understood on the immediate literal level. He used the word "literal" on one occasion as a way of insisting that the *details* of his images be attended to:

> Miss Edith Sitwell's analysis, in a letter to the *Sunday Times* of the lines:
>
>> The atlas-eater with a jaw for news
>> Bit out the mandrake with to-mor-
>>> row's scream
>
>> *Altarwise by owl-light*.
>
> seems to me very vague. She says the lines refer to "the violent speed and the sensation-loving, horror-loving craze of modern life." She doesn't take the literal meaning: that a world-devouring ghost creature bit out the horror of to-morrow from a gentleman's loins.[1]

No matter what the full meaning of *Altarwise by owl-light* may be, Thomas evidently wants us to see his "atlas-eater" as something which actually devours worlds and is specifically biting off a mandrake in the quoted lines. He drives the point home by going on to say: "This poem is a particular incident in a particular adventure, not a general elliptical deprecation of this 'horrible, crazy, speed-life.'" We trust that he is not denying the particular adventure all general significance, but just stressing that one must work from the literal level.

The trouble with the literal interpretation of some of Thomas' lines is not in seeing what happens but in believing it. Thomas has the boys drown cargoed apples in their tides. The boys have, in some unspecified sense, tides, in which they drown apples that are, in some unspecified sense, cargoed. One can imagine apples sinking in the sea; but can one *believe* that this is what Thomas wants us to imagine? There is actually good reason to do so. Thomas once wrote to Vernon Watkins concerning two lines from *I make this in a warring absence*, "A calm wind blows that raised the trees like hair / Once where the soft snow's blood was turned to ice":

> a wind had blown that had frightened everything and created the first ice and the first frost by frightening the falling snow so much that the blood of each flake froze.[2]

Again the lines are a particular incident in a particular adventure. They utilize the two common expressions for fear: "his hair stood on end" (the trees' hair, the branches) and "his blood froze" (here, the blood of each snowflake). The thought can be reduced to one word, "fear"; but Thomas requires us to see the literal event in the metaphor for fear: "the blood of each flake froze."[3] So that he would also, one can be sure, want us to see the apples drown in the tides — then we are free to see the event as another symbol of the ruin of harvest.

Of course, if we are asked to accept that cargoed

apples are drowned, we should also be assured that cargoed pears or plums wouldn't have done just as well. This assurance usually comes with an understanding of the metaphor involved; the words earn their place by a sort of second, hidden meaning (which is what "metaphor" implies). With the image of the snow's blood freezing, the middle stage was the common expression for fear. With the cargoed apples, no such midway point comes immediately to mind. "Cargoed" is an interesting word: the apples are ripe, heavy, cargoed with their own weight; and since cargoed, they are like ships that can sink. If there must be some thing for which the phrase is a metaphor, I suggest the apples are the breasts of the girls in the previous line. Compare "jacks of frost" in the second stanza:

> These boys of light are curdlers in their folly,
> Sour the boiling honey;
> The jacks of frost they finger in the hives.

"Jacks of frost" is a metaphor for icicles. The poet is playing on the name Jack Frost and also giving the image a sexual twist, the slang meaning of "jack," common enough in England, providing the male counterpart to the hollow hive of the female. The boys again bring "frozen loves" to their girls. If we also think of "jack of hearts" with its connotations of knavery, we have quite a complicated superstructure for the phrase. It is Thomas' practice to take some common item such as an icicle and describe it with deliberate strangeness to bring out certain constituent qualities. Thus in part II of *I see the boys of summer* the phrase "this four-winded spinning" describes the revolving globe of this planet in terms of appropriate qualities, its four-windedness and its spinning. Here the icicle image fits the boys of summer: it is a stiff, prodding weapon of destructive mischief, cold and male in its attack on female warmth.

Thomas sanctioned the search for double meanings in his poetry when he said that a line from *A grief ago:*

> The country-handed grave boxed into love

meant that "the grave had a country for each hand, that it raised those hands up and boxed the hero of my poem into love. 'Boxed' has the coffin and the pug-glove in it."[4] The grave is heavy-handed, so Thomas' image acts out the inherent event in the metaphor, giving the grave a country for each hand, hands heavy enough. The coffin, itself a box, is an unavoidable threat, a violent coercer like a heavy-handed boxer. In the same way as he would have said of "jacks of frost" that "it has male stiffness and icicles in it," so Thomas is unequivocally saying that "boxed" contains both the coffin and the pug-glove. This process of adding secondary and tertiary connotations to an image is a risky business. In the third stanza of *I see the boys of summer*, "fairy thumbs" comes with something of a jolt:

> I see the summer children in their mothers
> Split up the brawned womb's weathers,
> Divide the night and day with fairy thumbs.

Just for the sake of argument, are we to accept the connotations of homosexuality in this word? Or, if we refuse to do so, on what basis do we refuse?

Thomas can be ruthlessly double-edged if he wants to. Take a most poignant line from the later poem *In the white giant's thigh*. Dead women buried in the dust of the hillside pull the poet down to them:

> Now [the women] clasp me to their grains
>     in the gigantic glade.

"Grains" is dust, but it is also "groins." The embrace becomes sexual. Besides the verbal echo of "groins" in the word, "grains" actually means "groin" in a dialect meaning that Thomas could have known.[5] But, of all the possible verbal puns hovering around the word "grains" ("groans," "greens," "grins," and so on), we accept "groins" chiefly because it is pertinent to the major theme of the poem — the sexual longing of the childless women — while the alternatives make no such direct connection with the themes that were Thomas' preoccupation. "Fairy" is perhaps sufficiently explained by the delicate, diminutive thumbs that children in the womb might be imagined to have, and their magical, fairy-like dividing of night and day. If one were to press for a double meaning to help the word earn its place, the word "changelings" (a species of fairy) might come to mind: these are certainly children of mutability and change — and, possibly, in Thomas' logic, changelings.

We cannot, however, dodge the fact that Thomas knew exactly what he was risking with that word. In an unpublished letter to Trevor Hughes three months before the poem, he used the phrase "like a fairy" and felt compelled to go on: "It needed courage to say that 'like a fairy', for the young panto-mime ladies, gallivanting in gossamer nudity, have robbed the fairy of all but her woman's body. A fairy is not supernatural; she is the most natural thing in the world." Thomas in the New Year 1934 was "believing in" fairies. There is the literal fairy in "fairy thumbs," then. What about the slang "fairy"? He had used the word in conjunction with "epicene" in a Notebook poem 18 of March 1931. Yet the "fairy thumbs" in our poem is not revolting, as homosexuality was to Thomas ("It's the only vice, I think, that revolts me," he wrote in another unpublished letter about this time). The word "hermaphrodite" — used without disparagement in another early poem — gives us a better clue. If "fairy" is thought to contain both male and female, it is certainly polar; and the indeterminacy of sex is appropriate to the foetus image.

With this third stanza of *I see the boys of summer* we have a new locale, the womb of the mother; and we might wish to question the logic which has brought us from the harvest field of the first stanza to the womb of the third. The "particular adventure" has a strange sequence of events. Is there any narrative at all, in the ordinary sense of the word? Thomas tried to express his idea of narrative in an answer to an enquiry from *New Verse:*

> Narrative, in its widest sense, satisfies what Eliot, talking of "meaning," calls "one habit of the reader." Let the narrative take that one logical habit of the reader along with its movement, and the essence of the poem will do its work on him.[6]

A reader habitually expects *something* to happen to *someone* in a poem; Thomas intends to meet this expectation. His poems are filled with action; and the reader does find himself swept along the narrative line by force of habit, even though the different events are not in an accustomed sequence of cause and effect, of temporal and spacial contiguity. It seems like a surrealist world where actions follow one another without reason. But is it really surrealistic? Behind the many actions of the boys of summer we found the abstract concept of negation. The disparate actions have unity on that level. They are connected (as Webster's *NID* defines *disparate*) "by some notion of great generality or by some interest of extreme catholicity." Furthermore, the way in which the imaged actions succeed each other is not entirely haphazard. Disparateness is the essence of Thomas' style:

> A poem by myself *needs* a host of images, because its centre is a host of images. I make one image—though "make" is not the word; I let, perhaps, an image be "made" emotionally in me and then apply to it what intellectual and critical forces I possess — let it breed another, let that image contradict the first, make, of the third image bred out of the other two together, a fourth contradictory image, and let them all, within my imposed formal limits, conflict. Each image holds within it the seed of its own destruction, and my dialectal method, as I understand it, is a constant building up and breaking down of the images that come out of the central seed, which is itself destructive and constructive at the same time.[7]

A poet's rationalization of his own creative act may offer all kinds of traps; but here Thomas seems to give genuine help in understanding how to follow the "logic" of his images. Let us take our stanza two:

> These boys of light are curdlers in their folly,
> Sour the boiling honey;
> The jacks of frost they finger in the hives;
> There in the sun the frigid threads
> Of doubt and dark they feed their nerves;
> The signal moon is zero in their voids.

"Curdlers" of the first line breeds the "sour" of the second, utilizing the alternative meaning of sour: milk *curdles* but honey is made *unsweet*. The posing of citric sourness against lactic sourness is not astounding — but Thomas said nothing about violent contradictions. It is enough to see that the first image prompts the second, which is, however, not really a continuation of it but something new. Similarly, the "boiling honey" gives rise to "hives," which again involves a new image of negation: fingering and freezing. The boys then feed into their nerves the frigid threads (bred from "jacks of frost") of doubt and dark: a different image from the preceding and again "contradictory" in the sense that it thwarts our expectation of a continuing locale.

This breeding and contradicting process is essentially fanciful and undisciplined; its only logic is that of association of ideas. "Sun" in line 4 of the stanza above suggests "moon" for line 6; "nerves" in line 5 makes the moon a "signal" moon; and having fed on doubt and dark in line 5, the boys are possessed of "voids" in line 6. The signal moon, in keeping with the harvest theme of the first stanza, is the full moon (a sign of changing weather); the boys make its roundness a mere zero, an emptiness, so it ceases to be a signal. This is an effective image. Being cosmic in scope, it is the climactic incident in this series of "adventures." But, for most of us, this virtue is obscured by the disjointedness of the narrative. Thomas wants us to go with him along a literal narrative line; but in these early poems he does not give us the habitual narrative signposts, and it is something of an effort to hold on. This does not detract from the effectiveness of the images as symbolic of the central concept of the poem. The moon, traditionally a harvest and female fertility symbol, is made zero by the boys — this is very effective in communicating their destructiveness symbolically. Nor should our present difficulty with the narrative of disparate images prevent us from seeing that it is the very disparateness which ensures the broadness of the symbolized concept. The "jacks of frost" could be taken entirely on a sexual plane; but add the "signal moon" and the interpretation must be pushed further back into a more generalized notion beyond sex. Add the further images, and the final result is a concept of life and death which is as broad as it is because each image has helped to define its breadth. And this is where the discipline comes in. Each image must be shaped to perform this function of creating the final concept as well as carrying on a narrative line. No matter how casually the images are bred, they must meet the demands of this symbolic function. Thomas said:

Out of the inevitable conflict of images —
inevitable, because of the creative, recreative,
destructive and contradictory nature of the
motivating centre, the womb of war — I try
to make that momentary peace which is a
poem.[8]

The reconciliation is in the unifying concept shared
by all the images. We have a grip on the meaning of
a poem when we understand on what basic premise
the warring images are reconciled.

The womb symbolism of stanza three is self-
evidently consistent with the life-cycle theme of *I see
the boys of summer* as a whole:

I see the summer children in their mothers
Split up the brawned womb's weathers,
Divide the night and day with fairy thumbs;
There in the deep with quartered shades
Of sun and moon they paint their dams
As sunlight paints the shelling of their heads.

"Signal moon" of the previous stanza brought up the
subject of weather; here the womb has "weathers."
Weathers are the conditions through which time and
the seasons work their changes on the world. By
transposition they become the atmospheric conditions
within the human body, specifically here within the
"brawned," muscular womb. What does it mean to
"split up" these weathers? Since the children here
are presumably the unborn boys of summer, they will
be up to their usual tricks as agents of mutability.
Nowhere are time and change more dramatically
portrayed than in gestation, in which splitting up and
reduplication of cells occurs. Pregnancy makes us

very conscious of the calendar, makes its demands
continuously night and day. This vital sense of change
through time is utilized by the poet here. Not that
"splitting up weathers" need refer to any particular
stage of pregnancy; Thomas is not interested in taking
us into a real human drama. On one level, the thought
is very literal: the summer children take the weathers
of the womb (the conditions in the womb) and split
them up (an action of producing multiple from
single). It is as though the first day of Genesis were
repeated by each child within its mother, peace and
unity destroyed by the presence of another being,
the fight of opposites begun. One becomes two, two
becomes four: this is the development within the
stanza. The shades of color with which the children
paint their mother are "quartered," an indication of
increasing multiplicity (as in such birth poems as
*From love's first fever to her plague:* "And the four
winds, that had long blown as one"). "Quartered"
is a pun-word, since both the year and the month
have quarters, which are sometimes symbolized on
the calendar by a small circle shaded in quadrants.
The children are painting the seasons on their mothers.
"Dams" is some indication of the harshness of the act.
The birth of a child has often been seen by poets as
the beginning of the death of the parents. As the
child grows through nine months in the amniotic
deep of the womb, its first gift to the parent is a
sense of mortality. As the sun, the creative force,
paints the shelling of its head (creates the skull, the
pieced-together shell which gets a coloring of hair),
the child paints ("tarnishes" as it were) the mother
with the touch of age.

After his glance back at the boys of summer as an emblem of Time in the womb, the poet looks ahead, in the fourth stanza, to the boys' growing up. They will become "men of nothing," hollow men:

> I see that from these boys shall men of nothing
> Stature by seedy shifting,
> Or lame the air with leaping from its heats;
> There from their hearts the dogdayed pulse
> Of love and light bursts in their throats.
> O see the pulse of summer in the ice.

"Seedy shifting," a reminder that in a sense the gestation of the womb continues in the metabolism of the body, has unhealthy connotations in the words "seedy" and "shifting" (reminding one of "shifty"). After negating the harvest and their mothers, the boys now negate themselves. It is a vision of their ruin; they will leap away from their own heat of summer, crippling the air (a violent enough leap) and presumably themselves. Just as "lame" is apparently bred from "stature" and "leaping" from "shifting," so "dogdayed" comes from the "heats." Again there is a contradiction: the heat (dogdays are in July and August) now "bursts in their throats" — throbs, pulsates, in their throats. It is surprising that the boys should have so much "love and light" in their hearts. It would be more surprising if the image were less violent.[9] The reversal is from one extreme to another. The boys have all along been "of summer," but belying their summeriness with ice and cold. In these last three lines we begin to see the "pulse of summer in the ice." And even their heat is excessive. They are symbolic of polar opposites of whatever kind. As agents of change, they contain all weathers, and are capable of pulling each season slowly or violently into its opposite.


[2]

The "But" which starts off part II of *I see the boys of summer* suggests its opposition to the tone of accusation of part I. Here the boys speak for themselves and defend mutability:

> But seasons must be challenged or they totter
> Into a chiming quarter
> Where, punctual as death, we ring the stars;
> There, in his night, the black-tongued bells
> The sleepy man of winter pulls,
> Nor blows back moon-and-midnight as she
>     blows.

The first line is as close as we get to a direct statement of theme: seasons (standing for all the different states in the world and in life) must be fought against or they will stagnate. The "chiming quarter" (echoing "quartered shades," a previous symbol of mortality) is a place where clock-like monotony reigns. One has to ring star after star as though each were a bell-chime that had to be sounded punctually. Death is punctual and is ever present in the ticking of a clock. The sleepy man of winter is a deliberate opposite of the boys of summer. Representing stagnation, he pulls the bell ropes of death, the bell tongues in mourning black. He exists in the very dead of night ("moon-and-midnight") and he does not resist the dark, fails to answer the call in the night. There is no pulse of summer in his ice.

The boys, however, do blow back. They are great gainsayers:

> We are the dark deniers, let us summon
> Death from a summer woman,
> A muscling life from lovers in their cramp,
> From the fair dead who flush the sea
> The bright-eyed worm on Davy's lamp,
> And from the planted womb the man of straw.

"Deniers" is a key word. All the subsequent actions are denials — in a sense that we gradually become fully aware of: to deny is not only to pull down the positive good (though this was the emphasis of part I) but also to oppose the negative and produce good from it. To produce death from a woman in the summer of her life is obviously destructive denial; but the next image is the reverse. "Muscling life" (incidental echo of "brawned womb" here) is summoned from the opposite, "cramp," lack of muscles. ("Cramp," however, is a paradox word, since it is very expressive of the involuntary "death" in which lovers beget life.) "Davy's lamp," which has superficial associations with the drowned through Davy Jones, is the miner's lamp invented by Sir Humphrey Davy; and the bright-eyed worm is its flame, like a glowworm. Thomas uses "glow-worm" elsewhere as a paradox word: a worm, usually associated with the earth and death, is in this case a sparkling light. It is a geological fact that oil comes from the long-decayed organic deposits in the earth; like the glowworm, the flame too is connected with the dead, the "fair" dead, to complete the paradox. The dead produce the living flame. Another effective image of negative coming out of positive is "the man of straw" coming from "the planted womb," the womb planted with seed.

In the next stanza the boys continue their dual role:

> We summer boys in this four-winded spinning,
> Green of the seaweeds' iron,
> Hold up the noisy sea and drop her birds,
> Pick the world's ball of wave and froth
> To choke the deserts with her tides,
> And comb the county gardens for a wreath.

The boys are "green," virile, fresh — but green like seaweed, because of the iron content. Their greenness has a hard, metallic, ruthless quality inherent in it, and the world they live in, this four-winded spinning, is violent and inhumane. They hold up the noisy sea — one imagines a wave at its height arrested by these cosmic deniers — and drop the seabirds, presumably to destruction. They force the sea on to the deserts, choking them rather than parching their thirst. They search the county gardens not for the bouquet that the polite "county" might suggest, but for a stern wreath. Their greenness ends in a wreath, and then in the sharp holly:

> In spring we cross our foreheads with the holly,
> Heigh ho the blood and berry,
> And nail the merry squires to the trees;
> Here love's damp muscle dries and dies,
> Here break a kiss in no love's quarry.
> O see the poles of promise in the boys.

This stanza seems at first reading almost totally negative. Yet, it would be very strange for the poet to ask us to see "poles of promise" in the boys if such poles, positive as well as negative, had not been shown us. The positive is there, submerged in the apparently negative. For instance, within the anti-pastoral scene of the first three lines, there is a Christian symbolism that implies the opposite of destruction. The boys scratch a cross on their foreheads with holly (this itself reminds one of Christ's thorns), an act of cruelty and self-abnegation in the midst of gaiety. (The Elizabethan "Heigh ho" is both happy and sad; the berry is happy, the blood sad.) But the sign of the cross is also a blessing. Again, the nailing of the merry squires to the trees is not only an inhumanly perverse act but also a reminder of Easter, the crucifixion of Christ miraculously turned to good with the Redemption. The fortunate fall should indeed be merry. As an image for "poles of promise," is there anything more incisive than Christ on the Cross, depth of degradation signifying highest regeneration?

The two lines in which we might expect to see most clearly the "poles of promise" are

Here love's damp muscle dries and dies,
Here break a kiss in no love's quarry.

The first line is decidedly negative: "damp" is one of Thomas' ways of saying "life-containing," and dryness is death. Whatever part of the anatomy "love's damp muscle" might be, the line signifies the end of love. Does the breaking of the kiss in the next line mean the opposite, the beginning of love? Despite the negative sound of "break," there is rea-

son to think that it does. "Break" would normally
indicate that the kiss is destroyed, but think for a
moment of the logic of the image: breaking a kiss
in a quarry is basically a stone-breaking image. Here
we have the very making of the kiss, like a hammer
blow on a stone, a violent juncture. "Break" has the
same kind of positive implication that "bursts" had
in part I when it meant "pulsates." It is Thomas'
practice to use words of violence in order to speak
in hyperbolic terms of something essentially favored.
To "break a kiss in no love's quarry," then, is to
create love where there was none before, in the
quarry (suitably female) of no love. What more
direct opposite for "love's damp muscle" could be
found than the simple "no love's quarry"? The line
supplies the balancing positive pole, and we do, therefore, see the poles of life and death in the boys.


[3]

The single stanza of the third and last section of
*I see the boys of summer* suggests that it has four
times its apparent weight if it is to match the other
sections. It is a concentrated recapitulation and climax.

I see you boys of summer in your ruin.
Man in his maggot's barren.
And boys are full and foreign in the pouch.
I am the man your father was.
We are the sons of flint and pitch.
O see the poles are kissing as they cross.

Each of the lines is end-stopped; nowhere does

Thomas' propensity for short independent images reveal itself more clearly. As usual the question is, what are these separate "adventures" and what unifying idea gives them their coherence? Line 1, obviously a close parallel of the first line of the poem, summarizes the complaint against the boys in part I. Shorn of all particulars, the complaint is concentrated in the symbols "summer" and "ruin," with stress on the negative pole. Line 2 is negative, but without the saving implication of the positive pole. Man is in "his maggot," his fleshly body. His flesh, his mortal dross, is a maggot because a maggot symbolizes the corruption and decay to which the flesh is subject. It is the man of winter; his barrenness means there will be no blowing back. Thus, we have the larger contrast in the poem: polarity (challenging) versus nonpolarity (stagnation). The boys are half-destructive, but their destruction is essential to the life-cycle. Their polarity is expressed again in line 3. They are "full," indicating their potentiality for good; they are "foreign," which summarizes all their antagonism. The pouch, whether marsupial or scrotal, is polar, containing these opposites.

By all traditional esthetic canons, it is now far too late for the "I" observer to start playing a dramatic role in the poem; yet we have the line "I am the man your father was." The most sensible paraphrase of the line seems to be: I am the kind of man your father used to be. But this does not say much about the boys or the father, or the "I" for that matter. This failure on the literal level forces us immediately to the level of symbolic presentation. The "I" seems to be present as a convenient digit for constructing a symbolic structure. The "I" relates himself to the two generations older and younger, fixing himself midway in the life-span, thus giving the symbolic assertion: two poles (boys and father) with the central point (the "I"), a meeting point of youth and age. This, at least, is the conclusion toward which the poem is leading. "Flint and pitch," two extremes, spark and unite in the boys. And the poles kiss in the last line. Here Thomas would probably be thinking of the common sign for a kiss, a cross — but also, one can be sure, of the Christian connotation. Where everlasting life came at the moment of death, the positive and negative forces in the universe might be considered to have crossed most significantly.

This last line of the poem is a climax prepared for by the previous last lines:

(I)   O see the pulse of summer in the ice.
(II)  O see the poles of promise in the boys.
(III) O see the poles are kissing as they cross.

These key lines are linked by reiteration of sound, which helps to pull the poem together. Mutability in its traditional destructive aspects was the subject of part I until the end when the dual nature of destruction was hinted at. Part II stated directly the superiority of challenge over stagnation. The boys denied everything, and thus were partly creative. Part III recapitulated the previous ideas and expressed the dynamic balance between polar tensions, growth and decay, in each instant of experience. No wonder Thomas picked out this poem for the beginning of his first volume. It is the fullest statement of his basic view of the universe as a war of conflicting forces.

Since his own poetry is written in a warring of images, the poem also sums up his poetic method, implying the unity between poetry and life.

[4]

Thomas' early poetry has not appealed to those who like poetry to be *about something*. They have assumed that because it is difficult to see any central subject the poems do not communicate intelligibly but employ a kind of automatic writing. But we have seen, with this first poem at least, that Thomas does make a coherent assertion in spite of disparate imagery — indeed, because of disparate imagery. *I see the boys of summer* is a poem *about* polarity, and the disparate imagery demonstrates the extremes of the polar opposites. Direct statements do appear in the poem: "Seasons must be challenged," "O see the poles of promise," and so on. We shouldn't distrust these statements of theme just because they are direct and therefore exceptional. We might wish for more. We would certainly feel more secure in our interpretations generally if Thomas had divulged precisely what he meant to say in at least one poem. Then we could see how the interpretation and the poem fit together; we wouldn't have to work it all by deduction. Actually there is one such case. In a letter to Vernon Watkins, Thomas encloses *Into her Lying Down Head* and tells what it is *about*:

It is a poem about modern love. For some reason, I wrote a note under the poem in my copybook: All over the world love is being betrayed as always, and a million years have not calmed the uncalculated ferocity of each betrayal or the terrible loneliness afterwards. Man is denying his partner man or woman and whores with the whole night, begetting a monstrous brood; one day the brood will not die when the day comes but will hang on to the breast and the parts and squeeze his partner out of bed.[10]

Even in his paraphrase, Thomas cannot stop being the poet; he uses further images instead of explanations. The point, however, is clear: much of our love-making is insincere lust, devastating to human sensibility and ending in hatred. The three-part poem is long and complicated, but the paraphrase reassures us that it has coherence, that it is *about* something.

I

Into her lying down head
His enemies entered bed,
Under the encumbered eyelid,
Through the rippled drum of the hair-buried ear;
And Noah's rekindled now unkind dove
Flew man-bearing there.
Last night in a raping wave
Whales unreined from the green grave
In fountains of origin gave up their love,
Along her innocence glided
Juan aflame and savagely young King Lear,
Queen Catherine howling bare
And Samson drowned in his hair,
The colossal intimacies of silent
Once seen strangers or shades on a stair;

There the dark blade and wanton sighing her down
To a haycock couch and the scythes of his arms
      Rode and whistled a hundred times
      Before the crowing morning climbed;
Man was the burning England she was sleep-walking,
    and the enamouring island
Made her limbs blind by luminous charms,
Sleep to a newborn sleep in a swaddling loin-leaf
    stroked and sang
And his runaway beloved childlike laid in the
    acorned sand.

Once it is known that the "enemies" entering the marriage bed are the fantasy figures with which the partner is unfaithful (the poem concentrates on the woman's infidelities), the disparate images can all be interpreted in terms of this third party; their profusion expresses the enormity of the tragedy. Noah's dove of peace is bred dialectically from "enemies." It is a dove with a difference, now "unkind" and "man-bearing," bringing the rival instead of an olive branch. The whales that come in a "raping wave" are also in the *Ballad of the Long-legged Bait*, which is close to this poem in date and in the use of violent imagery for sexual union. The unlikely combination of Juan, young King Lear, Queen Catherine, and Samson, added to the "strangers or shades on a stair," serves by its very unlikeliness to emphasize the promiscuity. Lines 16-19, where the "blade" (a sharp fellow?) "dark" and "wanton" rides and whistles, expresses the sexual act by means of hay-cutting puns. In the last lines of part I, the woman is being made love to by the whole island of England ("Circe's swinish, coiling island" in the first printing); this

population of charming males "blinds" her limbs,
strokes and sings and lays her in the sand.

II

>There where a numberless tongue
>Wound their room with a male moan,
>His faith around her flew undone
>And darkness hung the walls with baskets of snakes,
>A furnace-nostrilled column-membered
>Super-or-near man
>Resembling to her dulled sense
>The thief of adolescence,
>Early imaginary half remembered
>Oceanic lover alone
>Jealousy cannot forget for all her sakes,
>Made his bad bed in her good
>Night, and enjoyed as he would.
>Crying, white gowned, from the middle moonlit
>stages
>Out to the tiered and hearing tide,
>Close and far she announced the theft of the heart
>In the taken body at many ages,
>Trespasser and broken bride
>Celebrating at her side
>All blood-signed assailings and vanished marriages in
>which he had no lovely part
>Nor could share, for his pride, to the least
>Mutter and foul wingbeat of the solemnizing
>nightpriest
>Her holy unholy hours with the always anonymous
>beast.

Part II continues the theme: while countless
male tongues (like baskets of snakes) moan around
the bedroom, betraying her infidelities, she confesses
to the night all the "vanished marriages" in which

her husband had no part. The rival is here pictured as a superman, "column-membered," a raping image out of her past, the thief of adolescence, a trespasser,[11] and an anonymous beast.

The "monstrous brood" of Thomas' paraphrase, the progeny of the myriad promiscuities, is only hinted at in the poem as we have it; and the picture of their forcing the partners out of bed is material enough for a part IV. The implication of conception is present in part III, but the tone is not so malicious as one might expect.

### III

Two sand grains together in bed,
Head to heaven-circling head,
Singly lie with the whole wide shore,
The covering sea their nightfall with no names;
And out of every domed and soil-based shell
One voice in chains declaims
The female, deadly, and male
Libidinous betrayal,
Golden dissolving under the water veil.
A she bird sleeping brittle by
Her lover's wings that fold to-morrow's flight,
Within the nested treefork
Sings to the treading hawk
Carrion, paradise, chirrup my bright yolk.
A blade of grass longs with the meadow,
A stone lies lost and locked in the lark-high hill.
Open as to the air to the naked shadow
O she lies alone and still,
Innocent between two wars,
With the incestuous secret brother in the seconds to
perpetuate the stars,
A man torn up mourns in the sole night.

And the second comers, the severers, the enemies
   from the deep
Forgotten dark, rest their pulse and bury their dead
   in her faithless sleep.

The male, female, libidinous, and deadly betrayal
is over, dissolving under the water veil. A seashore
image and then a bird image express the resting
period after the war of sex. The "bright yolk" and
"the seconds to perpetuate the stars" suggest conception, and the last line confirms it with the reference
to burying the dead. Thomas in other places implies
that the husband has much less to do with conception
than the wife and their ancestors. In the *Ballad of
the Long-legged Bait* it is "his fathers" who "cling to
the hand of the girl" and announce that "Time is
bearing another son." In *A grief ago*, the ancestors
again preside over conception: "Let her inhale her
dead, through seed and solid / Draw in their seas."
Thomas' view of childbirth, as we have seen with the
summer children in their mothers, brings out the cruel
antagonism between parent and offspring. In *It is the
sinners' dust-tongued bell*, the parents are a "plagued
groom and bride" and the child "the urchin grief."
At best, conception is the beginning of suffering; and
in *Into her Lying Down Head* it is the infidelities of
the marriage bed that produce the offspring. The
"enemies from the deep forgotten dark" create the
new enemy. So that the woman's sleep as well as her
loving is "faithless" in that she has conceived a grief
and a rival.

The periodical publication of the poem had a
more direct reference to the paraphrase's "monstrous
brood":

> Damned damned go down or caress to death
>     the sun-sized bridal bed's cruellest brood.

In the draft that Thomas had sent to Watkins earlier, this long line had made an even more direct statement of the horror produced by infidelity:

> The filth and secret of death is sweeter with
>     the sun than these inconstancies.

Thomas wondered if the line wasn't too "prosy."[12] The revision was thus deliberately more "obscure," as was the final rewriting:

> O she lies alone and still,
> Innocent between two wars,
> With the incestuous secret brother in the
>     seconds to perpetuate the stars.

The long line is here simpler in form, yet more taxing: the "brother" seems more significant than the "enemies." Has the man found kinship with his rival? If so, Thomas' paraphrase does not fully apply to the poem as it now stands.

We have gone far enough into this major poem to see that behind the complexity is a central assertion which only such complexity can fully communicate to the poet's satisfaction. Thomas' paraphrase of the poem is confirmation that our effort to find coherence in these difficult poems is warranted. What finally is left to trouble us is whether or not the intricacy is as valuable to the reader as it apparently is to the poet. Thomas' narrative of disparate images has seemed to some readers a mere play of empty forms. Donald Davie coined the word "pseudo-syntax" to denote a sentence that only *appears* to be communicating meaning but isn't, and has suggested that Thomas' "pseudo-syntax" is "radically vicious."[13] If Thomas' image-narrative only *appeared* to be telling about events, we should probably have to agree with Davie. But Thomas once said in a letter, "Try to Think in Things," and has elsewhere, as we have seen, asserted his desire to have his images taken seriously on a literal level. Any poet describes imaginary events. Some of Thomas' are especially hard to imagine; yet he asks us to do so. When he writes in *Altarwise by owl-light*, "Time tracks the sound of shape on man and cloud," he is depicting an event. Time (personified) tracks sound (like a sound track), sound which is really the expression of shape or form. Man and cloud are given their existence within time, as though they were ticked into shape. The line in the context of sonnet VII is another expression of mortality. The particular adventure in this line may not be very comfortable to contemplate, but Davie will not have it as an event at all:

> The verb "tracks" is completely devoid of meaning. What appears to be narrative ("Time," the agent, transfers energy through "tracks" to the object "sound") is in fact an endless series of copulas: "Time is tracking which is sound which is shape . . ." and so on. That the metaphors could in fact be broken down into successive meanings is irrelevant; even when the breaking down has been done for us, we cannot hold on to it when we return to reading the poem.[14]

In stating the problem in terms of the endurance

demanded of the reader, Davie has raised the issue of Thomas' poetry in its proper form. Such a line as the above is pseudo-syntax if we find ourselves unable to take the event seriously. In the words of John Bayley, the critic who has gone perhaps most searchingly into the problem of Thomas' obscurity:

> The critical uncertainty which must still be felt about Thomas' real status as a poet arises from the fact that we still do not know whether language is capable of what he tried to do with it; or rather whether the consciousness of the receiver can adapt itself to such a variety of linguistic uses and such a multiplicity of verbal stimuli.

Bayley adds: "Probably it can."[15] And one reader, at least, A. D. S. Fowler, is willing to challenge Davie's specific accusation:

> On five lines wrenched from Dylan Thomas's "Now stamp the Lord's Prayer," the only pathological specimen he examines in any detail, Davie puts forward only unsympathetic and unsupported reiterations that the "syntax cannot mime, as it offers to do, a movement of the mind . . . these sentences that seem to drive forward in time through their verbs in fact do no such thing. The verb 'tracks' is completely devoid of meaning." . . . One is irritated into replying: "The verb 'tracks' is *not* devoid of meaning: prove that it is." Thomas's syntax is not shown to be defective, except by criteria which would condemn equally Sidney,

Daniel, Milton, and, indeed, most of the poetry we value.[16]

With this positive note one can concur, if only on the grounds of personal experience. The "multiplicity of verbal stimuli" in Thomas' poetry does become easier to handle and more rewarding as time goes on. The "variety of linguistic uses" becomes less bewildering when one can see a certain basic methodology. Every image in Thomas has to be taken on its own merits and it is impossible to say, for instance, that Thomas is likely at any particular time to be employing a proverbial expression, a Biblical reference, or a Freudian symbol. These kinds of images occur often, but so do a hundred other kinds. The two broad lines of approach that we have found useful with the poems discussed so far are, first, each image in a poem is best looked upon as isolated, having its own internal logic and only superficial associations with adjacent imagery on the narrative level. We have seen how casually an image is born out of another, but this casualness and perhaps verbal similarity should not deceive us into thinking that the new image is not entirely new. The way to understand these images, if we are to read them in the spirit in which they were written, is to treat them first of all as literal events. Second, the full significance of a poem will be in the literal narrative plus the central concept inherent in the symbolic power of the wording. The generality of the symbolized concept is determined by the range of the imagery in the poem; the images receive their deeper significance, and the poem its coherence, from that generality.

[5]

By the time of *Deaths and Entrances* (1946)
Thomas had developed a more open and relaxed style
in a good many of his poems. The rigorousness of
our own approach can consequently be tempered.
Thomas gives us a more realistic setting in these
poems, more of a world we recognize. There is disparate imagery, but the assertion to which the images
are attached is usually clear. Thomas was aware that
he had become a more accessible poet:

> It is impossible to be too clear. I am trying
> for more clarity now. At first I thought it
> enough to leave an impression of sound and
> feeling and let the meaning seep in later, but
> since I have been giving these broadcasts
> and reading other men's poetry as well as
> my own, I find it better to have more mean-
> ing at first reading.[17]

The war thrust Thomas into contact with a wider
audience through his work in films and broadcasting.
But the war itself, as a subject, demanded a wider
audience. Thomas' reaction to the war was personal,
but the subject was public, and he found a new
authoritative voice with which to proclaim it. Typical of the new poem is *A Refusal to Mourn the
Death, by Fire, of a Child in London* (published
1945), whose title announces what it is *about*.

> Never until the mankind making
> Bird beast and flower
> Fathering and all humbling darkness
> Tells with silence the last light breaking

And the still hour
Is come of the sea tumbling in harness

And I must enter again the round
Zion of the water bead
And the synagogue of the ear of corn
Shall I let pray the shadow of a sound
Or sow my salt seed
In the least valley of sackcloth to mourn

The majesty and burning of the child's death.
I shall not murder
The mankind of her going with a grave truth
Nor blaspheme down the stations of the breath
With any further
Elegy of innocence and youth.

Deep with the first dead lies London's daughter,
Robed in the long friends,
The grains beyond age, the dark veins of her
    mother,
Secret by the unmourning water
Of the riding Thames.
After the first death, there is no other.

"Never until I die shall I say a word or shed a tear of mourning for this dead child." We don't here reach the main assertion through a series of "adventures." The assertion is clear; we merely have to recognize the understatement. In refusing to mourn, the poet utilizes the language and sentiments of intense mourning. His refusal to be elegiac becomes a great elegy.

The poem is not without its own set of difficul-

ties; for instance, the protracted compound adjective
stretched over the first three lines:

> Never until the mankind making
> Bird beast and flower
> Fathering and all humbling darkness.

With these run-on lines, a contrast to the end-stopped
lines of the *18 Poems*, we are forced to pay attention
to the individual word before, and momentarily
quite apart from, the meaning of the sentence as a
whole. The device works. The darkness is (1) man-
kind-making, (2) bird-, beast-, and flower-fathering,
and (3) all-humbling. It was there at the beginning
and will be there at the end. The way the poetry
holds apart the "making" and the "humbling" mim-
icks the life-span of man and the world. Again, an
adjective such as "round" comes out very strongly
when broken from its noun:

> And I must enter again the round
> Zion of the water bead.

"The round zion" is the static paradise to which man
returns. By stressing the circularity, the poet suggests
other associations: the life cycle, a zero, the world
in the waterdrop.

As though the poem were a discursive essay, the
initial statement of refusal to mourn is followed by
the reason for refusing:

> I shall not murder
> The mankind of her going with a grave truth
> Nor blaspheme down the stations of the breath
> With any further
> Elegy of innocence and youth.

The immoderateness of "murder" confirms the poet's high seriousness. To mourn would be to murder the child twice (we assume what we are not told: that the child was killed in an air raid) because all the words available are necessarily inadequate, over-solemn truths or thumbed elegies. The language here is loaded with connotations. The "mankind of her going" — a strange construction — communicates the worldwide implications of the child's death. The "stations of the breath," echoing "stations of the Cross," expresses the poet's resolution to keep his art sacred.

> Deep with the first dead lies London's daughter,
> Robed in the long friends,
> The grains beyond age, the dark veins of her
>    mother,
> Secret by the unmourning water
> Of the riding Thames.
> After the first death, there is no other.

This last stanza gives a further reason for the refusal to mourn. The earth with its dust and immortality has welcomed the child like an old friend or mother. This is not a Christian heaven; the round zion of the water bead is part of a river that does not mourn. But "after the first death, there is no other"; the consolation is that there is not another death to face.

The fact that the poem ends with an unadorned explanatory assertion shows how far Thomas has come in his aim to give more meaning at first reading. The meaning we look for in subsequent readings is, in a sense, extra. The ultimate significance is in the full power and depth of certain striking words. Take for another example the climactic stanzas of *A Winter's Tale* (also 1945):

For the bird lay bedded
In a choir of wings, as though she slept or died,
And the wings glided wide and he was hymned
    and wedded,
And through the thighs of the engulfing bride,
The woman breasted and the heaven headed

Bird, he was brought low,
Burning in the bride bed of love, in the whirl-
Pool at the wanting centre, in the folds
Of paradise, in the spun bud of the world.
And she rose with him flowering in her melting
    snow.

The image of the she-bird is not one of those short-
lived images of the early poems that immediately
fades and breeds another, different image. On the
contrary, it provides the central core of the poem.
The poem has its literal level: during a snowfall, a
she-bird comes to the man sitting by his fire in the
valley farmhouse. There are very real "puffed birds
hopping and hunting" in the poem; and this climax
is Leda and the Swan in reverse. But the final meaning
is in the symbolic connotations of certain words used
to describe the she-bird and the lover; for instance,
"whirlpool," which in becoming two words (whirl- /
Pool) communicates both destruction and the great
energy of life at its highest point of surrender. By
means of such words, the poet imparts to the reader
his sense of the mystical unity of love and death. It
should also be clear from this and the above examples
that there is frustration in trying to anticipate or
tabulate the ways in which Thomas puts extra meaning into his words. In the next chapter we go as far

as we can in identifying and describing Thomas'
special vocabulary of process words. But for the most
part there is no sure scheme. If "whirl- / Pool" gives
added meaning to *A Winter's Tale*, the poem itself
has made it possible for the word to do so. One relies
on the context and on the dictionary meaning of the
words.

# Chapter III

# *Process Poems*

*"To others caught
Between black and white"*

Thomas' inscription on
the August 1933 Notebook

HERE IN ITS SIMPLEST TERMS is the duality of the
world portrayed in *I see the boys of summer* and the
larger part of *18 Poems*. It is convenient to term the
poems that treat this struggle between black and
white "process poems." Process is the subject — obviously so in *A process in the weather of the heart*,
written two months before *I see the boys of summer*:

A process in the weather of the heart
Turns damp to dry; the golden shot
Storms in the freezing tomb.
A weather in the quarter of the veins
Turns night to day; blood in their suns
Lights up the living worm.

A process in the eye forwarns
The bones of blindness; and the womb
Drives in a death as life leaks out.

A darkness in the weather of the eye
Is half its light; the fathomed sea
Breaks on unangled land.

57

The seed that makes a forest of the loin
Forks half its fruit; and half drops down,
Slow in a sleeping wind.

A weather in the flesh and bone
Is damp and dry; the quick and dead
Move like two ghosts before the eye.

A process in the weather of the world
Turns ghost to ghost; each mothered child
Sits in their double shade.
A process blows the moon into the sun,
Pulls down the shabby curtains of the skin;
And the heart gives up its dead.

This smaller poem says much the same thing as *I see the boys of summer*. When the "golden shot storms in the freezing tomb," the boys of summer could very well be at work "denying" the coldness of the tomb with "golden shot," a metaphor for sunlight. Again much of the action occurs inside the human body. Night becomes day inside the veins; it is as though each corpuscle of the veins were a sun whose blood lights up the body (or one specifically worm-like part of the body). Again a counterpoise is maintained between positive and negative images. The sun imagery of the first six lines calls up the reference to blindness in the seventh. This poem has more formal statements of theme: "A darkness in the weather of the eye is half its light"; and the imagery that expresses the duality is more clear-cut: the division between light and dark is simply represented, for instance, by the two opposites, deep sea and un-fished land. Half of the sexual seed (from the pubic forest) "forks," which is a positive, vigorous action;

while half drops down during sleep. Life and death are two ghosts or images, each taking on the other's appearance; every individual is under their sway. The last three lines of the poem signify the end of the dual process in death.

Besides general similarities, much of the actual wording of this poem duplicates that of *I see the boys of summer*. Notably, the word "weather" recalls

> I see the summer children in their mothers
> Split up the brawned womb's weathers.

"Weather" is an effective "process" word. A speaker in Shakespeare says: "It is foul weather in us all, good sir, when you are cloudy." In Thomas, this equation of the sky with internal states has come a good deal further. One is hardly permitted to think of the sky any more, but of some seemingly no less physical atmospheric conditions existing within the flesh and bone of the body. If the inner processes of life and death are contained in the words "damp" and "dry," then the state of the processes at any time will logically be "the weather," the two weathers vying for dominance. The very strangeness of the rare plural "weathers"[1] and "*a* weather" (as opposed to *the* weather) makes these forms effective in signifying the strange forces beneath the surface of things. Several other words particularly suited to expressing process are common to the two poems, and occur elsewhere more or less coextensive with the poems whose subject is process; so that one can begin to talk of a "process vocabulary" as characterizing a "process poem."

The word "process" itself appears only four times in Thomas' poetry — in the poem we have been discussing. Process words are those that offer a good alternative for that key word. "Tides" is one such word. Like "weathers," the word is rare in the plural outside of Thomas' process vocabulary. We are accustomed to speak of "*the* tide," there being usually only one tide at a time. "Tides," as Thomas uses it, communicates a strange sense of the habitual rising and falling motions underlying universal flux.

> Where no sea runs, the waters of the heart
> Push in their tides.

These tides of *Light breaks where no sun shines*, like the tides in which the boys of summer drown the "cargoed apples" and with which they "choke the deserts," are more than a seaside phenomenon; they are the medium by which forces of change can be imagined as operating. In the words of *Before I knocked*, they are "tides that never touch the shores." In the same way, "eye" in the singular is often a process word. We see through our "eyes" (plural); the "eye" in Thomas is rather the globe within which forces of light and darkness clash. So that in our prototype process poem we find, "a process in the eye" and "a darkness in the weather of the eye"; and in *Light breaks where no sun shines*, "the secret of the soil grows through the eye"; and so on. Not every "eye" need be a process "eye," nor all "tides" process "tides"; but a count of these words and others like them, blunt though a count may be as a critical instrument, is impressive. "Tides" occurs eight times in six of the *18 Poems*, and only twice in the remainder of the poems (more than three times the number of lines). The more commonplace "tide" doesn't occur at all in *18 Poems*, but eleven times elsewhere. The process word "eye" occurs thirteen times in ten of the *18 Poems*, once in *I, in my intricate image* (which poem might be counted as the nineteenth of the *18 Poems*), and only eleven times elsewhere. On the other hand, "eyes" occurs only four times in *18 Poems*, but forty times elsewhere. Some other characteristic process words, with the ratio of their relatively high concentration in *18 Poems* (plus the nineteenth), are flesh 21:16, ghost 27:17, bone 22:33, blood 23:33, fork 7:5, bud 4:2, force 3:0, womb 8:7, vein 7:7, root 7:7, oil 6:3, wax 3:1, matter 3:1, skin 3:2, dry 16:13, damp 6:1, weather(s) 13:12.[2]

Generally speaking, we can say that process vocabulary (which is to say the process poem as well) has disappeared by the outbreak of war. Thomas used the plural "weathers" for the last time in 1938; and in that year we see him deliberately forgoing "weather" as a process word. In March 1938 he sent to Vernon Watkins a rewritten draft of *Not from this anger* (originally 20 April 1933 in the notebooks), with the line: "In a land without weathers." The poem is chronologically a pre-process poem, and this attempt by Thomas to tap the deeper process level produced a noticeable strain. Watkins must have remarked on it, for on 1 April 1938 Thomas wrote: "Before your letter came, I had cut out the ubiquitous 'weather' from the anticlimactic poem, and am revising it all."[3] He didn't revise the whole poem, but he did cut out the "land without weathers," substituting the present line: "In a land strapped by hunger."

"Without weather" meant that the land was without the working processes of nature. "Strapped by hunger" gives the same idea: the land is desolate. But the word "hunger" operates in its own image for desolation, not relying on previous connections with process themes. One "weather" couldn't make a poem a process poem. At the same time, for those who have previously felt its force, some of the process connotation stays with the word in its later more conventional usage, for example in *Poem in October* (perhaps begun 1939; finished 1944):

> There I could marvel
> My birthday
> Away but the weather turned around.

Or in the *Ballad of the Long-legged Bait* (1941):

> The boat swims into the six-year weather.

The contexts support the extraordinary meaning, the vestigial notion of underlying processes. The very fact that we can talk of vestigial meaning shows how strongly established is the use of "weather" as a process word.

Perhaps no other word can we be so sure about. Whenever we want to make a generalization about Thomas' use of words, we run up against one overriding generalization: that his words rarely have exactly the same meaning twice. Each new occurrence in an image is likely to call forth a new significance from the range of a word's possible meanings. Thomas was not being fair to himself when he said:

> I agree that each of my earlier poems might
> appear to constitute a section from one long

> poem; that is because I was not successful
> in making a momentary peace with my
> images at the correct moment; images were
> left dangling over the formal limits, and
> dragged the poem into another.[4]

If it were strictly true that these early poems were
all scoops from the same stream of images, then it
would be easy to explicate one poem by means of
another. The images, dangling over from one poem
to the next, would be common to both, and doubly
revealing. But we saw in the last chapter that Thomas'
images, despite the ultimate similarity in thought
content and a surface similarity of wording, are
usually quite distinct from one another. And although
we can identify certain words as "process" words,
the actual use of such words is not as mechanical as
a word count might suggest. They are not bricks, but
clay blocks to be molded differently in each image.
Such a word as "worm" (occurring in ten of the *18
Poems* and in only three later poems) is a good
process block, witness "the wormy winter" in *Especially when the October wind* (1934 version); but
it is used with a wide variety of denotative meanings
by Thomas: (a) charnel worm, (b) parasitic worm,
(c) phallic worm, (d) glowworm, (e) umbilical cord,
(f) Satan, and (g) the common garden worm. Given
this variety, in what respects can it be a called a
process word? For one thing, in its different meanings
it is very useful for making an image, which image
gives us the process theme. But why should it be
especially useful for making a process image? It is
simply that the word, whatever it denotes in the
image, cannot shake off its association with mortality.

If one's object is to communicate the idea of decay and death, one worm will perhaps do just as well as another; one gets variety of imagery within the single purpose.

On the other hand, Thomas did not perversely require that a word have a brand new meaning every time. Often when we suspect a rather extreme twist to a word, we find that the poet has moved in that direction elsewhere. "Man in his maggot" from *I see the boys of summer* is a case in point. We took "maggot" to indicate the man's flesh, his body. This occurrence of "maggot" is the last of seven (if we include those in the notebooks). It would be all to the good if the interpretation here were backed up by at least one of the seven. *Find meat on bones*, originally poem Forty Six in the February 1933 Notebook, has

> Rebel against the flesh and bone,
> The word of the blood, the wily skin,
> And the maggot no man can slay.

The rebellion here is against the body, the flesh and bone, blood and skin, and the "maggot," the symbol of decay, indicating the mortality of the whole body. We get even closer in poem Twenty Eight of the August 1933 Notebook, which begins

> Here lies the worm of man.

A dead man is speaking of himself lying under the ground, "worm" denoting the corpse itself. Thomas altered the line to: "Here lies the beast of man," which indicates that "worm" was roughly equivalent to "beast," the carcass of the man as opposed to his soul. Thomas apparently shied away from the use of "worm" here; six months later he did use the idea in *I see the boys of summer*, pushing it a stage further: "maggot" becomes the living body, barren in that it presages its own death. These are far-fetched images and readings; but two uncertainties, if they are found to have been fetched in the same way, may have the effect of increasing each other's certainty.[5]

[2]

The contending forces of growth and decay find their natural expression in antithetical imagery, one image posed against its opposite in imitation of the balance of forces. The likelihood of antithesis in a poem is a great help in explication. In *I see the boys of summer* the line "Here break a kiss in no love's quarry" had to be positive in order for the contraries to even out properly — there was at least that expectation to go on. Other process poems set up similar expectations in their rhetorical forms, notably *The force that through the green fuse drives the flower*, whose subtlety within antithesis is worth looking into:

The force that through the green fuse drives the
  flower
Drives my green age; that blasts the roots of trees
Is my destroyer.
And I am dumb to tell the crooked rose
My youth is bent by the same wintry fever.

The force that drives the water through the
     rocks
Drives my red blood; that dries the mouthing
     streams
Turns mine to wax.
And I am dumb to mouth unto my veins
How at the mountain spring the same mouth
     sucks.

The hand that whirls the water in the pool
Stirs the quicksand; that ropes the blowing wind
Hauls my shroud sail.
And I am dumb to tell the hanging man
How of my clay is made the hangman's lime.

The lips of time leech to the fountain head;
Love drips and gathers, but the fallen blood
Shall calm her sores.
And I am dumb to tell a weather's wind
How time has ticked a heaven round the stars.

And I am dumb to tell the lover's tomb
How at my sheet goes the same crooked worm.

As usual we look first for the dialectic breeding of
imagery. The gunpowder conceit of the first line
(the flower seen as an explosion at the top of its
stem, the fuse) supplies the "blasts" of the second
line, which, however, utilizes the alternative meaning
of "blasts" in the blighting of the roots of trees. The
disease element is retained in "fever"; and "blasts"
is recalled in "wintry," a third connotation. This is
a curious kind of balancing effect. Besides the literal
narrative, there is non-discursive communication in
the placing and permutating of the symbolic words

within the stanza frame. This presentational mode is part of the stuff of poetry — part of its magic, if not its meaning proper. We are chiefly concerned with meaning; but we should acknowledge the role of such balanced symbols in supporting, though unobtrusively, the balanced import of the assertions. Take, as a specially striking example, the "crooked worm" of the last line echoing the "crooked rose" of the first refrain. Such repetition binds a poem. An "unbound" poem gives quite a different sensation, which must affect the meaning in some way, though it seems impossible to speak of the effect in any but the vaguest terms. As a matter of fact, the link here has a direct bearing on meaning. The rose is "crooked" because it contains a "crooked worm." Derek Stanford is right to think of Blake's *The Sick Rose*.[6] Thomas surely had Blake in mind when he wrote the first draft in the August 1933 Notebook:

> The force that through the green fuse drives the
> flower
> Drives my green age; that blasts the roots of trees
> Is my destroyer.
> And I am dumb to tell the eaten rose
> How at my sheet goes the same crookèd worm,
> And dumb to holla thunder to the skies
> How at my cloths flies the same central storm.

We still have something of Blake's "howling storm" in the "wintry fever." The "worm" is split from the "rose"; but Blake's images now span the poem and the connection is telling.

Antithetical form is very clear in the first stanza: the force that, on the one hand, brings the flowering of youth causes, on the other hand, destruction, which is then emphasized in the refrain. The second stanza repeats the form:

> The force that drives the water through the
> rocks
> Drives my red blood; that dries the mouthing
> streams
> Turns mine to wax.

Again, the two forces, growth and destruction, operate both in nature and in the individual. The second refrain continues the theme, with a slight variation:

> I am dumb to mouth unto my veins
> How at the mountain spring the same mouth
> sucks.

Exactly parallel wording would have given, as the first refrain:

> I am dumb to mouth unto the spring
> How at my veins the same mouth sucks.

Besides avoiding exact repetition, the reversal adds an increment of meaning through a play on the word "mouth." "Mouthing streams" are streams at the mouth, the estuary. The mouth sucking at the mountain spring can be thought of as the estuary, sucking down the whole course of the stream into the sea. The force that drives the water through the rocks is the same as that which sucks it in at the mouth: in short, the creating and destroying forces are identical. This same mouth, the estuary, sucks at the veins. The poet is leading up to a leech image in stanza four, but here the image is of the bloodstream, the stream of life, beginning in youth, with time slowly sucking away vitality, pulling toward the estuary, death. The force that drives the blood also dries it; the force of youth pulls one on to age. The same idea is represented differently in the next stanza:

> The hand that whirls the water in the pool
> Stirs the quicksand; that ropes the blowing wind
> Hauls my shroud sail.

The force that whirls the water (positive action) stirs quicksand (betokening death). The force blows both the ship of life and the ship of death. The two forces are one.

Another extraordinary effect is achieved here. Imbedded in each side of the equation is a tacit counter-assertion. The hand whirling the pool brings up the idea of whirlpool, as much a symbol of destruction as the quicksand, which in turn has the under-suggestion of sands of life in the positive element "quick." And, similarly, to rope the blowing wind suggests a binding, constraining force; while the hauling of the sail, shroud or no, is very active, gives the impression of a voyage under way. These echoes, seemingly subversive to the image containing them, really support the theme, the point that the life and death forces are the same. When $A = B$, there is every reason for seeing B in A and A in B. Is this same kind of two-way cross current in the refrain?

> And I am dumb to tell the hanging man
> How of my clay is made the hangman's lime.

We certainly wouldn't see it unless we were looking for it. The poet's mortal clay is not only dead but is the receptor for dead flesh, doubly dead. Though the positive doesn't have much chance here, "lime" no doubt came down from "quicksand" (via quick-lime) and shares the same implication of "quick." The lime pit is, in a sense, cleansing. Positive effects can, according to Thomas' way of looking at things, come out of the macabre. This is the point of the next image:

> The lips of time leech to the fountain head;
> Love drips and gathers, but the fallen blood
> Shall calm her sores.

Time is a leech, which sucks at the fountain head of Love, making a sore wound. But the loss of blood, in keeping with archaic lore, is beneficial. The refrain of this stanza makes the same assertion of unexpected good coming from evil:

> And I am dumb to tell a weather's wind
> How time has ticked a heaven round the stars.

"Heaven" must be positive; Thomas would not use it ironically here.[7] When Time, usually the agent of destruction, ticks a *heaven* round the stars, it is un-expected, but that is the whole point — positive comes out of the usually negative.

As in certain lines of *I see the boys of summer* we have again the Christian doctrine of the fortunate fall. We cannot escape the Christian connotation in "heaven" and "fallen blood." "Fountain head," too, is very New Testament. Thomas elsewhere calls Christ "all glory's sawbones" (sonnet VIII), and "leech" is another name for doctor, Christ the doctor who saves us all, saves us from the "weather's wind" of mortality. This is not to say that we have here a

Christian poem. Thomas exploits the Christian concept of life coming out of death, just as he exploits
medieval medicine, just as, indeed, he exploits the
personal lament. How easy it would have been, were
this poem truly personal, to have said "calm *my*
sores" instead of "calm her [love's] sores." The personal references earlier are anonymous; the real subject is the idea of contending forces in nature and
the vital role of destruction. Of course, the forces
do cause dismay, and regret is the dominant response
to the world of flux. The refrains communicate this
tone, which is summed up in the final isolated couplet:

> And I am dumb to tell the lover's tomb
> How at my sheet goes the same crooked worm.

The poet is expressing his identity with the dead
lover, knowing himself to be mortal, the worm
already at his sheet as though it were his shroud. The
pathos here seems to set at nought the "heaven" of
the previous lines. At the end of his celebration of
the dual processes in nature, the poet emphasizes the
negative. We have learned to expect antithetical
statements in a process poem, but we cannot be too
stern if the poet eschews perfect regularity. Each
poem works out the antithesis in a way organic to
itself. It is natural that this poem should end at its
most elegiac. The poem is more than a bare statement
about forces. Our abstracting the conceptual meaning is not an effort to reduce the poem's stature, but
an effort to find the framework of absolute coherence
without which the images are merely suggestive. The
poem is, of course, all its constituent elements, all the
applicable connotations and symbolic implications, in-

cluding the elegiac tone. But the poem's "motivating center," as Thomas once put it, is the *idea* of the unity of contrary forces. And antithetical structure is one of the chief means of finding in the "womb of war" this center, this "momentary peace."

## [4]

Reserved for separate treatment are a small group of process poems that have the specific subject, dreams. *Our eunuch dreams* is the clearest of them. Indeed, it is gratifying to see how reasonable one of the "obscure" *18 Poems* can be. It is meticulously paragraphed in four sections, and it asserts the sensible values of the working world. One thing makes it, and the other dream poems, extraordinary: the precise nature of the indictment of the world of dreams.

I

Our eunuch dreams, all seedless in the light,
Of light and love, the tempers of the heart,
Whack their boys' limbs,
And, winding-footed in their shawl and sheet,
Groom the dark brides, the widows of the night
Fold in their arms.

The shades of girls, all flavoured from their
        shrouds,
When sunlight goes are sundered from the
        worm,
The bones of men, the broken in their beds,
By midnight pulleys that unhouse the tomb.

## II

In this our age the gunman and his moll,
Two one-dimensioned ghosts, love on a reel,
Strange to our solid eye,
And speak their midnight nothings as they swell;
When cameras shut they hurry to their hole
Down in the yard of day.

They dance between their arclamps and our
  skull,
Impose their shots, throwing the nights away;
We watch the show of shadows kiss or kill,
Flavoured of celluloid give love the lie.

The first two parts give the two worlds: first, dreams,
and then day-dreams, which is what the movies
amount to, in Thomas' view here. The dreams are
personified as ghosts rising nightly from their graves;
their actions are sexual and "flavoured of the shroud."
The "flavour" of celluloid is the same: sex and death.
The poet is driven to ask: Can either of these two
be the real world?

## III

Which is the world? Of our two sleepings,
  which
Shall fall awake when cures and their itch
Raise up this red-eyed earth?
Pack off the shapes of daylight and their starch,
The sunny gentlemen, the Welshing rich,
Or drive the night-geared forth.

The photograph is married to the eye,
Grafts on its bride one-sided skins of truth;
The dream has sucked the sleeper of his faith
That shrouded men might marrow as they fly.

Movies are cheating (welshing), dreams are equally deceiving. The question is a rhetorical one; neither of these two worlds will hold true in the world of daylight.

## IV

This is the world: the lying likeness of
Our strips of stuff that tatter as we move
Loving and being loth;
The dream that kicks the buried from their sack
And lets their trash be honoured as the quick.
This is the world. Have faith.

For we shall be a shouter like the cock,
Blowing the old dead back; our shots shall smack
The image from the plates;
And we shall be fit fellows for a life,
And who remain shall flower as they love,
Praise to our faring hearts.

In saying "This is the world" about movies and dreams, the poet is being sarcastic. "Have faith" is the turning point. The last section is a statement of positive action: the dreams are to be blown back, the screen figures shot at, and the values of waking life asserted.[8]

The full significance of *Our eunuch dreams* and its possibly over-optimistic ending is best seen through the perspective of three allied poems. The opening lines of *When once the twilight locks no longer* describe the birth and babyhood of the "I" of the poem, using sea imagery for the liquids of the womb and breast:

When once the twilight locks no longer
Locked in the long worm of my finger
Nor damned the sea that sped about my fist,
The mouth of time sucked, like a sponge,
The milky acid on each hinge,
And swallowed dry the waters of the breast.

When the galactic sea was sucked
And all the dry seabed unlocked,
I sent my creature scouting on the globe.

Then follows the images of the child's exploration
of himself, realizing and celebrating the world of daylight by holding "a little sabbath with the sun." However, the early version of this poem in the August
1933 Notebook has none of these images of exploration, but takes us immediately into the world of
sleep. The day is hardly introduced before the night
comes to destroy it:

When the galactic sea was sucked
And all the dry sea bed unlocked,
Rose the dry ghost of night to suck the day;
No hyleg but the Sleeper's star
Shone on this globe of bone and hair,
No star but sleep's was nodding in the sky.

Then follow six stanzas of nightmare images, which
were whittled down for the corresponding stanzas
of the final version coming after the exploratory lines.
The last stanza of the draft version intensifies the
connection between sleeping, dreaming, and death;
and, significantly, leaves us still inside the sleeper's
world:

There is no sweetness in the dead
I feel not in my sleeping blood;

Then sleep and dream, sleeps dreams and dies;
When once the twilight locks no longer
Locked in the long worm of my finger
I did unlock the Sleeper's eyes.

Ending thus, the early version shows itself to be entirely an exposé of the degrading aspects of dreams. So that when we come to the last two stanzas of the poem as printed we can see them in a much surer light. The next to last stanza recapitulates the poem: first the womb and nursing stages, then the exploration of the infant into the world of actuality, and finally a summary of the consequences of falling asleep.

When once the twilight screws were turned,
And mother milk was stiff as sand,
I sent my own ambassador to light;
By trick or chance he fell asleep
And conjured up a carcass shape
To rob me of my fluids in his heart.

The dead appear and rob the dreamer of "fluids." The poem is about the horror of dreams; and also, in the last stanza of the final version, about the joyful release into the waking world:

Awake, my sleeper, to the sun,
A worker in the morning town,
And leave the poppied pickthank where he lies;
The fences of the light are down,
All but the briskest riders thrown,
And worlds hang on the trees.

These are lines added later. Again, as in *Our eunuch dreams*, the poet's second thoughts were to emphasize the positive aspects of living.

The third dream poem, *I fellowed sleep*, takes us almost immediately into the world of sleep with which the previous two poems have made us familiar. The geography of the sleeper's journey is rather more complicated here because it is really two journeys from two separate draft poems in the August 1933 Notebook: (1) Thirty One, a short pessimistic poem, very much in the dream-death category, and (2) Twenty Two, a visionary poem, which gives us a heaven not a nightmare. Without knowing these early drafts we might find it difficult to see that the change in location in stanza four of the published poem involves a spiritual change to optimism. Dreaming, then, is an important matter to Thomas. When he says, "These are but dreaming men," he really is talking about dreams and not about some remoter subject, a subject which, naturally, one cannot grasp, because it doesn't exist. And the optimistic ending to all these three poems means that it is important to him that we should "breathe" in "the living air."

The clue to the importance of dreams is given in the early draft of *From love's first fever to her plague*, a poem which is a fairly straightforward account of an individual's development through different stages from conception to adolescence. Symbolic of the kind of experience in each period, a numerical value increases with increasing awareness: one, two, four, and then a jump to a million. The last line gives a twist to the conceit: "One sun, one manna, warmed and fed." With this glance back at a supposed single source of life-power, the poem as we have it ends satisfactorily. In its manuscript ver-

sion, however, the poem continues with a description
of youth, the stage that the poem has brought us to:

> Now that drugged youth is waking from its
>     stupor,
> The nervous hand rehearsing on the thigh
> Acts with a woman, one sum remains in cipher;
> Five senses and the frozen brain
> Are one with wind, and itching in the sun.

A hand on the thigh rehearsing acts with a woman —
this can only be interpreted as onanism. The numerical conceit is used to express the nullity of the act.
In cutting out these depressing lines Thomas produced, again, a more optimistic poem. By leaving
them in the notebooks, however, he has given the
key to the other dream poems. It is in the same stage
of youth, reached by the end of the second stanza
of *When once the twilight locks no longer*, that the
hero of that poem falls asleep:

> But when the stars, assuming shape,
> Drew in his eyes the straws of sleep,
> He drowned his father's magic in a dream.

A dream that drowns is a wet dream — the implication, as with the "drugged youth" of the previous
poem, is sexual waste. The same implication is in the
key line of the poem: "To rob me of my fluids in
his heart." The manuscript version of the poem is
full of specific references: "leaked their midnight
seed," "the seed of dreams," "Sleep is the winding
lover in my cloth." The pessimistic early draft of
*I fellowed sleep* has such lines as "I fathered dreams
as races from the loins" and "I fellowed sleep who
drained me with a kiss." Poem Eleven in the February

1933 Notebook has perhaps the most direct statement about loss of seed:

> In wasting one drop from the heart's honey
>     cells,
> One precious drop that, for the moment, quells
> Desire's pain, eases love's itch and ills,
> There's less remains.

This sexual waste is equivalent to death. There is the boy's blunt reference in the story "A Prospect of the Sea" to "death from playing with yourself." The manuscript version of *When once the twilight locks no longer* has the lines:

> Crow on my heap, O living deaths;
> There is no horror death bequeathes
> I cannot number on this sleepy hand.

The threat Thomas sees in dreams, then, is not fanciful but physical. Sexual waste becomes the chief symbol for all the other waste of youth in the land of dreams, day dreams, night dreams, or even movies. This is why the dreams are "eunuch" and "whack their boys' limbs." They are infertile; they "groom the dark brides," but "no children break, all flavored, into light" (this line a variant in the first printing of *Our eunuch dreams*). Sexual waste, standing for all waste, is equivalent to death in life: this is the essential significance of the three dream poems.

The fight between the forces of night and day, dreams and waking action, waste of sex and proper use of sex, is part of the universal antithesis of growth and decay. The dream poems fall readily under the heading of process poems. *A process in the weather of the heart* itself uses an image that could have come from a dream poem:

> The seed that makes a forest of the loin
> Forks half its fruit; and half drops down,
> Slow in a sleeping wind.

If we wanted to be very strict about a definition of "process poem," we perhaps would have to limit it to those which utilize images (images of sexual waste, for instance, as above) to express process, and exclude those which utilize process images to express something else, the stages of growth or the harm in sexual waste, for example. This strict category would be very small, perhaps only *I see the boys of summer*, *A process in the weather of the heart*, *The force that through the green fuse drives the flower*, *Light breaks where no sun shines*, and *All all and all the dry worlds lever*. After that one draws an arbitrary line.[9] Perhaps any poem that Thomas writes in praise of mortality, even later ones such as *Poem in October*, *Fern Hill*, and *Over Sir John's hill*, has process at the core. In practice, the word "process" serves to denote those poems containing a particular kind of diction, usually accompanied by antithetical structure, giving a sense of the interplay of forces beneath the ordinary events of life.

# Chapter IV

# *Distancing the Intimate*

> *"You can put all you have to say in a single sentence and it isn't a poem. You can say God is Love, or Love is God, and have done with it—go out and play golf."*
>
> Dylan Thomas in Utah, 1952

TO EXPRESS THE IMPORTANT and intimate facts of experience without seeming to blurt them out — this is the task the poet sets himself. Thomas in his youth made several important poems from the personal, and dangerously bathetic, subject of onanism. He did so by stating sexual waste not in terms unbearably close to the subject but in remoter images such as nightmare and graveyard figures. In his marriage poems, where the secrets of the marriage bed — so to speak — are in jeopardy, much of the energy generated is in the holding back, in the forging of configurations that let out the secrets with sufficient caution, turning into fine poetry what would otherwise be mere salacious information. That these controls are esthetic rather than prudish is clear from the shamelessly sexual subject that the words do, finally, communicate. Take, for instance, the vigorous representation of sexual union in the first two stanzas of *A grief ago:*

A grief ago,
She who was who I hold, the fats and flower,
Or, water-lammed, from the scythe-sided thorn,
Hell wind and sea,
A stem cementing, wrestled up the tower,
Rose maid and male,
Or, masted venus, through the paddler's bowl
Sailed up the sun;

Who is my grief,
A chrysalis unwrinkling on the iron,
Wrenched by my fingerman, the leaden bud
Shot through the leaf,
Was who was folded on the rod the aaron
Rose cast to plague,
The horn and ball of water on the frog
Housed in the side.

Our grammar books won't let Thomas get away
with "She who was who I hold." Actually few people
have qualms about using "who" for "whom" where
it feels natural to do so. But we might challenge the
second "who" on other grounds. Is it really needed
at all? Is there a significant change if we recast the
lines?

A grief ago
She who I hold [did such and such].

Two things are lost by dropping the "She who was
who I hold." First, the idea that the "she" now being
held is a somewhat different person from the "she"
who *was* being held a grief before; second, the uni-
versalizing that comes with this kind of "who," which
has something of the sense of "whoever at all." The
"she I hold" is a far too familiar body of bones. "She

who was who I hold" is the mysteriously estranged loved one. We are made more remote from the particular intimate act of love, but perhaps all the closer to the essential nature of it. The distancing is achieved here and elsewhere by using syntax as though it were a lock-gate, allowing meaning to come slowly through regulated compartments. This delay in completing the sense is important in dealing with intimate things; it avoids the danger of flippancy. Moreover, to disturb customary syntax is to affect normal space and time relationships. *A grief ago* takes place all within the few moments after sexual union, but by means of the syntax we are flashed back to genesis and forward to the day of judgment; the history of the world is concentrated into the moment.

Thomas' abnormal syntax may occasionally be confusing; but it is rare that grammatical requirements are not rigorously met. The first stanza of *A grief ago* is a good test case. If we italicize the three main verbs, the actions of the subject "she," and enclose in brackets appositional descriptive material (adverbs being put into parentheses), the stanza becomes:

> (A grief ago,)
> She [who was who I hold,] [the fats and
>     flower,]
> [Or, water-lammed, (from the scythe-sided
>     thorn,)
> Hell wind and sea,]
> [A stem cementing,] *wrestled* (up the tower),
> *Rose* [maid and male],
> Or [, masted venus,] (through the paddler's
>     bowl)
> *Sailed* (up the sun).

The stanza is clearly a "she did something" sentence. That "something" is one action; but Thomas uses syntax that will allow for three very active verbs, each with graphic adverbial adjuncts, while adding several appositional descriptions of the "she," all this with correct, though difficult, grammar.

Literary craftsmanship has traditionally met the challenge of blank paper by such devices of amplification and compression. *A Refusal to Mourn the Death, by Fire, of a Child in London* is in the same tradition as, though a good deal more serious than, Chaucer's *occupatio*, the rhetorical technique of confessing it to be beyond his skill to describe what he then goes on to describe. The "I am dumb to tell" of *The force that through the green fuse drives the flower* is the same device of volubly protesting a lack of words. And there are many other techniques. The rhetorical question, which goes at least part of the way to answering itself, is common in Thomas:

> What shall it tell me if a timeless insect
> Says the world wears away?
> (*Here in this spring*).

It structures the first two stanzas of *How shall my animal* and the opening lines of *Vision and Prayer*. Thomas has messengers within his poems. "I tell her this" in *A grief ago* is a good example. Quaintly, in *A Winter's Tale*, the tale itself is brought into the poem like a boat, "pale breath of cattle at the stealthy sail." *Poem in October* opens with the morning beckoning the poet with its harbor noises. In *Over Sir John's hill* the poet reads psalms in "the leaves of the water" and hears "death" in a shell. The first half of

the *Ballad of the Long-legged Bait* is mainly made
up of running commentary from a number of incidental personae such as "the dwindling ships" and
"the laughing fish." One happy form of amplification
is to express the negative of what *doesn't* happen in
order to communicate what *does:*

> . . . the lover's rub
> That wipes away not crow's-foot nor the lock
> Of sick old manhood on the fallen jaws
> > (*If I were tickled by the rub of love*);

or to pretend ignorance of which of two possibilities
pertains, where both (or neither, as in the case of
dreams and movies in *Our eunuch dreams*) apply:

> I know not whether
> Adam or Eve, the adorned holy bullock
> Or the white ewe lamb
> Or the chosen virgin
> Laid in her snow
> On the altar of London,
> Was the first to die
> > (*Ceremony After a Fire Raid*).

An extreme example of this use of the rhetorical negative is in the Prayer part of *Vision and Prayer*, where
the poet prays in the name of the wrong people:

> In the name of the lost who glory in
> The swinish plains of carrion
>
> . . . . . . .
>
> In the name of the wanton
> Lost on the unchristened mountain
>
> . . . . . . .

> O in the name
> Of no one
> Now or
>
> No
> One to
> Be  . . .

But he is praying, in their unholy or nonexistent
names, for the *opposite* of what he wants. He prays

> That he [Christ] let the dead lie though they moan
> For his briared hands to hoist them
> To the shrine of his world's wound
>
> . . . . . . .
>
> May the crimson
> Sun spin a grave grey
> And the color of clay
> Stream upon his martyrdom.

All this could have been done much more easily with
a single positive statement; but two wrongs make a
right — and also a poem.

The choice of metaphor, as well as the syntac-
tical arrangement, is an important factor in distancing.
The man in the street is often an expert at handling
sexual matters with images that utilize metaphoric
wordplay. Few would be unwilling to concede
Thomas supremacy in this area, however. See him
at work in the first stanza of *A grief ago*, where the
girl's motions are the focus of attention. Cementing
a stem, she wrestles up the tower; rises maid and
male; as a masted venus, she sails up the sun through
the paddler's bowl. These are images for the welcoming of penetration, a highly erotic subject; but
Thomas has managed to find words that communicate

the event without eroticism. "Masted venus" — why doesn't this image, a most dynamic way of saying that the female is completely possessed ("masted") by the male, strike us as prurient? One reason is the sharpness of the wording, the opposite of slyness. Further, the image, as well as being sexually symbolic, has to take its place in the literal image-narrative. The venus is masted *like a boat* and, in the next line, *sails*. The sailing image is remote from any pictorial representation of joined parts of the body.

Another description of complete penetration, in *The tombstone told when she died*, is a contrast:

> I died before bedtime came
> But my womb was bellowing
> And I felt with my bare fall
> A blazing red harsh head tear up
> And the dear floods of his hair.

Thomas himself was troubled by this warmer, closer imagery:

> The word "dear" fits in, I think, with "though her eyes smiled," which comes earlier. I wanted the girl's *terrible* reaction to orgastic [sic] death to be suddenly altered into a kind of despairing love. As I see it now, it strikes me as very moving, but it may be too much of a shock, a bathetic shock perhaps.[1]

Yes, the passage *is* moving and vivid (the "hair" is pubic hair), which is just what the imagery of *A grief ago* isn't. To be moved one must be struck by a familiar chord. Perhaps the most immediately moving lines in *A grief ago* are:

Tugged through the days
Her ropes of heritage.

They draw on a fairly conventional image of struggle
and oppression. But in these lines — and those from
*The tombstone told when she died* — Thomas is least
himself. He is most himself when he has forced us
to take a new view of something (a "masted venus"
for instance) by putting us at a distance from the
intimate.

[2]

Freud discovered that the unconscious or sleeping mind is a great coiner of euphemistic metaphors,
and that the coinage shows certain consistencies. To
know about the specific figures that the unconscious
mind repeatedly uses as metaphors should, on the
face of it, be useful in studying poetry. After all,
poetry is at one stage or another a heeding of the
sights and sounds from the muse in the unconscious.
But, strictly speaking, Freudian symbols arise from
the need of our minds "to give a *disguised* representation to their latent thoughts."[2] Freud is really dealing with what happens when the mind works against
itself. Only when we find an author *unwittingly* producing symbols we recognize as Freudian can we
apply Freud's theory — though one might challenge
the value of reading into a work levels of meaning
of which the author was not himself aware. Thomas
was very clear on this point. His answer to the *New
Verse* question on Freudian influence shows him to
be well aware of the significance of repression and

actively interested in combatting it. He wanted to go further than Freud:

> Poetry must drag further into the clean nakedness of light more even of the hidden causes than Freud could realize.[3]

Thus the applicability of Freud to Thomas seems severely limited. The symbolism behind which a repressed mind hides itself should be approached differently from the symbolism by means of which the poet consciously desires to reveal.

At the same time, the well-known Freudian symbols constitute a shared sexual language. Everything today is either concave or convex. Such a word as "crocodile" (used twice by Thomas) can gain a simple denotative meaning from being in the Freudian bestiary. Thomas must have known he was being Freudian in certain places — the dream sequences at the beginning of *Under Milk Wood*, for instance. Another case, perhaps, is in *Into her Lying Down Head*. A room generally represents a woman, and the snake is the most important symbol of the male member.[4] So we can decode the sexual event behind the words:

> There where a numberless tongue
> Wound their room with a male moan,
> His faith around her flew undone
> And darkness hung the walls with baskets of
> snakes.

As Thomas puts it: "Man is denying his partner man or woman and whores with the whole night."[5] The question, however, is whether or not we really need recourse to Freud. The associational logic that our dreaming mind is said to exhibit in its symbol-making is equally available to our waking mind. If the sleeping mind "deceives" itself with a dream of Aaron's rod, for instance, the poet should be able to use the same analogizing process in order to communicate deliberately the sexual significance. We simply do not need Freud to tell us that scythe, thorn, stem, tower, mast, paddle, and sun are male symbols, and fats, flower, and bowl are female; nor to divulge the secret of the water imagery in the mythology of *A grief ago:* "The people's sea drives on her"; "The dens of shape / Shape all her whelps with the long voice of water"; "Let her inhale her dead, through seed and solid / Draw in their seas." Water and the sea are naturally associated with conception and birth; the physical processes involve fluids at every stage, seminal to amniotic. And one does not feel especially relieved to find this association confirmed by Freud. What Freud contributes to an understanding of sexual imagery is just what we can now (post-Freudians that we are) most take for granted, i.e. that sexual matters will generally be imaged by some physically similar counterpart. One tussles with the intricacy of Thomas' imagery in somewhat the same manner as Freud tackled dreams, but trusting that the poet's creating, censoring, and selecting mind has a responsibility and skill that the dreaming mind does not; in short, that the distancing is esthetic rather than psychotic, conscious rather than the result of repression in the unconscious.

Let us see, then, with or without Freud, what we can make of perhaps the most obscure and involved sexual imagery in *A grief ago:*

[She] Was who was folded on the rod the aaron
Rose cast to plague,
The horn and ball of water on the frog
Housed in the side.

The context indicates that the girl is folded on
(wrapped around) a male rod. This rod is described
as the one which "the aaron rose cast to plague." In
the Biblical story, "Aaron stretched out his hand with
his rod, and smote the dust of the earth, and it became
lice." For the second applicable meaning of "plague"
we turn back to *From love's first fever to her plague*
where the word means "production of offspring."
Plague breeds, and children are a pestilence. So that
when the "aaron rose" (i.e. herself acting like Aaron)
casts the rod to plague, she can be said to be creating
children by means of it, "cast" recalling the fishing
image for sexual reproduction in *Ballad of the Long-
legged Bait*. The masculinity of "aaron" is softened
by an echo of the feminine "sharon rose." "Rose"
itself is a common symbol for the female. No one
can doubt what is going on when we have rod and
rose together. But no more than in previous instances
is the imagery erotic. The complexity makes its own
demands on our attention, and thus keeps us at a
distance from the sexual event.

"Horn and ball of water on the frog" is perhaps
even more difficult. Grammar indicates that the phrase
is equivalent to the "rod" above. "Horn," at least,
has well-established phallic connotations. "Ball" added
to "horn" is, one presumes, completing a stylized representation. "Of water" makes a connection with
"water-lammed" in the first stanza and the other
water imagery generally symbolic of insemination and

gestation. The horn and ball of water are "housed in the side" — the Miltonic sense of "side" as the womb. "On the frog" is not only grotesque but unclear. "Frog" probably has its root meaning of "jump." Brought into the poem because of the Egyptian plague of frogs — another of Thomas' superficial associations — the image evokes the sufficiently suggestive physical action, leap-frog. The wording "on the frog" denotes a continuous action, like "on the hop" or "on the make." One has no need to investigate what the phrase might mean to a patient of Freud's, but rather what possible ways there are of playing on the normal meaning of "frog" and "leap-frog." One enters Thomas' sexual imagery, like his other imagery, through the dictionary meanings and the verbal turns he seems likely to be making.

Provided there is an essential connectedness between the thing and the distancing image, the remoter the image the more esthetically effective it is. Hence the telling use of death imagery for sexual matters. Love and death are, paradoxically, both far apart and very close. This paradox, which gives the title of *A grief ago* its significance, is at the core of the conception stanzas of the poem:

> And she who lies,
> Like exodus a chapter from the garden,
> Brand of the lily's anger on her ring,
> Tugged through the days
> Her ropes of heritage, the wars of pardon,
> On field and sand
> The twelve triangles of the cherub wind
> Engraving going.

Who then is she,
She holding me? The people's sea drives on her,
Drives out the father from the caesared camp;
The dens of shape
Shape all her whelps with the long voice of
     water,
That she I have,
The country-handed grave boxed into love,
Rise before dark.

The night is near,
A nitric shape that leaps her, time and acid;
I tell her this: before the suncock cast
Her bone to fire,
Let her inhale her dead, through seed and solid
Draw in their seas,
So cross her hand with their grave gipsy eyes,
And close her fist.

Behind the wit of "And she who lies,/Like exodus a
chapter from the garden," which uses Old Testament
imagery to denote the resting of the withdrawn
couple, is the serious identification of the girl with
Eve and of the sexual act with the first sin against
purity in Eden. God's command to go out and mul-
tiply was coincident with His imposing the penalty
of mortality. It is as though death forces one to love.
Thomas gives us the image of the grave "boxing" the
girl into love. The grave has "countries" for hands,
countries a symbol of national and personal history
and endurance — as in the lines:

   [She] Tugged through the days
   Her ropes of heritage, the wars of pardon,
   On field and sand

The twelve triangles of the cherub wind
Engraving going.

The tug-of-war image represents the burden that the
Fall has imposed. The wind is the agent of death,
not only wearing the girl down, but engraving,
bringing her to her grave. Death is the lover who
leaps her — and then we have the lover as the herald
of doomsday and also, with the apocalyptic "suncock"
and its connotations of male potency, of birth. There
is a long literary tradition for lovers dying in sex,
but Thomas' is a far more serious use of the conceit
than probably any since the seventeenth century.
The dead hover over the conception; they are in a
mystical way the ingredients of life: "Let her inhale
her dead."

[3]

Thomas often expresses the sexual in religious
terms. With characteristic frankness and sacrilegious-
ness — frank and sacrilegious because the cross, as
something that has to be borne, cannot escape phallic
connotations in this poem — the "old ram rod" of
Lament sighs:

When I was a man you could call a man
And the black cross of the holy house.

Thomas can say with truth, "I know the legend / Of
Adam and Eve is never for a second / Silent in my
service" (Ceremony After a Fire Raid). In a sense,
the religious merely serves for esthetic purposes. The
range of basically non-sacred religious imagery runs
from the casual

And the sabbath rang slowly
In the pebbles of the holy streams
>                    (*Fern Hill*)

to the emphatic

> No. Not for Christ's dazzling bed
>                 ('*If my head hurt a hair's foot*').

At times Christ is used as a simile:

> The young stars told me,
> Hurling into beginning like Christ the child
>                  (*Unluckily for a Death*).

But then we have the reverse situation. Christ appears as Himself in some poems, and metaphors are then found for Him. And just as Christ is used rather cavalierly in figures of speech, so are rather cavalier figures of speech found for Christ. There is sometimes real doubt whether Christ is being praised or defamed. In the Buffalo notebooks, an undated epigram reads, in part:

> If God is praised in poem one
> Show no surprise when in the next
> I worship wood or sun or none.

One of Thomas' first published poems, in *Adelphi* (September 1933), has the same duality:

> No man believes who cries not, God is not,
>
>         .    .    .    .    .    .    .
>
> Believe and be saved. No man believes
> Who curses not what makes and saves.
>
>         .    .    .    .    .    .    .

> And this is true, no man can live
> Who does not bury God in a deep grave
> And then raise up the skeleton again.

The same scorn seems to appear in such poems as *Incarnate devil* and *Shall gods be said to thump the clouds* to say nothing of more juvenile poems left in manuscript. But *Before I knocked* is a different matter; it is a harsh, sincere reaction to the idea of Christ's mortality:

> You who bow down at cross and altar,
> Remember me and pity Him
> Who took my flesh and bone for armour
> And doublecrossed my mother's womb.

This harshness, and the "Jack of Christ" in other poems, is a deliberate distancing device, whose effect lies in the commitment to a deity that one dares disparage. Thomas talked of his father's atheism, an atheism which

> had nothing to do with whether there was a god or not, but was a violent and personal dislike for God. He would glare out of the window and growl: "It's raining, blast Him!" or, "The sun is shining — Lord, what foolishness!"[6]

Thomas' own attitude to Christ is probably closer to his father's than to that of Hopkins or Francis Thompson, say. Even in his most devotional poem, *Vision and Prayer*, Thomas has achieved distancing (paradoxically) by getting so close to the birth of Christ that it ceases to be a sentimental nativity and becomes the birth of the poet's own child in the next room.

To avoid identifying the chief character, certainly one way of distancing, is one of the several means used in Thomas' other main Christian document, the sonnet sequence *Altarwise by owl-light*. In the first sonnet he is "the gentleman," and "that gentleman of wounds" (which helps); but he is other things as well:

> Altarwise by owl-light in the half-way house
> The gentleman lay graveward with his furies;
> Abaddon in the hangnail cracked from Adam,
> And, from his fork, a dog among the fairies,
> The atlas-eater with a jaw for news,
> Bit out the mandrake with to-morrow's scream.
> Then, penny-eyed, that gentleman of wounds,
> Old cock from nowheres and the heaven's egg,
> With bones unbuttoned to the half-way winds,
> Hatched from the windy salvage on one leg,
> Scraped at my cradle in a walking word
> That night of time under the Christward shelter:
> I am the long world's gentleman, he said,
> And share my bed with Capricorn and Cancer.

We have previously glanced at the "atlas-eater" lines in taking up Thomas' complaint that Edith Sitwell didn't read them literally. Thomas gave the "literal" reading:

> a world-devouring ghost creature bit out the
> horror of to-morrow from a gentleman's
> loins.[7]

In other words, this is a form of castration. One thinks immediately of sonnet VIII:

> I by the tree of thieves, all glory's sawbones,
> Unsex the skeleton this mountain minute.

Again, the religious is expressed in sexual terms, the violence of the crucifixion being like a castration, the sacrifice a self-castration. Gods of other cultures have performed this act; but the whole problem is made more difficult in sonnet I by the castration's being performed by a strange creature described first as a dog and then an atlas-eater. And Thomas doesn't clarify too much in his further "literal" interpretation of the lines. There is no hint of the Christian key:

> A "jaw for news" is an obvious variation of a "nose for news", and means that the mouth of the creature can taste already the horror that has not yet come, or can sense its coming, can thrust its tongue into the news that has not yet been made, can savour the enormity of the progeny before the seed stirs, can realise the crumbling of dead flesh before the opening of the womb that delivers that flesh to to-morrow. What is this creature? It's the dog among the fairies, the rip and cur among the myths, the snapper at demons, the scarer of ghosts, the wizard's heel-chaser.[8]

Trying to make the creature seem a literal atlas-eater with a jaw for news, he keeps re-phrasing the image. He tries to find synonyms for the dog among the fairies. But, imagination having got the better of analysis, he is in effect writing a continuation of the poem. We are left to do the analyzing. The creature that bites out the mandrake is, in its simplest terms, biting out a symbol of mortality; the creature senses the "crumbling of dead flesh" and bites it out. The event just before this in the poem is syntactically an exact parallel: "Abaddon in the hangnail" cracks off from Adam.[9] "Adam" is Christ the Man, the second Adam, in this crucifixion scene. "Abaddon in the hangnail" is the devil, the devil in the flesh, another symbol for sin and mortality. The event is the Redemption. Man is being released from sin and death through the physical violence done to Christ's body. Who performs this physical violence? In the first image, the Abaddon cracks off without an agent being present. In the castration image proper, the agent is the "atlas-eater," whom Thomas describes as a "world-devouring ghost creature." Let us take him up on that word *ghost*, and postulate the Holy Ghost, who certainly is a "wizard's heel-chaser" (i.e. "a dog among the fairies") in the sense brought out in Milton's "Nativity Ode," one of Thomas' favorite poems, the pagan gods fleeing before Him. It is perhaps better not to stick to the conventional Trinity. Rather let us put it that the spiritual element in the Christ figure is working the miracle of Redemption on the physical Christ, the "sawbones" (doctor, who heals, saves) aspect of Christ operating on the "skeleton" Christ, as sonnet VIII has it. After all, it is none other than Christ himself who gave himself up to torture and death. This is a one-man drama, which Thomas splits into multiple roles.

It is basic to Thomas' idiom that a person should divide and walk on two levels, and see himself walking there. The Godhead does this in *Before I knocked*:

I, born of flesh and ghost, was neither
A ghost nor man, but mortal ghost.
And I was struck down by death's feather.
I was mortal to the last

Long breath that carried to my father
The message of his dying christ.

The ordinary individual can be a trinity in himself:

My hero bares my side and sees his heart
Tread, like a naked Venus,
The beach of flesh, and wind her bloodred plait
        (*My hero bares his nerves*);

I sent my creature scouting on the globe,
That globe itself of hair and bone
That, sewn to me by nerve and brain,
Had stringed my flask of matter to his rib
        (*When once the twilight locks no longer*).

We have to be sure of this ingrained notion of split-identity in Thomas, because it is the only reasonable key to the first sonnet.[10] For Christ is not only on the Cross (and, as we have seen, the Redemption involves more than one aspect of His personality), but He is also the Christ child in the cradle:

[The gentleman of wounds]
Scraped at my cradle in a walking word
That night of time under the Christward shelter.

The "Christward shelter" gives us the nativity scene; there is no point in trying to imagine the poet in a Swansea cradle. The use of "my" is just another example of the "me-Him" split that we come across so often in Thomas. Here Christ just off the Cross comes to visit the newly-born Christ. The Nativity is put against the backdrop of Calvary. It is as though the Babe were being told the significance of His incarnation "in a walking word" by the Christ who has just "Hatched from the windy salvage on one leg." "Hatched" is the key word in the sonnet. It refers to the crucifixion: "on one leg" is a grotesquely simple way of speaking of the upright of the Cross, and "the windy salvage" is this world of mortality, a "salvage" because it is the thing saved by Christ. Though used to indicate death, "hatched" has at the same time all the connotations of birth, birth into everlasting life, Christ's second nativity. Thomas' sonnet sequence on the significance of Christ, then, begins appropriately with the Nativity as the subject of the first sonnet — but the Nativity approached so obliquely that we have to shed all conventional sentiments by the time we arrive at it. This is the final aim of distancing: not to obscure, but to prevent us from rushing in with the hackneyed, with our own notions rather than the poet's.

# Chapter V

# *Last Poems*

WE HAVE ATTEMPTED TO SEE what lies behind the obscurity of Thomas' early poetry; with the last poems we have to ask what lies behind their comparative clarity. The "Note" to the *Collected Poems*, dated November 1952, seems especially applicable to the later poems of the volume: they were written "for the love of Man and in praise of God." But behind that solemnity one can hear the poet's alternative phrasing to John Malcolm Brinnin in July 1951: "poems in praise of God's world by a man who doesn't believe in God."[1] The answer to the riddle posed by these statements is perhaps best sought in the poems themselves, for instance in *Over Sir John's hill* where universal mortality is symbolized in the actual scene from the poet's window overlooking the estuary of the Taf and Towy at Laugharne, South Wales. God is mentioned twice in the poem; we seek the significance of these two allusions:

Over Sir John's hill,
The hawk on fire hangs still;

In a hoisted cloud, at drop of dusk, he pulls to
    his claws
And gallows, up the rays of his eyes the small
    birds of the bay
And the shrill child's play
Wars
Of the sparrows and such who swansing, dusk,
    in wrangling hedges.
And blithely they squawk
To fiery tyburn over the wrestle of elms until
The flash the noosed hawk
Crashes, and slowly the fishing holy stalking
    heron
In the river Towy below bows his tilted
    headstone.


Flash, and the plumes crack,
And a black cap of jack-
Daws Sir John's just hill dons, and again the
    gulled birds hare
To the hawk on fire, the halter height, over
    Towy's fins,
In a whack of wind.
There
Where the elegiac fisherbird stabs and paddles
In the pebbly dab-filled
Shallow and sedge, and 'dilly dilly,' calls the loft
    hawk,
'Come and be killed,'
I open the leaves of the water at a passage
Of psalms and shadows among the pincered
    sandcrabs prancing

And read, in a shell,
Death clear as a buoy's bell:

All praise of the hawk on fire in hawk-eyed dusk
   be sung,
When his viperish fuse hangs looped with flames
   under the brand
Wing, and blest shall
Young
Green chickens of the bay and bushes cluck,
   'dilly dilly,
Come let us die.'
We grieve as the blithe birds, never again, leave
   shingle and elm,
The heron and I,
I young Aesop fabling to the near night by the
   dingle
Of eels, saint heron hymning in the shell-hung
   distant

Crystal harbour vale
Where the sea cobbles sail,
And wharves of water where the walls dance
   and the white cranes stilt.
It is the heron and I, under judging Sir John's
   elmed
Hill, tell-tale the knelled
Guilt
Of the led-astray birds whom God, for their
   breast of whistles,
Have mercy on,
God in his whirlwind silence save, who marks
   the sparrows hail,
For their souls' song.
Now the heron grieves in the weeded verge.
   Through windows
Of dusk and water I see the tilting whispering

Heron, mirrored, go,
As the snapt feathers snow,
Fishing in the tear of the Towy. Only a hoot owl
Hollows, a grassblade blown in cupped hands,
    in the looted elms
And no green cocks or hens
Shout
Now on Sir John's hill. The heron, ankling the
    scaly
Lowlands of the waves,
Makes all the music; and I who hear the tune of
    the slow
Wear-willow river, grave,
Before the lunge of the night, the notes on this
    time-shaken
Stone for the sake of the souls of the slain birds
    sailing.

Do sparrows have souls? In what theological
sense can they possibly be saved? Or, to recast the
question in keeping with the parable nature of the
poem, do human beings (with their "shrill, child's-
play wars") have immortal souls whose destiny depends on God's mercy being evoked by prayer? The
same kind of question attends the basic courtroom
metaphor in the poem. As often before, Thomas is
acting out a common expression: "We are all condemned to die." In the traditional religious sense we
are *condemned* by Adam's original sin, and are personally *saved* by the redemption of Christ. The use
of "save," "blest," "mercy," etc. in the poem suggests
the traditional approach; but the poem doesn't really
go beyond the mere suggestion. The word "guilt" is
used, but without seriously indicating in what sense
the small birds (or we unknown soldiers) are guilty.

Although Sir John's hill puts on the black cap for our death sentence, there is no real judgment as there is no real crime. Where a little sermonizing of the scene might be expected in the poem, one looks in vain. The hawk-executioner, especially, might have been given moral import; but the poet's intention seems to have been quite the opposite.

It is worth-while looking closely at the language used to describe the hawk, and this is one case where there is little doubt as to the kind of decision that produced the particular wording. Harvard College Library has the working papers for this poem, and although they are extensive and cumbersome (forty-seven sheets for the single poem), we can with a high degree of accuracy follow the poet from the first conception to the completed poem. Some phrases are worked and reworked up to forty-one times. We are given an opportunity to see exactly what kind of pains Thomas took. Pertinent to our concern with the personality, if any, of the hawk is the phrase "halter height" in the second stanza of the poem:

> . . . and again the gulled birds hare
> To the hawk on fire, the halter height, over
> Towy's fins.

As we might expect, the words are descriptive and symbolic at the same time. The hawk catches the last rays of the sun and is "on fire" — this is apt description. But it is also symbolic, connected to the doomsday-explosion symbolism running through the poem, by which the hawk is viewed as a gunpowder fuse ready to go off. Thus, the hawk is as much a metaphor for the symbolic fire as the fire is a meta-

phoric way of describing the hawk. The poet's efforts
in the work sheets are directed toward finding the
diction that will successfully act this double role,
symbolic description and descriptive symbolism.

The "hawk on fire" in the passage above began,
it seems, quite simply as the "high hawk." What
appears to be the next draft incorporates both the
gallows and the gunpowder images in "the hempen
firing hawk," a foreshadowing of the final phrase,
"the hawk on fire, the halter height." The work
sheets often show that first thoughts are the best,
but the poet proves it to himself by trying out alternatives. In subsequent rewritings of this part of the
poem we find him substituting different phrases while
simply recopying the adjacent lines. He introduces
a brutal image of slaughter: "the skinning hawk."
Then, as though to soften somewhat the picture of
tearing flesh, the hawk is abstracted to one aspect
of itself, its height above the bay. Thus we have
"the skinning height" that the small birds hare to.
But "skinning" is subsequently replaced by a reversion to the gallows theme with "the hanging height."
Soon "hanging," not quite right, is intensified to
"lynching." "The lynching height" appears several
times in the drafts while the poet adjusts such phrases
as "over the river Towy finned," neatened to "over
Towy's fins." Then there is one particular three
square inches of a page in which Thomas lists further possibilities—"dusky height," "hempen height,"
and "hempen caudle height." "Caudle," a sweet drink,
is appropriate to the gaiety with which the little
victims fly up to their death. But, further, "hempen
caudle" has been used by Shakespeare to mean "a

hanging," and no doubt Thomas was thinking of following suit.[2] But neither this nor any of the others seems to have been as satisfactory as "lynching height," which is used as a stand-by until finally crossed out in favor of "halter height" near the end of the work on the poem.

"Halter height" is not the choice that might have appealed to some poets. It is more cold and bloodless than "skinning" and "lynching," for instance. The only explanation for Thomas' passing over these more violent words is that their connotations must have been undesirable. They both imply vindictiveness; whereas "halter" does not. The work sheets show Thomas deliberately finding a neutral adjective for his killer-hawk. He does not want death to appear hateful. As for "hempen," which is neutral enough, it gives perhaps an unwanted notion of texture; the hawk is not a sack but a noose. There was possibly nothing wrong with "hanging height" except commonplaceness. "Halter" says the same thing as "hanging" but more interestingly. "Halter" is also the harness for a driven animal. Besides the point that death is amoral and unjudging, Thomas seems to want to say that mortality is a burden taken on by all. Like the sea of *A Refusal to Mourn the Death, by Fire, of a Child in London*, we are all "tumbling in harness"; and the "halter" here signifies the final pull of that harness.

Death is not just (or unjust), Sir John's hill is not judging, the birds are not guilty, the heron is not holy, and God is not, in any meaningful sense, merciful. What, then, are we to think of a poem in which such adjectives are applied to such individuals?

Perhaps we should bear in mind, to begin with, that the common expression "condemned to die" does not, when one thinks about it, really mean condemned, *punished* by death. It is just a way of saying "shall or will die" — simple futurity. But there is a rightness about "condemned"; it corresponds to the feeling of grievance against death. The word is not irresponsible; neither, I think, is Thomas. The poem may be expressing only the *fact* of death, and such words as "guilt" may be empty of intellectual content; but a form of meaning is communicated to the emotions, the reader's compassion is guided. One usually frowns on poetry that has vague emotional wording without precise denotation. Such a dismissal would not, I think, meet the case here. Thomas should be given credit for expressing truly the chief tenet of the non-religious: that the intellect cannot handle the fact of death, and that it is sternness, rebellion, hatred, self-pity, compassion — some naked emotion — with which we are left to face the situation. From among these emotions it is Thomas' inclination to choose compassion and to use the words, new or old, which will succeed in expressing it for him.

We get a closer look at the God of *Over Sir John's hill* in a prose note about a projected long poem to be entitled *In Country Heaven*, of which that poem along with *In country sleep* and *In the white giant's thigh* would form separate parts. The frame for the pieces is the scene in heaven when God hears of the end of the world:

> The godhead, the author, the milky-way farmer, the first cause, architect, lamplighter, quintessence, the beginning Word, the an-

thropomorphic bowler-out and black-baller,
the stuff of all men, scapegoat, martyr,
maker, woe-bearer He, on top of a hill in
Heaven, weeps whenever, outside that state
of being called his country, one of his worlds
drops dead, vanishes screaming, shrivels, ex-
plodes, murders itself. And, when he weeps,
Light and His tears glide down together,
hand in hand. So, at the beginning of the
projected poem, he weeps, and Country
Heaven is suddenly dark. Bushes and owls
blow out like candles. And the countrymen
of heaven crouch all together under the
hedges and, among themselves in the tear-
salt darkness, surmise which world, which
star, which of their late, turning homes, in
the skies has gone for ever. And this time,
spreads the heavenly hedgerow rumour, it
is the Earth. The Earth has killed itself. It is
black, petrified, wizened, poisoned, burst;
insanity has blown it rotten; and no creatures at all, joyful, despairing, cruel, kind,
dumb, afire, loving, dull, shortly and brut-
ishly hunt their days down like enemies on
that corrupted face. And, one by one, these
heavenly hedgerow-men, who once were of
the Earth, call one another, through the long
night, Light and His tears falling, what they
remember, what they sense in the submerged
wilderness and on the exposed hairsbreadth
of the mind, what they feel trembling on the
nerves of a nerve, what they know in their
Edenie hearts, of that self-called place. They
remember places, fears, loves, exultation,

misery, animal joy, ignorance and mysteries, all *we* know and do not know.

The poem is made of these tellings. And the poem becomes, at last, an affirmation of the beautiful and terrible worth of the Earth. It grows into a praise of what is and what could be on this lump in the skies. It is a poem about happiness.[3]

Dylan Thomas, supposedly the lyric poet, the singer of the self, is in these last poems responding perhaps as fully as any writer of our time to the basic problem facing mankind in the atomic age, the problem of total annihilation. Furthermore, his response is particularly suited to what C. S. Lewis would call our post-Christian era or what Albert Camus would call the age of absurdity. For Thomas' God, both in the prose account and in the poems, is not a religious entity at all in the normal sense of a presiding Being whose presence controls or at least justifies our existence. Thomas' God does nothing to alleviate the absurdity of the position of rational man in an irrational universe; Thomas' God does nothing to explain death in terms of higher values. As the eternal sympathetic spectator, He simply weeps, offering none of the usual consolations. It is the Last Day of Non-Judgment:

> And all your deeds and words,
> Each truth, each lie,
> Die in unjudging love
> (*This side of the Truth*).

One can see why Thomas said he didn't "believe in God" — not the usual God, anyway. His own God has perhaps only one function: to make death less fearful. Or, looked at the other way round, that miraculous force which — not for any arguable reason but nevertheless effectively — makes death less fearful, he calls God.

Some of the early poems saw death as a threat, a "running grave." In the first London days it was understood that the poet would die within a few years.[4] There is reason to believe that he had had vague intimations from a doctor. But one detects no real sense of imminent death until the last poems, in which Thomas seems to gauge his life-span exactly. *Poem on his Birthday* (his thirty-fifth) acknowledges the approaching death (four years later). Yet he meets it with an increased momentum of life:

> . . . the closer I move
> To death, one man through his sundered hulks,
> The louder the sun blooms
> And the tusked, ramshackling sea exults;
> And every wave of the way
> And gale I tackle, the whole world then,
> With more triumphant faith
> Than ever was since the world was said,
> Spins its morning of praise.

And the *Author's Prologue* (1952), with which he sealed his life's work, is written

> For you to know
> How I, a spinning man,
> Glory also this star, bird
> Roared, sea born, man torn, blood blest.
> Hark: I trumpet the place,
> From fish to jumping hill! Look:
> I build my bellowing ark

> To the best of my love
> As the flood begins.

It need not, therefore, be a mystery why the hawk is praised in *Over Sir John's hill:*

> All praise of the hawk on fire in hawk-eyed
>     dusk be sung.

His call is seductive: "Dilly dilly, come and be killed." And it is blithely answered: "Dilly dilly, come let us die." This poem about death is a celebration; "it is a poem about happiness." The Thief in *In country sleep*, like the hawk, is not really an enemy. He is "sly," as the conceit demands; but he is also "sure." The dominant mood of the poem is assurance. Thomas' message to his sleeping child is that the Thief will not leave her forsaken. To paraphrase a very complicated sentence: she has a faith that each night Death comes to dispel her fear that he will leave her to grieve he will not come. Sleep is a small death, and confirms each night death's presence in the world.

> My dear this night he comes and night without
>     end my dear
>                         Since you were born:
> And you shall wake, from country sleep, this
>     dawn and each first dawn,
> Your faith as deathless as the outcry of the ruled
>     sun.

The sun, no less than mere mortals, is "ruled" (or "chained," as it was in a draft). One's sustaining faith is two-edged: life is given security by being bounded by death.

> Death can be personified and symbolized; pathos

is a ready emotion. But a fulness of life cannot successfully be shown as a person or a symbol. It has
to be described in its particulars so that every word
upholds the assertion of value with an intrinsic
buoyancy. "Buoyancy" is hardly definable; much
depends upon poetic effects whose qualities — though
one can talk bluntly about alliteration and rhyme —
fortunately defy analysis. Poetic effects should not
demand admiration, but should keep us admiring un-
awares. The exuberant life recalled by the dead
women of *In the white giant's thigh* is so detailed and
passionate that one hardly notices that the poem is
written in quatrains; the "daughters of darkness flame
like Fawkes fires still," but their longing for children
(a *symbol* of affirmative life, if you will) is so keen
that one doesn't remark how very alliterative they
are. In this example from stanza two of *Over Sir
John's hill:*

> There
> Where the elegiac fisherbird stabs and paddles
> In the pebbly dab-filled
> Shallow and sedge . . . ,

one can feel that the sound of "there where" goes
very well with the idea called for by "elegiac," and
that the verse ensures the shallow is sufficiently filled
with dabs. One does not count consonants to prove
how many fish. Suffice it to say that the words flick
one's attention from object to action to object in a
real, active world. We might, however, be permitted
one question: Is "sedge" added to "shallow" for
more reason than the sound effect? It introduces a
useful but inconsequential detail — "sedge" is marshy

grass. But this doesn't prevent our repeating: Is this word alliteration-determined? Does anything else help it deserve its place?

The question can be answered satisfactorily when we go further into the meaning of "sedge" — and with the aid of the Harvard work sheets. Funk and Wagnall's Dictionary gives a second meaning: "A flock of herons or similar birds." The word has the same meaning as "siege" as listed in the *OED:* "The station of a heron on the watch for prey." It is then technically correct for Thomas to have his fisherbird in a "sedge," and it is all to the good to have this further note added to the theme of universal predatoriness. Thomas' intention is evident in the work sheets. A circled note reads: "Sedge is a lot of herons." Near it is the phrase, "a sedge of heron stilts." The poet did not use this ready-made combination. Elsewhere, however, he was having trouble finding a meaningful word to fit a much-favored sound pattern. Throughout the drafts we find the variants: "shallow and shadow," "shallow and shade," "shallow and stones," "shallow and shelves." Thomas' discovery that "sedge" is loaded with two meanings suitable for his context, as well as having the right sound, made "shallow and sedge" the natural end to the search. This phrase, unlike "the hawk on fire, the halter height," for instance, may not add too much to the serious symbolic thread of the poem; but the very vitality of such descriptive language deepens the significance of a song in praise of mortality, which can be said to succeed in so far as the diction vies with life itself in being active and many-sided.

It seems beside the point to add that Dylan

Thomas died young, that he died amidst hullabaloo in New York City. His last work, *Under Milk Wood*, was a great comedy; his last words were a humorous play on "roses" and "Rose's" (lime juice);[5] and, most of all, his last poems give a sense of what it is to live well and die well, so that even an unillusioned age, "a lump in the skies," might feel that, in some inexplicable way, life is a blessing and death is a *good* night.

# *Abbreviations*

Thomas' works:

| | |
|---|---|
| *18P* | *18 Poems* (London: The Sunday Referee and the Parton Bookshop, 1934) |
| *25P* | *Twenty-five Poems* (London: J. M. Dent & Sons, 1936) |
| *ML* | *The Map of Love* (London: J. M. Dent & Sons, 1939) |
| *Portrait* | *Portrait of the Artist as a Young Dog* (London: J. M. Dent & Sons, 1940) |
| *DE* | *Deaths and Entrances* (London: J. M. Dent & Sons, 1946) |
| *Selected Writings* | *Selected Writings of Dylan Thomas* (New York: New Directions, 1946) |
| *ICS* | *In Country Sleep* (New York: New Directions, 1952) |
| *CP* (Brit.) | *Collected Poems 1934-1952* (London: J. M. Dent & Sons, 1952) |
| *CP* (U.S.) | *The Collected Poems of Dylan Thomas* (New York: New Directions, 1953) |
| *QE* (Brit.) | *Quite Early One Morning* (London: J. M. Dent & Sons, 1954) |
| *QE* (U.S.) | *Quite Early One Morning* (New York: New Directions, 1954) |

LVW                 *Dylan Thomas: Letters to Ver-*
                    *non Watkins* (London: J. M.
                    Dent & Sons, and Faber &
                    Faber, 1957)

Manuscript Sources:

BBC                 The British Broadcasting Corpo-
                    ration
BM                  British Museum
Hanley              The collection of T. E. Hanley
M.I.T.              The Massachusetts Institute of
                    Technology
Notebook            Lockwood Library of the State
                    University of New York at
                    Buffalo

Periodicals:

*Botteghe*            *Botteghe oscure*
*CP&P*                *Contemporary Poetry and Prose*
*LLT*                 *Life and Letters To-day*
*NEW*                 *New English Weekly*
*NS*                  *New Stories*
*NV*                  *New Verse*
*O'London's*          *John O'London's Weekly*
*SGSM*                *Swansea Grammar School Maga-*
                    *zine*
*S Ref*               *Sunday Referee*
*20thC Verse*         *Twentieth Century Verse*

# Appendix I

# *Chronology of Composition*

> *"The opossums are un-*
> *satisfactory, I know."*
>
> Dylan Thomas to
> Vernon Watkins, 1938

THERE IS A MELANCHOLY CONVENIENCE in the fact that Dylan Thomas prepared his *Collected Poems* in the year before his death. The volume, like a last will and testament, contains all the poems that he wished to leave to the world. It is, in fact, a compilation of all five of his previously published volumes reproduced in sequence with very little alteration.[1] Scholars and critics thus have an apparently settled corpus by which to judge Thomas' development in style and subject matter. Unfortunately the definitiveness of the *Collected Poems*, as far as chronology is concerned, is more apparent than real. The order in which Thomas wrote his poems is quite different from the order in which they were published, so that statements about his development based on the sequence of the *Collected Poems* have had only limited validity.

The major source of information for the chronology of composition is the collection of Dylan Thomas' notebooks for the years 1930 to 1934 (with gaps), now at the Lockwood Memorial Library of the State University of New York at Buffalo.[2] Not only did Thomas date a poem when he first copied it into his notebook, but he also generally dated the revisions as he went back to the notebooks time and time again up to 1941. The poet's *Letters to Vernon Watkins* is the chief authority for the date of poems after the notebooks end in 1934. In surprisingly few cases are we left without circumstantial evidence to give a better date than that of first publication. The *Bibliography*, compiled by J. Alexander Rolph in 1956, has been invaluable throughout.

The poet's schoolboy publications for the most part are not serious, and are definitely inferior to other poems he was writing at the time.[3] By December 1930, when as editor of the *Swansea Grammar School Magazine* he printed his *Captain Bigger's Isle* (first line: "Captain Bigger was the skipper of the steamer *Duke of York*"), he had already composed the early versions of *How shall my animal* and *Today, this insect*. And before he left school at sixteen and a half he had written *The spire cranes* in a form close to its final published state in *The Map of Love* eight years afterwards.

The existence of such delayed publication of early poems is the most notable discovery to be made in the chronology. About half the poems in Thomas' two middle volumes, *Twenty-five Poems* (1936) and *The Map of Love* (1939), had their origin in that amazing burst of creativity in the two years prior to *18 Poems* (1934). Moreover, it is exactly these poems — some of them hardly revised at all — that are usually cited as indicating a trend toward clarity in Thomas' mid-career. "C.B.S." reviewing *Twenty-five*

*Poems* in *New Verse* (Christmas 1936) divided the volume into "sense" and "nonsense" poems: the nine "sense" poems are all early, revised poems.[4] We can now see that the "trend toward clarity" was really a recourse to early poems that Thomas had refrained from including in *18 Poems*.

While in the following Chronology emphasis is on Thomas' poetic output,[5] some attempt has been made to list prose and other writings, and to give biographical mileposts where they are known.

## SCHOOLBOY POEMS

Born Swansea 27 October 1914. Entered Swansea Grammar School September 1925 (aged almost 11); left July 1931 (aged 16¾). An editor of the *SGSM* from July 1929. Publications there consist of 27 poems (including one later as an Old Boy), various parodies and notes, two short stories, and two essays: "Films" and "Modern Poetry." Schoolboy poems also appeared in *Western Mail* (14 January 1927) and *Boys Own Paper* (February 1927).

Thomas quotes from 5 of his early poems (c. 1929) in his story "The Fight" and from another in "Reminiscences of Childhood." In the BM are typescripts of 8 poems possibly pre-1930, including "third person plural" poems done in collaboration with Daniel Jones.[6]

Two lines from a poem submitted in a competition appear in *Everyman* (10 October 1929). Thomas was a winner of the BBC Poetry Competition in February 1933 with *The Romantic Isle* (not extant) broadcast 28 June 1933.

## BUFFALO NOTEBOOKS

1930 Notebook: "Mainly Free Verse Poems" — numbered 1 to 42 (plus 4 deleted poems) from 27 April 1930 to 9 December 1930. The BM has typed copies of 18 of these poems. This Notebook contains the ancestor of *How shall my animal.*

1930-1932 Notebook: "Mainly Free Verse Poems" — numbered I to LVVVI (plus 6 unnumbered poems) from December 1930 to July 1932. The BM has typed copies of 9 and autographs of 2. This Notebook contains early versions of *To-day, this insect, The spire cranes, Why east wind chills, The Hunchback in the Park,* and *Out of the sighs.*

A Notebook for July 1932 to January 1933 is not extant, but certain poems possibly belong to this period: (1) 8 poems for which the BM has typescripts, including an early version of *Especially when the October wind;* (2) early versions of such published poems as, possibly, *Once it was the colour of saying, When all my five and country senses see, Should lanterns shine, Then was my neophyte, That sanity be kept,* and *Do you not father me.*

February 1933 Notebook: "Poems" — numbered One to Fifty Three, from 1 February 1933 to 16 August 1933, with five gaps. The BM has typed copies of 5 poems, and autographs of 2; Hanley has typescripts of 7. This Notebook contains early versions of *Was there a time, After the funeral, On no work of words, I have longed to move away, On the Marriage of a Virgin, See, on gravel paths, O make me a mask, And death shall have no dominion, Out of the Pit, Not from this anger, First there was the lamb on knocking knees*, *We lying by seasand*, *Incarnate devil*, *No man believes*, *The tombstone told when she died*, *Why east wind chills*, *Greek Play in a Garden*, *Here in this spring*, *Find meat on bones*, *Ears in the turrets hear*, *The Woman Speaks*, and *Shall gods be said to thump the clouds*.

August 1933 Notebook: Numbered One to Forty One, from 17 August 1933 to 30 April 1934, with two gaps. The BM has typed copies of 5 poems; Hanley, 7. This Notebook contains versions of *The hand that signed the paper*, *That the sum sanity*, *Grief thief of time*, *The seed-at-zero*, *Before I knocked*, *My hero bares his nerves*, *In the beginning*, *Love me, not as the dreaming nurses*, *I fellowed sleep*, *The force that through the green fuse drives the flower*, *From love's first fever to her plague*, *When once the twilight locks no longer*, *Light breaks where no sun shines*, *This bread I break*, *A process in the weather of the heart*, *Foster the light*, *Our eunuch dreams*, *Where once the waters of your face*, *I see the boys of summer*, and *If I were tickled by the rub of love*.

Red Notebook: Ten short stories written between 28 December 1933 and October 1934: "The Tree," "Martha," "After the Fair," "The Enemies," "The Dress," "The Visitors," "The Vest," "Gaspar, Melchior, Balthasar," "The Burning Baby" and "Mr. Tritas On The Roofs" (or "Anagram").

## Swansea Journalism

On staff of *South Wales Daily Post:* first piece "Nellie Wallace's Mimicry" (15 July 1931); last piece "Genius and Madness Akin in World of Art" (7 January 1933). Thomas did 7 articles on local poets in *Herald of Wales;* a poem *Youth Calls to Age* accompanies that on 23 April 1932. *Herald of Wales* also published *Greek Play in a Garden* on 15 July 1933 (from Notebook 7 July 1933).

*Swansea and West Wales Guardian* published *That the sum sanity* on 8 June 1934 (revised from Notebook 24 August 1933), and several journalistic pieces.

### London Publications Before 18 Poems

1. *NEW* 18 May 1933—*And death shall have no dominion* (from Notebook April 1933); revised in Notebook February 1936 for *25P.*

2. *Adelphi* September 1933 — *No man believes* (from Notebook 23 May 1933).

3. *S Ref* 3 September 1933—*That sanity be kept* (no MS extant).

4. *S Ref* 29 October 1933—*The force that through the green fuse drives the flower* (from Notebook 10 October 1933); reprinted *18P.*

5. *S Ref* 7 January 1934 — *Love me, not as the dreaming nurses* (from Notebook 18 September 1933).

6. *NEW* 25 January 1934—*Out of the Pit* (from Notebook 16-20 April 1933).

7. *S Ref* 11 February 1934—*A process in the weather of the heart* (from Notebook 2 February 1934); reprinted *18P.*

8. *Adelphi* March 1934—*The Woman Speaks* (from Notebook July 1933).

9. *Listener* 14 March 1934—*Light breaks where no*

*sun shines* (from Notebook 20 November 1933); reprinted *18P*.

10. *NEW* 15 March 1934—"After the Fair" (from Red Notebook November 1933).

11. *S Ref* 25 March 1934—*Where once the waters of your face* (from Notebook 18 March 1934); reprinted *18P*.

12. *NV* April 1934 — *Our eunuch dreams* (from Notebook March 1934); reprinted *18P*.

Thomas' award of the Book Prize is in *S Ref* 22 April 1934. After several visits, Thomas took up residence in London in November 1934 with periodic "return journeys" to Swansea.

13. *O'London's* 5 May 1934—*Ears in the turrets hear* (emended from Notebook 17 July 1933); full version *25P*.

14. *NV* June 1934—*When once the twilight locks no longer* (from Notebook 11 November 1933); revised for *18P*.

15. *NV* June 1934—*I see the boys of summer* (from Notebook April 1934); reprinted *18P*.

16. *NS* June-July 1934—"The Enemies" (from Red Notebook 11 February 1934).

17. *NV* August 1934—*If I were tickled by the rub of love* (from Notebook 30 April 1934); reprinted *18P*.

18. *Adelphi* September 1934—Reviews of poetry.

19. *Criterion* October 1934—*From love's first fever to her plague* (from Notebook 17 October 1933); reprinted *18P*.

20. *NV* October 1934—"Answers to an Enquiry."

21. *Listener* 24 October 1934—*Especially when the*

*October wind* (revised from BM version); re-printed *18P*.

22. *S Ref* 28 October 1934—*Foster the light* (from Notebook 23 February 1934); revised for *CP&P* May 1936, and reprinted *25P*.

23. *NEW* 22 November 1934—"The End of the River."

24. *Adelphi* December 1934 — "The Tree" (from Red Notebook 28 December 1933).

25. *NV* December 1934—*My world is pyramid* (no extant MS); reprinted *18P*.

26. *NV* December 1934—Review of Stephen Spender's "Vienna."


## Composition of 18 Poems

Published 18 December 1934. In April 1934 Thomas' choice for his first volume was 9 poems published or about to be (items 4, 7, 8, 9, 11, 12, 14, 15 above, and *That the sum sanity* revised from its Swansea publication), plus two poems in the August 1933 Notebook, *Before I knocked* and *Not forever shall the lord of the red hail;* "and about 6 or 7 others." Thomas changed his mind about the last poem, about *That the sum sanity*, and about item 8, *The Woman Speaks*. As the book was delayed through the summer, Thomas wrote and included *If I were tickled by the rub of love* (item 17), *I dreamt my genesis* (c. May 1934), *All all and all the dry worlds lever* (c. July 1934), *My world is pyramid* (c. August 1934; item 25), and *When, like a running grave* (c. September 1934). To these were finally added items 19 and 21 above, and revisions from the August 1933 Notebook: *My hero bares his nerves* (17 September

1933), *In the beginning* (18 September 1933 and April 1934), and *I fellowed sleep* (5 October and 27 November 1933).

### COMPOSITION OF <u>TWENTY-FIVE POEMS</u>

Published 10 September 1936.

1. *I, in my intricate image*—written c. December 1934-March 1935; published *NV* August-September 1935.

2. *Hold hard, these ancient minutes in the cuckoo's month*—probably written c. April-May 1935; published *Caravel* March 1936.

3. *A grief ago*—probably written May-June 1935.

4. *How soon the servant sun*—written for publication, with item 3, in *Programme* 23 October 1935.

5. *Now*—usually associated with item 4; first published *25P*.

6. *Do you not father me*—rewritten c. July 1935 from a version in typescript (c. October 1934); published *Scottish Bookman* October 1935.

7. *Incarnate devil*—from Notebook 16 May 1933; revised for *S Ref* 11 August 1935 (revision copied in Notebook 20 January 1936).

8(a). *Grief thief of time*—first stanza from Notebook 26 August 1933; revised in Notebook "Donegal August 1935."

9(a). *Altarwise by owl-light* (sonnets I-VII) — probably written Summer 1935; published *LLT* December 1935.

10. *The hand that signed the paper*—emended from Notebook 17 August 1933 for publication, with items 11 and 12, in *NV* December 1935.

11. *I have longed to move away*—revised from Note-

book 1 March 1933 (revision copied in Notebook 13 January 1936).

12. *Should lanterns shine*—probably from early version c. 1932.

Thomas was in Swansea preparing *25P* during December 1935-February 1936, and completed the following:

8(b). *Grief thief of time* — second stanza from Notebook 26 September 1933, revised; whole poem published *Comment* 1 February 1936.

9(b). *Altarwise by owl-light* (sonnets VIII-X)— published *CP&P* May 1936 and July 1936.

13. *Was there a time*—from Notebook 8 February 1933; thorough revision in Notebook December 1935; published *NEW* 3 September 1936.

14. *Here in this spring*—from Notebook 9 July 1933; thorough revision in Notebook January 1936; first published *25P*.

15. *Find meat on bones*—from Notebook 15 July 1933; revision interlined January 1936; published *Purpose* April-June 1936.

16. *Why east wind chills*—from Notebook 1 July 1933 (with ancestor 12 September 1931); thorough revision in Notebook 21 January 1936; published *NEW* 16 July 1936.

17. *Foster the light* — from Notebook 2 February 1934; early version published *S Ref* 28 October 1934; rewritten for *CP&P* May 1936.

18. *This bread I break*—from Notebook 24 December 1933; published *NEW* 16 July 1936.

19. *The seed-at-zero*—early version in Notebook 29 August 1933; later version *25P*.

20. *Shall gods be said to thump the clouds*—from Notebook August 1933; thoroughly revised for *25P*.
21. *Out of the sighs*—from Notebook 7 June and 1 July 1932; revised for *25P*.
22. *Ears in the turrets hear*—from Notebook 17 July 1933; short version in *O'London's* 5 May 1934; full version *25P*.
23. *To-day, this insect*—early version in Notebook 18 December 1930; completely rewritten for *25P*, and published *Purpose* October-December 1936.

The volume was expanded from *Twenty-Three Poems*[7] by the addition of:
24. *Then was my neophyte* — possibly from early version c. 1932; published with item 23 above.
25. *And death shall have no dominion*—early version in Notebook April 1933; published *NEW* 18 May 1933; revision in Notebook February 1936; published *25P*.

OTHER PUBLICATIONS BETWEEN *18P* and *25P*

Poems not included in *25P*: *Poet: 1935* (from Notebook 31 March 1933) in *Herald of Wales* 8 June 1935; *Before we mothernaked fall* (from Notebook 16 September 1933) in *NEW* 30 July 1936.

Reviews in *Morning Post* (26), *Adelphi* (4), *Bookman* (1).

Stories later in *ML*: *Criterion* (2), *Comment* (1), *Transition* (1).

Other stories: "The Lemon" in *LLT* Spring 1936; "The Burning Baby" (from Red Notebook

September 1934) in *CP&P* May 1936; "The Horse's Ha" in *Janus* May 1936; and "The School for Witches" in *CP&P* August-September 1936.

## COMPOSITION OF THE MAP OF LOVE

Proofs March 1939; published 24 August 1939.

1. *We lying by seasand*—from Notebook 16 May 1933; revised for *Poetry* (Chicago) January 1937; revision copied in Notebook September 1937.
2. *It is the sinners' dust-tongued bell*—written 1936; published *20thC Verse* January 1937.

Married Caitlin Macnamara in Cornwall, July 1937. Resident alternatively at Blashford, Ringwood, Hants, and at Laugharne, South Wales. Llewelyn Thomas born January 1939.

A. "Exhausters"[8]

3. *I make this in a warring absence*—finished November 1937; published *20thC Verse* January-February 1938.
4. *How shall my animal*—finished March 1938 (ancestor in Notebook 9 December 1930); published *Criterion* October 1938.
5. *A saint about to fall* — finished October 1938; published *Poetry London* February 1939.
6. *'If my head hurt a hair's foot'*—finished March 1939; published *Poetry London* April 1939.

B. "Opossums"[9]

7. *The spire cranes*—from Notebook 27 January 1931; revised November 1937; published *Wales* March 1938 and *Poetry* (Chicago) August 1938, along with items 8, 9, and 10.

8. *O make me a mask*—from Notebook 31 March 1933; revised in Notebook November 1937.

9. *Not from this anger*—from Notebook 20 April 1933; revised in Notebook January 1938.

10. *When all my five and country senses see*—probably revised c. January 1938 from early version c. 1932.

11. *After the funeral*—from Notebook 10 February 1933; revised March-April 1938; published *LLT* Summer 1938.

12. *On no work of words*—from Notebook 16 February 1933; rewritten in Notebook September 1938; published *Wales* March 1939.

13. *The tombstone told when she died*—from Notebook July 1933; revised in Notebook September 1938; published *Seven* Winter 1938.

[not in *ML*] *I, the first named* — written October 1938; published *Seven* Winter 1938.

14. *Twenty-four years*—written October 1938; published *LLT* December 1938.

15. *Once it was the colour of saying*—written December 1938 (probably from early version c. 1932); published *Wales* March 1939.

16. *Because the pleasure-bird whistles*—written January 1939; published *20thC Verse* February 1939.

C. Stories

Most (probably all) of the stories in *ML* had their inception during 1933-34.[10] They were collected, with slight revision, from periodical publication: "The Visitor" (from Red Notebook April 1934) in *Criterion* January 1935; "The Enemies" (from Red Notebook 11 February 1934) in *NS* June-July 1934; "The Tree" (from Red Notebook 28 December

1933) in *Adelphi* December 1934; "The Map of Love" in *Wales* Autumn 1937; "The Mouse and the Woman" in *Transition* Fall 1936; "The Dress" (from Red Notebook March 1934) in *Comment* 4 January 1936; "The Orchards" (based on Red Notebook "Anagram" October 1934) in *Criterion* July 1936.

Except for the title story they were not among the prose pieces published since *25P*: "A Prospect of the Sea" in *LLT* Spring 1937; "The Holy Six" in *CP&P* Spring 1937; "Prologue to an Adventure" in *Wales* Summer 1937; "In the Direction of the Beginning" in *Wales* March 1938; "An Adventure from a Work in Progress" in *Seven* Spring 1939; "The True Story" and "The Vest" (from Red Notebook 20 July 1934) in *Yellow Jacket* May 1939.

Other prose: 10 fiction reviews for *NEW* between March 1938 and December 1939. Thomas' "Tribute to Auden" in *NV* November 1937 was probably written in February 1937.

## Composition of Portrait

Proofs January 1940; published 4 April 1940. These stories, probably written immediately prior to publication, were collected with slight alteration: (1) "A Visit to Grandpa's" in *NEW* 10 March 1938; (2) "One Warm Saturday" — finished July 1938; (3) "The Peaches" *LLT* October 1938; (4) "Old Garbo" in *LLT* July 1939; (5) "Extraordinary Little Cough" in *LLT* September 1939. In August 1939 Thomas was working on the stories for a December 1939 deadline. (6) "Just Like Little Dogs" in *Wales* October 1939; (7) "The Fight" in *LLT* December 1939; (8) "Patricia, Edith, and Arnold" in *Seven* Christmas

1939; (9) "Where Tawe Flows"; and (10) "Who Do You Wish Was With Us?" — finished by early December 1939.

## POETRY 1939

Thomas resident in Laugharne.

*Unluckily for a Death* — first version finished May 1939; published *LLT* October 1939; rewritten for *DE*.

*To Others than You* — written May 1939;[11] published *Seven* Autumn 1939 and *DE*.

*When I Woke* — written c. July 1939; published *Seven* Autumn 1939; revised for *DE*.

*Paper and Sticks* — written for publication in *Seven* Autumn 1939; reprinted *DE*, but not *CP*.

*Once below a time* — written December 1939; published *LLT* March 1940; not in *DE*, but reprinted *CP*.

## WARTIME WRITING

At Blashford, January-April 1940; at Sea View, Laugharne, April-June 1940.

*There was a Saviour* — written January-March 1940; published *Horizon* May 1940 and *DE*.

*The Countryman's Return* — written March 1940; published *Cambridge Front* Summer 1940; not in *DE*.

*Into her Lying Down Head* — written March-June 1940; published *LLT* November 1940; slightly revised for *DE*.

At John Davenport's house, Marshfield, Wilts, June 1940-January 1941.

*On a Wedding Anniversary* — probably written July 1940; published *Poetry London* 15 March 1941; revised for *DE*.

*Love in the Asylum* — possibly written Summer 1940; published *Poetry London* May-June 1941 and *DE*.

*Request to Leda* — published *Horizon* July 1942; not in *DE*. This "Homage to William Empson" was one of the parodies in the unpublished satirical novel *The Death of the King's Canary* written with John Davenport c. July-August 1940.

BBC scripts for Latin American Service: (1) "Duque de Caxias" August 1940; (2) "Cristobal Colon" October 1940; and (3) "March of the Czech Legion" — finished February 1941 (not used).

*Deaths and Entrances* — written c. September 1940; published *Horizon* July 1942 and *DE*.

At parents' home, Bishopston, near Swansea, January-April 1941.

*Ballad of the Long-legged Bait* — begun in 1940, finished February 1941; published *Horizon* July 1941 and *DE*.

*On the Marriage of a Virgin* — from Notebook 22 March 1933; revised in Notebook January 1941; further revision June-July 1941; published *LLT* October 1941 and *DE*.

At Richard Hughes' Laugharne Castle, May-August 1941.

"Adventures in the Skin Trade" — initiated August 1940, written mainly May-June 1941; first section published *Folios of New Writing* Autumn

1941, remaining sections *New World Writing* November 1952 and May 1953.

*Among those Killed in the Dawn Raid was a Man Aged a Hundred* — written July 1941; published *LLT* August 1941 and *DE*.

*The Hunchback in the Park* — from Notebook 9 May 1932; revised in Notebook 16 July 1941; published *LLT* October 1941 and *DE*.

London and environs, August 1941-June 1944.

*A Dream of Winter*—poem commissioned by *Lilliput* for photo captions January 1942.

Film scripts include: (1) "These Are the Men," released April 1943; (2) "The Three Weird Sisters"; (3) Lockwood MSS: "The Unconquerable People"; a documentary on a girls' reformatory; and a film synopsis of Maurice O'Sullivan's *Twenty Years A Growing*; (4) "Our Country" — published *Wales* Autumn 1943; and (5) "The Doctor and the Devils" — finished October 1944, prepared for publication 1947, published 1953.

BBC performances as actor/reader on 19 September 1941, 25 May 1942, 29 November 1942, and 8 August 1943. "Reminiscences of Childhood" — written for BBC Wales broadcast 15 February 1943; published *Listener* 25 February 1943 and *QE*

*Last night I dived my beggar arm* and *Your breath was shed* — probably written from early versions; published *Poetry London* c. April 1944; not in *DE*.

*Ceremony After a Fire Raid* — finished for publication in *Our Time* May 1944; in *DE*.

Carmarthen, July - September 1944; Newquay, Cardiganshire, September 1944-September 1945.

*Poem in October* — possibly begun in Laugharne, October 1939; finished August 1944; published *Horizon* February 1945.

*Vision and Prayer* — finished August 1944 (probably begun for daughter's birth a year before); published *Horizon* January 1945.

*Holy Spring* — finished November 1944; published *Horizon* January 1945.

"Quite Early One Morning" — written for BBC Wales; recorded 14 December 1944, broadcast 31 August 1945; published *Wales* Autumn 1946.

The following poems were finished in the period prior to the proofs of *DE*, December 1944-April 1945:

*A Winter's Tale* — in *Poetry* (Chicago) July 1945.

*A Refusal to Mourn the Death, by Fire, of a Child in London* — in *New Republic* 14 May 1945 and *Horizon* October 1945.

*Lie Still, Sleep Becalmed* — in *LLT* June 1945.

*This Side of the Truth* and *The Conversation of Prayer* — in *LLT* July 1945.

*Fern Hill* — in *Horizon* October 1945.

*In My Craft or Sullen Art* — in *LLT* October 1945.

*Deaths and Entrances* (book) — published 27 February 1946.

## POET AS PERFORMER

Chelsea, October 1945-March 1946; Holywell Ford, Oxford, March 1946-April 1947

Thomas did about 50 broadcasts in this period

as reader, mainly for John Arlott in BBC Eastern
Service. Specially written broadcasts were:

1. "Memories of Christmas" — BBC Wales 16 December 1945; published *Listener* 20 December 1945 and *QE* (Brit.); revised for *Harper's Bazaar* December 1950 and *QE* (U.S.);

2. "Welsh Poets" — BBC Eastern 5 January 1946; in *QE;*

3. "On Poetry" — BBC Light 18 June 1946 — discussion with James Stephens; appears in part in *QE;*

4. "This is London" — BBC African 15 July 1946;

5. "Wilfred Owen" — BBC Eastern 27 July 1946; in *QE;*

6. "How to Begin a Story" — BBC Home 8 October 1946; published *Listener* 17 October 1946 and *QE;*

7. "What has happened to English Poets?" — BBC North American 16 October 1946 — a discussion;

8. "Holiday Memory" — BBC Wales 25 October 1946; published *Listener* 7 November 1946 and *QE;*

9. "Walter de la Mare as a Prose Writer" — BBC Third 30 November 1946; published *Living Writers*, ed. G. H. Phelps (1947), and *QE;*

10. "The Crumbs of One Man's Year" — BBC Home 27 December 1946; published *Listener* 2 January 1947 and *QE;*

11. "Oxford-Princeton"—BBC North American, recorded 29 December 1946;

12. "Sir Philip Sidney" — BBC West of England 24 January 1947; in *QE;*

13. "Return Journey" — written February 1947 for BBC Home, recorded 2 April 1947, broadcast 9 May 1947; in *QE*.

Thomas answered "Questionnaire" in *Horizon* September 1946.

Italian visit, April-August 1947.

*In country sleep* — begun in 1946, finished July 1947; published *Horizon* December 1947.

South Leigh, Oxford, September 1947-March 1949.

"Conversation About Christmas" — written for *Picture Post* 27 December 1947.

During this period Thomas did a further 50 broadcasts, notably reading Satan's part in *Paradise Lost*, W. H. Davies' *The Autobiography of a Supertramp*, and as a performer in several plays produced by Louis MacNeice. Specially written broadcasts were (1) "A Dearth of Comic Writers" — BBC Light 14 February 1948 — discussion with Arthur Calder-Marshall; in part in *QE;* and (2) "The English Festival of Spoken Poetry" — BBC Third 30 July 1948; published *Listener 5* August 1948 and *QE.*

Address to Scottish P.E.N.; published *Voice of Scotland* December 1948.

Film script: "The Beach of Falesa" — written 1948; published posthumously *Harper's Bazaar* August 1959.

Resident in Laugharne from April 1949.

*Over Sir John's hill* — written in Laugharne; published *Botteghe* December 1949.

Specially written broadcasts: (1) "Living in Wales" — BBC Scottish 23 June 1949; (2) "On Edward Thomas" — BBC Wales 29 July 1949; (3) "On Reading One's Own Poems" — BBC Third 24 September 1949; in *QE;* and (4) "Swansea and the Arts" — BBC Wales 24 October 1949.

Stage appearance in reading of William Blake's "An Island in the Moon," produced by Eric Capon 16 February 1950.

"How to Be a Poet" — written for *Circus* April 1950 and May 1950.

1st visit to U. S., 21 February to 31 May 1950.

*In the white giant's thigh* — finished by September 1950; published *Botteghe* 1950 with a note.

Broadcasts: (1) "Three Poems" — BBC Third 25 September 1950; in *QE*; (2) "Poetic Licence" — BBC Home 13 December 1950 — discussion with George Barker, Roy Campbell, and W. R. Rodgers; (3) "Persian Oil" — BBC Home 17 April 1951 — written after a visit to Persia, January 1951; (4) "The Festival Exhibition 1951"—BBC Wales 19 June 1951; in *QE*. There were 11 other broadcasts as actor/reader in this period.

*Poem on his Birthday* — presumably begun October 1949, finished July 1951; published *World Review* October 1951.

*Do not go gentle into that good night* — possibly begun 1945; finished by July 1951; published *Botteghe* 1951.

*Lament* — possibly written c. July-August 1951; published *Botteghe* 1951; revised for *ICS*.

"Llareggub (A Piece for Radio Perhaps)" — in progress spring and summer 1951; published *Botteghe* 1952.

*In Country Heaven* (unpublished poem) — probably finished c. October 1951.

*In Country Sleep* (book) — compiled c. November 1951 for publication 28 February 1952.

Review of Roy Campbell's *Light on a Dark Horse* in *Observer* 16 December 1951.

2nd visit to U. S., 15 January to 16 May 1952.

"I am Going to Read Aloud" — introduction to readings, recorded M.I.T. 7 March 1952; published posthumously *London Magazine* September 1956.

Review of Amos Tutuola's *The Palm-Wine Drinkard* in *Observer* 6 July 1952.

*Author's Prologue* — written for *CP*; broadcast 26 October 1952; in *Listener* 6 November 1952.

Introduction and Selections from Edgar Lee Masters' *Spoon River Anthology* — written summer 1952; broadcast posthumously 23 January 1955; published *Harper's Bazaar* June 1963.

"The Followers" — in *World Review* October 1952.

*Collected Poems* (Brit.) published 10 November 1952.
Father's death, December 1952.

BBC readings: (1) poetry of Robert Lowell and Theodore Roethke, recorded 16 July and 1 August 1952; Lowell broadcast 14 October 1952; (2) Vernon Watkins' *Three Ballads* 14 January 1953; (3) four "Anthologies" produced by Aneirin Talfan Davies, BBC Wales, broadcast 1, 8, 15, 22 March 1953; and (4) "A Painter's Studio," BBC Television April 1953; published *Texas Quarterly* Winter 1961.

William Foyle Poetry Prize, January 1953.

3rd visit to U. S., 16 April to 3 June 1953.

*Under Milk Wood* — first solo reading 3 May 1953, Cambridge, Mass.; first cast performance 14 May 1953, New York Poetry Center; published posthumously *Mademoiselle* February 1954 and *Observer* 7 and 14 February 1954.

"A Visit to America" — introduction for readings, recorded M.I.T. 11 May 1953; rewritten for BBC recording 28 September 1953; broadcast posthumously 30 March 1954; published *Listener* 22 April 1954 and *QE*.

"The International Eisteddfod" — written for BBC Wales 13 July 1953; in *QE*.

"A Story" — written for BBC Television 10 August 1953; published *Listener* 17 September 1953 and *QE* (U.S.).

"Laugharne" — written for BBC Wales, recorded 5 October 1953, broadcast 5 November 1953; in *QE*.

4th visit to U. S., arrived 19 October 1953, died 9 November 1953.

At time of death Thomas was working on *Elegy*, published posthumously *Encounter* February 1956.


It is impossible in a short space to indicate the degree of conjecture or certainty in dating works and events. One problem that should be discussed is typified by *When all my five and country senses see*,

a short poem in *ML* which seems of early vintage but
for which there is no extant MS. On what basis may
we categorize it as a revised poem? One main argument is from style: it is short, rather languid in tone,
and easeful compared with the poems of major effort.
Line-breaks are handled with a natural flair. Note
the fanciful, almost flippant, imagery of the first ten
lines, where the five senses are gaily interchanged:

> When all my five and country senses see,
> The fingers will forget green thumbs and mark
> How, through the halfmoon's vegetable eye,
> Husk of young stars and handfull zodiac,
> Love in the frost is pared and wintered by,
> The whispering ears will watch love drummed
>     away
> Down breeze and shell to a discordant beach,
> And, lashed to syllables, the lynx tongue cry
> That her fond wounds are mended bitterly.
> My nostrils see her breath burn like a bush.

"The whispering ears will *watch*" and "My nostrils
*see*" — in a weightier poem such forced transpositions
of the senses would be torn and twisted in the relentlessly changing imagery; here there is a consistency.
The idea is stated in the first line: we are to imagine
all our five senses as *seeing*. What each sees is the
downfall of love in its own particular area, Love
being a continent with a country for each sense. This
fact in itself betrays the poem's minor status, the fact
that it has a simple central conceit, "just a curious
thought said quickly," as Thomas remarked about a
previous minor poem.[12] The final four lines, which
reveal the poem to be quite a regular sonnet, complete
the thought: the heart is to be imagined as energizing

a substitute for the other senses, a sixth sense capable of alone taking over the domain of love:

> My one and noble heart has witnesses
> In all love's countries, that will grope awake;
> And when blind sleep drops on the spying senses,
> The heart is sensual, though five eyes break.

Thomas is saying that the heart is the real, bountiful source of sensual love. This kind of ingenious conceit, which might supply a single line in a major poem, indicates a juvenile effort when it motivates the whole.

The argument from style and content is backed up by other considerations. For one thing, *When all my five and country senses see* was published alongside three revised poems, *The spire cranes*, *O make me a mask*, and *Not from this anger*, in *Poetry* (Chicago) August 1938, in which Thomas had published another juvenile poem, *We lying by seasand*, the previous year. To add to this guilt by association, we have evidence in the letters to Vernon Watkins. Four months after sending *The spire cranes* to Watkins, Thomas forwarded another batch of poems to be typed. "Here are 4 poems," he writes, himself distinguishing the major from the minor, "two short simple ones, done fairly quickly, a conventional sonnet, and one I have spent a great deal of time on."[13] *O make me a mask* and *Not from this anger* were two of the poems, the "short simple ones." The long poem was *How shall my animal*. This leaves the "conventional sonnet," which can only be *When all my five and country senses see*. Though Watkins' note does not quite jibe,[14] Thomas confirms in his next letter that he had sent that poem along with the others in the previous one:

> The opossums are unsatisfactory, I know.
> Before your letter came, I had cut out the
> ubiquitous "weather" from the anticlimactic
> poem, and am revising it all; I will conquer
> "rebellion in"; and "eyed" tongue shall,
> momentarily, become "lashed."[15]

Here Thomas is promising to revise the batch of smaller poems. Apparently they were sent off to *Poetry* without revision: the "weather" appears there in *Not from this anger*, and "rebellion in" in *O make me a mask*. There is no "eyed" tongue in these two poems, nor any sign of such a thing in their draft versions. "Eyed tongue" is in the *Poetry* printing of *When all my five and country senses see*: "And, lashed to syllables, the eyed tongue talk" (line 8). There can be little doubt, therefore, that this poem is the "conventional sonnet" previously mentioned, and consequently one of the "opossums" of the minor strain.

The opus was *How shall my animal*, a poem which poses another problem of categorization. Though it has a very early version in the 1930 Notebook, the sheer amount of effort the poet expended on it later — transformation a better word here than revision — forces the poem into the opus category. "I had worked on it for months," he told Watkins on 1 April 1938. The result is one of his most complicated and unyielding poems.[16] *After the funeral* is another crux. It had a series of preliminary drafts, beginning with twenty-five lines in the February 1933 Notebook, where it is not about any specific person. On the death of his aunt, Thomas turned the poem into a personal elegy. The draft that he sent to Watkins had fifteen lines. For the final version he added a long parenthesis in the middle of the poem; and a new ending came, according to Watkins, "in a rush." This last comment, added to the poet's reliance on the early draft for ideas and phrasing, makes it impossible to classify *After the funeral* with the laboriously worked poems of Thomas' main stream. Again the poet himself suggests the correct value judgment: "I'm making it longer and, I hope, better than any of my recent simple poems."[17] The implication is, however, that it is basically one of them.

Similar arguments are available for the few other doubtful cases.[18] *Twenty-four years*, the poet's October birthday poem for 1938, is a crossroads. Thomas admits it is built on a single line from an early (non-extant) poem.[19] But one feels that the poem is new, a new strong statement — a twenty-fourth birthday poem not an eighteenth. *Because the pleasure-bird whistles*, written for the New Year 1939, poses the same problem. When we see Thomas writing fairly straightforward poems not from laziness but from an apparently conscious effort to achieve a maximum effect in a new way, then we must logically discard the two categories, major and minor. It is as though Thomas had warmed to the idea of writing clearer poems. The revising of old poems, while obviously not in the main stream of Thomas' development, seems to have produced a change in the main stream. The result is a line of major and unobscure poems.

This is the probable truth about the trend toward clarity in Thomas' middle period. Because of the practical need to increase his output of poems to more than one a year, Thomas turned out the "opossums," which, to use his own word, were "unsatisfactory." The notebooks help us to see why they are unsatisfactory: to put it bluntly, he was reversifying old poems. It is the so-called difficult poems of this period that are the product of Thomas' full powers and most serious effort. At the same time, Thomas could not have helped realizing that the lesser poems were successful in a way his "exhausters" were not. We can presume, then, that he was led to develop a new conscious style, one which grows to perfection in *This Side of the Truth* and *In My Craft or Sullen Art*, careful poems of Thomas' highest effort.

# Appendix II

# *Textual Cruxes*

*"P.S. It's a full stop after 'ice' in the last verse."*

Dylan Thomas to
Vernon Watkins,
13 November 1937

THOMAS' PREFATORY "Note" to the *Collected Poems* has been taken to imply that he prepared a definitive text. But, as Appendix I showed, that volume was indeed a mere *collected* poems, very little selection or editing having occurred. The few slight changes seem inconsequential or even accidental. A few misprints were corrected in the later printings of the volume; a few still remain. These are taken up here, along with any other cruxes which might be thought to require emendation.

This is not to say that the *Collected Poems* is a bad text; on the contrary, it is extremely good. But studying Dylan Thomas is difficult enough without having to worry about the reliability of the text. The aim of this Appendix is to settle a few of our suspicions, by taking up all the cases that have come to light. It may be assumed that the English and American texts are identical unless otherwise stated.

*Author's Prologue*
l. 24 — *Listener* and several MSS have "strangers" set

off by commas. The less urgently vocative *CP* version seems preferable.

l. 51 — to be followed by a stanza break, not totally clear in *CP* (U.S.), though the later printings of *CP* (Brit.) doubly emphasize it by numbering the lines 1 to 51 and 51 to 1.

*I see the boys of summer*
I, ll. 3 & 20 — the commas, not present in MS or periodical printing, are unnecessary but inoffensive.

*When once the twilight locks no longer*
l. 3 — *NV*, *18P*, and *Selected Writings* all have "dammed." The "damned" of *CP* is a pun that one would wish to save Thomas from. Unfortunately it exists in the Notebook version 11 November 1933; and, writing to Vernon Watkins on 27 April 1946, he includes the phrase: "locked in these damned days. . . ."

*Our eunuch dreams*
II, l. 8 — *CP* (U.S.) has "showing"; apparently a misprint for "throwing" in *CP* (Brit.) and all other versions, including MSS.

*When, like a running grave*
ll. 42 & 44 — *CP* adds a superfluous comma after the parentheses; early typescript had commas but not the parentheses; *18P* had parentheses but not the following commas.

*From love's first fever to her plague*
l. 11 — followed in *18P* by a line omitted in *CP:*
    "And to the miracle of the first rounded word,"
— probably a deliberate deletion.

l. 18 — the internal comma was changed to a semicolon by the editor of *Criterion*, also the final comma of l. 23 — both felicitous emendations.

### Light breaks where no sun shines

l. 16 — *Listener* is strictly correct in omitting the comma after "fenced." Notebook and *18P* has the comma; but an early typescript does not.

### I fellowed sleep

l. 4 — the apostrophe in *18P* " 'planing-heeled" serves to explain the image.

### I dreamed my genesis

l. 4 — an end comma would allow the "I" subject to be brought down for the verb "shuffled" (l. 5), which is otherwise without a subject.

### My world is pyramid

l. 20 — the internal comma is puzzling, perhaps best omitted? *NV* had a semicolon, which was more confusing still.

### I, in my intricate image

II, l. 8 — periodical printing, supported by two MSS, has "the Cadaverous gravels" in keeping with the capitalized "Cadaver" of III, l. 31.

II, l. 18 — one MS gives authority for an end comma. As it stands with a semicolon (or with the period of the first printing) the previous stanza has no finite main verb, and the "Bring" becomes vocative rather than (better) the transitive main verb.

### This bread I break

l. 6 — early printings of *CP* (Brit.) had misprint "wind" (taken from *25P*), later corrected to "wine."

*Out of the sighs*
l. 19 — followed in Notebook and early typescript by a line omitted in *25P* and *CP:* "And, sleeping, made me dream" — which explains the grammatical construction of the following phrase, "How much was happy," which, as it now stands, is awkwardly dependent on "Feeling."

*A grief ago*
l. 17 — the omission of the end comma in *Programme* is the one variant that pleases.

*How soon the servant sun*
l. 1 *et al.* — in *Programme* dashes set off the parenthetical passages; *25P* supplied parentheses and omitted the commas in ll. 1, 2, 3, 5, 9, 12, and 24. Strangely *CP* restored the unnecessary commas.

*Ears in the turrets hear*
ll. 12 & 22 — superfluous commas, only appropriate if there are also commas after "island" (l. 10) and "ships" (l. 21) as in MS.

*Foster the light*
l. 25 — superfluous comma in *CP*, not present in periodical printing or *25P*.

*I have longed to move away*
l. 8 — *CP* (U.S.) has misprint "From" instead of "For" in all other printings.

*Grief thief of time*
l. 22 — the *Comment* variant "to-day" is plausible but almost certainly not correct.

*Altarwise by owl-light*
*Sonnet IV*
l. 8 — "boy" was "lad" in *25P* and periodical printings; the apparently inconsequential change breaks the off-rhyme scheme.
l. 10 — *CP* (U.S.) has misprint "shrowd" ("shroud" in all other printings).
l. 11 — first printing in *LLT* had "Love's a reflection of the mushroom features," thus making clear the verbal status of the " 's," which, as it stands in *25P* and *CP*, can easily be taken for a possessive, leaving the sentence apparently without a main verb.
*Sonnet V*
l. 5 — both periodical printing and *25P* have end comma; both have end semicolon in l. 10: neither variant seems to clear up the punctuation problem in this sonnet.
*Sonnet VIII*
l. 12 — this famous line was "Unsex my skeleton . . ." in its periodical printing, an illuminating variant.

*I make this in a warring absence*
ll. 37-38 — *CP* (Brit.) puts these two lines with the lines following, thus violating the stanzaic pattern preserved in MS and other printings.

*Not from this anger*
l. 7 — followed by stanza break in Notebook and periodical printing; in *ML* a page division obscures this fact.

*The tombstone told when she died*
l. 10 — followed by stanza break in versions up to *ML*, which again obscures this fact because of pagination.

*'If my head hurt a hair's foot'*
l. 19 — "none" repeated only once in the version sent to Vernon Watkins and printed in *Kenyon Review*. The third Hopkensian "none" appears in *Poetry London* and *ML*.

*The Conversation of Prayer*
l. 18 — *CP* (U.S.) has "his made grave" following Hanley MS, *LVW*, and *New Republic*; *CP* (Brit.) has "his true grave" following *LLT* and *DE*.

*To Others than You*
ll. 18-19 — *Seven* printing adds comma after "That"; the version in *LVW* omits the end comma of l. 19: either alternative is more strictly correct than *CP*.

*Into her Lying Down Head*
II, l. 19 — *LLT* and *LVW* have "Celebrating at his side" — a reading appropriate to the sense.

*Do not go gentle into that good night*
l. 5 — early printings of *CP* (Brit.) had "has forked" following a typescript; later corrected to "had forked."

*Ceremony After a Fire Raid*
l. 18 — followed in *Our Time* by a one-word line: "Give" — omitted in *War Poets* (1945) and subsequent printings, leaving the poem rather misshapen.

*Once below a time*
I — the roman numeral "I" missing in *CP* (U.S.).

*When I Woke*
l. 19 — "death-stagged"—probably a deliberate emendation (along with others) from "death-staggered" in periodical printing.

*Ballad of the Long-legged Bait*

l. 77 — "smoothe" is a strictly incorrect form for the verb.

l. 107 — "Sussanah's" appeared in *CP* over proofreader's query; *Horizon* had correct "Susannah's."

*Lament*

l. 44 — *CP* (U.S.) has "Slung"; all other sources have "Slunk."

*In the white giant's thigh*

l. 20 — followed by new page in *CP* (Brit.); probably *CP* (U.S.) should show stanza break, which appears in periodical printing and *ICS*.

l. 56 — *CP* (Brit.) still prints "desires" following *ICS* instead of "desirers" which has MS authority as well as that of other printings.

At least one obvious mistake in "The Visitor" should be added: the girl Rhianon was called Millicent in an earlier draft; this name was left unchanged on one occasion on about the third page of the story.

# Notes

## CHAPTER I

1. Portrait by Bill Brandt, *Harper's Bazaar* LXXXVIII (February 1954), p. 129.

2. "Poetic Manifesto," *Texas Quarterly*, IV (Winter 1961), 48.

3. *Ibid.*, p. 47. At M.I.T. in 1952 he added Robert Service, Stevenson, Eskimo Nell, the *Boys Own Paper*, Keats, Burns, and Dostoevsky to the list; see "I am Going to Read Aloud," *London Magazine*, III (September 1956), 14.

4. Daniel Jones, "Dylan Thomas: Memories and Appreciations," *Encounter*, II (January 1954), 10; in E. W. Tedlock, ed., *Dylan Thomas: the Legend and the Poet* (London: Heinemann Publishers, 1960), p. 17; and in John Malcolm Brinnin, ed., *A Casebook on Dylan Thomas* (New York: Thomas Y. Crowell, 1960), p. 281.

5. Geoffrey Grigson, "Recollections of Dylan Thomas," *London Magazine*, IV (September 1957), 40.

6. *Adelphi*, X (June 1935), 179-181. The scope and accomplishment of Thomas' brief bout of reviewing for *Adelphi* is remarkable: new poetry by Soutar, Montgomerie, and Salt (September 1934), Gandhi's devotional lyrics (January 1935), new poetry by Lyle Donaghy, John Lehmann, and Ruth Pitter (February 1935), a poetical tract by Alfred Haffenden (February 1935), the Clare (June 1935), and a survey of world literature by R. D. Jameson (October 1935).

7. The following list from a manuscript at the Lockwood Library, State University of New York at Buffalo, is apparently the fare, both humorous and serious, that Thomas was preparing for his audiences:

> Poem—Yeats/Poem—Norman Cameron/Poem—Mcneice/ Chard Witlow—H Reed/Naming of Parts—H Reed/Potpourri from a Summer Garden—John Betjeman/2 Grotesques — Robert Graves / The Great Grandmother — Robert Graves/Hospital in Poona—Alun Lewis/Have I a Wife—LAG Strong/Carol—John Short/Poem—William Morgan/Poem—Edward Thomas/Poem—Walter de la Mare/Poem—Vernon Watkins/Poem—W. H. Auden/

Poem—W. S. Graham/Poem—George Barker/Poem—
Ruth Pitter/Waterfall—Norman Nicholson/Poem—Bernard Spencer / Poem — Hardy / Blake / Herbert / Smart /
Peele/Hopkins/D. H. Lawrence—Ship of Death/Browning/Wm. Barnes/Frank O'Connor translation/John Clare
(Foolish, fond)/Vaughan

8. "I am Going to Read Aloud," *London Magazine*, III (September 1956), 14. Thomas would have seen Norman Cameron's translation of *Bateau ivre* in *New Verse* (June-July 1936); and certainly the *Ballad of the Long-legged Bait* is like Rimbaud's poem. But, after Thomas' pointed remark, there seems no reason to take general similarities as indicating "a faithful parody of *Bateau ivre*," as William York Tindall puts it in *The Literary Symbol* (New York: Columbia University Press, 1955), p. 155, or to speak of the *Ballad* as "deriving almost certainly from Rimbaud's *Bateau ivre*" as Derek Stanford does in *Dylan Thomas: A Literary Study* (London, Neville Spearman, 1954; New York, Citadel Press, 1954), p. 119. See also Henry Treece, *Dylan Thomas: 'Dog Among the Fairies'* (2d ed.; London: Ernest Benn; New York: de Graff, 1956), pp. 45-46. There have been plenty of sea journeys. The most striking characteristic of the *Ballad* is the allegorizing of the sexual life-cycle: a girl-bait on the man's fishing rod being made love to by a host of sea creatures until a climax is reached and the boat returns to land. If a parallel for this central allegorical action were to be found, then we could begin to talk of sources. *Bateau ivre* is no such analogue. One is indebted to Raymond Garlick's editorial in *Dock Leaves*, V (Spring 1954), 4, for reference to a stanza from Donne's *The Baite*:

> When thou wilt swimme in that live bath,
> Each fish, which every channell hath,
> Will amorously to thee swimme,
> Gladder to catch thee, than thou him.

Here is a partial parallel. But since Donne's image goes no further than this, being merely a lover's conventional compliment, these four lines can hardly be considered a source. In *A Reader's Guide to Dylan Thomas* (New York: the Noonday Press, 1962), p. 251, William York Tindall is less insistent on the parody: "But reading seems unnecessary for an image so inevitable as this for all the caught."

9. An examination of the *Ballad* work sheets at the Lockwood Library was made by Patricia Earle Speyser in an unpublished M.A. thesis (State University of New York at Buffalo, 1959).

10. John L. Sweeney, Introduction to *Selected Writings of Dylan Thomas* (New York: New Directions, 1946), p. xvi.

11. David Aivaz, "The Poetry of Dylan Thomas," *Hudson*

*Review*, III (Autumn 1950), 401. G. S. Fraser in *Dylan Thomas* (London: Longmans, Green, 1957), p. 14, makes a similar connection between Rilke and *Should lanterns shine*.

12. *Dylan Thomas: Letters to Vernon Watkins* (London: J. M. Dent & Sons, and Faber & Faber, 1957), p. 105; hereafter cited as *LVW*. A passing reference to Rilke in a review in *Adelphi*, IX (February 1935), 318, is still later than the poems in question.

13. This does not exhaust, of course, the question of literary influences on Thomas. It merely suggests that the onus is on those who wish to show such influences. The matter has been taken up at length by Giorgio Melchiori in *The Tightrope Walkers* (London: Routledge & Kegan Paul, 1956). Melchiori gives an initial nod to the accepted influences on Thomas: Welsh, the Bible, Hopkins, Joyce (p. 222); but his subsequent discussion repudiates the influences one by one in finding basic differences instead of similarities. There is evidence in letters that the poet most highly regarded by the young Thomas was William Blake. Thomas wanted to be a "mystical" poet. References are made to Blake at various times in the ensuing chapters, but no attempt will be made to hold up Blake as a "source."

14. For the second edition of his book, Henry Treece left out entirely the section dealing with Welsh influence — perhaps on the advice of Glyn Jones, whose authority on Welsh forms he had used. In *Dock Leaves*, V (Spring 1954), 25, Glyn Jones writes:

> My friend Henry Treece in his book . . . gives several examples of what he believes to be *cynghanedd* in Dylan's poetry. Tambimuttu in numbers 11 and 13 of *Poetry London* makes similar claims on behalf of Welsh influences. Miss Kathleen Raine, writing in *The New Statesman* at the time of the poet's death, uses words which I feel must mean that she too credits him with a knowledge of Welsh metrics. My own view is that any traces of *cynghanedd* in Dylan Thomas's poetry derive not from a direct study of Welsh prosody, but are present either by accident or as a result of the influence upon him of Hopkins, whose knowledge of this involved subject was considerable.

15. I am indebted to Meredydd Evans for pointing out one example of *cynghanedd* in Thomas (perhaps the only one, and almost certainly accidental), l. 11 of the first part of *Vision and Prayer*:

> To the *burn* / and \**turn* / of \**time*,

which is a most casual line of English poetry compared with the Hopkins:

The down-*dugged* / \*ground-*hugged* / \*grey.

Thomas stated his own attitude to the "bardic forms" in "Welsh Poets" written for the BBC in 1946, in *Quite Early One Morning* (London: J. M. Dent & Sons, 1954), pp. 149-150; (New York: New Directions, 1954), p. 112; hereafter cited as *QE*.

> These forms rely on a great deal of assonance and alliter-ation and most complicated internal rhyming; and these effects in English have, in the hands of the few who have attempted to use them, succeeded only in warping, crab-bing, and obscuring the natural genius of the English language.

See also Aneirin Talfan Davies, "A Question of Language," *Yr Einion*, IV (1953), 27.

16. Daniel Jones in Tedlock, p. 18. It is the syllabic nature of the stanza forms of *Vision and Prayer* that makes the achievement there quite different from that in George Herbert's *Easter Wings*, which hugs the safety of the iambic line. The Vision stanza goes from 1 to 9 syllables and back to 1 (the reverse of this in the Prayer stanza), each line rhythmically unique. Again there are lapses:

| | | | | | | | | | | | | | | | | | | |
|---|---|---|---|---|---|---|---|---|---|---|---|---|---|---|---|---|---|---|
| I | 1 | 2 | 3 | 4 | 5 | 6 | 7 | 8 | 9 | 8 | 7 | 6 | 5 | 4 | 3 | 2 | | 1 |
| | 1 | 2 | 3 | 4 | 5 | 6 | 7 | 8 | 9 | 8 | 7 | 6 | 5 | 4 | 3 | 2 | | 1 |
| | 1 | 2 | 3 | 4 | 5 | 6 | 7 | 8 | <u>8</u> | 8 | 7 | 6 | 5 | 4 | 3 | 2 | | 1 |
| | 1 | 2 | 3 | 4 | 5 | 6 | 7 | 8 | 9 | 8 | 7 | 6 | 5 | 4 | 3 | 2 | | 1 |
| | 1 | 2 | 3 | 4 | 5 | 6 | 7 | _ | 9 | 8 | 7 | <u>7</u> | 5 | 4 | 3 | 2 | | 1 |
| | 1 | 2 | 3 | 4 | 5 | 6 | 7 | 8 | <u>10</u> | 8 | 7 | 6 | 5 | 4 | 3 | 2 | | 1 |
| II | <u>10</u> | 8 | 7 | 6 | 5 | 4 | 3 | 2 | 1 | 2 | 3 | 4 | 5 | 6 | <u>8</u> | <u>8</u> | | 9 |
| | 9 | 8 | 7 | 6 | 5 | 4 | 3 | 2 | 1 | 2 | 3 | 4 | 5 | 6 | 7 | 8 | | 9 |
| | 9 | 8 | 7 | 6 | <u>4</u> | 4 | 3 | 2 | 1 | 2 | 3 | 4 | 5 | 6 | 7 | 8 | | 9 |
| | 9 | 8 | 7 | 6 | 5 | 4 | 3 | 2 | 1 | 2 | 3 | 4 | 5 | 6 | 7 | 8 | <u>10</u> | |
| | <u>11</u> | 8 | 7 | 6 | <u>6</u> | 5 | 4 | 3 | 2 | 1 | 2 | 3 | 4 | 5 | 6 | 7 | 8 | | 9 |
| | 9 | 8 | 7 | 6 | 5 | 4 | 3 | 2 | 1 | 2 | 3 | 4 | 5 | 6 | 7 | 8 | | 9 |

Most of the *18 Poems* are regularly iambic (the syllable count and the metrical beat go together in the pentameter). An excep-tion is *I dreamed my genesis*. The syllable count is 12 7 10 8, and consistently so, while the rhythm is irregular:

> I dreamed my genesis in sweat of sleep, breaking
> Through the rotating shell, strong
> As motor muscle on the drill, driving
> Through vision and the girdered nerve.

From limbs that had the measure of the worm, shuffled
Off from the creasing flesh, filed
Through all the irons in the grass, metal
Of suns in the man-melting night.

These first two stanzas are enough to show the tight rhyme
scheme utilizing near-rhymes and the rhyming of accented with
unaccented syllable, e.g. "*driv*ing:*nerve*," "*meta*l:*night*," "*jour*ney:
*man*," "*muzz*led:*gas*," and so on. All these strictures smack of the
Welsh. But there is nothing like *Vision and Prayer* and *I dreamed
my genesis* in Welsh poetry. Though undeliberately Welsh in
some respects, they should be taken as completely unique.

17. The work sheets of *Over Sir John's hill* (47 sheets), along
with those of the *Author's Prologue* (94 sheets), were presented
to Harvard College Library in 1955 by Oscar Williams as a
memorial to Gene Derwood.

18. The count is

| | | | | | | | | | | | |
|---|---|---|---|---|---|---|---|---|---|---|---|
| 5 | 6 | 14 | 15 | 5 | 1 | 15 | 5 | 14 | 5 | 14 | 14 |
| 5 | 6 | 13 | 14 | 5 | 1 | 13 | 6 | 13 | 4 | 13 | 14 |
| 5 | 6 | 13 | 14 | 4 | 1 | 14 | 4 | 15 | 5 | 14 | 13 |
| 5 | 6 | 14 | 14 | 5 | 1 | 14 | 4 | 14 | 4 | 13 | 13 |
| 5 | 6 | 14 | 14 | 6 | 1 | 13 | 5 | 14 | 6 | 14 | 13 |

*Into her Lying Down Head*, of which Thomas said, "I've
never worked harder on anything, maybe too hard: I made it
such a difficult shape, too" *LVW*, p. 92), has a syllable count of
impressive consistency in its three stanzas as they now stand:

| | | | | | | | | | | | | | | | | | | | | | |
|---|---|---|---|---|---|---|---|---|---|---|---|---|---|---|---|---|---|---|---|---|---|
| 7 | 7 | 8 | 11 | 9 | 5 | 7 | 7 | 11 | 8 | 11 | 7 | 7 | 11 | 9 | 11 | 11 | 8 | 8 | 20 | 9 | 15 | 15 |
| 7 | 7 | 8 | 11 | 9 | 5 | 7 | 7 | 11 | 8 | 11 | 7 | 7 | 12 | 8 | 11 | 11 | 7 | 7 | 20 | 9 | 14 | 16 |
| 8 | 7 | 8 | 11 | 10 | 6 | 7 | 7 | 11 | 8 | 10 | 7 | 6 | 11 | 9 | 11 | 12 | 7 | 7 | 20 | 9 | 17 | 17 |

In an earlier printed version the long line in the last stanza had
nineteen syllables and was followed by five lines instead of three.
The revision was a normalization. With *Unluckily for a Death*,
on the other hand, revision meant loss of strict syllabic regularity
and rhyme-scheme, but the second version seems otherwise a
great improvement. It is hard to tell exactly what Thomas required of himself in this matter.

19. As reported by Marjorie Adix, "Dylan Thomas: Memories and Appreciations," *Encounter*, II (January 1954), 14; in Tedlock, p. 62; in Brinnin, *Casebook*, p. 286.

20. Marjorie Adix, in Tedlock, p. 63; in Brinnin, *Casebook*,
p. 287. I am indebted to Roberto Sanesi for retelling the story of
Thomas' reading habits during the summer months of 1947 on the
Island of Elba. Dylan, the story goes, spent each afternoon with

a different book, lying in the sun on a rock in the middle of the bay, and on finishing would throw the book into the sea.

21. As printed in *QE* (U.S.) p. 20. The earlier version appears in *QE* (Brit.), p. 21.

22. A revealing comment occurs in *LVW*, p. 82, where Thomas refers to the adjective "blacked" in *There was a Saviour:* "I had, quite apart (that is absurd, I mean secondarily to) from the poem, the blackout in mind."

23. I am indebted to A. E. Trick for his personal reminiscence that the inception of the poem was with some middle-aged men in business clothes whom Thomas saw wading on the seashore — "summer boys in their ruin." No particular of that epiphany survives in the final poem, unless briefly in the fourth stanza of part I. The "boys of summer" in the poem are not ruined men acting like boys but boys actively ruining.

## CHAPTER II

1. Henry Treece, *Dylan Thomas: 'Dog Among the Fairies'* (London: Lindsay Drummond, 1949), p. 149. (This valuable appendix is not included in the second edition.)

2. *LVW*, p. 31.

3. The Notebook version of *Incarnate devil* (16 May 1933) at the Lockwood Library has an early try at the same image:

> Before we sinned we knew all evil,
> Hearing in snow that turned to ice
> The sibilant horror of the devil's voice.

4. Treece, 1st ed., p. 149.

5. Ralph N. Maud, "Obsolete and Dialect Words as Serious Puns in Dylan Thomas," *English Studies*, XLI (February 1960), 1-2.

6. "Answers to an Enquiry," *New Verse* (October 1934), p. 7.

7. Treece, 2d ed., p. 37. In the original letter, now in the Lockwood Library, the two sentences following the quoted passage are:

> Reading back over that, I agree it looks preciously like nonsense. To say that I "let" my images breed and conflict is to deny my critical part in the business.

He is anticipating and negating the implication that the poet is not in control of his poem.

8. *Ibid.*

9. In *New Verse* it is the "dog-dayed pulse / Of doubt and dark" that bursts in their throats.

10. *LVW*, p. 92.

11. "Celebrating at his side" — the line as sent to Vernon Watkins and as printed in *Life and Letters To-day* is surely correct: the enemy and the wife are at the husband's side.

12. *LVW*, p. 92.

13. Donald Davie, *Articulate Energy* (London: Routledge & Kegan Paul, 1955), p. 129.

14. *Ibid*, p. 126.

15. John Bayley, *The Romantic Survival* (London: Constable, 1957), p. 196.

16. A. D. S. Fowler, review in *Essays in Criticism*, VIII (January 1958), 83.

17. As reported by Marjorie Adix in Tedlock, p. 62; in Brinnin, *Casebook*, p. 285.

## CHAPTER III

1. "Weathers" is not rare in Thomas. It is found in the early Jarvis stories of *The Map of Love*, and in the genesis poem, *In the beginning:*

> In the beginning was the mounting fire
> That set alight the weathers from a spark.

Also in *I, in my intricate image:*

> They climb the country pinnacle,
> Twelve winds encounter by the white host at pasture,
> Corner the mounted meadows in the hill corral;
> They see the squirrel stumble,
> The haring snail go giddily round the flower,
> A quarrel of weathers and trees in the windy spiral.

This stanza was in danger of slipping into the merely pastoral; but the word "weathers" gears it firmly to the world of process beneath the scenery. These are no pretty breezes moving the trees. A similar effect is achieved in *Hold hard, these ancient minutes in the cuckoo's month:*

> Down fall four padding weathers on the scarlet lands,
> Stalking my children's faces with a tail of blood.

The "weathers" belong to a beast, which uses them as claws, weapons of mortality and change, on the children. "Weathers" are the innumerable ever-changing facets of a state of existence; so that "wood of weathers" in *Altarwise* (sonnet II) and "the outside weathers" in *How shall my animal* are both periphrases for this mortal world, bringing in the special idea of being subject to process.

2. Josephine Miles, a pioneer in the field of word counts, has

attempted in *The Continuity of Poetic Language*, University of California Publications in English, XIX (1948-1951), pp. 304-402, to make critical judgments on the basis of frequency of words in a poet's work. One suspects, however, that her shrewd insights come more from reading the poets than from counting their words. The method of taking partial samples is invalid. In the case of Thomas, for instance, she counted adjectives, nouns, and verbs in the first 1,000 lines of *Selected Writings* (1946). But several words, listed because they occurred ten times or more turn up much less frequently later in the volume. "Face" and "word" occur only twice later, "bell" only once, and "tower" not at all; whereas "night," "water," and "bird" are used about twice as often as before. "Flesh" occurs eleven times in two poems not included in the *Selected Writings*. Using a complete count of the *Collected Poems*, we would have to emend Josephine Miles' list of Thomas' most-used words rather drastically. *Adjectives:* subtract two of the "rainbow colors" ("golden" and "red"); add several of what might be called eschatological adjectives: "long," "black," "old," "last," and "still." *Nouns:* subtract nine — "bell," "tower," "word," "land," "mouth," "voice," "weather," "boy," and "face"; add ten — "wind," "dark," "ghost," "fire," "flesh," "hill," "bed," "cloud," "star," and "wound." *Verbs:* subtract "drive" and "drop"; add several verbs of observation and utterance — "sing," "see," "cry," "hear" — as well as "die" and "come." These changes place Thomas' vocabulary very much more in line with that of his contemporaries. He has now 21 (rather than 17) of the 30 majority words of the 1940's; 15 (rather than 13) of the 37 minority words; 15 high-frequency words (rather than 11) shared with at least one other poet of the time; whereas words used with high frequency by Thomas alone are reduced from 12 to 10. The fact that the poet's total vocabulary, viewed statistically, differs so little from that of his fellow writers indicates the limited use of a total count in making literary judgements. Some refinement can be achieved by showing the most-used words in chronological groupings:

| *CP* (3800 lines) | *18P* & *25P* (1500 lines) | *ML* (400 lines) |
|---|---|---|
| man 90 | man 53 | love 14 |
| love 89 | time 47 | eyes 12 |
| sea 89 | sea 41 | heart 11 |
| sun 82 | death 38 | stone 10 |
| time 79 | love 36 | tongue 9 |
| night 64 | blood 34 | sea 9 |
| death 62 | sun 32 | red 8 |
| dead 61 | light 27 | mouth 8 |
| light 61 | wind 27 | black 8 |

| heart 57 | ghost 26 | grave 8 |
| blood 56 | dead 25 | lie 8 |
| one 50 | flesh 25 | house 8 |

| *DE* (1100 lines) | *ICS* (500 lines) |
|---|---|
| sun 33 | night 23 |
| sea 32 | black 15 |
| dark 27 | hill 13 |
| love 27 | love 12 |
| light 24 | sun 12 |
| dead 24 | man 10 |
| water 23 | high 9 |
| man 22 | wood 9 |
| birds 21 | sleep 8 |
| night 21 | house 8 |
| time 20 | heron 7 |
| heart 20 | dew 7 |

His most-used words, it could be argued, reflect Thomas' pre-occupation during the four periods. 'Man" and "time" dominate the early volumes. The middle poems are more romantic with "love," "eyes," and "heart." *Deaths and Entrances* is a celebration of nature: "sun" and "sea." The very last poems are brooding: "night" and "black." What partial truth there may be in these summary comments is not proved by the word count — for several reasons. (1) The sample counted, even though it is the total possible, is not large enough to give the results statistical validity. (2) The list shows glaring contradictions. If *Deaths and Entrances* is so celebrational, why all the occurrences of "dark"? If the last poems are brooding, why "love" and "sun" so high on the list? (3) The count cannot take into consideration the chronology of composition, since so many of the poems are half-revised. (4) Finally and chiefly, no word count can reflect the several meanings of a single word. The numerical result shows Thomas to be a sea poet. But the sea from which dreams and corpses come, or to which Christmas memories roll, or through which the processes of nature operate, is quite different from the sea beside which lovers lie or in which the girl-bait is dragged. Only when certain words are found to be repeated to the same effect in the same group of poems can a count begin to confirm one's judgment about the type and quality of the vocabulary.

3. *LVW*, p. 40.

4. Treece, 2d ed., p. 37.

5. It is never out of place to look at Blake in relation to Thomas' early poems. In "The fields from Islington to Marylebone" we find:

> He [Satan] withered up the Human Form
> By laws of sacrifice for Sin,
> Till it became a Mortal Worm,
> But O! translucent all within.

For a portrayal of man literally in his maggot, see Blake's frontispiece "What is Man" to *The Gates of Paradise*, reproduced in the Everyman edition of Blake, p. 292, a volume that the young Dylan almost certainly had access to.

6. Stanford, pp. 59-60.

7. "Heaven" was a later addition to the poem. The manuscript version had:

> Love drips and gathers, but the fallen blood
> Shall make her well.
> And I am dumb to tell the timeless sun
> How time is all.

"Shall make her well" is clearly positive; and "time is all" should be too. Time is the enemy of man, yes, but not of the "timeless" sun ("timeless clouds," as it was in another draft), which is thought of as everlasting, not subject to wearing down by time. Revision made the ending unequivocal.

8. If we need confirmation that the subject of *Our eunuch dreams* really is dreams and movies, the notebook version (Thirty Seven in the August 1933 Notebook) ends with a clear summary of the issues:

> Which is the dream, and which the photograph?
> And which is life, is death?
> This is the world which whispers in our breath:
> This is the world. Have faith.

Dreams and movies are indistinguishable, both are death. And the draft ends with the voice of reality. There was a "jarring" optimism even in the revised stanza, according to Thomas in a letter to Grigson; he offered his editor a "less false" alternative to "Have faith" in the words "Suffer the world to spin." But the poem was printed without the substitution.

9. A possible line would enclose: (1) *Find meat on bones* (July 1933), perhaps the first poem in the notebooks to have process as its subject. Thomas had talked about process in *Especially when the October wind* and *Here in this spring* before this; but here disparate imagery gives a sense of process. Antithesis throughout: Find meat on bones (+) that soon have none (−), etc. (2) *Ears in the turrets hear* (July 1933). A simple statement of constraint as opposed to release. (3) *Shiloh's seed* (August 1933). (4) *Before I knocked* (September 1933). This and the last poem utilize the conception of Christ to express the operation of forces. (5) *My hero bares his nerves* (September

1933). The flesh-spirit duality ("mortal ghost") applied to the poet's own self. (6) *In the beginning* (September 1933). The duality in a Genesis setting. (7) *Grief thief of time* (August 1933). Opposite of genesis; the waste of human material. (8) *From love's first fever to her plague* (October 1933). Process vocabulary gives added dimension to the development of the individual from conception through embryo to youth. (9) *Foster the light* (February 1934). Antithetical exhortation. (10) *Where once the waters of your face* (March 1934). The sea is an arena for interplay of forces. Negative condition, with previous positive condition expressed in the adverbial "where" clauses. (11) *When, like a running grave* (c. September 1934). Predominantly images of decline. (12) *I dreamed my genesis* (c. May 1934). Death and rebirth. (13) *My world is pyramid* (c. August 1934). (14) *I, in my intricate image* (1935). (15) *Do you not father me* (1934-35). (16) *Hold hard, these ancient minutes in the cuckoo's month* (1935).

## CHAPTER IV

1. *LVW*, p. 44.

2. Sigmund Freud, *The Interpretation of Dreams* (London, 3d ed., 1937), p. 334. The italics are mine.

3. Thomas, "Answers to an Inquiry," *New Verse*, No. 11 (October 1934), p. 9.

4. Freud, pp. 336, 339.

5. *LVW*, p. 92.

6. As reported by Marjorie Adix, in Tedlock, p. 66; in Brinnin, *Casebook*, p. 288.

7. Treece, 1st ed., p. 149.

8. *Ibid.*, pp. 149-150.

9. There has been a tendency to read "cracked" in this line as a past participle. But an examination of the contextual syntax shows that "cracked" can be no other than the past tense verb, and that the line is a complete sentence: "Abaddon in the hangnail *did crack* from Adam." See Ralph N. Maud, "Thomas' Sonnet I," *Explicator*, XIV (December 1955), art. 16.

10. We cannot here ignore another key that has been offered, Elder Olson's astronomical interpretation of the sonnets, which takes up most of the sixth chapter of *The Poetry of Dylan Thomas* (Chicago: University of Chicago Press, 1954). If the constellation Hercules were really the main hero of the poems, as Olson postulates, then this would certainly be a major factor in making more oblique our approach to the Christian core. But Thomas' acquaintances have not revealed that the poet had a vital interest in star maps, nor does Olson suggest that such an interest exhibits itself anywhere in the poet's writings other than

the sonnets. His theory is based on internal indications only. When the opening lines of sonnet I,

> Altarwise by owl-light in the half-way house
> The gentleman lay graveward with his furies,

are taken by Olson to describe the constellation Hercules setting toward the west with Scorpius, Draco, and Serpens Caput, his neighboring "furies" in the night sky, we are being asked to agree that this interpretation not only fits the poem but is *demanded* by it — since there is no sound reason why it should otherwise occur to us. The burden of proof is unbearably great. When sonnet VIII ("This was the crucifixion on the mountain") states quite definitely its subject matter, when Biblical references in every sonnet suggest a religious and specifically Christian theme, and when we have the gentleman called five lines later "that gentleman of wounds," it would seem strange if the quoted lines should not pre-eminently and immediately demand a Christian, rather than Herculean, interpretation. In order to give Hercules a certain position in the night sky, Olson was obliged to take "owl-light" as "night" rather than the more correct "dusk," which we can take to be the shrouding of the sun at Christ's death. "Half-way house," according to Olson, is the "autumnal equinox"; but surely the phrase ties up with the "half-way winds" of later in the poem, both symbols of mortality, this-worldliness. The "half-way house" will be the whole transitory world — a halting-place midway between two stages of a journey (see the *OED*). The "furies" are best seen as Christ's earthly passions and sins, which die with Him. He lies "graveward" in the sense that he is making for the grave; also he is in the position of an altar in a church ("altarwise" as defined in the *OED*), the living prototype of our common symbolic cross. In order to explain "altarwise," Olson makes an amazing side-step, discarding altogether his picture of the night sky and substituting an alternative system where Hercules represents the sun "moving southward as the year wears on, in the direction of the constellation Ara, the Altar; hence 'altarwise'" (p. 68). But the suffix *-wise* indicates manner not direction. If Dylan Thomas had ever set himself the fantastic job of laying clues for the expert in astronomy, the meticulousness of mind so required would at least have supplied "altarbound" or "altarward." To take the "gentleman" to be Christ does not make this a simple poem, but it does mean that the ingenuities here are the same kind as we have found in other poems of Thomas'. Were "gentleman" to stand for Hercules, it would be little more than a subterfuge to avoid giving the name; whereas the anonymity of "gentleman" is appropriate for Thomas' "Jack Christ." And further, an ear for Thomas' wordplay will give us "*gentle* man" as an expression of Christ's meekness. For further discussion see Ralph N. Maud, "Dylan Thomas Astro-navigated," *Essays in Criticism*, V (April 1955), 164-168, and Monroe C. Beardsley and Sam Hynes, "Misunderstanding Poetry: Notes on Some Readings of Dylan Thomas," *College English*, XXI (March 1960), 315-322.

## CHAPTER V

1. John Malcolm Brinnin, *Dylan Thomas in America* (Boston: Little, Brown, 1955), p. 128; in Brinnin, *Casebook*, p. 208.

2. "Ye shall have a hempen caudle then, and the help of hatchet" — *Henry VI*, pt. 2, IV. vii. 95. When the *OED* records only one other instance of this kind of comic reference to hanging (in the Marprelate Epistles), one is intrigued by the question of where Thomas got the phrase in the first place if not from the *OED* itself. Perhaps he knew his early Shakespeare histories and Marprelate tracts better than one might suppose?

3. "Three Poems," in *QE* (U.S.), pp. 178-180. See also note to *In the white giant's thigh*, *Botteghe oscure*, No. 6 (November 1950), pp. 335-337. *In Country Heaven* (unpublished) is a verse rendering of this prose explanation.

4. R. B. Marriott writes in *Adam International Review*, No. 238 (Dylan Thomas Memorial Number, 1953), p. 31: "In 1935, when first I knew Dylan Thomas, he said: 'I shall be dead within two years.'" In contrast we have Phillip Burton quoting Thomas as saying in 1952: "I've got another twenty, or perhaps twenty-five, years to live. . . ." (*Ibid.*, p. 36). The last poems do not reflect that view.

5. Brinnin, *Dylan Thomas in America*, p. 274:

Dylan waked and dozed intermittently. "The horrors" were still there, he said — "abstractions, triangles and squares and circles." Once he said to Liz, "You told me you had a friend who had d.t.'s. What was it like?" "He saw white mice and roses," said Liz. "Roses plural?" asked Dylan, "or Rose's roses, with an apostrophe?" Then Liz said, "You know, Dylan, one thing about horrors — just remember, they go away, they do go away —" "Yes," said Dylan, "I believe you." As she sat beside him holding his hand in hers, she suddenly felt his grip stiffen. When she looked at Dylan his face was turning blue. A quick call to Dr. Feltenstein brought an ambulance that took Dylan to St. Vincent's Hospital.

## APPENDIX I

1. See "Note" dated November 1952 in *Collected Poems 1934-1952* (London: J. M. Dent & Sons, 1952) and undated in *The Collected Poems of Dylan Thomas* (New York: New Di-

rections, 1953). These two editions differ in pagination but not in the text. The five constituent volumes are *18 Poems* (London: The Sunday Referee and the Parton Bookshop, 1934), *Twenty-five Poems* (London: J. M. Dent & Sons, 1936), *The Map of Love* (London: J. M. Dent & Sons, 1939), *Deaths and Entrances* (London: J. M. Dent & Sons, 1946), *In Country Sleep* (New York: New Directions, 1952). *Paper and Sticks* (in *DE*) was dropped while the *Collected Poems* was in proof. *Once below a time*, not previously included in a volume, was added in *CP*, as was *Author's Prologue*.

2. The four poetry Notebooks at the Lockwood Library are presently being prepared for publication. Manuscripts presented to the British Museum by Trevor Hughes confirm many points and, in the case of *Especially when the October wind*, fill a striking gap. Documents in the Harvard College Library and in the T. E. Hanley collection are also corroborative. Communications concerning like manuscripts or relevant information are solicited. Enquiries may be addressed to the author, Lockwood Library, State University of New York, Buffalo 14, New York.

3. Only three Notebook poems appeared in *Swansea Grammar School Magazine*. *Orpheus* in *SGSM* July 1930 is a traditional pastoral, thoroughly deleted in the 1930 Notebook. *Two Images* in *SGSM* April 1931, dated 28 and 29 December 1930 in Notebook, both prompted the poet's later marginal "Ugh."

4. See also Treece, 2d ed., chap. viii, *passim*; Stanford, pp. 64, 73; W. S. Merwin, "A Religious Poet," *Adam International Review* (1953), p. 75; Randall Swingler, "Recent Verse," *New English Weekly* (1 October 1936), pp. 409-410. The few poems of Thomas' congenial to David Holbrook, dealt with under "The True Voice of Dylan Thomas" in his book *Llareggub Revisited* (Cambridge: Bowes & Bowes, 1962), p. 191, are early ones:

> It would be interesting to know under what circumstances these poems in which a true voice or partly true voice appears — *Should lanterns shine, I have longed to move away* and *Out of the sighs* — were composed. At what points of personal balance was Thomas able to contemplate his predicament with some objectivity. . . . Perhaps the most revealing of the true poems is *O make me a mask. . . .*

The chronology answers the question. These poems cannot be held to reveal valuable moments of self-awareness in the mature Thomas. The "true voice" of Dylan Thomas remains in the long, difficult poems.

5. A tabulated representation of the poetic output appears in Ralph N. Maud, "Dylan Thomas' *Collected Poems*: Chronology of Composition," *PMLA*, LXXVI (June 1961), pp. 292-297.

6. See Tedlock, p. 17; Brinnin, *Casebook*, p. 280.

7. Charles Rare Books, Catalogue Forty-One, lists "Proof of *Twenty-Three Poems* 1936. Advance proof copy in printed drab wrappers, actually *Twenty-five Poems* lacking *And death shall have no dominion* and *Then was my neophyte*, with two versions of *To-day, this insect*, one of which was never published."

8. With reference to the term "exhausters," what Thomas wrote to Vernon Watkins on 13 November 1937 about *The spire cranes* (originally a January 1931 poem) applies equally to his practice for the previous couple of years (*LVW*, p. 31):

> I've done another little poem: nothing at all important, or even (probably) much good: just a curious thought said quickly. I think it will be good for me to write some short poems, not bothering about them too much, between my long exhausters.

What he had done with *The spire cranes* was to regularize and reduce by about half a very free short-lined poem from the 1930-1932 Notebook, retaining the thought and much of the wording. In contrast, the "long exhauster" *Poem to Caitlin* later entitled *I make this in a warring absence* took "roughly a year" to finish; a single line would occupy Thomas for many days (*Ibid.*, p. 30). The difference in tone and achievement between the two poems is great, and immediately apparent. The fact that Thomas was interested in revising early poems is significant in itself; but the main point here is that Thomas' real development as a poet can only be seen by putting to one side the minor strain, the revamped poems, thus isolating his main line of creativity.

9. Watkins coined the engaging term "opossum" to make a contrast with "opus" (*Ibid.*, p. 40). Though Thomas apparently never revealed to his correspondent that these short poems were revisions, he at least put an appropriate value judgment on them. To Henry Treece he frankly explained that he had written the "straight" poems of *25P* "quite a long time before the other poems," and referred to the early notebooks in a letter dated July 1938.

10. This was the period in which Thomas had ambitions for a Jarvis novel. Glyn Jones in "Dylan Thomas — The Other Man," *Western Mail* (21 April 1958) mentions bringing away with him from his first visit to Thomas (about April 1934) "typescript copies of, among others, 'The mouse and the woman,' 'The visitors,' and 'The enemies.'" He also recalls Thomas working on "The Orchards" at that time.

11. Thomas wrote of *To Others than You:* "Here is a new short poem, nothing very much" (*LVW*, p. 68). At least two lines were not new: (1) "Desireless familiar," as Thomas' letter

indicates, came from "The Orchards," and (2) "My friends were enemies on stilts" came from Notebook poem 2 April 1933. The "opossums" apparently continue into *DE*. *When I Woke* goes back to a February 1933 Notebook poem for its opening line (see also *Ibid.*, p. 41). *The Hunchback in the Park* and *On the Marriage of a Virgin*, published in 1941, were drafted almost ten years earlier.

12. See note 8.

13. *LVW*, p. 39.

14. *Ibid.*, p. 37. Watkins indicates that the fourth poem was the draft of *After the funeral*. The simplest explanation is that five poems, not four, were enclosed, and that Thomas added this unfinished poem without including it in his count.

15. *Ibid.*, p. 40.

16. An indication that *How shall my animal* should be taken as a major effort is that Thomas sent it to *Criterion*, a periodical with "an established snob-appeal," where he had planned to send his previous major poem, the poem to Caitlin (*Ibid.*, pp. 33, 31). That poem, if sent, was rejected; *How shall my animal* was accepted. Place of publication, as we have seen with the revised poems sent to *Poetry*, is generally a good indication of the value Thomas placed on a poem, in turn a guide to how he wrote it, whether easy revision or hard driving.

17. *Ibid.*, pp. 57, 40.

18. The contents of *ML* are divided into two groups in the Chronology. A similar division for *25P* is more difficult. The undisputably "major" poems are *I, in my intricate image, A grief ago, Hold hard, these ancient minutes in the cuckoo's month*, and *Altarwise by owl-light*. The teasers *Now* and *How soon the servant sun* were acknowledged to be in a special category (*Ibid.*, p. 16). *To-day, this insect* was exhaustively rewritten from its early version. *Find meat on bones, Foster the light, Grief thief of time, Do you not father me* might best be considered as part of the major effort that produced *18P*. The suggestion that *Then was my neophyte* is a revised poem is completely conjectural. In December 1936 Thomas considered it the best poem in the book.

19. *Ibid.*, p. 48.

# Index of Thomas' Poems

After the funeral, 124, 133, 146-147, 172.

All all and all the dry worlds lever, 80, 128.

Altarwise by owl-light, 21, 47-48, 70, 97-101, 124, 129-130, 153, 163, 167-169, 172.

Among those Killed in the Dawn Raid was a Man Aged a Hundred, 137.

And death shall have no dominion, 124, 126, 131, 171.

Author's Prologue, 113, 142, 149, 161, 170.

Ballad of the Long-legged Bait, 3-4, 42, 45, 62, 85, 91, 136, 155, 158.

Because the pleasure-bird whistles, 133, 147.

Before I knocked, 60, 96, 99-100, 125, 128, 166.

Before we mothernaked fall, 131.

Captain Bigger's Isle, 122.

Ceremony After a Fire Raid, 85, 94, 137, 154.

Conversation of Prayer, The, 138, 154.

Countryman's Return, The, 135.

Deaths and Entrances, 136.

Do not go gentle into that good night, 141, 154.

Do you not father me, 124, 129, 167, 172.

Dream of Winter, A, 137.

Ears in the turrets hear, 125, 127, 131, 152, 166.

Elegy, 143.

Especially when the October wind, 63, 124, 127-128, 166, 170.

Fern Hill, 15, 80, 95, 138.

Find meat on bones, 64, 125, 130, 166, 172.

First there was the lamb on knocking knees, 124-125.

Force that through the green fuse drives the flower, The, 65-72, 80, 84, 125-126, 128, 166.

Foster the light, 125, 128, 130, 152, 167, 172.

From love's first fever to her plague, 31, 77-78, 91, 125, 127-128, 150, 167.

Greek Play in a Garden, 125-126.

Grief ago, A, 23, 45, 81-84, 86-88, 90-94, 129, 152, 172.

Grief thief of time, 125, 129-130, 152, 167, 172.

Hand that signed the paper, The, 125, 129.

Here in this spring, 84, 125-130, 166.

Hold hard, these ancient minutes in the cuckoo's month, 129, 163, 167, 172.

Holy Spring, 138.

How shall my animal, 84, 122, 124, 132, 145-146, 163, 172.

How soon the servant sun, 129, 152, 172.

Hunchback in the Park, The, 124, 137, 172.

I dreamed my genesis, 128, 151, 160-161, 167.

I fellowed sleep, 77-78, 125, 129, 151.

I have longed to move away, 124, 129, 152, 170.

I, in my intricate image, 61, 129, 151, 163, 167, 172.

I make this in a warring absence, 22, 132, 153, 171-172.

I see the boys of summer, 13-40, 57-59, 64-65, 70, 80, 125, 127-128, 150, 162.

I, the first named, 133.

If I were tickled by the rub of love, 85, 125, 127-128.

'If my head hurt a hair's foot,' 95, 132, 154.

In Country Heaven, 110-112, 114, 142, 169.

In country sleep, 110, 114, 140.

In my Craft or Sullen Art, 138, 148.

In the beginning, 125, 129, 163, 167.

In the white giant's thigh, 25, 110, 115, 141, 155, 169.

Incarnate devil, 96, 125, 129, 162.

Into her Lying Down Head, 40-46, 89, 135, 154, 161, 163.

It is the sinners' dust-tongued bell, 45, 132.

Lament, 94, 141, 155.

Last night I dived my beggar arm, 137.

Lie Still, Sleep Becalmed, 138.

Light breaks where no sun shines, 60, 80, 125-126, 128, 151.

Love in the Asylum, 136.

Love me, not as the dreaming nurses, 125-126.

My hero bares his nerves, 100, 125, 128, 166.

My world is pyramid, 128, 151, 167.

No man believes, 95, 125-126.

Not forever shall the lord of the red hail, 128.

Not from this anger, 61-62, 124, 132-133, 145-146, 153.

Now, 129, 172.

O make me a mask, 124, 132-133, 145-146, 170.

On a Wedding Anniversary, 136.

On no work of words, 124, 133.

On the Marriage of a Virgin, 4, 124, 136, 172.

Once below a time, 135, 154, 170.

Once it was the colour of saying, 124, 133.

Orpheus, 170.

Our eunuch dreams, 72-74, 76, 79, 85, 125, 127-128, 150, 166.

Out of the Pit, 124, 126.

Out of the sighs, 124, 131, 152, 170.

Over Sir John's hill, 6, 80, 84, 103-110, 114-115, 140, 161.

Paper and Sticks, 135, 170.

Poem in October, 5-6, 62, 80, 84, 138.

Poem on his Birthday, 113, 141.

Poet: 1935, 131.

Process in the weather of the heart, A, 57-60, 79-80, 125-126, 128.

Refusal to Mourn the Death, by Fire, of a Child in London, A, 50-53, 84, 109, 138.

Request to Leda, 136.

Romantic Isle, The, 123.

Saint about to fall, A, 132.

See, on gravel paths, 124.

Seed-at-zero, The, 125, 130.

Shall gods be said to thump the clouds, 96, 125, 131.

Shiloh's seed, 166.

Should lanterns shine, 124, 130, 159, 170.

Spire cranes, The, 122, 124, 132, 144-145, 171.

That sanity be kept, 124, 126.

That the sum sanity, 125-126, 128.

Then was my neophyte, 124, 131, 171-172.

There was a Saviour, 135, 162.

This bread I break, 125, 130, 151.

This Side of the Truth, 112, 138, 148.

To Others than You, 135, 154, 171.

To-day, this insect, 122, 124, 131, 171-172.

Tombstone told when she died, The, 87-88, 125, 133, 153.

Twenty-four years, 133, 147.

Two Images, 170.

Unluckily for a Death, 95, 135, 161.

Vision and Prayer, 84-86, 96, 138, 159-161.

Was there a time, 124, 130.

We lying by seasand, 4, 125, 132, 145.

When all my five and country senses see, 124, 132-133, 143-146.

When I Woke, 135, 154, 172.

When, like a running grave, 113, 128, 150, 167.

When once the twilight locks no longer, 74-76, 78-79, 100, 125, 127-128, 150.

Where once the waters of your face, 125, 127-128, 167.

Why east wind chills, 124-125, 130.

Winter's Tale, A, 53-55, 84, 138.

Woman Speaks, The, 125-126, 128.

Your breath was shed, 137.

# ENTRANCES TO DYLAN THOMAS' POETRY

It is surprising that Dylan Thomas' reputation rests on so few poems that are well understood. His poetry moves like an iceberg; nine-tenths of its power and weight is under the surface. In reaching below the surface, ENTRANCES TO DYLAN THOMAS' POETRY is concerned with the precise nature of Thomas' obscurity—or, rather, the precise nature of our difficulty with Thomas' poetic idiom.

In this study by Ralph Maud the reader is asked to enter Thomas' poetry without preconceptions and, from a close reading of certain texts, to establish first principles for interpretation. In his approach to the meaning of the poems, Dr. Maud uses the available aids to explication: Thomas' own statements about his poetry, manuscript sources, word and syllable counts, biographical and critical material. A selected number of poems from the different periods of Thomas' development are thoroughly explored for meaning, notably: *I see the boys of summer, A Refusal to Mourn the Death, by Fire, of a Child in London, The force that through the green fuse drives the flower, Our eunuch dreams, A grief ago, Altarwise by owl-light,* and *Over Sir John's hill.* Through these the author investigates Thomas' recurring themes, his poetic idiom, and his artistic disciplines.

ENTRANCES TO DYLAN THOMAS' POETRY, concludes with two reference appendices. Appendix I presents the first full chronology of composition of Thomas' works, including newly uncovered Swansea and London publications. Appendix II lists the textual cruxes in the British and American editions of COLLECTED POEMS.

Ralph Maud, English-born of Welsh ancestry, has been a student of Thomas' poetry for many years and has published numerous articles on his work. He is co-editor with Aneirin Talfan Davies of THE COLOUR OF SAYING, an anthology of poems of other poets which Thomas recited before audiences in England and America. With the aid of an American Council of Learned Societies grant, he spent the year 1961-62 in Dylan Thomas country — Swansea, Soho, and elsewhere.

His appointment to the faculty of the State University of New York at Buffalo in 1958 brought him into contact with the Lockwood Library, where are stored Thomas' Notebooks dating from 1930 to 1934 and other holograph material. These sources made it possible for him to expand his knowledge of Thomas' poetry through textual research and combine that critical method with his feeling for the poet and his work.

# UNIVERSITY OF PITTSBURGH PRESS

C

## Date Due

| | | |
|---|---|---|
| BC3M 84 | | |
| BC 4 M 85 | | |
| May 15 | | |
| | | |
| | | |
| | | |
| | | |
| | | |
| | | |
| | | |
| | | |
| | | |
| | | |

971    Morton, Desmond, 1937-
Mor      A short history of Canada / Desmond Morton.
         Edmonton : Hurtig, [1983]
           295 p.


         1. Canada - History.  I. Title.
         0888302533                        1996576 NLC
         0888302525 pb                     1996584

# A Short History of Canada

## Desmond Morton

Hurtig Publishers Ltd.
Edmonton

Hurtig Publishers
10560 105 Street
Edmonton, Alberta

**Canadian Cataloguing in Publication Data**

Morton, Desmond, 1937–
     A short history of Canada

     Includes index.
     ISBN 0-88830-253-3 (bound).—ISBN
0-88830-252-5 (pbk.)

1. Canada—History.   I. Title.
FC164.M67      971      C83-091280-0
F1026.M67

Printed and bound in Canada
by Friesen Printers

# Contents

Foreword / 6

PART I    Different Histories / 8

1/New Nation / 9
2/Cartier's Quebec / 16
3/English Canadians / 29
4/United Canadas / 40
5/Lower Provinces / 52
6/The Great Northwest / 61

PART II    A Mari usque ad Marem / 70

1/Confederation / 71
2/Nation-Building / 80
3/National Policy / 92
4/Political Revolution / 106

PART III    "The Century of Canada" / 118

1/Flourishing / 119
2/Questioning / 132
3/National Crisis / 145
4/Dead Ends / 158
5/The Depression / 173

PART IV    Middle Age, Middle Power / 188

1/Mr. King's War / 189
2/Prosperity / 204
3/Recession / 220
4/Confusion / 234

PART V    A Country Shared / 246

1/Liberation / 247
2/Affirmation / 263
3/Futures / 278

Index / 283

# Foreword

A nation, said Ernest Renan, is a people that has done great things together in the past. It is not bound by language or by a common culture but by a shared experience. History is what Canadians have in common.

Canadians believe that their history is short, boring, and irrelevant. They are wrong on all counts. The choices Canadians can make today have been shaped by history. The governors of New France launched arguments that federalists and independentists repeat in present-day Quebec. Early fur traders illustrated economic laws that modern-day resource development unconsciously follows. Canadians trying to understand the problems of political leadership deserve a second look at the arts of Sir John A. Macdonald and Mackenzie King.

In each generation, Canadians have had to learn how to live with each other in this big, rich land. It has never been easy. For those who ignore history, it is doubly difficult. This book has been written to make it a little easier for Canadians to know and understand their country.

It would not have been written without the inspiration and firm prodding of Mel Hurtig. That inspiration has been reinforced—unconsciously and perhaps grudgingly—by generations of students at Erindale College, the Mississauga campus of the University of Toronto. Some of them have been new Canadians, committed to an adopted country, yet puzzled by it and reluctant to take its truths for granted.

Because of them, there will never be a final history of Canada. This is a guidebook to take its readers a certain way. The future is for them to make.

More than most of my books, this one has profited from the patient care and perceptiveness of my editor, Sarah Reid, and of my wife, Jan. Both deserve whatever claims the book may have to be readable. Where it fails, they could not prevail over stubbornness. David Shaw, as designer, has been all that an author could wish. Clara Stewart has been more than a typist. She and Kathie Hill have reminded me that readers deserve wit and clarity as well as facts.

They want accuracy too, and there I have profited from Erindale colleagues, notably Paul Fox and Eric Sager. They bear no responsibility for any persistent errors. Few institutions have demonstrated more consistently that vague but real virtue called collegiality than Erindale. It is to a college in the new city of Mississauga that this book is dedicated. Erindale sums up for me the past and future of Canada.

# PART I

# Different Histories

# 1 / New Nation

At midnight on July 1, 1867, church bells rang out from Lunenberg to Sarnia. In Ottawa, militia artillery fired the first round of a hundred-gun salute. Crowds cheered the explosions and waited as the militiamen laboured in the dark with rammers and sponges. At dawn, four million people awoke as citizens of a new Dominion of Canada. Some of them, in New Brunswick and Nova Scotia, might resent their fate, but a two-day weekend (for July 1 fell on a Monday) was too rare a treat to be shunned. Picnics, lacrosse tournaments, cricket matches, and excursions focused the day's excitement. Farm families united around groaning kitchen tables. On Toronto's waterfront, a huge ox would roast all day so that dripping hunks of meat could be distributed to the poor.

Carefully respecting the ban on Sabbath labour, George Brown arrived at the offices of his *Globe* that midnight, determined to do editorial justice to events he had helped to cause. Throughout the morning hours, his pen filled page after page with history, statistics, and hope for the new Dominion. Only at dawn was Brown finished. Solemnly he pledged that "the teeming millions who shall populate the northern part of this continent, from the Atlantic to the Pacific shall, under a wise and just Government, reap the fruit of well-directed enterprise, honest industry and religious principles." By then, the express trains that normally carried the *Globe* to readers across the old province of Canada West had departed without it. Brown's hopes would go largely unread.

In the summer of 1867, they were no more than hopes. Confederation covered only 370,045 square miles (958 416.5 km²), a mere tenth of British North America. Three colonies had become four provinces, but the northern edge of the new provinces of Ontario and Quebec ran vaguely along the watershed that drained into the St. Lawrence and the Great Lakes. The population—3,816,680 by official count—was a tenth as large as that of the bustling, powerful nation to the south. Many Canadians wondered how long they would survive the American boast of a "manifest destiny" to rule the entire continent.

George Brown's Dominion Day mood allowed no dismay. Small as it was, Canada's population was at least as large as America's had been when the Thirteen Colonies won their independence in 1783. Confederation itself was proof that the divisions between a million French Canadians and two and a quarter million Canadians of British origin could be overcome. If there remained differences of race, region, and religion, prosperity would dissolve them. The *Globe*'s readers could share the editor's intoxication with statistics, marvelling at every aspect of the young country's potential, from ship-building to the vast deposits of rock oil near Petrolia.

In his day, Brown had flailed at the corruption and waste of the railway builders but now he celebrated their achievements: 2149 miles (3458 km) of track in Quebec and Ontario alone, backed by canals, roads, bridges. The Grand Trunk, with 1277 miles (2055 km) of rail, was the world's largest system. Almost two of those miles rumbled across the St. Lawrence River at Montreal on the world-famous Victoria Bridge, completing a line that ran unbroken from Sarnia to Portland, Maine. And soon there would be more. Confederation was nothing if not a guarantee that new rail lines would snake their way east to Halifax and perhaps west across the fabled Rocky Mountains to the Pacific.

Prosperity would depend on the *Globe*'s most faithful readers, the farmers. Across the Dominion, there were more Canadians in farming than in any other occupation. If there was an average farmer of the time, he owned from fifty to one hundred acres, cultivated twenty of them, grew seventy-two bushels of wheat, owned eight cattle and a team of horses. In fact, soil and climate created vast differences. Quebec farmers were poorer, on average, than those in Ontario or the agricultural regions of the Maritimes, but they were recovering from several grim years of depression. Surplus offspring had left for New England mill towns and were sending home the hard-earned sums that would allow the family farm to diversify into dairying. Much of Ontario, soil exhausted and crops ravaged by Hessian fly, was now sliding into its own rural depression.

Social scientists and statisticians barely existed in the 1860s to warn people of national trends. Canadians who gathered for barter or gossip at the local inn or general store knew only of a daughter marrying a man from "the Boston states" or of sons gone homesteading in Kansas. Only the census, every ten years, identified trends: Canadians were leaving the land, and many of them were leaving Canada. Meanwhile, people lived their lives for the most part within the limits of family and community. They looked to politicians not for social or economic programs but for bridges, wharves, and post offices, and sometimes for a personal place on the public payroll.

In spite of localism, broad legislative programs existed. Egerton Ryerson had crusaded tirelessly to make the rural communities of Upper Canada establish and tax themselves for their own public schools. Ontario could boast of the results (and grumble at the cost). In Lower Canada, Ryerson's dynamic counterpart, Pierre Chauveau, became the first premier of the new province of Quebec. The struggle for schools was hard; in the lower provinces, it was not yet won. Rural communities saw no need for those "charitable and eleemosynary institutions" the new constitution assigned to the provinces. Rural families made room for their own orphans, elderly, and insane. If the treatment was sometimes harsh and misguided, were the few publicly-run poor houses, orphanages, and asylums any better? Even police forces had no place in a rural Canada. Magistrates had to turn to the militia or recruit special constables if criminals defied the majesty of the law. A frightened rural community could make its own laws, as the Black Donnellys of Lucan, near London, discovered in 1880. When their sense of justice was aroused, rural communities could also defend their own. The Megantic outlaw, Donald Morrison, was hidden from the law for three years in the 1880s when his Eastern Township neighbours found no crime in his alleged arson and accidental manslaughter.

Farming lay at the heart of Canadian society and economics in 1867. Closely linked were the other resource industries of fishing and logging. Indeed, there was little distinction. However harsh or inhospitable the coastline, every fishing family cultivated a few acres of vegetables and hay. Settlers on the edge of the Canadian Shield forced the thin soil to grow hay and oats for the logging camps where they and their sons spent the winters. Wheat, square

11

timbers, and fish made up most of the $80 million in exports with which the new Dominion hoped to pay her way in the world.

The future, of course, would be different. It lay not so much with the resource frontier as with the cities that controlled the trade and transportation routes. Once it had been rivers and harbours that made cities, now it was railways that confirmed or denied urban ambitions. The Victoria Bridge confirmed that Montreal would continue as the metropolis of Canada, the first city of 100,000 people. Quebec, with 59,699, would slowly wither as her poor rail connections undermined her claim to be the great port of the St. Lawrence timber trade. Toronto, with 56,092 citizens, would grow because of the river of railway tracks across her waterfront—the Grand Trunk, the Great Western, and her own creation, the Northern, reaching to Collingwood, Lake Huron, and the West. Halifax with 29,582 people and Saint John with 28,805 were the fourth and fifth cities of the Dominion and dominated their own provinces. Their huge merchant fleets allowed Brown to boast of Canada as a great new maritime power. But in the Victorian mansions, where the shipowners displayed their wealth, already there were fears that great ports might become backwaters.

If railways decided the fate of cities, they also created new reasons for urban growth. The costly self-sufficiency of small market towns, producing their own tools, furniture, and boots, ended with the railway. Mass markets justified mass production, costly machinery, and armies of persuasive salesmen. Necessities made locally or in the home could now be supplied year-round with a variety and quality few local tradesmen could hope to match. By 1867, manufacturing employed fifteen per cent of Canadian workers and produced twenty per cent of Canadian wealth. The Massey family's reaper and mower won a prize that year at the Paris Exposition. What could better typify the hopes of Confederation than a Yankee-style pride in home-grown inventiveness? What was more Canadian than delight at foreign recognition? More significant for Canadian development was the process that would carry Daniel Massey's little foundry at Bond Head to the town of Bowmanville and finally, by 1878, to the growing metropolis of Toronto.

The merchants and industrialists of the expanding cities were, for the most part, self-made men: once-penniless clerks and artisans who had saved their money, seen their chance, and seized it. Some were Americans; a disproportionate number, perhaps because they were apprenticed so young and in such a hard school, were Scottish immigrants. Few of these hard-bitten achievers (including George Brown), could spare much genuine sympathy for those who had failed in the struggle for wealth. Confederation coincided with an era when skilled workers were losing the struggle for near-equality with their employers and superiority over the unskilled. Ancient crafts, from shoemaking to typography, were being undermined by new technologies. By luck and strong organization, the printers would save themselves; other occupations would disappear or decline in status.

The average worker in Confederation Canada—almost as mythical a being as the average farmer—echoed the rhyme that "a dollar a day is very good pay." That might be true for labourers; a skilled worker expected twice as much or more for a work week of six days and sixty hours. A mixed blessing of industrialism was that women now found paid work, though at barely half a man's wage. Children earned far less. An employee, of course, paid for his own holidays—even Dominion Day and Christmas —and took his own risks with old age, sickness, and injuries on the job. The cyclical certainty of hard times was met from a worker's meagre savings. Those responsible for municipal relief did their best to make sure that any applicant had first considered starvation as a serious alternative.

Urban, industrial workers were a minority. Most Canadians still worked in a wageless, pre-industrial economy, often, like Gaspé fishermen, in debt to their merchant suppliers. Rural-minded Canadians had no sympathy with arguments for shorter hours, higher wages, or labour unions. When workers in Hamilton and Toronto imitated British industrial workers by demanding a nine-hour day, the Halifax *Witness* delivered an editorial sermon most of its readers would instinctively echo:

In this new country, where every man who strives may advance in social power and rank, to teach men subordination to class movements is to deprive them of those noble opportunities for personal advancement which are the peculiar glory and advantage of this continent.

If many Canadians pretended to ignore class differences, their political, religious, and cultural leaders offered plenty of alternatives. They began with the barriers between the two "founding nations" of French and English. Few, in the first Dominion census, escaped either category: 202,991 Germans were by far the largest exception, but the census-takers found only 125 Jews and 11 "Hindoos." Yet British origins could hide historic and bitter differences. The 846,414 Irish (far the largest of the "British groups") had brought with them, refreshed by an ocean voyage, all the hatreds of Green and Orange. They played them out in frequent midsummer riots in Montreal, Toronto, Saint John, or wherever the fires could be struck.

More than the differences of language and culture, the architects of the new Dominion had tried to accommodate the bitter quarrels of Catholic and Protestant. Few politicians had escaped the temptation or the risks of mixing religion and politics. It was misleading, of course, to claim that Protestants were united (the census distinguished six varieties of Presbyterian and eight of Methodist). Nor were all Canadians united in Christianity (the census also found 1884 "pagans" and 20 atheists, almost all from Ontario).

For Brown's Toronto, for the twenty thousand people of the sweltering little logging town of Ottawa, for Montreal businessmen with renewed visions of a transcontinental empire, Confederation was a triumph. For others, half-devoured by the long struggle with the land, the forest, or the sea, it was a matter of deep indifference. For some, like those who draped the entrance to the Halifax *Chronicle* in black bunting, or those who gathered at Montreal's *Institut Canadien* to hatch schemes to bring down that "sell-out," George-Etienne Cartier, Confederation was already an enemy before it was born.

It was Cartier, the man of action, not words, who had urged, cajoled, and manoeuvred his fellow French Canadians into Confederation. The man who had composed *Avant tout, soyons Canadiens* ("Before All Else, Let's Be Canadians"), who sang it in his rough, raucous voice whenever the company could endure it, was also the man who insisted that Confederation created a "new nation." It was, Cartier insisted, only within a new political nation of British North America that the cultural nation of French Canada could be safe from American conquest or English assimilation.

The new Canadian nation was not the outcome of a long

14

struggle for liberation or even of the effort, so common in nineteenth-century Europe, to revive a half-buried language and culture. The Dominion had no common language or agreed-upon symbols. Even the beaver, "a most respectable animal," as Sir William Dawson of McGill University acknowledged, was "a type of unvarying instincts and old-world traditions. He does not improve and becomes extinct rather than change his ways." Canadians certainly shared a climate—harsh, interminable winters that might, if one believed the dangerous new doctrines of Charles Darwin, breed out the feeble and the weak-willed. Winters were more popular with the wealthy than with workers who faced routine wage cuts and layoffs when the cold months approached. Canada's image as "Our Lady of the Snows" would repel the investment and immigration which so preoccupied the Fathers of Confederation.

July 1, 1867, was a time of hope and fresh beginnings. In fact, Confederation had not broken with the past. Unlike the American revolutionaries, who deliberately concealed their borrowings from colonial tradition, the Fathers of Confederation built deliberately, pragmatically, and cautiously from their own historical experience. They and their critics carried their memories intact across the narrow divide of the first Dominion Day. The history of Canada as a single transcontinental nation begins from that day.

The histories of Canada had begun long before.

# 2 / Cartier's Quebec

For George-Etienne Cartier or any other *Canadien*, Canada's history began not in 1867 but in 1534, when another Cartier had made his landfall on the Gaspé shore of the Baie des Chaleurs. By erecting a cross and claiming the continent for His Most Christian Majesty, Francis I, Jacques Cartier had posted the French bid for North America.

The bid ignored the claims of Indians or Inuit, established for thousands of years since their ancestors had crossed the Alaska land-bridge from Asia. Even Europeans had staked an earlier claim; Vikings, driven west from Iceland to the coast of Labrador, Newfoundland, and perhaps even New Fngland, had recorded their discoveries in Norse sagas. Basque and Breton fishermen had come regularly, returning under strict oaths of secrecy about the origins of their rich catches. In 1497, when the boastful John Cabot came back to Bristol to report schools of codfish so dense "they sometimes stayed his shippes," he merely broke a trade secret.

Cartier had come for a different form of wealth. He had been enticed by vague Indian claims of a wealthy "Kingdom of the Saguenay" and by the great river that he hoped would lead past the rapids of Lachine to a western ocean. When the gold he brought home on his third voyage proved to be iron pyrites, the St. Mâlo seaman was discredited. Anyway, France was too deep in the wars between Catholic and Huguenot to care about distant lands. Seventy years would pass before the French came again. This time, Samuel de Champlain would make them stay.

No nation could ask for a nobler founder than Champlain. Navigator, soldier, visionary, a Protestant turned Catholic by conviction, a man of Renaissance curiosity and eternal fortitude, Champlain created New France. A few bleak winters spent on the

Bay of Fundy persuaded him to try elsewhere. Fate then took him back to Cartier's great river, the "Father of Waters." Where Cape Diamond rears up to narrow the St. Lawrence River, Champlain and a few men built their *habitation* in the autumn of 1608.

Champlain's business, financed by court favourites and Rouen merchants, was the fur trade. In its name, he made alliances with Algonquin Indians; fought their dreaded enemies, the Iroquois; journeyed to the Huron country that is now central Ontario; and sent young Frenchmen to learn Indian languages and lifestyles as the first *coureurs de bois*.

Champlain has been condemned for provoking the Iroquois, but his intervention only speeded up the inevitable. Enemies and climate had driven the Iroquois south of the Great Lakes. Their longhouse culture of cornfields and tribal alliances gave them a strength and a stability no other northern Indians possessed. On the other hand, they lacked rich sources of good furs or the swift canoes to carry them to the new European trading posts. Anyone who has tried skinning a rabbit with a stone knife or boiling water in a clay pot will not wonder why Indians were soon desperate for the steel knives and copper kettles the Europeans traded for their furs. Lacking furs and canoes, the Iroquois used their military power to become the middlemen between the stolid Dutch traders at Albany and the Huron and Algonquin suppliers. If these tribes went to the French, they would be punished or even destroyed by the Iroquois.

For almost a century, war with the Iroquois was a recurrent, tragic fact of life for the struggling French settlement. The war made every settler a soldier and a potential victim of death by torture or brutal captivity. One result was a legend of an embattled people, defended by heros such as Adam Dollard of the Long Sault and such heroines as Madeleine de Verchères. Only divine inspiration could have spared the few hundred colonists or the frail outpost of Montreal, established in 1642 by Paul de Chomédy, Sieur de Maisonneuve. In the legend of *Canadien* survival, there was little room for sympathy with the Indians, caught between powerful European rivals and struggling with their own ingenuity and courage to defend their interests.

To Champlain and to others, New France meant more than furs or war. The fur trade was a vital commercial foundation for a greater purpose: the conversion of the Indian people. As part of the price for their furs, the Algonquins and the Hurons had to take back with them black-robed missionaries with their strange incantations and their epidemic infections. It was a heavy penalty for the magnificent European goods. In five years, almost half the Hurons had perished.

If commerce led to conversion, Champlain saw that colonization was vital to both. European settlers would give the Indian converts a demonstration of the Christian life while they laboured to make New France self-sufficient.

The interlocking of commerce, colonization, and conversion was Champlain's plan, sustained against adversity, failures, and the first English conquest by the Kirke brothers in 1629. It was Maisonneuve's plan when he established Montreal in defiance of the Iroquois peril. It was the vision that Jesuit missionaries reported in the *Rélations,* the brilliant propaganda newsletters which attracted funds for their enterprise from the ladies and gentlemen of the French court. The plan sent Jesuits to Huronia in the 1630s. A generation later, the few Huron survivors of European diseases and Iroquois invasions withdrew from a devastated land. Only in 1662, when a newly-powerful Louis XIV finally extended his royal government to his remote and embattled subjects, was Champlain's concept altered.

In fact, the three elements of Champlain's scheme had never worked together. Traders preferred to leave their customers as they found them. Missionaries were scandalized by trading morals and methods. Colonists rarely measured up as role models for the few Indian converts. As well, they were too attracted to the freedom of the fur trade, too busy defending themselves from the Iroquois, and often too untrained as farmers to be successful producers. The *habitants*, as they proudly called themselves (in distinction from the proper term of *censitaire* or "tenant") cleared trees and laid out the characteristic strip farms running back from the river banks, but even the Iroquois peril could not persuade them to leave their own land and live in forts and villages. With effort and good weather, the settlers could enjoy a rude plenty. As often, however, the colony was close to starvation. Always the annual trading fleet had to make room for food and livestock as well as for the cloth, hardware, and brandy the fur trade demanded.

Under royal government, the missionary impulse weakened.

The autocratic Bishop François Montmorency de Laval established a stern tradition of religious authority in the little colony, but the officials of Louis XIV could be certain of royal backing against any bishop's pretensions. It was far harder for them to resolve a dilemma which persisted throughout the French regime and, in some form, has remained with the leaders of French Canada ever since. Were the people of New France to be *habitants,* cultivating their small colony in the valley of the St. Lawrence, or were they to be *voyageurs,* carrying the fur trade, Catholicism, and French influence throughout the continent?

The instructions of Louis XIV's minister of colonies, Jean-Baptiste Colbert, were clear. His Intendant, or business manager, Jean Talon, must expand the population, improve farming and develop industries in a compact, self-contained colony. Talon and his successors did their best to obey. Shiploads of women were brought over to provide brides and to balance the sexes in the male-dominated colony. Though immigration slowed to a trickle after 1700, impressive rates of natural increase sent the population of New France soaring from only three thousand at the start of royal government to sixty thousand a century later. As in the English colonies to the south, the legal and administrative structures of the old world were simplified and adapted to the new. Seigneurs served as settlement agents, and any who fancied themselves as feudal lords could swiftly be brought to earth by a rude reminder from the Intendant.

The seigneuries along the St. Lawrence and its tributaries formed one version of New France. On his farm, the *habitant* could fish or hunt. The long strip of land, rolling back from the river to the forest, would be divided among his sons. Rents and taxes were low. An efficient, reasonably cheap court system allowed the *habitant* to indulge a proverbial delight in lawsuits. Officials and clergy might seem all-powerful but they were also paternal. The forest and the fur trade were outlets for the ambitious or the discontented. Since officers' appointments in the colonial garrison were reserved for the sons of influential colonists, there was even access to the lower rungs of the French aristocracy. By the 1750s, visitors from the old world claimed that a new kind of French people was emerging along the banks of the St. Lawrence.

The pressure to expand created another version of New

France. As Talon complained, his efforts to create a compact settlement were undone by the unscrupulous but plausible rogue Louis XIV had appointed governor of the colony. Sent to the new world to escape his creditors, Louis de Buade, Count Frontenac, saw only one way to rebuild his fortune and return in splendour to court. Whatever it might cost in renewed war or humiliating treaties, Frontenac had to reach past the Iroquois and revive the fur trade. First he built a fort at Cataraqui (now Kingston) where the St. Lawrence becomes Lake Ontario. Then he sent Robert de la Salle to build another fort at Detroit. Soon agents for the trade, missionaries, and *coureurs de bois* reached out along the Great Lakes, the Ohio and the Mississippi rivers, and north to Hudson Bay to find new Indian bands, new converts, and, above all, new sources of fur.

For governors, soldiers, and ordinary *habitants* there was really no other source of wealth. A journey to the West, with its dangers and back-breaking labour, netted a *voyageur* enough to buy the livestock or land that might turn subsistence farming into a chance to support a wife and family. A successful licence at a trading fort could give a young officer the quick fortune he wanted to support the status of minor nobility in France. Governors and even intendants took their cut of fur-trade revenue, from selling licences to taking a share of the fur price. Nothing else was as profitable. Talon developed shipbuilding and the iron deposits at St. Maurice near Trois-Rivières, but never with commercial success. Only when the French king poured a fortune into fortifying Louisbourg and into wartime garrisons could corruption provide an alternative source of wealth. By then, the fate of the French regime was sealed.

The price of expansion was a far more dangerous rivalry than the Iroquois or the Dutch had represented. The English colonies, sheltered behind the Appalachians, looked as compact and settled as the seigneuries on the St. Lawrence. In fact, they were quarrelsome, divided, and, by the 1750s, ready to explode beyond their borders.

Two dissident *coureurs de bois*, Pierre Radisson and Médard Chouart des Groseillers, bedevilled by Talon's restrictions on the fur trade, had managed to interest English merchants in the opportunities of Hudson Bay. In 1670, the English established the

Company of Adventurers Trading into Hudson's Bay. There is now no doubt that the French were more skillful at trading with the Indians than the English. Their goods, from Europe's leading manufacturing nation, were superior to most that the English could supply. The long Indian wars had forced the *Canadiens* to become tough, efficient wilderness soldiers. What the French lacked in the developing struggle for North America was a powerful navy and the will to match the thousands of English emigrants who left annually for the Thirteen Colonies. Embattled in Europe, France was forced to treat her remote colonies as valued but sacrificial pawns.

In a game of historical might-have-been, the compact colony of New France might have escaped conquest by a sort of armed neutrality. That never seemed possible. The frontier wars, with their lightning raids, burnings, and massacres, cried out for vengeance. A legacy of fear and hatred of the Iroquois and their American backers grew up in New France, to be matched with equally horrifying memories in New England and northern New York. Even more significant was the role that the expansionist fur trade came to play in French strategic thinking.

At the French court, New France was only a pawn in a European power game. Louis XIV's decision to occupy New Orleans, and the later plan in the 1750s to build a belt of French forts along the Ohio and Mississippi rivers were part of complex schemes to help France's Spanish allies and to distract the British. They owed nothing to the commercial needs of the fur trade for there were few pelts to be gained from the Ohio region. The French-Canadian militiamen who struggled and died in the brutally mismanaged expedition to build Fort Duquesne (at present-day Pittsburgh) were expendable pieces in a board game played far away at Versailles. When first the Virginians, under George Washington, and then the British, under General George Braddock, were sent reeling back from the Ohio valley in humiliation or defeat, the French congratulated themselves. In fact, by provoking the stronger British, the French strategists had sealed the fate of New France.

Blockaded by the Royal Navy, preoccupied by wars with its European neighbours, France could spare only a few thousand regular troops to back its gamble in the new world. Louisbourg, the vast fortress built on Cape Breton Island to protect the

21

approaches to the St. Lawrence, fell in 1758 because France had too few warships to relieve it. The French military commander in New France, the Marquis de Montcalm, detested his superior, the Canadian-born governor, Pierre de Rigaud, Marquis de Vaudreuil. Their bitter rivalry, far more than the gross corruption of the last Intendant, François Bigot, doomed the colony. Though Montcalm's outnumbered regulars won against incredible odds, notably at the battle of Carillon or Ticonderoga in 1758, the general's insistence on mixing Canadian militia with his soldiers was a big factor in their defeat on the Plains of Abraham in the following year. An almost accidental last-minute victory by General James Wolfe and his redcoats was made certain by confused tactics in the French ranks. In the fall of Quebec, the French and the Canadiens discovered how little they had in common.

In September 1760, with Quebec in British hands and Montreal surrounded, the surviving French troops burned their standards, boarded ships, and went home. So did most of the merchants and leaders of the colony. The remaining Canadiens, abandoned in the hands of their enemies, would retain an enduring suspicion of remote imperial strategies and their bloody consequences.

It had taken a century and a half to create New France but now the French were finished with it. To the French Ministry of Marine, the colony had represented huge costs, small returns, and no advantage that fishing concessions off Newfoundland could not match. Voltaire's blunt dismissal of Canada as "several acres of snow" became the official consensus. The British seemed hardly more interested. His Majesty's new Province of Quebec would be made as hospitable to British settlers as the imposition of English law and an elected assembly reserved for Protestants could make it. Narrow boundaries for the new colony cut off the fur-trading hinterland, but incoming British merchants would presumably find other ways to become rich. The conquered Canadiens would undoubtedly accept the blessings of the new regime and become English-speaking, if not necessarily Anglican.

Nor for the last time, however, the Canadiens defied the inevitable. The first British governor, General James Murray, and his successor, Sir Guy Carleton, detested each other, but their aristocratic souls both rejoiced in the ordered, rural, and seemingly dutiful society that had survived the capitulation of 1760.

Under its Catholic clergy and a scattering of remaining seigneurs and merchants it was, claimed Murray, "perhaps the bravest and best race upon the Globe." To both governors, it was intolerable that the handful of shifty merchants and camp followers who had accompanied the British army to Montreal and Quebec should now monopolize power simply because British law excluded Catholics. Murray's good will was immediately apparent. The Catholic bishop of Quebec had died on the eve of the conquest. Without a bishop, no new clergy could be ordained. With Murray's help, a successor was chosen, sent to France to be consecrated (since the Catholic church was illegal in Britain), and returned to Quebec. The British gained a staunch clerical ally.

The British had imagined that a flood of settlement would soon help anglicize Quebec. Few people came. By 1772, Sir Guy Carleton, Murray's successor, had absorbed an obvious point: "barring a catastrophe shocking to think of [Carleton probably meant smallpox], this country must, to the end of time, be peopled by the Canadian race." A more troublesome principle followed: they must be governed by institutions and practices familiar to them. Carleton's arguments persuaded the British government. The Quebec Act of 1774 restored the kind of regime Quebec's clergy and seigneurs desired. The Church regained its legal right to tithes and the seigneurs regained the old civil law. The earlier promise of an elected assembly vanished. If the community of English-speaking merchants at Montreal raged at this betrayal, they were more than compensated. The huge fur-trading hinterland to the west, removed from Quebec in 1763, was now restored. Indians and traders would not be disturbed by settlers.

Carleton could not foresee that his Quebec Act would help drive the Thirteen Colonies to open revolt, but he was certainly confident that the Act would rally both the Indians and gratified *habitants* to the British side. He was disappointed. When Americans invaded Quebec after the Declaration of Independence in 1775, the clergy and seigneurs appealed almost in vain for people to rally to Carleton's aid. The Americans, as they advanced to besiege Quebec City, had little better success in winning over the *Canadiens*. Only when starving Americans began to raid livestock and food supplies, leaving worthless paper from the Continental Congress as payment, did the *habitants* choose sides. By the spring of 1776, the Americans had been driven away.

23

The American Revolution undermined Carleton's prediction. Quebec would not be forever *Canadien*. Ten thousand Loyalist refugees poured into the province up the old invasion route of the Richelieu River and across the Niagara River. Beyond the seigneury of Longueuil, Loyalists and German veterans of the war were granted land.

The cataclysm of the American Revolution forced the British to reconsider the government of the scattered colonies that remained to them. Once again it was Carleton (now Lord Dorchester) who tried his ingenuity. He would split the old province of Quebec. Beyond Longueil, Upper Canada would develop as a model British society that *Canadiens* and Americans could admire—and perhaps even ask to join. The eastern portion, Lower Canada, would also have an elected Assembly, an appointed upper house or council, and an executive—replicas of the British Commons, Lords, and Cabinet—but the *Canadiens* would also keep their language, their civil law, and their religious institutions. The Act of 1791 confirmed the arrangements.

And the *Canadiens* seemed to prosper. If a high birthrate is a symptom of a nation's well-being, rarely have a people been happier. The sixty thousand *habitants* of 1760 were a hundred and ten thousand by 1784 and three hundred and thirty thousand by 1812. The Colbert-Talon dream of a compact, prosperous rural society was fulfilled. The methods were primitive—farmers piled their manure on the ice to float downriver at the spring breakup—but wheat production climbed and seigneurial fortunes rose. The long war between Britain and revolutionary and Napoleonic France that began in 1793 awakened few old loyalties among Lower Canadians. Instead, wartime scarcities promoted wheat exports and a growing timber trade from the St. Lawrence. The Church opened colleges to train its clergy. Wealthier *habitants* sent their sons to train for such professions as law and medicine.

The avocation of these newly-educated *Canadiens* would be politics. The aging anglophile seigneurs and local notables who had represented the *Canadiens* in the Assembly in its early years soon gave way to younger, more critical men. Politics provided an outlet for new grievances. Despite their dramatic population growth, the *Canadiens* felt threatened. Land that their children would someday need was now being granted to Americans who had not even been Loyalists. Quebec's new Anglican bishop,

Jacob Mountain, made no secret of his hope that a state-endowed "Royal Institution," through its schools, would systematically anglicize the French. Through the Assembly, French-Canadian politicians could fight back.

In spite of the *Canadien* predominance, there were signs that Lower Canada *was* becoming anglicized. By 1812, most of the thirty thousand Montrealers spoke English. So did a majority in Quebec City. Whether the French-speaking merchants were vanishing through intermarriage, deliberate preference for the seigneurial life, or because of brutal competition, the business of Lower Canada was being done in English. Beyond those who purchased seigneuries as a source of income, few merchants cared about the over-population or the shrinking harvests of the rural districts. Their concerns lay with the fur trade or improving the St. Lawrence route to the wheat and potash trade of a thriving Upper Canada. Financing canals to get past the St. Lawrence rapids would cost money. Like most prudent men, the Montreal merchants wanted others to foot the bill.

In Lower Canada, the Assembly soon became the battleground where *Canadiens* could challenge the harsh verdict of the conquest. Their leader, Etienne Bédard, taught the young notaries, doctors, and lawyers that *Canadiens* could win their fight by using the institution the British themselves most admired: Parliament. By 1810, Bédard's determination had led him to prison. However, with war imminent on the American frontier, the British removed his antagonist, Sir James Craig, replacing him with a more sympathetic (and bilingual) governor, Sir George Prévost. In French Canada, Craig's name would remain a symbol of English oppression to the *Canadiens*.

The War of 1812 rarely crossed the Lower Canadian border. When it did, both *Canadiens* and the Assembly could take pride in their patriotic role. Among the officers of the French-Canadian militia was Louis-Joseph Papineau. Eloquent, handsome, seemingly self-confident, Papineau was the logical choice for Speaker of the Assembly in 1815. A professed believer in British institutions, Papineau was also a proud and by no means benevolent seigneur and, thereby, a firm guardian of French Canada's most basic institution. Above all, Papineau was a man of words, concealing a tragic streak of indecision behind billowing rhetoric.

25

In the wake of the War of 1812, there was much that was seriously wrong in Lower Canada—economic stagnation, crop failures and declining yields, over-population in the seigneuries. Montreal's English-speaking merchants urged reunion of the Canadas and costly improvements of the St. Lawrence route; Papineau and the *Canadien*-dominated Assembly refused. When the merchants pushed their ideas with the appointed council and executive in 1822, Papineau and his allies visited England to defeat the reunion plan. Far from returning triumphant and grateful, Papineau came home disillusioned by Britain and her institutions. Every issue was soon reduced to an uncompromising battle between Papineau and his *patriotes* and those he sweepingly denounced as a "Chateau Clique" of *bureaucrates*. Leaving more moderate allies in his wake, Papineau set an increasingly radical course, halting all public works, preventing payment of official salaries, and making administration of Lower Canada almost impossible.

Papineau's goals were unclear. In religion he was almost a free thinker; as a seigneur, he was highly conservative. At times, he preached the merits of an American-style republic. Above all, he denounced the control of patronage by the governor's appointed advisers. This issue had strong appeal for the growing *Canadien* elite of educated professionals, condemned to remain as ill-paid village notaries and doctors. Constitutional arguments also aroused English-speaking followers like Wolfred and Robert Nelson, ready to believe that British liberties were at stake. George-Etienne Cartier, studying law and sharing the circle of Montreal's French-speaking elite, was only one of scores of ardent young men who took up the *patriote* cause.

In the Lower Canadian countryside, the mood was different—grimmer. The growing population had become a terrible burden. The narrow strips of land, subdivided for the sons in each generation, could be split no more. Seigneurs, French and English, had become oppressive landlords with no Intendant to restrain them. The land could no longer support its people. Wheat fly and exhausted soil produced shrinking yields. For the first time, a class of landless labourers appeared.

Since the end of the long European war in 1815, a tide of immigration had swept up the St. Lawrence. Most of it had moved on to Upper Canada or the United States; often only the poorest remained. So did the cholera epidemics. The first of them invaded Lower Canada in 1832. Hundreds died miserably from a plague no medical knowledge could cure, and there were those who echoed the *patriote* orators who insisted that the British had deliberately plotted the death of the *Canadiens*. Suspicion and hatred were mutual. The old cordiality of a merchant class that had intermarried, learned French, sometimes even converted to Catholicism, was not inherited. British governors, assailed by hostile *patriote* politicians in the Assembly, also worried about the growth of a rancorous, bitter "English party" in Montreal. The violent attacks by journalists like Adam Thom and the military drill of young men in the Doric Legion only spurred Papineau's followers to fresh extremism in language and tactics.

In 1837, the clash came. Three years before, Papineau had compiled every imaginable Lower Canadian grievance into what he called "Ninety-Two Resolutions" and despatched them to London. The Assembly, he promised, would let the colony stagnate until Britain acted. In 1837, Lord John Russell's Whig government sent its reply, in the form of the "Ten Resolutions." These instructed the governor to reject the Assembly's demand for executive power, ordered him to give hard-pressed officials their back pay, and to govern the colony with or without an elected Assembly.

It was a terrible year to provoke a political conflict. While the colony had stagnated, tensions had risen. Endless rains in the summer and autumn of 1837 had ruined crops. In the United States, President Andrew Jackson's anti-banking crusade had led to a commercial collapse that affected Montreal. Huge, sodden rallies of *habitants* gathered to hear Papineau, echoing his outrage but ignoring his unexpected appeals for prudence and patience. Papineau's indecision was beginning to show, just as the avalanche of anger he had helped to build was beginning to move. Angrier, harder men, like Wolfred Nelson, a wartime surgeon, began drilling men at St. Dénis.

In Montreal, both the *patriotes* and the English drilled. When the governor banned the Doric Legion, it reformed under another title. Suddenly there were clashes; one violent riot threatened Papineau's house and only the arrival of British troops saved it. Fearing arrest, Papineau fled to the countryside. The cautious, peace-seeking Lord Gosford resigned as governor; Sir John Colborne, one of the British army's ablest soldiers, succeeded him.

Given time and a united leadership, the *patriotes* of 1837 might have been a formidable force. At St. Dénis on November 23, Nelson's men drove off two hundred British regulars. Young George-Etienne Cartier shared in that victory, but Papineau had fled St. Dénis, slipping across the border to Vermont. Other *patriotes,* like Louis-Hippolyte La Fontaine, hurried to Quebec City in a vain effort to make peace. An impatient Sir John Colborne gave the rebels no more time to drill or debate. Beaten at St. Dénis, the British troops mounted a swift counter-attack on the rebel centres on the Richelieu River. With the winter freeze-up, Colborne sent his men north of Montreal to crush rebels at St. Eustache. His ill-disciplined irregulars spread across the countryside, leaving the *habitants'* homes blazing behind them. Colborne would be remembered in the historical mythology of French Canada as *"Vieux Brûlot,"* the Old Firebrand.

Long after the futility and self-interest of Louis-Joseph Papineau and the *patriotes* had been forgiven, the bitter memory of fire and sword would remain. As in 1760, the *Canadiens* had been defeated. The bitterness of a second conquest engulfed the Lower Canadian leaders, leaving them paralysed and despairing. Others would have to find strength and ingenuity to survive.

# 3 / English Canadians

English-speaking people in Lower and Upper Canada had a different memory of their history—sometimes several different memories. To them, Canada dated from John Cabot's discovery of his "New Founde Lande" in 1497. The French had been the hereditary enemy, conquered in 1759 when James Wolfe led his soldiers up the narrow, ill-guarded Anse au Foulon to occupy the Plains of Abraham.

All memories are selective. Most English Canadians forgot those New Englanders, ransomed from Indian captors, who so fully joined in the life of New France that they refused to go home. Men from Wolfe's army, most of them Scots, stayed, married, and also assimilated, becoming ancestors of such French-speaking Quebec premiers as J. G. Ross and Daniel Johnson. The English also forgot the deft calculation which had helped persuade French diplomats to abandon New France. With no threat from Quebec, the French had reasoned, the American colonists would fight each other. Within fifteen years of the capitulation at Montreal, Britain and her American colonies were indeed at war. Within a decade of the Quebec Act of 1774, the British had absorbed their worst defeat of the century.

The Treaty of 1783, ending the American Revolutionary War, left Britain with the cold, unprofitable remnants of the continent. Perhaps something might be made of them. After all, Montreal still sat astride the only route to the heart of America. The vast interior of the continent had changed hands too often to assume that the Treaty of 1783 was the last word. Preferring profits to politics, most of the American merchants at Montreal had remained loyal. British garrisons and their Indian allies would continue to hold the interior until the claims of dispossessed Loyalists were satisfied. That might be a long time.

For the moment, the top priority was to cope with the columns of refugees pouring into the province of Quebec. Tools, rations, and livestock were as necessary as land. Bewildered officials, wrestling with problems of wilderness logistics, were cursed as hard-hearted or corrupt. In the wake of the war, ten thousand Loyalists were struggling to build homes and farms in the forests along the upper St. Lawrence or below the Niagara escarpment. Iroquois of the Six Nations, forced into exile as British allies, found their own pockets of settlement up the Grand River. Pennsylvania Germans, bound by language and culture as well as loyalty, drove and floated their big Conestoga wagons even further up the valleys of the Grand, the Speed, and the Eramosa rivers.

History is preoccupied with politics, ideas, and movements. In the 1790s, as perhaps in any age, these were luxuries only a few could enjoy. For pioneers in a harsh and unfamiliar land, survival was a preoccupation, to be achieved only through relentless, backbreaking work. The forest was the enemy. Huge first-growth trees resisted the puny axes and saws of the settlers as they struggled to clear fields or even to break through the overhanging gloom to the sun. The forest accentuated loneliness. Pioneers were described as being reduced to an unsmiling grimness by loneliness and labour. Women faced the terror of childbirth without even a neighbour to help. A single careless blow with an axe could cripple a man or leave him to die in the stench and agony of gangrene. The dark side to pioneer life was only partly veiled by the almost frantic revelry of militia reviews, barn-raisings, and "bees," or by the fervour of camp meetings summoned by Methodist circuit riders, the best agents of frontier Christianity.

Yet politics and ideals mattered because they gave shape to the thousands of individual struggles for survival. Newcomers they might be, but the King's "old subjects" from below the border had strong views about the political society they wanted. When they turned from their grinding tasks, they could count on outspoken leaders to state their case. Sir John Johnson, superintendent of Indian affairs in New York, became a leading Loyalist in the Canadas. It was he who led the campaign to split the colony to help guarantee an elected Assembly for at least Upper Canadians. William Smith, the former Chief Justice of New York and now of

30

Quebec, argued for a federation of all the British North American colonies, a precursor for the eventual idea of Confederation in 1867.

The British response was both generous and conservative. The Constitutional Act of 1791 created the two Canadas sought by Johnson, provided them both with the structure of governor, executive council, and elected assembly, and fostered institutions which, in the hopes of Colonel John Simcoe of Upper Canada, might create "the very image and transcript" of English society. Since taxes had provoked the American Revolution, in the Canadas, government would be financed by reserving a seventh of all land for the Crown. Another seventh would finance an established Protestant clergy. Though proposals for a titled aristocracy in the Canadas were abandoned, insistence that legislative councillors possess up to six thousand acres was intended to foster the keystone of the English constitution, a well-entrenched landed gentry.

If Champlain was the founder of New France, Upper Canada was almost as much the creation of John Simcoe. A successful commander of Loyalist troops, Upper Canada's first Lieutenant Governor could not resist trying to reverse the verdict of the American Revolution. With incredible optimism, Colonel Simcoe imagined that he could make his raw, backwoods colony so attractive that Americans would repent their disloyalty and renew their allegiance. His energy matched his ambition. Survey parties vanished into the forest to lay out the gridiron of concession and side roads that still shape rural Ontario. Soldiers and settlers drove highways of the future through swamp and bush—Yonge Street north from Lake Ontario to Lake Simcoe; Dundas Street west from Yonge Street to Hamilton and to the tiny inland settlement of London. The Kingston Road struggled eastward to the garrison town where Frontenac had once built his fort. At the junction of these roads was the muddy little village of York, set in malarial lakeside swamps, where Simcoe moved his capital. London, his first choice, had been vetoed as too remote. From his little bungalow, Simcoe dictated letters, dispatches, instructions, and promoted a flood of proposals for everything from hat-making to a mining industry.

Simcoe's energy was guided by a dream. To prosper, Upper Canada would need far more than the fourteen thousand people

31

who had reached it by 1791. As a bustling, progressive success story, the province would be a haven for all who, Simcoe boldly predicted, would be weary of the mismanagement and corruption of the American republic. Unmoved by the warnings and protests of Loyalists, Simcoe boldly invited any of His Majesty's late subjects to renew their allegiance in return for excellent free land. Moreover, people came. Allegiance was a small matter on the frontier; land was everything. Upper Canada, particularly its lower peninsula between Lake Erie and Lake Huron, was directly in the path of the American frontier surge. Simcoe's critics sneered at "late Loyalists" but the ox-teams with their overloaded wagons poured into the colony. By 1811, almost ninety thousand people had settled in Upper Canada and distinctions between early and late Loyalists had been worn down by the common pioneering experience.

By then, however, Simcoe had been gone for fifteen years. He was not even knighted for his services. His successors were lesser men, reluctant exiles in a colonial backwater of long winters and steaming, mosquito-ridden summers. Most of Simcoe's vision left with him, but the people still came, for by now even the colony's tiny elite had realized that their huge land grants would be worthless without the pressure of settlement. A fertile tract surrounded by prospering farms would grow in value. In the meantime, one might live respectably on the salary and profits of government office.

If Upper Canada seemed a backwater to British officials, it was the front line in British-American relations. South of the Great Lakes, the British clung to their old trading posts, holding out for compensation for the Loyalists and unconsciously encouraging the Indians to resist the advance of American settlers. In 1791, a small American army was destroyed by the Indians. The British were blamed, even though they had warned the Americans of the danger. Britain's government saw the folly of another war with the United States at a time when the French Revolution was blazing on their own doorstep. In 1794, they conceded the futility of their hopes of receiving Loyalist compensation and withdrew, abandoning their Indian allies to the tide of American settlement. The result was the decisive defeat of the Indians, under their great chief, Tecumseh, at the Battle of Fallen Timbers.

Other factors heightened Anglo-American hostility. In the

long war that dragged on in Europe (with brief intervals) from 1793 to 1815, neutrals found little sympathy. Even the Swiss and the Swedes became involved. American ships were seized and boarded by British and French alike. The lure of war profits helped the ships' owners to adjust, but American opinion boiled at each insult to the young flag. Bitterness grew as one moved west, to mingle with outrage at alleged British backing of the Indians. In the 1812 elections, the western states sent angry "warhawks" to Congress, demanding that President James Madison declare war and promising swift and easy conquest of Canada. "I verily believe," boasted one of them, young Henry Clay of Kentucky, "that the militia of Kentucky are alone competent to place Montreal and Upper Canada at your feet." In June 1812, Madison delivered his message: there would be a second War of Independence.

Most people called it the War of 1812 and shrouded it with myths. On paper, Clay was right. Seven and a half million Americans could overwhelm half a million British subjects, a fifth of them "late Loyalists." Major-General Isaac Brock, with fifteen hundred regulars to defend Upper Canada, concluded that he would have no help from his legislature and very little from local magistrates and militia colonels unless he won some rapid victories. Backed by Indian allies such as Tecumseh and his Shawnee warriors, Brock seized the initiative. A handful of regulars and Indians captured the American fort at Michilimackinac, holding the entire Middle West for the rest of the war. While American state militias debated whether to cross the border and aged generals left over from the Revolutionary War trembled for their scalps, Brock and Tecumseh captured an entire army at Detroit. In the final battle of 1812, at Queenston Heights, Brock died, but his angry redcoats and a revived Upper-Canadian militia hurled American invaders back across the Niagara River.

That one year, 1812, gave Upper Canada most of the national myths it would ever have, from Brock's leadership to the gallantry of the militia (which, for the most part, had waited until the regulars and the Indians determined the outcome of the war). The struggle continued for two more years of hard-fought victories, painful setbacks, and murderous devastation of frontier communities. The Americans would remember the war for a series of ship-to-ship battles, forgetting the fighting that ravaged the Upper

33

Canadian landscape. In fact, the Americans lost the war by 1814 because of the British naval blockade, while their strength, resources, and new regular army steadily grew in the inland campaigns. In 1813, American control of Lake Erie allowed raiding parties to ravage Upper Canada from Sandwich to Norfolk. In 1814, American shipwrights were outbuilding the British dockyard at Kingston. Once the Americans won Lake Ontario, Upper Canada would fall.

Instead, British negotiators had ended the war even before its last—and almost its bloodiest—battle was fought at New Orleans. The war changed no boundaries, brought no reparations, avenged no wrongs. The Canadian hope that somehow the old fur-trading hinterland might be restored turned out to be forlorn. Upper Canadians seeking compensation for burned-out farms and slaughtered livestock would get no reparations from the Americans who had done the deed. They must look to Britain, and the British, exhausted after a generation of war, could not afford to be generous.

From the War of 1812, English Canadians took both proud and bitter memories. In Lower Canada, they felt a pleasing, if temporary sense of solidarity with the French Canadians. The battle at Chateauguay was hardly Waterloo, but a French Canadian, Colonel Charles de Salaberry, had commanded both British regulars and his own *Voltigeurs* in driving off the Americans. Upper Canadians could be proud of Queenston, the murderous battles of Stoney Creek and Lundy's Lane, and the odd little legend of Laura Secord driving her cow through the American lines to warn Lieutenant James Fitzgibbon of an enemy attack. Even more important were the memories of those who had stood loyal and unafraid in the early days of disloyalty and confusion. Archdeacon John Strachan, the Scottish convert to Anglicanism, with his megalithic convictions of righteousness, had faced American invaders with the same resolution he would show to Methodists and unbelievers. John Beverley Robinson had shown courage on the battlefield and brutal resolution at the Ancaster assizes. Robinson's prosecution had sent eight late-Loyalist traitors to the gallows and had confirmed him, though he was barely out of his teens, as Upper Canada's Attorney General. In Upper Canada, the Loyalist tradition had always been questionable. The War of 1812 gave the colony's elite new credentials of loyalism. If there was a

Family Compact in Upper Canada, it was really an unspoken alliance of those who had led and organized the colony in its most threatened years, who had run great risks and who expected the rewards.

As the colony struggled after 1815 to rebuild from wartime wreckage and to adjust to an economy no longer fed by huge British military spending, Upper Canada's leaders cancelled Simcoe's old welcome to Americans. By insisting on war, the American warhawks had helped to cancel a process that might have led to peaceful absorption of the colony by the United States. Upper Canada would now be British, though at a cost. The tide of superbly-qualified American frontiersmen would pass south of the Great Lakes, making the shores flourish with farms, cities, and industries, while Upper Canada stagnated. Certainly immigrants came to the colony after 1815, lured by promises of land and opportunity, but they came from a Britain where there were now "too many spoons for the broth." Very few had the skills or the capital to transform wilderness into crude but productive farms. In time, the "late Loyalists," with their mixed allegiance, would be submerged in a tide of English, Irish, and Scottish settlers, but Upper-Canadian land-owners would still grumble that abstract principles had hurt their profits.

The post-war colony was full of grumblers. In part, this was because a generation of relentless labour had paid off. Pre-war settlers had won the leisure to observe the Upper-Canadian scene. With a franchise broader than most Britons would enjoy until 1832, there were few barriers to political participation for prosperous farmers or tradesmen. Newspapers were few and costly, and their proprietors depended on government advertising, but they also satisfied an appetite for gossip and controversy. A red-wigged tempestuous newcomer named William Lyon Mackenzie was one of those who filled this need. An honest man with a huge bump of self-righteousness, Mackenzie travelled the backwoods and filled his *Colonial Advocate* with the grievances he uncovered, together with serialized novels, moral tracts, helpful hints, and the reports of curiosities that he loved to collect.

The grievances were many and most grew out of jealousy of the greener fields on the American side of the lakes. Upper Canada seemed a backwater, short of bridges, roads, and other public works vital to a pioneer society. By American standards, officials were grossly overpaid. Land policies which left vacant the tracts of crown and clergy land, adding to the weary trek of farmers to their markets, were inevitably blamed on corruption. In a province that was Methodist if it was anything, how dare Archdeacon Strachan claim to the British government that Upper Canada was Anglican? There was really no mystery: Strachan wanted the clergy reserve revenues for his own denomination. In young Egerton Ryerson, the Methodist dissenters found an eloquent and fearless champion.

The history of Upper Canada has been dominated by one-sided versions of its political struggles. Historians have been captivated by the persuasive venom of Mackenzie's editorials; they have treated the slogans of reformers as though they were factually true. Probably Upper Canada's leaders were as honest and conscientious as the times allowed, their fault was their conviction that they must manage everything in the colony, including successive lieutenant-governors. Like most elites, they saw no distinction between their own best interests and those of the community. They succumbed to the dangerous error of treating critics, from Robert Gourlay to Robert Baldwin, as mortal enemies.

Whatever monetary cranks like Mackenzie might claim, the colony needed the Bank of Upper Canada, but did the bank need to be switched, by legislative chicanery, from Kingston to York? The elite also backed William Hamilton Merritt's Welland Canal with its own funds, but, when the project ran beyond their means, they had no hesitation in using Upper Canada's credit. It was a shrewd stroke to invite British investors to create the Canada Company as an agency to market the crown and clergy reserves and then, by agreement, to force the company to develop the huge Huron Tract between Guelph and Goderich. Was it wise, though, to impose Strachan's son-in-law as the company's Canadian manager?

Oligarchies are rarely self-critical. Upper Canada's leaders could sometimes seem petty and vindictive in their use of power; they did not defy the law. When sons of York's elite threw Mackenzie's press into the harbour, a court ordered prompt and generous compensation. Mackenzie's own speeches and editorials were evidence to contemporaries that free speech prevailed in Upper Canada. Leading reformers like Dr. William Baldwin and his eloquent son, Robert, often found the excitable editor an embarrassment, but Mackenzie's following of farmers and small-town tradesmen was valuable to their loose coalition. Unlike Papineau's *patriotes* in Lower Canada, who commanded a one-sided majority in the Assembly, the reformers and the Tory oligarchy in Upper Canada each commanded only a knot of loyal supporters. Other members floated with the wishes and needs of their frontier constituents, stern against corruption but eager to bargain for a badly-needed bridge. In any case, the Assembly could be ignored by legislative and executive councillors who believed themselves appointed for life.

That conviction was suddenly challenged. In a seeming political cataclysm, Britain's Whigs came to power after more than half a century of Toryism. In the excited political mood, it seemed the Radicals might not be far behind. The turmoil was easily exaggerated. The new men were as wealthy and almost as cautious as the old. The great Reform Bill of 1831 gave Britons the franchise Canadians had enjoyed since 1791. A succession of Whig aristocrats at the colonial office differed little from their Tory predecessors though they were a little more willing to listen to professed "Reformers" from the colonies and to give credence to claims of "Family Compacts" and "Chateau Cliques." When John Beverley Robinson grumbled about Mackenzie having received a hearing in London for his absurd charges, he was dismissed as Attorney General for his indiscretion. In 1836, when the Whigs chose a successor to the valiant Sir John Colborne, some Upper Canadians erected banners welcoming their new Lieutenant Governor as "A Proven Reformer."

Sir Francis Bond Head certainly had radical ideas. No previous governor had worried about Upper Canada's depleting resources or about the land and hunting rights of the Indians. Unlike Colborne, who listened to the oligarchy, Bond Head listened to himself. He appointed Reformers like Baldwin to his executive and dismissed them when they insisted on their own policies. Bond Head is remembered as a figure of fun who conducted official audiences with his short legs stuck rigidly out in front of him. He was the would-be dictator who took the field in the 1836 Assembly elections, raised the loyalty cry, and drove most of the Reformers, including Mackenzie, from their seats.

Most sensible Reformers licked their wounds and bided their

time. Assembly elections in Upper Canada swung regularly from Tory to Reform as settlers voted alternately for public works or political fireworks. Certainly there were differences in 1836. The post–1815 flood of British settlers had begun to have political significance. Some signs were ugly. Reformers complained that Tory bullies had attacked their voters at London—though that did not prevent a Reform victory. Orangemen, the Protestant extremists who had been banned in Ireland, surfaced in the eastern districts of Upper Canada to back Bond Head's loyalty call. They were dangerous allies.

For William Lyon Mackenzie, defeat was intolerable. In 1834, he had enjoyed a brief taste of power as the first mayor of a newly incorporated city of Toronto—the old York. A long visit to the United States convinced him that only republican institutions would give Upper Canada the cheap, honest government its yeoman-farmers needed. To Mackenzie, defeat in 1836 was not an electoral mishap but an act of tyranny enforced by a British governor and a corrupt oligarchy. From the analysis came the only possible remedy: revolution.

As in Lower Canada, the times encouraged revolutionary language among angry, American-born farmers in the townships north and west of Toronto. An economic depression had descended on Upper Canada, aggravated by Bond Head's insistence that banks and business houses must keep their doors open and pay off panic-stricken creditors even at the cost of needless ruin. It was no secret in Toronto that both Canadas faced rebellion, but Bond Head sent every soldier he could find to reinforce the British garrison in Lower Canada.

When Mackenzie shared his plans for proclaiming an Upper Canadian republic, most Reformers were aghast. Robert Baldwin drew away. Others decided that Mackenzie's threat, however foolish, might frighten the governor into concessions. Dr. John Rolph, the veteran Reform politician Mackenzie had designated as president of his provisional government, talked discreetly to both sides. In the rural townships, simpler men believed in "Little Mac," read his hurriedly-printed manifesto and heeded his call: "Up then brave Canadians. Get ready your rifles and make short work of it."

The work would be short. On December 4, 1837, unaware that Papineau's rebellion had already collapsed, a few hundred men began to gather at Montgomery's Tavern on Yonge Street, a few miles north of Toronto. It was a demoralizing prospect, with rain and wind, and Mackenzie himself in a state of rage and indecision. In Toronto, it was no better. Old Colonel Fitzgibbon, Laura Secord's confidant of 1813, pleaded desperately with Bond Head to abandon his complacency. News of the rebel gathering turned complacency into panic. Then, thanks to Fitzgibbon and a tough young Tory from Hamilton, Allan MacNab, the governor's allies rallied. At dawn on December 7, untrained militia marched up Yonge Street behind bagpipes and bands to meet the frightened, ill-armed rebels. In a few minutes, the battle was over.

Mackenzie fled, sheltered by men and women who risked everything for his safety until he reached the United States. Militia and Indians patrolled every road, checked every barn, and sent sad little groups of prisoners to face jail, trials, and transportation to Britain's penal colonies. There can rarely have been a rebellion that found fewer supporters at the time or more admirers afterwards.

The Rebellion of 1837 failed because it never had a chance of success. Mackenzie had sought to reverse not only the election of 1836 but the rejection of the United States in 1812. Many of his followers would pay a bitter price for his leadership. The absurd little battle north of Toronto was followed by repression far beyond anything seen in Lower Canada in 1837–38. Two of Mackenzie's lieutenants died on the gallows; ninety-two people were sent to penal colonies. In the aftermath, hundreds of prosperous but resentful settlers left for the United States. Yet, as Mackenzie's biographer, William Kilbourn, has argued, perhaps the Rebellion cleared the air. Some of the violence and unreasoning invective went out of Upper Canadian politics. A fresh start was possible, and most of the old players would be gone.

# 4 / United Canadas

The 1837 rebellions were the first formative experience for Cartier, John A. Macdonald, and many of the politicians who launched Confederation thirty years later. Even in the lower provinces, Confederation with the Canadas revived old fears of the violence and disloyalty of 1837. In fact, the rebellions ended an era. They could be bathed in a romantic aura because the old antagonisms died so quickly. Within a decade, Papineau and Mackenzie returned to communities where their luckless followers had been hanged. They were sputtering political relics. Old friends and enemies were too busy making money and finding political compromises to care.

In 1837 Britain was still euphoric at the accession of the young Queen Victoria. The Canadian rebellions had come as a shocking embarrassment. A shaky Whig regime might silence at least some critics by despatching "Radical Jack," Lord Durham, to solve the Canadian problem. As Governor-in-Chief and Lord High Commissioner, Durham's power extended to all of British North America. Unfortunately, it did not reach as far as Bermuda, though it was there that he sent his eight leading *patriote* prisoners, liberating the rest. It was wise clemency but Durham's English enemies crowed that he had exceeded his jurisdiction. After a bare four months, an ailing, exasperated Durham quit. Two years later he had died, after years of chronic ill-health.

Those four summer months of 1838 made his reputation. A man of firm liberal convictions did not need long to reverse the judgements of his military predecessors. The commercial dreams of Montreal merchants and Robert Baldwin's political frustrations made sense to Durham; the claims of French Canadians or the Upper-Canadian oligarchy did not. Durham did not have to talk to people, to reach conclusions obvious to any intelligent European liberal. "There can hardly be conceived a nationality more destitute of all that can invigorate and elevate a people," Durham reported of the *Canadiens*. They had no history, no literature, and, accordingly, no future. He spent ten days in Upper Canada, one of them with Robert Baldwin, others devoted to convivial attempts to improve relations with Americans at Niagara Falls. The journey sufficed to convince the Governor General that there indeed was a "Family Compact" to be dispossessed.

Both judgements were highly dubious but they lay at the heart of Durham's analysis. So did two solider facts. The Montrealers were right: Canada was an economic unit and the split beyond Longueuil had done great economic harm. Baldwin was right too: colonial self-government was a farce if the governor's officials and advisers could ignore the elected Assembly. The best constitutional experts had insisted that sovereignty could never be split. This, Durham insisted, was nonsense. There were powers vital to a colonial role—foreign affairs, for example, or even crown lands—which Britain must continue to exercise through its governors. There were many more powers which the colonists could be left to manage.

The Canadas must be reunited, Durham insisted, both for economic reasons and to assist the inevitable assimilation of the French. In a single Assembly, their numbers would give them a small majority, but the tide of immigration promised that it would not be for long. In subjects of colonial interest, the executive council must depend on the Assembly for support. No more than in Britain should a colonial administration continue without the confidence of the elected chamber. The Canadas also needed municipal governments so that the Assembly would no longer ring with controversies better settled at the local parish pump.

In time, Durham's report would be much admired. When it first appeared, it was cordially abused. Then, as often happens, large parts were implemented, and small, but significant, features were not. The Act of Union of 1840 created the United Provinces of Canada. The large debt of Upper Canada was merged with the modest debt of Lower Canada. English would be the language of government and legislature, but even the temporary risk of an Assembly dominated by ex-*patriotes* was avoided. Each of the old colonies would have forty seats. Nor was Durham's notion of "responsible government" to be entertained. Governors General would choose their advisers and manage the Assembly as best they could.

The British might be forgiven their caution. Throughout 1838, rebel exiles and their warm-hearted American hosts had plotted feverishly. Secret societies called Hunters or *Chasseurs* proliferated. The border became an armed camp; the internal conflict of 1837 became, for many Canadians, a patriotic struggle against American invasion. Hours after Durham's departure, a new *patriote* thrust crossed the border south of Montreal. Within a week, Colborne's men had crushed the invaders but leniency in Lower Canada was given no second chance. Twelve *patriotes* were executed and fifty-eight Lower Canadians were sent to the Australian penal colonies.

In Upper Canada, the drawn-out border conflict and the savage repression discredited Mackenzie and his Tory enemies alike. When Lord Sydenham, the veteran politician chosen to manage the awkward new Union, summoned his first Assembly at Kingston in 1841, Robert Baldwin's moderate Reformers won an easy ascendancy. In Lower Canada, the mood was utterly different. Their rebellion crushed, their leading *Canadiens* gave way to despair. Yet life went on and the new game would have to be played. Durham's verdict might be appealed. Already the young François-Xavier Garneau had set out to defy Durham's judgement that French Canadians had no history by writing it in massive detail. Etienne Parent, editor of *Le Canadien,* argued, like Bédard before him, that the British constitution could still be the best safeguard for French-Canadian survival. Forget Durham's errors, Parent urged, go to the Assembly and fight for his idea of responsible government.

The suggestion would be adopted, without much acknowledgement, by the ablest colonial politician of the 1840s. Louis-Hippolyte Lafontaine was a plump Montreal lawyer with a fancied likeness to Napoleon and a comparably authoritarian personality. He had split from Papineau in 1837, suffered a brief and beneficial martyrdom in prison, and now was prepared to teach the *Canadiens* how to survive in the new regime. The principles, most of them announced to the voters of Terrebonne in 1841, were clear enough; winning support took a little longer. French Canadians must forget the divisions which had separated the anti-clerical Papineau from the Church or middle-class leaders from *habitants*. Clergy and people must form a tight alliance of faith and nationality. Next, they must be pragmatic and progressive in order to build an alliance with the Upper Canadian Reformers. Together, they must dominate the new Assembly and in time they would win the constitutional struggle.

The essence of Canadian political history in the 1840s is the slow completion of Lafontaine's strategy. Lafontaine's alliance with the Reformers was sealed when, defeated in Terrebonne, he accepted Baldwin's invitation to campaign for an Assembly seat in Mackenzie's old territory north of Toronto. Later, Lafontaine would return the favour for Baldwin. Together, their supporters almost dominated the Assembly. A succession of governors did what they could. Sir Charles Metcalfe, Sydenham's successor, was in constant pain from a fatal cancer, but he did better than most. He waged the 1844 election campaign virtually as his own party leader, using arguments against patronage and its corruption which a Whiggish breed of Canadian constitutional historians later preferred to ignore. At stake in responsible government, he insisted, was the determination of Baldwin and Lafontaine to distribute offices and public works as spoils to their followers. Metcalfe was perfectly right. High-sounding arguments about British parliamentary institutions and vice-regal tyranny camouflaged the fact that colonial politicians wanted to reward followers and punish opponents in a very American fashion. Lafontaine argued that it was wiser to sprinkle appointments, commissions, and salaries among the frustrated professionals of Lower Canada, than to let them plot new *patriote* uprisings.

Britain did more for the Canadas than send a new constitution and a succession of able but unhealthy governors to enforce it. Durham had also underlined the desperate need for public works on the St. Lawrence rapids, so long delayed by Lower Canada's political impasse. In the 1820s, Britain had spent far more than she wanted to on fortresses and the Rideau Canal in the event of a repetition of the War of 1812. Now, more grudgingly, she guaranteed huge loans. The colonial economy, lagging as usual behind an American recovery, spurted forward.

Hardship in the 1830s had helped drive emigrants from Britain; the prosperity of the 1840s was what now attracted them to Canada. The appeal had to be strong. Big, leaky timber ships from Quebec crammed their "'tween-decks" with steerage passengers, doubling the owner's revenue at whatever cost in human misery. Despite the quarantine station at Grosse Ile, the cholera came up the river. So did the old country quarrels of Orange and Green, of Connaught-men and Cork. Canadians complained that better-fitted and more prosperous immigrants most often had plans to continue to the United States. But still, people came, filling the new counties of Canada West (Upper Canada), sending the population climbing at twice the rate of that in Canada East (Lower Canada). For the first time, too, many immigrants came without the means or prospect of acquiring land. The Irish, driven out by poverty, overcrowding, and then by the terrible potato famine of the 1840s, formed the first waves of that huge, anonymous, forgotten army of labourers who dug the canals and would build the railways, the mines, and the cities of a developing Canada.

Prosperity and then famine in the 1840s had a revolutionary impact on British colonial policy. Long before, in narrow intellectual circles, the radical ideas of Adam Smith, Thomas Malthus, and Jeremy Bentham had gently undermined old convictions about the necessity of maintaining a self-sufficient empire. Surely, as the greatest manufacturer and trader in the world, Britain should be the greatest foe of all constraints against free trade? Buying timber or wheat in the cheapest market rather than from Canada or New Brunswick would not only benefit Britain, it would remove a hidden tax from the poor.

The Canadas were a good illustration of why the new free-trade ideas made sense. Huge spending on defence and the continuing cost of a garrison only aggravated the Americans and brought no return to Britain. The Rebellions of 1837 surely proved that British colonial policies had failed. Prosperity in the early 1840s showed that protection was not needed. The Irish famines were aggravated by tariff barriers to cheap food. The complex system that had protected the markets of English landowners and colonial farmers alike crumbled.

Nothing happens overnight. Even in the 1820s, Canadian timber and wheat had had to compete harder in the British market, yet it was hard for colonials to see that arrangements they took for granted could ever fundamentally change. Whig or Tory, British politics seemed so immovable. Prosperity is also an anaesthetic, and in the 1840s everything was booming. In 1841, twelve thousand tons of shipping cleared the port of Quebec; in 1846, the total reached forty thousand tons. In Montreal that year, died Joseph Masson, the wealthiest merchant in Canada and a reminder that *Canadiens* too could prosper in trade. Even the church put its money into canal companies, steamships, banks, and the first little portage railways. A visitor to Toronto in 1842 marvelled: "All is in a whirl and a fizz and one must be in fashion; everything and everybody seems to go by steam." There was money for education too. As Chief Superintendent of Schools for Upper Canada, Egerton Ryerson had moved on from Methodist concerns to launch a public system of "non-discriminational schools." For the rest of his life, he would bully, prod, and inspire the cause of public schools. Strachan's dream of an Anglican monopoly of higher education crumbled as Presbyterians and Methodists used prosperous times to launch their own colleges. In Montreal, Bishop Ignace Bourget brought back the Jesuits and helped to revive a dream as old as Champlain, the conversion of an entire continent. French Canadians as far away as Oregon and as near as Toronto became bishops. Bourget too was an educator.

Disasters are rarely predicted and seldom come singly. Montreal had lavished hope and capital on its new canal system as the great route to the Atlantic, not only from Canada West but from the central United States. The Irish canallers had dredged a way across the Niagara peninsula, built locks to pass the Lachine and Soulanges rapids, and cleared a way from Montreal to Detroit. No sooner had they finished than the Americans dropped their duties and enticed traffic down the Erie Canal from Buffalo to the Hudson River. Wheat exports through Montreal dropped in the year 1848 from 3.9 million to 2.2 million bushels. As the Irish famine of the 1840s dumped shiploads of penniless, starving people in Canadian ports, the triumph of free trade in Britain wiped out Canada's only real export market. If that were not enough, Americans seized the Oregon territory on the remote Pacific coast and demanded that the boundary be set at 54.40', vowing war if they did not get their way. British territory would be shut off from the ocean.

Considering all this, it seemed almost irrelevant that the latest Governor General, Lord Elgin, was allowed to concede the principle of responsible government to a Lafontaine-Baldwin ministry after its election success in 1848, or that he would open the ensuing legislative session with a speech in both English and French. By now, the Canadian Parliament had moved from Kingston to a new building in Montreal—a suitable gesture to the commercial (and largely English-speaking) metropolis of the United Provinces. In the circumstances, though, with Montreal's merchants facing utter ruin and thousands of people unemployed at the busiest season, Lafontaine and Baldwin showed a surprising lack of tact. The first test of their new power, designed to bury forever the bitterness of 1837, was a Rebellion Losses Bill for Lower Canada. *Patriotes* and innocents alike would be recompensed for the depredations of *Vieux Brûlot,* Sir John Colborne, and his Montreal militiamen.

English Montrealers were furious. The bill was a political insult to cap their economic misery. A mob pillaged and burned the new parliament buildings. Lord Elgin was stoned and threatened. Leading businessmen went farther. If Britain had abandoned them, why not seek annexation with the United States? Among the names on the angry manifesto were Alexander Tilloch Galt, William Molson, John Redpath, and a future Prime Minister, John Abbott. Louis-Joseph Papineau's name was there too, with those of a clutch of ardent new admirers who already called themselves *rouges,* from the ribbons and banners of revolutionary red they had adopted.

Even as the English crowds raged through Montreal, the annexationists had their answer. That year, there had been huge finds of gold in California, fuelling an economic boom that would last (with breaks) to the early 1870s. Despite its growing conflict over states' rights and slavery, the United States surged with growth. Canada followed. When they stopped complaining long enough to check their ledgers, merchants discovered that the British markets had not dried up after all and now the Americans might also become buyers of Canadian wheat and timber. In 1854, Elgin's successor, Sir Edmund Head, went to Washington to find out. He returned with a ten-year Reciprocity Agreement which almost wiped out the border for natural products, including fish from the lower provinces. It had not been easy. Southern congressmen backed the treaty only when Head promised it would keep the colonies British. As slaveholders, they wanted no more "free soil" states. Other politicians merely wanted entertainment. Head boasted that his agreement had "floated through on champagne."

Baldwin and Lafontaine retired, their work complete. Canada had its framework of government, education, and municipalities.

George-Etienne Cartier would soon complete a modernized civil code for Canada East which would see the gentle extinction of seigneurialism. In ten years, the *Canadiens* had taken a constitution designed to destroy them and made it work for them. Indeed, they now rather liked the Act of Union. If it had been fair in 1840 to give each province equal representation, it would surely be fair for a long time, even if Canada East now had only 1,111,566 people to the West's 1,396,091.

The old issues were gone and so were old alliances. As always, there were those who were fed up with compromise. Youthful *rouges* from the old *patriote* strongholds of the Richelieu valley stirred with nationalist passion and a nervous anti-clericalism. It seemed impossible that they could ever make common cause with the austere Protestant farmers in the "great western peninsula" of Canada West, with their anger at privilege, corruption, and government spending. "Clear Grits," they called themselves, "pure sand and not a particle of dirt." In the 1850s, though, the big, craggy-faced Scot named George Brown who had created the Toronto *Globe* and who never questioned his own wisdom, would take the Grits in hand. They would be purged of Americanism and disciplined. Above all, Brown reminded them, Protestant English Canadians must show as much solidarity as the French or their own religion and rights might be forfeit.

Those who held power had outgrown such preoccupations. Lafontaine's men, re-mustered by Cartier, now called themselves *bleus,* to contrast with *rouges.* They were, appropriately, cool realists from a province that had learned pragmatism. There were Baldwinites, too, like the cunning Francis Hincks, but more and more weight lay with the Tories, with heirs of the Family Compact and Metcalfe's 1844 campaign. Yet, whether it was the gawky young lawyer from Kingston, John A. Macdonald, or old Sir Allan MacNab, once Bond Head's adviser and champion in 1837, these also were pragmatists. "Railways are my politics now," MacNab blandly confessed. The title of their party, the Liberal-Conservatives, surely welcomed anyone who wanted a share in power.

MacNab was typical. The railway boom had crossed the Atlantic. Cities, towns, and nimble speculators pestered the legislature for charters, planned routes, and interviewed contractors. Francis Hincks went to London to negotiate a line to Halifax with representatives from the lower provinces. Angry Maritimers felt cheated when the Canadians pulled out. Torontonians had even better reason to cry foul when the same Francis Hincks was caught out, with the mayor of their city, in an ingenious stock swindle with their beloved Northern Railway. Hincks dropped out of sight, but railway promotion was irresistibly corrupting.

In 1850, Canada had about 55 miles (88.5 km) of track. Four years later, Sir Allan MacNab's Great Western Railway covered 254 miles (408.6 km) from Niagara to Windsor. Hincks' London visit had not been wasted. The great British contracting firm of Peto, Brassey, Jackson & Betts persuaded itself that there would be profit from a vast trunk railway through Canada from Portland, Maine, to the American Middle West. No one seems to have warned them about rivers, politicians, labour costs, or the effect of Canadian winters on track, locomotives, and rolling stock. By 1861, the line was complete to Sarnia but the company's largely-British shareholders had to recognize that the Grand Trunk was not only effectively bankrupt, but that the system would never pay a penny unless even more money was poured into it. To illustrate their imperial vision, Grand Trunk interests bought control of the Hudson's Bay Company and fantasized about the profits to be made from a real trunk railway across the continent. Meanwhile the company had to find a scheme to keep conductors from "deadheading" passengers for free trips, the cheapest way to get their tracks standardized to the North American gauge, and how to relate British railway technology to Canada's winters.

Booms end and love affairs cool. By the late 1850s, both fates befell railways in Canada. Politicians who had shared in the "great barbecue" were suddenly suspect. In the pattern of double-barrelled ministries which Lafontaine and Baldwin had established as a makeshift for their un-United Province, George-Etienne Cartier and John A. Macdonald had emerged as leaders. In the prevailing morality, Cartier saw no sin in being both Attorney-General and the Grand Trunk's well-paid lawyer. Indignation at railway corruption could unite George Brown and the party he preferred to call "Reformers" with Antoine-Aimé Dorion's *rouges*. An Assembly with a large number of "shaky fellows," "loose fish," and "waiters-on-providence" (as Macdonald scornfully called independents) meant that no unpopular government was safe for long.

Trivial, emotional issues are always the trickiest. After Montreal's violent behaviour in 1849, the province's capital alternated (on a costly three-year cycle) between Quebec and Toronto. A firm choice of a capital had to be made. Tactfully, the choice was left to Queen Victoria, guided by pleasant little watercolours done by officers of the Royal Engineers. Photography might have been safer. The Queen chose Bytown, an ugly lumber town on the Ottawa River. Not even monarchists accepted the choice and the Cartier-Macdonald government fell; Brown and Dorion had a chance to govern. Two days later, when the Assembly members had recovered their composure, the Reformers and *rouges* were defeated. This "double shuffle" returned Macdonald and Cartier to power and left Brown fuming on the sidelines.

By now the Upper Canadian Reformers had an issue the *rouges* did not share: representation by population. Supporters made it a slogan, "Rep by Pop," and the issue lent itself to simple emotions. Late in 1852, after Upper Canadians had drifted home from the long legislative session at Quebec City, the French members voted to impose Catholic public schools on an overwhelmingly Protestant Canada West. Brown and his followers were outraged at such sectarian meddling; they held firmly to the doctrine that separated church and state. With Brown's inspiration, still more grievances were developed against the Lower Canadians. By the 1850s, Canada West's share of the population had become a large and growing majority. The equality of representation imposed by the Act of Union in 1840 had become anathema.

By the 1860s, "Rep by Pop" had taken hold as a popular cause in Canada West, and support for Macdonald's Liberal-Conservatives diminished at each election. The slogan pitted English against French and, since religious prejudices outweighed race, Protestant against Catholic. Orange riots in the towns of Canada West were matched by Catholic violence when apostate priests, Gavazzi and Chiniquy, insisted on evangelizing in Montreal and Quebec for Protestantism. With no efficient police forces to control mobs and the British garrison cut by the need to send troops to the Crimea and India, the province reluctantly organized a five-thousand-man "volunteer militia." The forebear of Canada's armed forces found its primary role as a riot police.

The thought of sectional conflict might have been farther

from people's minds if the example of violence had not been so near at hand. Canadians formed the largest group of immigrants to the United States; hundreds of thousands of *Canadiens* who had trekked to the New England cotton mills, easing the poverty and over-population of Canada East, kept their relatives aware of American events. Meanwhile, the American slavery issue was brought to Canada West by hundreds of black fugitives, helped into British territory by the men and women of the "Underground Railroad." Blacks in Canada experienced plenty of racial discrimination, but their presence was a reminder of the "irrepressible conflict" tearing the United States apart. When it came in April 1861, the American Civil War divided Canadians as well. Both sides also recognized that the American crisis could easily develop into a threat to Canada as well.

To most Canadians, defence and foreign policy were British responsibilities. Even Canada's tiny volunteer militia was left to languish after a few early years of enthusiasm. Suddenly, war was imminent. President Lincoln's Secretary of State, W. H. Seward, publicly declared that war with Britain might rally the divided states. Others argued that the conquest of Canada could compensate for the departed Confederacy. When an American warship removed Confederate delegates from a British mail steamer, Britain had a solid justification for a declaration of war. In an instant, the British forgot their colonial indifference. At no thought of the cost, thousands of regular troops were despatched to Canada to forestall an American invasion.

They were still there in 1862 when the provincial Assembly rejected a modest defence program and threw Macdonald and Cartier out of power. While Reformers and *rouges* gained for a couple of years, British public opinion reacted in fury. The hot, patriotic sympathy for the endangered Canadians curdled into resentment at so foolish and ungrateful a people. Moreover, as the huge military potential of the United States was mobilized for the Civil War, British strategists came to the cold realization that they could never repeat the victories of the War of 1812. A report in 1864 by a trusted staff officer confirmed the conclusion: without efforts no British government could afford, the Canadas were indefensible.

That was a secret no colonist could be allowed to know, but it lent harsh urgency to the British determination that something be done about the North American colonies. It was a determination shared by a number of influential private investors in the Grand Trunk Railway. In Canada, too, there was a growing sense that radical change must come. George Brown's detested rival for the Reform leadership, John Sandfield Macdonald, plaintively urged his own solution—that no major issue would be settled without a double majority from each province. Not even the *Canadiens* were much impressed. Even supporters of some sort of federal system for the two provinces no longer seemed bold enough, though their ideas intrigued Cartier and some of his associates.

By 1864, the two Canadas seemed trapped in their own histories and limited by their own geographies. Both would be dramatically changed.

# 5 / Lower Provinces

Beyond the mouth of the St. Lawrence lay four proudly self-reliant British colonies. John Cabot's crew was almost certainly not the first to see Newfoundland when the *Matthew* sailed into the future harbour of St. John's in 1497. The history of these colonies would have been the oldest in North America if Basque, Portuguese, French, and English fishermen had left records of their voyages and discoveries.

Since they had no cheap source of salt, some fishermen, notably the west-country English, needed to go ashore. The cod must be landed and dried on long racks, or "flakes." To do more, to develop whole colonies of fishermen on this distant shore, would give them a six-week head start before the rival fleets could arrive from England. Men might be left to guard and repair the flakes, but a few early attempts at settlement convinced the English that Newfoundland, with its harsh climate and thin soil, could never support serious agriculture. People came anyway, ignoring laws and periodic attempts at deportation, somehow surviving the hardships. Mass starvation remained a hazard of Newfoundland life as late as the 1820s.

In later years, on the rare occasions when Maritimers thought about what they insisted on calling "Upper Canada," they frequently deplored the incessant squabbles of French and English, Catholic and Protestant. Yet their own region had the same troublesome diversity and the same propensity to quarrel with neighbours and subjugate them if they could. Indeed, this existed within each colony. There was a distinction few people in either region fully appreciated. The Canadians were forced together in their lives and their quarrels by the long, indivisible avenue of the St. Lawrence and the Great Lakes. Each of the lower colonies developed as a ring of shoreline settlements. People depended on themselves and their chosen neighbours. If they sought space, they could look out to sea. In all but Prince Edward Island, much of the interior was a rocky, inhospitable wilderness. Very few river valleys—the St. John, the Miramichi, the St. Croix—beckoned farmers and timber merchants inland. Between the shore and the forest, the more favoured regions offered a chance to farm. Towns and cities developed at harbours. There was timber for ships and housing and export, but for generations, the only real wealth of the region came from the sea.

Most Acadians were heirs of the few French who had remained in the area when Champlain had chosen to move up to the St. Lawrence. Tossed, for a few turbulent years, between French adventurers and New England pirates, the Acadians were then left to themselves for a century. They learned to dike the rich bottom land of the Minas Basin against the Fundy tides. In 1713, when the Treaty of Utrecht transferred Acadia to the British, perhaps sixteen hundred Acadians were included. It seemed to make no difference to them.

Unhappily for the Acadians, war outpaced fishing and subsistence farming as an industry for the region. The French settlers and the friendly Micmac and Abenaki Indians had provided a passive flank defence for New France. After 1720, they were supplemented at the far corner of Ile Royale by the huge new French fortress of Louisbourg. For all its strength, a British naval squadron and New England militia took the fortress in 1745, only to see it returned to the French by English diplomats. As the French hurried to repair the damage, the British countered by developing the huge natural harbour of Halifax. With its forts, its dockyard, and its garrison mentality, Halifax became a city that subsisted on government and thrived on war. Having ignored the Acadians, both sides now demanded their loyalty. Old loyalties favoured the French, but neither Quebec nor Louisbourg sent protection. Instead, backed by the harsh rules of war, British troops rounded up thousands of Acadians in 1755 and sent them south to be scattered among the Thirteen Colonies. In 1758, with Louisbourg taken again, more Acadians were expelled.

The dispersal was neither complete nor permanent. Many Acadians fled into the woods; others returned when the war was over to find their farms sold to American speculators. The returning Acadians went on to Ile St. Jean and Ile Royale—renamed respectively by their English conquerors Prince Edward Island and Cape Breton Island. Others went to the St. John River valley and later to the Madawaska. The French government, which prudently limited its North American commitments to fishing rights on Newfoundland's French shore, sent Acadians to inhabit the tiny islands of St. Pierre and Miquelon, all that remained of Champlain's great venture.

Like the Acadians, the American settlers who took their place and who spread themselves along the southern and western shores of Nova Scotia largely ignored the self-important little government of merchants and officials at Halifax. They sent home grim corrections to the glowing propaganda which had enticed them to "Nova Scarcity," but, while New Englanders' minds turned to revolution, Nova Scotia's Yankees turned their few leisure thoughts and moments to the "New Light" movement, a passionate religious revival. With a British fleet and garrison at Halifax, the few sparks of revolt in the 1770s were swiftly extinguished, and the missionaries of the "New Awakening," alarming though they seemed to Halifax Anglicans, sought revolutions in morals, not governments. Merchants in Halifax and other ports made too much money from the war to feel rebellious.

The Revolution came to Nova Scotia anyway. Loyalists arrived in shiploads from Boston in 1776, and then tens of thousands more came after the British had abandoned New York in 1783. It was a flood of bitter, defeated exiles, who had suffered much and lost everything for the Crown. The thirty thousand who came to Nova Scotia were not like the toughened farmers who went to Upper Canada. At Shelburne, where a large townsite with special districts for servants and for blacks had been laid out to welcome them, thousands of once-wealthy Loyalists landed. Promptly, they set to work planning a city hall, street names, and where to house the little fire engine presented by King George III. Unfortunately, no labourers appeared to build their houses. Not even the toughest frontiersmen could have tilled the rocks and swamps beyond the town. A little poorer and wiser, most Loyalists moved on.

At Halifax, Governor John Parr and his council lost patience with "New York office-grabbers." The answer, as in the Canadas but for different reasons, was separation. In 1784, New Brunswick and, for good measure, Cape Breton, became separate colonies. The leading Loyalists were delighted. In New Brunswick, they would build a society that would become "the most gentleman-like on earth." Whole regiments, under their officers, would settle on grants up the St. John River, with colonels and captains receiving much larger grants to support their social status. Fredericton, safe from American attack up the river, would be a little gem of a capital. In a verdant paradise, Tory values would thrive.

Reality was different. The first fleet reached Saint John on May 18, 1783, to find bare rocks, swamps, and an endless vista of burned-over forest. As the ships departed, one woman felt such a terrible loneliness that ". . . although I had not shed a tear through all the war, I sat down in the damp moss with my baby and cried aloud." A second fleet, with thirty-five hundred people, arrived at the end of 1785 with no time to do more than pitch tents or erect crude huts before winter descended. Brave men simply lay down on the frozen earth and died.

Many Loyalists left. Others accepted the ruin of their dreams and made the best of it. When the huge trees of the St. John valley were cleared, the soil was good enough for farming, and the timber slowly formed the basis of a major industry. Saint John grew slowly as a commercial centre, gradually justifying the premature charter that made it the first city of British North America. Behind the genteel Loyalist myth was a hard-grubbing, impoverished existence, mocking the memories of cultivated life in New York or Boston. More than a few Loyalists took their chances and slipped back to the United States, making links that others would later join.

New Brunswick was a victim of emigré illusions. Cape Breton was the little colony almost everyone but its Highland settlers forgot. Both were spared the casual disaster inflicted on Prince Edward Island. In a display of greed blatant even for the time, English speculators fastened on the island as soon as it was transferred from France in 1763. Sixty-seven "proprietors" drew lots for sixty-seven equal townships of twenty thousand acres on which they promised to pay quit-rents, develop the fishery, and establish a hundred Protestant settlers within the decade. Only one of them, Samuel Holland, kept his promise. Two others made a feeble attempt. The rest simply waited for squatters to occupy the land and then sent agents to collect the rent. As a result, what was potentially the richest Maritime colony never grew up. By dint of keeping the ear of the British government in London, the proprietors could milk the settlers and do nothing in return. Settlers had no incentive to improve the land or even their homes. They were even reluctant to build schools or churches. Every political issue seemed to focus on the distant "grantees" and on the officials who always seemed to enforce the proprietors' rights and condone their broken promises.

Loyalist leaders in the Atlantic colonies had concocted a grandiose economic role for their new home. The rich business of supplying food to Britain's slave islands in the Caribbean would be barred to the rebel Americans and switched to the loyal provinces. As rebel Americans looked on, rich cargoes of food and timber would travel south in Nova Scotia and New Brunswick ships. West Indies rum and sugar would move east across the Atlantic. It was absurd. It was only because of the squatter-farmers of Prince Edward Island that the Maritimes could feed themselves much less the West Indies. In any case, Britain was determined to make friends, not enemies, of the King's late subjects, the Americans.

The salvation of the Atlantic regions came with war. The struggle with Revolutionary France that began in 1793 and ended with the final defeat of Napoleon in 1815 transformed the economy of each of the lower provinces. The naval weakness of Revolutionary France guaranteed near-immunity to the ships and ports of the colonies, but wartime fleets and garrisons meant customers who paid in gold. French victories in Europe, and French alliances which closed off vital supplies sent British agents searching for replacements. When Baltic ports would no longer supply the Royal Navy's timber and spars, the forests of North America had available, if inferior, substitutes. Merchants shifted their operations to Saint John and the mouth of the Miramichi. In Newfoundland, the peacetime arguments against allowing local settlement and fishing collapsed. In 1809, the huge, unexplored mass of Labrador had been passed back to Newfoundland as though in recognition that the island colony now mattered. By war's end, St. John's had become capital of the island's fishing industry, and in 1817 the first resident governor arrived.

The war was a spur to ship-building in every major port of the region. Even minor harbours set up stocks to build schooners for the rich wartime cargoes. There was another more risky but vastly more profitable trade in "privateering," a form of licensed piracy on enemy merchant ships. For young Samuel Cunard and other Halifax merchants, privateering became the foundation of huge shipping fortunes.

As for the War of 1812, it was the bonanza on top of good fortune. While Upper Canada fought for its existence, New Brunswickers lived in peace with their American neighbours. The furious speeches about seamen's rights and taming British pride had only been Yankee bluster. Humiliation, felt the New Englanders, was a small price to pay for the huge profits they could draw from wartime trade. By declaring war, President Madison had destroyed the most lucrative mercantile era the northeastern states could remember. They might cheer the victories of the few American frigates but they would not fight the war. British colonists had no such inhibitions. Battalions from Newfoundland and New Brunswick fought in the defence of Upper Canada. Privateers found new and richer prey. In the final months of the war, British troops brushed aside feeble resistance to occupy much of Maine. Intercepted American customs revenue helped endow Halifax's Dalhousie University.

Whatever many a Maritimer might secretly wish, war could not last forever! Peace brought an economic collapse. In Halifax and Saint John, firms went bankrupt by the hundred. The shacks and shanties of St. John's vanished in a huge fire in 1816, and by the following winter ships brought pathetic appeals for food to fend off imminent starvation. Methodist missionaries newly arrived in Newfoundland tactlessly chose the moment to blame Catholics for the terrible predicament of the area. Religious riots enlivened the misery.

Yet the prosperous years had left their mark. Halifax's Province House stood as the finest public building in British North America and an Education Act in 1811 had pioneered secondary education in Nova Scotia. The cheap labour of French and American prisoners had built streets and fine houses. Even Prince Edward Island had found the first few leaders to resist the grantees. The nervous Scottish philanthropist, Lord Selkirk, had given the island an influential voice in London as well as a few hundred Highland settlers. Shipping and timber might be sluggish in the first post-war years but protection would last for thirty more peacetime years. Then, as in the Canadas, American markets would be sought.

In the language of development, the war years had given the lower provinces as good a chance for economic take-off as they would ever have. Memories of a golden age of Maritime prosperity would be shared by only a few. The lives of Maritime farmers, seamen, loggers, and fishermen could be brutally hard and financially precarious. Shipping records show a terrible toll of lives in vessels that were helpless in a winter storm on a lee shore, where lighthouses were rare and life-saving non-existent. Romantic images of lumber camps and the spring log drives overlook the reality of bad food, dangerous work, and a record of disease, crippling injury, and early death. In the colonial assemblies, employers were in control, whether they spoke as Tories or Reformers. The first unions in British North America had appeared among Halifax and Saint John longshoremen during the War of 1812. Afterwards, the appearance at regular intervals of laws banning them suggest that at least feeble workers' organizations persisted.

By the 1850s, workers in Saint John had enough self-confidence to announce their wage-rates in newspaper advertisements, and civic officials welcomed union floats and marchers in the city's periodic processions. The reason was simple. The flood of immigration largely bypassed the Atlantic colonies, adding only a healthy quota of Irish to the region's population. Workers were scarce enough to command a price, and merchants and mill-owners were prosperous enough to pay it.

Workers with bargaining power because of skills or local scarcity were the exception. Coastal fishermen, particularly in Newfoundland, had no such advantages. Most of them were soon hopelessly in debt to fish merchants who supplied their needs and kept them dependent. The transfer of the merchants to Newfoundland brought few benefits beyond providing St. John's with a small middle class and the beginnings of a cultural and social life the people of the bays and outports would rarely glimpse. A pattern of debt and deference developed in Newfoundland with even more serious social consequences than the antagonism of proprietors and tenants in Prince Edward Island.

All of the colonies had assemblies, even Cape Breton until it returned to Nova Scotia in 1820. Everywhere, cosy local oligarchies monopolized power, resembling Upper Canada's Family Compact in all but its energy and creativity. Political opposition was much slower to develop, perhaps because of the tradition of expecting little from government. Farmers, the obvious critics of urban elites, remained few and scattered. Assemblies were like unambitious town councils, willing to share out modest public works and then adjourn. Would-be reformers seemed easy to isolate as "trouble-makers." In Newfoundland, a short-lived experiment in parties degenerated into such a bitter Catholic-Protestant conflict that in the 1840s, by common consent, the Assembly was suspended for six years. When it revived, the old divisions remained, but Catholics proclaimed themselves Liberals and Reformers while the Protestant communities along the north coast would call themselves Conservatives. In New Brunswick there were no real parties at all until the 1850s when the issue of prohibiting liquor finally split the colony. Prohibitionists, or "smashers," rallied behind a young Saint John druggist named Samuel Leonard Tilley. His opponents, the "rummies," preferred to consider themselves Conservatives.

Nova Scotians could be disdainful of such crude and primitive politics. Largest and wealthiest of the colonies, Nova Scotia's economy diversified from fishing, farming, and ship-building to mining and a little manufacturing. The province had slowly outgrown its self-perpetuating merchant elite and perhaps even its parade of stuffy soldier-governors. Thomas McCulloch's Pictou Academy gave early notice that brains and ability could be found outside Halifax. In 1835, a young Haligonian journalist, Joseph Howe, made himself a hero of the hinterland, first by denouncing the Halifax oligarchy and then by winning acquittal when he was tried for libel.

Like Mackenzie in Upper Canada, Howe was the angry spokesman for Nova Scotia reform, but he was no rebel. His pride combined with an almost mystical faith in Britain and her constitution. He denounced the 1837 risings not only for delaying Nova Scotia's constitutional progress but for their disloyalty. He would carry vestiges of this mistrust of the Canadas for a very long time. Through the 1840s, Nova Scotia Reformers articulated and then urged Lord Durham's idea of responsible government. In 1846, new instructions to the governor, Sir John Harvey, made the change. It was done, boasted Howe, "without the shedding of a drop of blood, . . . the breaking of a pane of glass." On February 2, 1848, James Uniacke, Howe, and the Reformers took power. Cautiously, and in their own time, the other lower provinces followed suit. In New Brunswick, local politicians themselves delayed party government until 1856. Even then, they were moved more by embarrassment at being last than by real party differences.

Constitutional change came slowly because societies in the lower provinces were smaller, less deeply divided by great issues. Ambitious men like Howe combined immense pride and devotion to their communities with an acute yearning for new worlds to conquer. "Boys, brag of your country," he told Nova Scotians. "When I'm abroad, I brag of everything that Nova Scotia is, has or can produce; and when they beat me at everything else, I turn around on them and say: 'How high does your tide rise?'" Yet Howe *wanted* to be abroad, and he pestered the British shamelessly for appointments. He dreamed boldly. Howe promoted railways and promised listeners that in their lifetime they would hear train whistles in the distant Rocky Mountains. Like growing numbers of Canadians, some Maritimers had a vision that reached as far as British North America. Others, and Howe was among these too, dreamed of an imperial federation in which Nova Scotia might someday be an equal partner with England and Scotland.

Behind the dreams came nagging practical worries. Free trade had frightened the Maritimes as badly as the Canadas, and the ten-year Reciprocity Agreement with the United States, signed in 1854, was vital for the region's fish and timber trade. If the American market should vanish, could the Upper Canadians ever provide a substitute? There was an urgent need for a connecting railway through British territory. It was easy to blame Hincks and the Canadians for the earlier failure, but the real problem remained the route through New Brunswick. Military considerations insisted that it follow the line of meagre little Acadian settlements along the north shore; New Brunswick politicians insisted that it come down the Maine border, along the St. John River valley, to Fredericton and Saint John, where most of their voters lived.

By the 1860s, the maritime colonies faced tough choices. It was not conservatism but a sense of dangerous, uncontrollable choices that hung over the Confederation debate in the Maritimes.

# 6/The Great Northwest

People emigrating to Canada have had an awkward tendency to assume that nothing much worthwhile has happened before their arrival. Champlain presumed that Indians would be honoured to transform themselves into good Catholics and subjects of his king. The Loyalists, in both Nova Scotia and Quebec, insisted that these colonies should be readjusted to meet their desires. The British immigrants who poured into Canada after 1815 felt obliged to correct the obvious "Americanism" of Upper Canadians. Later waves of immigration have felt equal freedom to make over the country in their own image and to denounce opposition as intolerant and old-fashioned.

The Canadian Northwest has been a particular victim of such assumptions. The amiable Canadian assumption that the West is somehow "new" and the North is newer still, ignores the fact that these regions have probably known human habitation longer than any others on the continent. The two hundred thousand Indians who met the Europeans in the 1600s were heirs to millennia of experience which probably began in the far Northwest. Fragmentary archaeological evidence suggests that they may have encountered even earlier human inhabitants. The ways of the Indian (and the amazing Inuit north of the sub-Arctic tree line) were very old indeed.

The long native heritage was at least as valuable to the early European invaders as any technology they brought from Europe. The light birchbark canoes of the Algonquins covered distances at a speed that astonished the first explorers, and their snowshoes made travel possible in the winter. The concoction of buffalo meat, fat, hair, and berries the Indians called pemmican might seem nauseous to Europeans but it was the only food nourishing and light enough to carry travellers across the Great Plains. From the tough, adaptable Naskapi of Labrador to the sophisticated Indian culture of the Pacific coast, native people were the best guides to adapting to the new continent. Only their lack of formal records and writing barred them, by pure convention, from having a "history."

In the sixth of Canada covered by the United Provinces and the Atlantic colonies, the 23,035 Indians who remained by 1861 had been bullied and enticed into the life pattern devised by Sir William Johnson, the first British superintendent of Indians. It was Johnson who devised the treaties of surrender and the reserves which shaped the Indian policies of both Canada and the United States for two centuries. As a means of easing consciences and removing Indians, treaties and reserves were a success; as a basis for equality between Europeans and native people or as fair compensation, Johnson's system would prove a failure. Unfortunately, no one then or later offered acceptable alternatives.

Beyond the limits of the settled colonies, there was no Indian policy at all and no need for it. In five-sixths of British North America, whites and native people lived in what, theoretically, was a simple market relationship of willing seller and willing buyer. Europeans had manufactured goods; Indians had furs. Simplicity was deceptive. Both sides brought bitter national, commercial, and private rivalries to the transactions. As the Iroquois had shown, there was nothing primitive in the Indians' understanding of competition, middle men, or the benefits of playing one tribe of white men against another. From the European side, too, there was nothing simple about a trade that depended on the vagaries of fashion, conducted a thousand or more miles from the nearest seaport among complex and therefore unpredictable people.

Whatever criticisms might be made of the beaver's habits and intellect, there was an excellent reason for adopting the hardworking rodent as a Canadian symbol. Instinct and common sense would have pulled traders and explorers southward in America; the beaver pulled them north. The best pelts came from the colder regions. Diplomacy, not furs, pushed the French into their southward venture into the Ohio valley in the 1740s. So far as commerce, not aggrandisement, was their goal, traders had every reason to stay north of the Great Lakes and well above the invisible line that a later age would identify as the forty-ninth

62

parallel. If the British wanted to share the continent with an expansive United States the beaver's natural preferences kept Canadians away from the American juggernaut.

That was why the trading rivalry that mattered most in North America was not between the French and the Dutch and English merchants who operated from Albany. A pair of disaffected French traders, Pierre Radisson and the Sieur de Groseillers, showed the English where real profits could be made, and the "Governor and Company of Adventurers of England Trading into Hudson's Bay" acted. There was literally almost nothing on the European maps to explain what Charles II meant by "Rupert's Land" in the 1670 Hudson's Bay Company charter. When the clerks wrote about waters draining into Hudson and James bays they were describing the vastest empire any private company ever controlled.

The English posts, perched nervously at the mouths of the Moose, the Albany, the Churchill, and the other rivers draining into the bay, transformed the fur trade. English trade goods were by no means superior to most that the French could offer, and the methods were cautious to the point of timidity. The Indians had to make their own toilsome way across the barren "starving country," but the Company's ships could come direct from England, cutting off a thousand miles of portages and trans-shipments, and getting closer to the best furs than any French trader could.

The French were forced to fight back. In brilliant campaigns, three of them led by the Canadian-born sailor, Pierre le Moyne d'Iberville, the Hudson's Bay Company posts were steadily captured and destroyed. By 1713 only one remained. Then, for reasons of European diplomacy, they were restored. In the years of quasi-peace, the French tried other tactics, planting their own posts up-river from the English, proclaiming alliances and allowing licences to men such as La Vérendrye and his sons who would probe as far as Lake Winnipeg in search of new business. The tactics worked, though the Indians were shrewd enough to share part of their trade with the English. The Crees, new middle men in the northern trade, understood even better than the Iroquois the virtues of competition.

After 1760, France was gone, but her complex, aggressive trading system of forts, depots, and highly-organized canoe brigades was simply inherited by the Scottish and New England merchants who followed the British armies into Montreal. The *bourgeois* or boss might now speak another language, but the *voyageurs* still gathered in the spring to make their marks on the careful, notarized contracts and then to set off in their heavily-laden *canots de maître*. They were small, tough men who could paddle twenty hours a day, measuring distances by the time it took to smoke a pipe of tobacco. At Grand Portage they met the smaller canoes of the wintering partners, as far away again from the distant posts. As they transferred their loads and dickered over the trade goods that custom allowed each *voyageur,* the "pork-eaters" from Montreal wondered whether the freedom and adventures of their western counterparts outweighed the hardships and long winters. The men of the upper country, the *pays d'en haut*, were different. Many took Indian wives, vital intermediaries in the trade, cementing in fact and in custom the trading alliances of white and native. In time, these would be mothers of a new mixed-blood people. Their sons and daughters would grow up divided between Indian ways and the Scots-Presbyterian or *Canadien*-Catholic heritage of a trader or *voyageur* father. The French-speaking would be Métis; the English-speaking "country born" or half-breeds.

Nothing in 1760 had ended the rivalry of the Hudson's Bay Company and the "pedlars from Quebec." Indeed, the "pedlars" themselves were in ruinous and sometimes murderous competition. Outsiders rarely understood how costly and risky the trade was. It took four or five years of packing, storage, and transportation before goods ordered in England could actually be paid for. Traders carried an impossible load of debt and even a small disaster could mean ruin. Business logic dictated the only possible solution, a cartel. A first small experiment in 1770 led by 1787 to the fully-grown North West Company. Systematically its few rivals were included or wiped out. The last was the short-lived XY Company, formed by traders driven from the southwest by the Americans.

It was the "Nor'westers," the wintering partners and their servants, who learned from the Indians how to live in the West and to find their way along its rivers and lakes. The rough American, Peter Pond, reached Lake Athabaska in 1778. Alexander Mackenzie, seeking a way over the mountain barrier, first followed the river that would bear his name in 1789. He called it "River of Disappointment" after it had led him to the ice-floes of the Arctic Ocean, but he persisted. With better navigational instruments and after terrible dangers, he could mark his name on a rock near the Dean Channel on July 22, 1793; the first white man to travel overland to the Pacific Ocean. Others followed; between them, Simon Fraser and David Thompson confirmed the shape of the great rivers and mountain ranges of the Pacific slope. Their purpose, almost always, was business.

The North West Company waged a desperate, Montreal-based struggle to fend off Americans like John Jacob Astor from the south and the Hudson's Bay Company from the north. The HBC responded, questioning its old policy of waiting for trade. "The sleep by the frozen sea," as scornful critics termed the Company's policy, had to end. The benefits of cheapness (and of leaving the Indians undisturbed) no longer weighed in the ledger. In 1774, Samuel Hearne, having explored on his own as far as the Coppermine River and the Arctic Ocean, went inland to build an HBC post at Cumberland House. Other posts soon followed. Rival posts competed with all the cunning and occasional violence their traders could devise.

By 1811, the Hudson's Bay Company had a new strategy. For years, those few veterans of the trade who loved the country or who would not abandon their Indian wives had settled in the relatively sheltered valley of the Red River. Their half-breed and Métis offspring had settled there too, the former turning to farming, the latter to the more adventurous but indispensable life of the buffalo hunt. The annual slaughter of the huge animals that seemed to supply every need of prairie life provided the Nor'westers with their pemmican. As part of their rivalry with the hated HBC, Nor'westers assured the Métis that, through their mothers' blood, they were the true and only inheritors of the land. Young people, growing up proud in the lore of two cultures, took pleasure in seeing themselves as a "New Nation" with the semimilitary structure of the buffalo hunt as their first cultural institution. Leaders like Cuthbert Grant gave the Métis a sense of power. In law, of course, that old charter of 1670 was clear—the Red River valley was part of Rupert's Land. The philanthropic Lord Selkirk, having settled destitute Scottish Highlanders in Prince Edward Island and Upper Canada, now purchased a big block of

Hudson's Bay Company stock and proposed to settle still more of his people on its highly recommended Red River land.

In 1811, the Company gave Selkirk 106,000 acres at the forks of the Red and the Assiniboine rivers for his colony. To every imaginable pioneering misery, from frost and floods to grasshoppers, Selkirk's settlers could add an extra calamity: the utter hostility of the Nor'westers and their Métis allies. Nor'westers saw no mystery in the Hudson's Bay Company's motive in planting a colony across their main route to the West and on top of their most basic food supply. Led by Cuthbert Grant and encouraged by the "New Nation" argument that the land was theirs, the Métis harrassed the unhappy Highlanders and trampled their crops. At Seven Oaks in 1816, Grant and his Métis shot down twenty-one men from the colony and mutilated some of the corpses. The remaining settlers were driven out, finding refuge at the far end of Lake Winnipeg.

Selkirk took rapid vengeance. Collecting Swiss mercenaries, disbanded after the War of 1812, he headed west. At Fort William, now the Nor'westers' trans-shipment base, he seized prisoners and trading goods and sent his men on to restore the colony. The nervous settlers returned to the Red River, and both Métis and Scots seem to have come to a surprisingly smooth reconciliation. The whole dispute entered the courts which, unfortunately for Selkirk, were held in the distinctly pro-Nor'wester atmosphere of the Canadas. By the time he had finished with judges, lawyers, and charges of false imprisonment, both the philanthropist's fortune and his health had withered away.

Even the battle with Selkirk was too much for the North West Company. Dissident partners plotted joining with the rival company. Sir Alexander Mackenzie, the explorer, had urged such a merger years before. The logic of monopoly was, as usual, inescapable. In 1821, the Hudson's Bay Company absorbed its competitor, cut the long link with Montreal, and secured a twenty-one-year licence for its monopoly from the British government. The Nor'westers, with their reputations for audacity, endurance, and the wild drinking of their Beaver Club, joined their old rival or applied their capital to other commercial dreams in Montreal. Some of them sank into obscure poverty.

In the West, a short, stout Scot named George Simpson emerged as "the little emperor" of the Hudson's Bay domain. By

1839, he had cut out most of the competing posts, reduced costs, and firmly suppressed any costly schemes for settlement or administration. He also established his headquarters in Montreal, though his strict supervision hardly slackened. In 1841, teams of paddlers took him from Fort Churchill on Hudson Bay to Astoria at the mouth of Columbia in only eighty-four days.

Astoria was part of the Pacific domain Simon Fraser and David Thompson had won from John Jacob Astor for the Nor'westers. Politically, its status was controversial. Britain and Spain had drifted close to war in 1790 over the ownership of Nootka Sound, but the firmness of Captain George Vancouver had made the Spanish accept a diplomatic withdrawal. The War of 1812 had proved a great setback for Americans like Astor, but the tide of history was on their side. In 1818, Britain and the United States had agreed to joint occupation of the distant Pacific coast, and in 1839, the Hudson's Bay Company settled a potential threat from the Russians in Alaska by trading them food supplies for a post.

Sensible Company officials knew that they held the coast on borrowed time. American missionaries had entered the Oregon territory, traders had followed, and troops to protect them were not far behind. So were settlers, pouring through the mountain passes into the rich valleys. Company officials hurried to harvest furs. In 1846, Oregon was gone, passed to the United States, and the whole coast would have followed as American politicians and editors cried for "Fifty-four-forty or fight." But a new fort had been opened at the tip of Vancouver Island, and British diplomats held firm behind a weak hand. They insisted that the international boundary along the Great Plains, the forty-ninth parallel, be extended over the mountains and pushed through the Straits of Juan de Fuca. (Even then, no one knew that San Juan Island straddled the line, and another war scare would occur in 1860 before the Americans won that prize.)

All things considered, British North Americans were lucky in their boundary settlement. As usual, they were utterly unprepared for war, and this time the Americans really were in a fighting mood; they went off and fought the unfortunate Mexicans instead. As for the Hudson's Bay Company, it had suffered a serious blow. The Company's prestige depended on an aura of permanency, summed up by the rude version of the letters on its flag— "Here Before Christ." Canadians and imperial-minded Britons awoke at last to the realization that a trading company was a very feeble steward for choice territory. The new free-trade ideology was utterly out of sympathy with government-licensed monopolies. Still, actually doing something would be troublesome too, and the Company got a second chance. In return for promising serious colonization within five years, it was given Vancouver Island to manage as a crown colony.

Even if the Company could have changed its ways, in 1849 every conceivable colonist set off for the gold fields of California. A few retired officials, two tiny parties from the Red River, and some accidental tourists were all that the Company could muster by 1851 when a hardened veteran of the Company service, James Douglas, became governor. People seemed to have forgotten about the colony until suddenly, in 1858, British Columbia had its own gold rush. Thousands of miners, prospectors, and hangers-on poured up the Fraser valley and on to new discoveries in the Cariboo. It was the moment for a tough old autocrat, and Douglas rose to the occasion in the full knowledge that he faced another Oregon. A separate mainland colony was proclaimed. A smart detachment of Royal Engineers arrived, not as a garrison but as road-builders and as discreet backing for an extraordinary one-man embodiment of a ruthless brand of British justice, Matthew Baillie Begbie. It would take months before the Colonial Secretary in London could consider a sentence, Judge Begbie informed one convicted murderer: "but you will not be interested in what he decided, for you are to be hanged Monday morning."

By 1866, both the gold and the rush were gone, leaving two tiny colonies, two capitals (at Victoria and New Westminster), and one large debt—for roads were not built cheaply through the mountains. With much grumbling, the colonies were reunited, the Company relinquished its power (in 1867), and in 1868 the capital was restored to Victoria. The nearby British naval base at Esquimalt provided some reassurance and a source of gunboats for frequent expeditions to overawe coastal Indians.

The Company had prided itself on maintaining good relations with Indians—mainly just by leaving them alone. Now growing numbers of missionaries found a humanitarian audience in Britain for their sometimes scurrilous allegations of Company neglect or sharp practice. A tiny British garrison in Red River, sent ostensibly for the Oregon crisis, was needed to maintain dwindling Company authority. Neither the troops nor the military pensioners who replaced them were much use as police.

In 1849, Guillaume Sayer appeared at the Red River court to be found guilty of breaking the Hudson's Bay Company's monopoly. Since he brought several hundred fellow Métis with him, the judge prudently decided that no punishment was in order. The high-wheeled Red River carts would be free to screech and squeal their way south to St. Paul as they pleased. The Métis had become formidable. In 1851, as their women and children sheltered behind the carts and loaded their rifles, the buffalo hunters slaughtered attacking Sioux at the battle of Grand Côteau.

The Company itself also collected its supplies from St. Paul. Steamboat and railway connections were now better than the old route from the Bay. Old links with Canada revived. So did Canadian interest. The Company had deliberately given the impression that the prairies were a sub-Arctic wasteland and the harsh experience of the Selkirk settlers had confirmed the image. French-Canadian missionaries to the Métis, mindful of the Jesuit *Relations* and the blessings of martyrdom, exaggerated their sufferings. The Grit farmers of Upper Canada were unimpressed. Like their American cousins, they looked on the frontier as a heritage for their sons, and they had not the slightest respect for the Hudson's Bay Company. When, in 1857, the British Parliament appointed a Select Committee to review the Company's licence renewal, George Brown and his Reformers made sure that Canada was present in strength.

Precise information on the area was still scarce. In 1857–58, two expeditions, one British and the other Canadian, set out to report on prospects for western settlement. John Palliser for the British concluded that the wooded parklands of the Red, Assiniboine, and North Saskatchewan river valleys were suitable for agriculture, but the treeless prairie to the south was too arid ever to be farmed. Henry Youle Hind, a professor of chemistry at the University of Toronto, delighted his Canadian sponsors by reporting rapturously on prospects for the entire region. Strong supporting evidence came opportunely from Lorin Blodgett, an American, who showed that lines of identical temperatures ran northwest and southwest, not along latitudes. Farming *was* possible. Suddenly, a new shape for British North America became an exciting prospect.

# PART II

# A Mari usque ad Marem

# 1 / Confederation

In an almost continent-wide coincidence, by the 1860s all British North Americans had been obliged to take thought for their future. A decade of railway-building had shown that it was possible to break the barriers of distance and climate but at a cost that no single colony could afford. The railway boom had also brought foreign investors to the region. Their perspective was broader, if no less self-interested, than that of local people and their politicians. However parochial they might be, all British North Americans could understand the threat of the United States.

In 1847 the Americans had absorbed Texas and California with quite unnerving speed. In the 1850s the Fraser and Cariboo gold rushes might well have been pretext enough to gain British Columbia. South of the little Red River colony, Minnesota was now a state and its politicians made no secret of their annexationist intentions. By 1861 Americans were preoccupied with their Civil War but, as the Montreal-Irish orator D'Arcy McGee warned, war was an appetite that grew with feeding. Even after four years of fighting and half a million dead, the United States' military strength seemed to keep on growing. If Washington wanted a pretext to turn northward, one would not be hard to find.

A few young Canadians, captivated by the South's romantic image, had helped Confederates use Canadian bases to plot their attacks. Some of the Southerners launched a murderous raid on St. Albans, Vermont, escaped to Canada, and went free. The furious Americans promptly closed their borders, enforced the use of passports, and announced that the cherished Reciprocity Agreement would end in 1866. It was one more reason for the British colonies to look to each other, if only as substitute markets.

Some form of union was no new idea. A British staff officer

had suggested it as early as 1783. William Smith, the Loyalist Chief Justice of Quebec, had devised a scheme for a central legislature in 1785. Among the ideas that had cascaded through William Lyon Mackenzie's mind was a colonial union. Lord Durham had promoted the notion when he had summoned lieutenant-governors and their councils to meet him in 1838. James W. Johnson, Howe's opponent in Nova Scotia, had been so impressed with Durham's idea that he had pushed the proposition during the 1850s. So had British governors like Lord Elgin and his able successor, Sir Edward Head. It was hardly astonishing. The colonies were all British—Canada East no less than the others—and they all lived in the shadow of the largest, if not necessarily the happiest, federal union in the world.

If the military and economic threat from the United States was the firmest prod in making the British colonies consider closer union, the breakdown of American federalism was also a useful warning. The real issue in the Civil War, as contemporaries understood matters, was not slavery but states' rights. The South's "peculiar institution" had led to secession in 1861 but it was the claim of state sovereignty that had allowed the Confederacy to raise armies and had paralysed the will of the rest of the nation. Federalism might seem a logical answer to the problems of the United Provinces or even of British North America as a whole, but the experience of the best available example was not reassuring.

Still, the experiment had to be considered. In 1859, when the Reformers of Canada West had met in convention, impatient in their demands for representation by population, George Brown had led them to consider some form of federalism as a possible compromise. The year before, the one-time annexationist and voice of Montreal business, Alexander Tilloch Galt, switched from the Reformers to Macdonald and Cartier on condition that they take up the notion of a British North American federation. Cartier and Macdonald did as little as was necessary to retain a valuable new partner; neither man was much taken with constitutional novelties.

By the spring of 1864, the idea was no longer a novelty but an opportunity. If Macdonald could not stem the tide of votes to Reform and "rep by pop," his career would end. Cartier could now foresee a political battle his *Canadiens* could not win. Two years of feeble government under John Sandfield Macdonald had proved to all but the stubborn Reform leader that a double majority drawn from each of the United Provinces would not work. Sandfield Macdonald's bitter rival, George Brown, saw both the need and an opportunity. By 1864, there had been two elections and four governments during three very dangerous years. Outsiders knew that Brown and the Tory leader, John A. Macdonald, were mortal enemies. The bibulous opportunist and the self-righteous autocrat hated each other. They might also use each other.

On June 14 a short-lived Macdonald-Cartier government was defeated. In the confusion George Brown rose to announce his willingness to enter a coalition pledged to find a way out of the constitutional impasse. An ecstatic but tiny French Canadian *bleu* clambered up the massive Brown and embraced him while the House cheered. By June 30, under the titular leadership of Sir Etienne-Pascal Taché, a veteran of the War of 1812, the Great Coalition was announced. Its constitutional policies were easily drawn from a legislature committee, chaired by Brown through much of the 1864 session. What was needed was a place to present them. News that leaders of three of the Atlantic colonies would meet at Charlottetown on September 1 suggested the opportunity. At once the Canadians asked for and received an invitation.

Maritime union, the original Charlottetown topic, was at least as old an idea as British North American federalism. It was just as obvious and just as impossible. It was a favourite of British lieutenant-governors like John Manners Sutton and Arthur Gordon in New Brunswick. How better might they advance the region (and their own careers)? Nova Scotians fancied the idea if only because they would obviously dominate the union, but it took all of Gordon's persuasion to make New Brunswick's Premier Tilley even a lukewarm supporter. As for Prince Edward Island, it was thought best to hold the Maritime Union Conference in Charlottetown to make sure that the Island's leaders showed up. Indeed, it may have been only the unexpected inquiry from the Canadians that ensured that the Conference happened at all.

In the circumstances, the Charlottetown Conference was an unexpected triumph for the Canadians. Since the Maritimers had nothing much to discuss, they cheerfully agreed to hear their visitors. Well-briefed and rehearsed, Macdonald, Cartier, Brown, and Galt each spoke brilliantly in their field of expertise. Lavish entertainment ashore and on the Canadians' ship, the *Queen Victoria,* made the first week of September pass like a dream. Next the Canadians and their hosts moved on to Halifax and then to Saint John with more speeches, banquets, and toasts and an agreement that all would meet at Quebec on October 10.

The Quebec meeting was longer, tougher, and much more specific. It almost began with tragedy when the *Queen Victoria,* sent to collect delegates, wives, and marriageable daughters, nearly foundered in a storm. At Quebec, Newfoundland was represented as well. So was Britain. Colonel W. F. D. Jervois, who believed Canada to be indefensible, obediently went to Quebec to tell delegates that a modest military effort could keep British North America safe. Details of discussion at the closed meetings are sparse and one-sided, taken largely from minutes kept by Hewitt Bernard, Macdonald's secretary, and from the letters sent home by George Brown to his young wife. Once again, the Canadians were the best-prepared, and almost all the seventy-two resolutions adopted between October 10 and 28 were their work.

The speed and good humour of the meetings concealed real differences. Macdonald made no secret of his preference for a single legislative union. Federalism, he insisted, had been discredited by the American experience. To a large degree, he had his way. Confederation, as it emerged from Quebec, gave the central government infinitely greater powers than Washington possessed. In the division of responsibilities, the future Section 91 not only gave the central power a healthy list of tasks to ensure "peace, order and good government" but left any "residual" or unspecified powers to the centre as well. Provincial responsibilities were so modest as to be almost municipal in scope— education, local roads and improvements, and "charitable and eleemosynary institutions." Moreover, provinces would be limited to the meagre revenue from direct taxes and their laws would be suspended or even disallowed by the central authority.

Yet Macdonald did not win. It was his partner and closest ally George-Etienne Cartier who insisted on a federal system. On behalf of his French-Canadian colleagues, Cartier argued that the provincial powers which would be their only bulwark against an even larger Anglo-Saxon majority, would be very real indeed. "Property and civil rights," for example, was the phrase from the old Quebec Act that had guaranteed the *Canadien*'s identity; it must now be a provincial concern. Cartier's chief ally was a short, bespectacled Ontario reformer named Oliver Mowat. In the light of events, an astonishing amount of discussion was focused on the proposed upper house of the new federal Parliament, and even that debate concentrated on the provincial shares, not the decisive fact that all senators would be federal appointees.

At the end of October 1864 the Confederation agreement was set. Many delegates headed on to Montreal, Toronto, and the West to see the vast potential of provinces most of them had never visited and to share the heady excitement of banquet oratory. Both the coalition and the British, contented midwives for the process, could congratulate themselves on an easy victory.

In Canada, the coalition government approached the provincial Parliament with some confidence. Meeting for the last time at Quebec, with their speeches recorded and published, members tackled the Confederation issues with energy and occasional flashes of vision. Some criticisms were predictable. The intercolonial railway demanded by Nova Scotia would be too costly; financial terms for the lower provinces were too generous. French Canadians obviously had much to lose. Cartier and his deputy Hector Langevin did their utmost to keep nervous *bleus* in line, boasting of the powers left for the new province of Quebec and insisting that *Canadiens* would now be masters in their own jurisdiction. A. A. Dorion and the *rouges* condemned the new arrangement as fatal to French Canada, and a number of younger *bleus* like Honoré Mercier abandoned their allegiance. Minorities would have minorities of their own. The elderly Christopher Dunkin, speaking for the English of Canada East, predicted that too many interests—regional, racial, religious, and political— would persist in the new Confederation to allow any new national community to develop. His warnings would be remembered.

Macdonald, Cartier, Brown, and especially the fiery D'Arcy McGee, cajoled, persuaded, and occasionally lifted their supporters' emotions above mundane criticisms. As they spoke, the great Civil War was winding to its end and the threat of the blue-clad Union armies hung over the debate. If the Americans came, talk of local rights, and especially of French-Canadian survival, would be academic. Everyone knew it. The vote was decisive. Members from Canada West voted 54–8 for Confederation; from

Canada East the margin was 37–25, though the French-speaking majority was only four. The next business, a $2-million loan for fortifications, passed swiftly, and the leading ministers left at once for London to pursue both matters with the British.

Confederation had passed, though more painfully than its architects in Canada had expected. In the lower provinces, it was another story. The euphoria of September 1864 had vanished by November when the delegates came home. It was obvious almost at once that neither island colony would join. Prince Edward Island delegates had opposed "rep by pop" at Quebec and had lost. Was that a foretaste of Confederation? Times were good; the little island would manage on its own. It could even afford its own railway without going on bended knee to Canadians. Newfoundland too would turn its back. St. John's, where political and business power met, was closer to London than to the newly designated capital of Ottawa. Its merchant elite had no plans to share power. Hard times had justified sending delegates to Quebec, but now fish prices were climbing again, prosperity began to breed confidence, and the Water Street merchants of St. John's spread the word: Confederation meant conscription and Canadian taxes. In the 1869 election, the pro-Confederates lost.

In Nova Scotia, James Johnson and Charles Tupper had brought the Conservatives to power back in 1864, so at least time was on their side. Opinion was not. Joe Howe had left politics in 1863. Perhaps he had squandered some of his influence by his anti-Catholic bigotry but his power was immense. At times Howe had backed a North American union but his real dream remained an imperial federation with Britain. Early in 1865, Howe acted. The pro-Confederation editor of the Halifax *Chronicle* was fired. Soon, the paper's columns carried "The Botheration Letters," brilliant invective against Confederation and its sponsors. The author was anonymous but every Nova Scotian knew the voice of their most outspoken politician—Joe Howe. Tupper, premier since 1864, could feel his support slipping.

Across the Bay of Fundy, matters were even worse. Tilley did not have time. His Liberals had held office for a decade, accumulating splits and enemies. An election was due and Governor Gordon insisted that it be held before the legislature could endorse the Quebec Resolutions. The anti-Confederates were ready. Tilley, they said, had sold New Brunswickers for eighty cents a head—the $200,000 the Quebec proposals would pay the colony for its customs revenues. By the end of March 1865 Tilley was out and his old enemy, Albert J. Smith, was in.

Without the two island colonies, Confederation could go forward; without New Brunswick to link Nova Scotia to central Canada, it was dead. Somehow, the idea must be resuscitated. The British would do their utmost to help. A pro-Confederate governor arrived in Nova Scotia and in New Brunswick Arthur Gordon got new orders to help Tilley if he could. The Canadians in London got a guarantee for their fortification loan and a vague but seemingly valuable pledge that if they would take their own defence seriously, "the Imperial Government fully acknowledged the reciprocal obligation of defending every portion of the Empire with all the resources at its command." That was an answer to Maritimers who insisted that Confederation would tie them to a defenceless interior.

Unknowingly, the Americans helped as well. The termination of Reciprocity, with its accompanying fishing agreements, in 1866 hurt the lower provinces as much as Canada. Albert Smith had boasted that he could get a better deal from Washington than from any Confederate politician. He returned empty-handed and humiliated. His support began to crumble.

The huge American armies had disbanded with astonishing speed after the Civil War, but they left a bitter residue. In the cities of the North, the Fenian Brotherhood, pledged to liberate Ireland from English rule, had recruited widely among the Union's Irish soldiers. By recruiting hardened veterans with ready access to arms and American sympathy, the Fenians planned to form an army to conquer Canada and hold her hostage for Ireland's freedom. It was a wild scheme, growing ever wilder in the reports sent by informers and secret agents to British and Canadian authorities. Thousands marched, applauded fiery speeches, and went home; there were hundreds, patriots and unemployed, who might act. In response, British troops and Canadian militia trained, planned, and occupied frontier posts. Border towns buzzed with rumours and false alarms.

Suddenly, the rumours came true. At Fort Erie on May 31, 1866, sixteen hundred Fenians scrambled ashore. By June 3, they had all fled or been captured, but not before they had defeated two small forces of Canadian militia. At Pigeon Hill, just over the

Vermont border, another eighteen hundred Fenians camped for a day before American authorities seized their leaders and supplies. The most fatuous but also the most significant incursion had ended a month before when Fenians clustered on the Maine border had tried to raid Campobello Island. For New Brunswick, it was traumatic. Not even in the comic-opera Aroostook War in the 1840s, when the contested boundary with Maine had finally been settled, had the colony felt so threatened. Now a few hundred confused, ill-led Fenians suddenly made a union with Canada appear sensible. Smith's support collapsed and the lieutenant governor discreetly used his power to require a new election. Funds from Montreal reinforced the cause of Confederation. This time Tilley was triumphant.

Both Tilley and Charles Tupper avoided asking their legislatures to endorse the Quebec Resolutions. Instead, they sought a mandate to negotiate still better terms in Britain. The hint was hardly needed. The Canadians had manoeuvring room and the British were now almost beside themselves with eagerness. The reasons were unflattering. British investors feared for their money in the hands of any of the individual colonies. Some of them had vast plans at stake, from expanding the Grand Trunk to creating a transcontinental railway line. Politically, the doctrines of free trade and imperial separation had reached their height. "I cannot shut my eyes to the fact that they want to get rid of us," an unhappy Galt reported from London in 1865. "They have a servile fear of the United States and would rather give us up than defend us, or incur the risk of war with that country."

When delegates from Canada, Nova Scotia, and New Brunswick met in London at the Westminster Palace Hotel, the mood of the Quebec Conference had revived. Tilley and Tupper got better financial terms and the educational rights of religious (though not linguistic) minorities were improved. The Intercolonial Railway, merely discussed before, became a legal obligation. In their own draft, the Canadians, monarchists to the core, had proposed that their creation be termed, "the Kingdom of Canada." The British warned that American sensibilities might be aroused. The devoutly Christian Leonard Tilley offered both an alternative and a national motto by thumbing his bible to Psalms 72:8: "He shall have dominion also from sea to sea, and from the river unto the ends of the earth."

Without particular ceremony or sense of occasion, the British Parliament passed the act as Canadians had designed it, correcting a word or phrase here or there as legislative draftsmen advised but giving the colonials, for the first time, a constitution that was as home-made as it could be. One lapse went unnoticed: nowhere did the British North America Act, 1867, explain how the colonists would share in its future amendment.

Lawyers and historians would amuse themselves for more than a century with debate about what the Fathers of Confederation had really meant by all their torrents of words between 1864 and 1867. Were the Quebec Resolutions a treaty, inviolable by the participating provinces? Macdonald and Cartier certainly said so to fend off would-be amenders in their Canadian Parliament but they cheerfully altered terms when they got to London in 1866 and they would change them later. Was the Act a compact, either among the three original colonies, or among the two founding nations of French and English, or even, most far-fetched, among all current and future provinces? Such a notion would become fashionable in the 1880s, supported by the diligent collection of random quotations. As an historical interpretation of what happened in the 1860s, the compact theory is absurd. Before and long after Confederation, sensible Canadians have understood that peace, order, and good government in their country have depended on the reasonable long-run harmony of French and English. That notion was not embodied in the British North America Act; it was left for ensuing generations to rediscover or neglect at their peril.

# 2 / Nation-Building

Confederation had been a means to many ends. By 1867, one purpose mattered more than the others: the bid to establish a transcontinental nation. Sir John A. Macdonald, newly knighted and summoned as the Dominion's first Prime Minister, would never forget that goal.

First he must form a government. The big gothic-style buildings at Ottawa and the timid bureaucrats of the United Provinces would form a suitable foundation. Few officials would leave the lower provinces. As for the new governments of Ontario and Quebec, they would start from scratch. Forming a cabinet was harder. In the Canadas, ministers had represented interests as well as departments. That would continue but it was now so much more complex. Quebec, for example, must have four ministers: one for the English Protestants and the others to balance the rivalry of Montreal and Quebec City. There was no room there for the brilliant D'Arcy McGee: he would have to wait. Nine months later, still a mere MP, McGee lay dead in the Ottawa slush, the victim of a Fenian bullet.

By November 1867 Macdonald was ready to face elections. The outcome reflected the Confederation debate. In Nova Scotia, only Tupper survived the anti-Confederate tide. New Brunswick split narrowly for Tilley. Quebec went solidly for Cartier's *bleus*. In Ontario, where George Brown had worked since 1865 for a Reform sweep, the *Globe* publisher lost his own seat. Sir John A. Macdonald was exultant. In Ontario, Macdonald shrewdly invited Sandfield Macdonald to head a "patent combination," a coalition of Tories and old Reformers. Again Brown was worsted. In Ottawa, the Dominion's first Parliament would pit 108 government supporters against a mixed bag of 72 *rouges,* Reformers, and Maritime anti-Confederates.

Safe in power, Macdonald had much to do. Joseph Howe's campaign to repeal Confederation was making no headway in Britain but Nova Scotia's bitterness was not allowed to fester. By 1869, Howe had accepted as "better terms" a richer subsidy than the original eighty cents a head and, despite the resulting cries of treason, had joined Macdonald's cabinet. Newfoundland would not come for eighty years yet; her 1869 election saw to that. (In 1895, Canada had another chance—but balked at the cost of $5 million in financial help. A generation of Newfoundlanders concluded that Canadians were a mean-minded folk.) Prince Edward Island was different. The fatal lure of railways had left the tiny colony $3 million in debt. Frightened island politicians turned to Ottawa and got terms they could not refuse: complete transfer of the provincial debt and hard cash to buy out the notorious "proprietors." By 1873, the island was a province.

A far more nerve-wracking issue to Macdonald was holding the West. At last the Americans were moving. In 1867, they bought Alaska from the Russians for $7.2 million and they sent a consul to the Red River. Canada saw that it was time for her legal haggling with the Hudson's Bay Company to end. In 1868, Cartier and William McDougall went to London and simply purchased Rupert's Land for $1.5 million and a guarantee that a twentieth of the land in the fertile belt would remain with the old Company. Formal transfer would come soon, "at a date to be determined." Meanwhile, Canada would send survey crews and a road-building gang to link the Red River settlement with Lake Superior.

It was really too good to be true. McDougall, the long-time campaigner for the Northwest as an outlet for farmers' sons, would become governor. An appointed council and a small police force would keep the peace and shut out American trouble-makers. Warnings from Catholic missionaries and aged Hudson's Bay officials were discounted. Cartier, the perennial optimist, knew that all would be well. McDougall reported that he had dependable informants among Canadians at the Red River.

Both men were wrong. The Canadians, with their knowing-newcomer arrogance, were detested. Company authority, shrinking since 1849, vanished under the strain of the unpopular land transfer. English-speaking settlers might accept their fate; the Métis would not. Their disciplined hunting organization made them a force. Their old belief that as the "New Nation" they had

81

inherited the land gave them a unifying cause. They were backed by Catholic priests, fearful of an influx of Protestant farmers. Still, Métis resistance might have been mere grumbling without young Louis Riel. The ambitious son of a respected father, Riel had gone to Montreal for a classical education. He had found no vocation for the Church or the law and had drifted home qualified for no career but politics. The man and the moment met. The combination derailed Macdonald's transcontinental plans. A national council of the Métis became the real authority in the Red River.

McDougall actually helped the Métis. As the would-be governor approached, the Métis formed a committee, mustered their forces, and seized Fort Garry, the Hudson's Bay Company's main base. No sooner had McDougall crossed the border than Métis guards expelled him. On December 1, the frustrated official again stepped a few feet over the boundary line, proclaimed Canadian sovereignty, fluttered a Union Jack in the icy wind, and retreated to his hotel room to command all loyal Canadians at the Red River to support his authority. The few Canadians who did so promptly found themselves in the freezing cells of Fort Garry. Louis Riel finally had an argument for proclaiming his provisional government: no other power existed in the colony.

In Ottawa, Macdonald was aghast. By his folly, McDougall had revealed Canadian impotence to Americans and Métis alike. If annexationists wanted a pretext to interfere, they would have a whole long winter before Canada could do anything. A steady stream of visitors and intermediaries, from old Joe Howe to Donald A. Smith, Hudson's Bay Company commissioner in Montreal, set out for the Red River. Riel met most of them with threats and legitimate suspicion. Smith proved by far the ablest. With patience and shrewdness, he manoeuvred Riel and the varied factions in the colony into stating their demands, choosing delegates, and despatching them to Ottawa. Riel's ambitions, after all, were not bizarre: he wanted Red River to be a province like the others. If the French could become Canadians, so could the Métis.

Unfortunately for Donald Smith, Riel and many other people, the patriotic Canadians in the Red River knew nothing of Macdonald's patient strategy. Their loyalty and their injured pride demanded more heroic action against the man McDougall had designated as a rebel. In February 1870 a new and even more bungled assault was mounted; once again the perpetrators were swiftly captured by Métis horsemen. This time, the mood was different. Riel's authority was slipping. Dissuaded by Smith and the community from executing C. A. Boulton, one of the Canadian leaders, he seized on smaller fry. Tom Scott, a big, raw-boned Ontarian, had already been savagely beaten for insulting his guards. On March 4, 1870, after a Métis court martial, he was taken out and shot. "We must make Canada respect us," Riel told Smith in melancholy justification.

It was worse than a crime; it was a blunder. Scott was an awkward martyr. Since he had earlier led a strike over unpaid wages and was certainly an Orangeman, most historians have generally agreed with Riel that Scott must have been a man of bad character. No one should be shot on such evidence. Contemporary opinion declared his death a murder. Reports from the Red River stoked the fires of Ontario Protestantism. Brown, the *Globe*, and the Grits had an issue the smallest mind could understand: Macdonald was bargaining with a murderous rebel. Quebec, at first dismayed by the killing, rapidly decided, after the Ontario furor, that Riel must be forgiven. Riel's friends in Montreal were long-suffering but loyal. They now regarded the Métis as guardians of a part of the French-Canadian patrimony most Québécois would rather admire from a distance.

Macdonald kept his eye on his purpose. Red River delegates were escorted past Ontario law officers, their desires were met, and they returned triumphant with virtually all any of them had sought. The colony would become the eleven-thousand-square-mile province of Manitoba. The duality of French and English, Catholic and Protestant, as it had existed in 1870, was secure forever. There would even be an upper and a lower house for the provincial legislature and, best of all, Ottawa would pay the bill. Only one desire was unsatisfied: an amnesty. It had been promised and expected, but that was before Scott died.

To confirm the transfer from what officially had been British sovereignty to Canadian rule, a joint Anglo-Canadian military expedition would show the flag to Americans, Indians, and the disaffected. With a mixture of land hunger, curiosity, and vengeful patriotism, young Ontarians flocked to join; young *Canadiens* did not. The Red River expedition of 1870 turned out to be a logistic triumph, navigating the old *voyageur* route from Port Arthur to Fort Garry without losing a man. It was also a political misfortune, introducing the young Dominion to the West as a punitive authority. A small garrison remained in Manitoba until 1877. As for Riel, he prudently fled before the approaching troops. A stabler and more robust personality might well, like Mackenzie and Papineau, have resumed a conventional political career, most probably in the Conservative ranks. Certainly Riel remained a hero to his Métis people, but by killing Scott he had robbed himself of immediate recognition as the founder of Manitoba.

The Red River was only one part of the West. In contrast, drawing British Columbia into Confederation proved deceptively simple. When gold ran out the miners departed, leaving behind a largely British and Canadian elite of officials, ranchers, and professionals, and a very large debt. The colony's leaders would have preferred the status quo; some merchants eagerly agitated for annexation with the United States. The editor of the Victoria *Colonist* (a Nova Scotian named William Smith who had renamed himself Amor de Cosmos) insisted that the Canadians be approached. A new British governor agreed, and, in the summer of 1870, two delegates made their laborious way to Ottawa via San Francisco. Macdonald was away, spending a restful summer in Charlottetown, but Cartier was on the job eager to make a coup. British Columbia needed money: for purposes of subsidy, Ottawa would pretend that it had sixty thousand people instead of twenty-eight thousand. (No one had even counted the colony's Indians—a loosely estimated eighty-two thousand!) The delegates hoped for a wagon road across the Rockies; Cartier had not forgotten the old Grand Trunk dream—British Columbia would have a full transcontinental railway within a decade of joining Confederation. It was an offer British Columbia could not possibly reject. By July 20, 1871, it was a province.

Between British Columbia and the Red River lay what an officially-sponsored traveller, Captain William Butler, called "The Great Lone Land," peopled by Indians, a few Métis, and even fewer white trappers, traders, and missionaries. Herds of buffalo, sole livelihood for the inhabitants, headed relentlessly towards extinction. Repeating rifles and an American slaughter policy, designed to starve the warlike Sioux Indians, devastated the herds. Canada could not afford Indian wars. Her officials set out to negotiate a system of Indian treaties and surrenders with reserves,

84

payments, medals, and a "medicine chest" as incentives for each band to clear the land for settlers. Ottawa could not stop there. The savage slaughter of an Indian party in the Cypress Hills and the establishment of American whiskey-traders at Fort Whoop-up in Canadian territory were warnings of early trouble. The mounted police force that had been planned for the Red River was revived. Policemen traditionally wore blue, but scarlet tunics would leave no doubt that a different sovereignty prevailed above the forty-ninth parallel. The North West Mounted Police was Macdonald's fondest creation. Canadians would later pretend that they were uniquely devoted to law and order. In fact, the peace and good order of the remote territories were practical necessities if American cavalry or vigilantes were to have no excuse for invading Canadian soil.

That soil would now also have to support a railway. Cartier's pledge was almost as worrying to his colleagues as MacDougall's folly had been in 1869. A three-thousand-mile railway from Montreal to the Pacific was a huge undertaking, especially at a time when Ottawa was pouring money into the Intercolonial Railway. The Pacific line would have to be a private venture, financed, if possible, by huge western land grants. Fortunately, two rival syndicates were bidding for the contract. Senator David Macpherson in Toronto was Macdonald's old friend, but he was a front for the Grand Trunk and no vote-conscious government would dare help that greedy and unloved company. In Montreal, the ruthless shipping magnate, Sir Hugh Allan, formed a rival group secretly backed by American railroad interests. Allan had money and he used it, buying up newspapers, young lawyers, even priests, to pressure Cartier and the entire Tory government.

With his national achievements and prosperity, Macdonald should have been impregnable. He was not. The Riel affair had turned both Ontario and Quebec against him. At the end of 1871, Ontario Liberals had used Riel and the Red River to batter Sandfield Macdonald into defeat. In Quebec, conservative Catholics concluded that the Church should resume the kind of political leadership it had exerted after the conquest. The pragmatic and corruptible *bleus* must be disciplined; the anti-clerical *rouges* must be destroyed. In New Brunswick, a new provincial government had belatedly introduced a single tax-supported non-denominational school system, deliberately rejecting the Ontario model of dual public and Catholic schools. French and Catholic protests had led nowhere. In Ottawa, the Conservatives refused to disallow the New Brunswick act, insisting that central governments should not interfere in provincial jurisdictions. It was an argument as important to Quebec as to any province but furious Catholics and *Canadiens* were not appeased. In 1871, Quebec's ultramontane bishops approved a "Catholic Program" and commanded faithful voters to support candidates who endorsed it. It was a weapon primarily against *rouges* but it was also designed to split the *bleus* and to shatter the convenient alliance that Lafontaine had forged in the 1840s. The Macdonald government was in trouble.

In politics, problems never come singly. By 1871, the British had claimed their price for Confederation: liberation from North American entanglements. Eager to save money and worried by the new power of Germany in Europe, William Gladstone's Liberal government wanted Britain's colonial garrisons brought home. The troops stayed just long enough to join the Red River expedition and to fend off the last Fenian attacks in 1870, but by the fall of 1871, red-coated regulars remained only at Halifax. A few hundred Canadian gunners, hurriedly recruited to guard abandoned forts, were no substitute for the $6 million a year the British garrisons had represented for the Canadian economy.

Since, as Colonel Jervois had concluded in 1864, Canada was indefensible, the British decision made military sense. It made equal diplomatic sense, for Canada's sake, to clean the slate of Anglo-American grievances. The list was long, ranging from Britain's responsibility for Confederate commerce-raiders to American negligence in the Fenian raids. Long before the plenipotentiaries met in Washington in 1871, with Sir John A. Macdonald a reluctant participant, the scenario could be predicted. Americans would bluster and threaten; the British would retreat. Canadian claims against the United States would be traded against American claims on Britain. So it happened. Canadian expectations, from fishing rights to hard cash, scattered in the wind when the Treaty of Washington was signed. Exasperated by his supercilious fellow British delegates, Macdonald had to accept their argument that lasting peace with the Americans was an inestimable benefit. The problem was that voters would not estimate it either.

Winning re-election in 1872 had become a desperate struggle, to be waged by every trick in the book. To the despair of its chief engineer Sandford Fleming, the Intercolonial was used as a vast funnel to pour contracts and patronage into the Maritimes. In Ontario, where George Brown had had his striking printers arrested, labour votes might be garnered by a law legalizing unions. Employers were reassured by an even tougher law against most strike activities. It was not enough. Everywhere, government candidates faced trouble. "Confederation is only yet in the gristle," a worried Macdonald wrote to a friend, "and it will require five years more before it hardens into bone." It was the kind of argument that usually precedes questionable expedients. Already Cartier had turned for cash to Sir Hugh Allan, and, as the campaign intensified, Macdonald followed. "I must have another ten thousand," he wired the magnate's solicitor in August 1872. "Will be the last time of asking. Do not fail me."

Macdonald won—narrowly—with 104 seats to 96, but there were too many "loose fish" on both sides to be certain. In Montreal, Cartier had lost his seat. In Ontario, farmers were furious that Macdonald had not rescued Reciprocity at Washington. Without Manitoba and a solid British Columbia, now eager for the railway, there would have been no victory. Sir Hugh would have his reward. For a million acres of land no official had ever seen and a list of other conditions, the government handed Allan a railway charter—on condition that his American partners be cut out. The old rogue agreed. The partners did not. Had they not fed most of the money to Allan for the election? The opposition would soon have the proof. A secret raid on the office of Allan's solicitor delivered a bag of evidence, including Macdonald's desperate message. Either $350,000 or $162,000 had been poured into the campaign. In any case, when even the Prime Minister earned only $8000 a year, the sum was enormous. The conclusion was obvious. "The Government got the money," explained Edward Blake, Ontario's Liberal premier, "and Sir Hugh Allan the Charter."

Brown, Blake, the dour Alexander Mackenzie, and other Ontario Liberals had always insisted that Macdonald was crooked as well as tricky. At last they had proof. Committees, a Royal Commission, and procedural delays could not stop the "loose fish" from swimming to safety. Among them, no defection counted more than that of Donald Smith, the successful negotiator of Red River. On November 3, fuelled by discreet glasses of gin, Macdonald offered a superb defence, but fatigue and alcohol sent him to bed for two days. By the time he revived on November 5, his government had collapsed. Members simply switched sides.

Macdonald's career was finished as certainly as anything in politics can be certain. His party might well follow him into obscurity. The Liberals could inherit his achievements—if they could form a government. The obvious leaders—Blake, Brown— would not serve. It was left to honest, grim Alexander Mackenzie, the immigrant stonemason who had made good in Sarnia, to become Canada's second Prime Minister and to create some unity out of the factions that had sat in opposition. On one thing they and the country could agree: wickedness must be condemned. The elections, spaced over weeks and with open voting, so that safe Liberal seats showed the trend, gave Mackenzie 138 of the 206 seats. The Conservatives held a mere 67, almost half of these in Quebec. From Manitoba came a solitary independent, willing to risk signing his name and taking his oath before fleeing for safety. The signature was that of Louis Riel.

In opposition, Liberals had assailed every nation-building policy, from better terms for Nova Scotia to the great railway. It had been easy for Macdonald to convince supporters, including Lord Dufferin, the latest Governor General, that Confederation was unsafe in Liberal hands. Yet Mackenzie had backed the project and he backed it still. The change of government brought rational, overdue reforms. Electoral corruption would surely be harder if voters used a secret ballot and if general elections occurred on the same day, not at the government's convenience. The Supreme Court, promised in the British North America Act, was created as a sop to nationalists—and promptly undermined by allowing appeals to continue to the Judicial Committee of the Privy Council in London. At Kingston, Mackenzie opened a tiny Royal Military College of Canada to train not simply officers but the engineers that a young country needed.

Yet governments inherit far more than they create. By 1876, the Intercolonial was complete to Halifax but Mackenzie's ruthless efforts to prune away corruption and waste never could correct the wandering tracks or the politically-appointed employees. The ICR was a cautionary tale for enemies of public enterprise.

When Mackenzie cancelled the Allan contract and announced that the promised Pacific railway would be built in slow stages and by the government, British Columbians claimed betrayal and promised secession. Mackenzie's critics promised another dose of corruption. What they got was painful progress from the Lakehead to the thriving little town of Winnipeg.

Progress was slow for an unexpected reason: Canada was suddenly deep in an economic depression.

The post-Confederation years had been a hot Indian summer of prosperity, continuing two decades of almost unbroken growth. Regions and industries might occasionally suffer a little but recovery came soon. Even the loss of Reciprocity in 1866 had seemed relatively painless. Good times had made Confederation easier to promote. Assuming debts, building railways, and improving transfer payments from Ottawa seemed a good idea when revenues grew even faster than spending, from $14 million in 1867 to $25 million in 1874. The first signs of trouble were visible in 1873, with banks failing in distant Vienna and trade and credit suddenly contracting. By 1874, the danger signs were so obvious that businessmen and politicians changed the subject. By 1875, the economic slump was unmistakable.

As usual, many individuals and whole communities escaped with no more than worries; some prospered so mightily that some economic historians would later deny that a depression had occurred. Contemporaries knew better. Revenues, based on import duties, fell drastically. Innocent of theories of counter-cyclical financing, Mackenzie's government set a public example of cost-cutting and, with deep regret (for free trade was Liberal gospel in Canada as well as Britain) raised tariff rates to seventeen and a half per cent. George Brown went to Washington on Mackenzie's behalf, negotiated and actually won a new reciprocity treaty only to see it trampled to death in a protectionist United States Senate. No wonder there was no money for British Columbia's railway. In a grudging compromise, extorted by British mediators, Ottawa agreed to spend $2 million a year and complete the line by 1890.

The economic crisis, with its thousands of hungry unemployed, spread to every part of Canada. By grim coincidence, the timber and shipping industries which had built the prosperity of both the Maritimes and the St. Lawrence faced new problems. The age of "wooden ships and iron men" was passing. Iron, and soon steel, hulls displaced the great ships which had drifted down the ways in Saint John, Quebec, and a dozen other Canadian ports. Nova Scotia's coal mines and a primitive iron industry could not hope to compete with British yards. Prudent merchants could shift their capital to new investments; seamen and shipyard workers simply had to move away. At Quebec and Montreal, *Canadien* shipbuilders waged violent battles for the jobs of Irish longshoremen. In Saint John, long, hopeless strikes brought the city's proud labour unions to the edge of extinction. In 1877, a disastrous fire left thirteen thousand homeless. It was a common enough catastrophe but it was almost more than the beleaguered New Brunswick city could endure.

Labour violence shifted easily to the old issues of sect and race. In 1875, Toronto police fought bloody battles to protect Catholic marchers from Protestant mobs. In Montreal, Orange processions organized to protest the local killing of members were simply banned. After the Liberal victory in 1874, Catholic Programmists no longer divided their fire between *rouges* and *bleus*. Bishop Bourget and his supporters now waged virtual holy war on the Liberals, provincial and federal, Catholic or secular. Clergy, thundering from their pulpits, had no trouble reminding the faithful that Heaven was blue and Hell was not. In 1877, the young Wilfrid Laurier was beaten in a savage by-election in his native Drummond-Arthabaska. Weeks later, he won a seat in Quebec-East. Quebec City's Archbishop Taschereau had an old hatred for Bourget and the Jesuits and a discreet affection for conservative young Liberals. Nothing was ever quite as monolithic as it seemed in French Canada.

Wilfrid Laurier and the Liberals would have a future. The frail, handsome lawyer insisted that he was the heir of Englishmen like Gladstone and Bright, not of European anti-Catholic liberals. Yet, for Liberals as a whole, that Gladstonian free-trade heritage brought political paralysis. The depression did not lift, as conventional wisdom insisted it should. Sir Richard Cartwright, the big, bewhiskered, blustering man who served as the Liberals' Minister of Finance, was an ex-Tory with a convert's fanaticism. Free trade was his gospel and he would not change it, whatever arguments might be offered by powerful deputations of businessmen and manufacturers. If Americans sent tariffs soaring, they were wrong and free trade was right. A wealth of conventional wisdom sustained him. So did his Prime Minister.

Sir John A. Macdonald thought differently. He had somehow survived his own despair, a near-defeat in Kingston, and inevitable party disaffection. Perhaps it was simply his durable, unquenchable charm. "When fortune empties her chamberpot on your head," he told a friend in 1875, "smile, and say 'we are going to have a summer shower.'" The shower had ended. Memories of the Pacific scandal were buried now by awareness of a depression, misery, hopelessness, and a government seemingly unwilling to do anything to help. Tariffs were not a heresy to Macdonald—nothing was if it won votes. Prominent manufacturers, fed up with American dumping of goods over the seventeen-and-a-half-per cent tariff barrier, had a point. They also promised more financial support than Hugh Allan had ever mustered. A summer of political picnics across Ontario in 1876 and another in 1877 taught Macdonald what people wanted and how to put his case.

Once again, Macdonald assured them, he would be the nation-builder, urging not "protection" but a "National Policy," a "judicious readjustment of the Tariff," to "benefit the agricultural, the mining, the manufacturing and other interests of the Dominion."

On September 17, 1878, for the first time in their history Canadians voted on the same day. Mackenzie was utterly confident. There might be local setbacks but huge meetings had cheered him and the rightness of his policies. Macdonald's sly scheme to tax ninety-five per cent of Canadians for the benefit of five per cent would surely destroy the Conservative party.

Instead, it destroyed Mackenzie. The 1874 election was more than reversed, with 142 Conservatives to only 64 Liberals. The popular vote, when the last figures trickled in, of 52.5% for the Tories to 46.3% for Liberal candidates. It seemed that voters preferred Macdonald drunk to Mackenzie sober; warm humanity to dry integrity.

At sixty-three, Sir John A. Macdonald could resume his work.

# 3 / National Policy

In only ten years, the Dominion had met most of the goals of Confederation. Seven provinces and the huge North West Territories ran from one ocean to the other. In 1880, when the British transferred to Canada their claims to the Arctic, Canadians heard of a third ocean few had considered in 1867. In Ottawa, the French-English stalemate was over. Even under the Liberals, Macdonald's policy of strong central government had largely prevailed. In the bad times of the 1870s, most people blamed politicians, not Confederation.

Now Macdonald was free to implement his "National Policy" and to retire triumphant. To most Canadians, it was now "NP"; as comforting and vague as any good political slogan. Sir Leonard Tilley would manage the details of the new tariff, and the corridors outside his office thronged with business deputations. More powerful capitalists met discreetly with Macdonald in a comfortable Toronto hotel room the suspicious *Globe* promptly christened "the Red Chamber." The NP forged a new alliance of business and government and so long as Liberals raged at protection capitalists would cling to the Tories as though their economic lives depended on it.

On March 14, 1879, Tilley finally announced the new tariffs. Amid the inevitable grumbling one thing was clear: from textiles to farm machinery, Canadian manufacturers could depend on a safe national market. Making that market grow was the next priority. The recipe was simple. By filling the empty Northwest with people, a flood of natural products could pour eastward to pay for a returning flow of manufactured goods. The Pacific railway must be hurried forward not simply to reassure British Columbians but to serve the government's prime economic strategy. Mackenzie's policy was too slow to suit anyone.

The most promising private developer was a Montreal-based syndicate that had bought out a bankrupt railway running from St. Paul, Minnesota, north to Winnipeg. At its head was the respectable George Stephen of the Bank of Montreal, but there were also fuzzy links with J. J. Hill, promoter of the Northern Pacific Railroad. Stephen's major partner was the man who had deserted Macdonald in 1873, the ubiquitous Donald A. Smith. Macdonald hardly hesitated; grudges were not his style. For $25 million in cash, twenty-five million acres along the line, a twenty-year monopoly and permanent exemption from local taxes on its property, Stephen's syndicate would build the line.

Again the Liberals thundered at the prodigality of the terms and the lack of guarantees. Their outrage aligned Macdonald and business more closely. The new railway would create a huge corporation whose fortunes would be bound to the Conservative party. But there were enemies too. In London, officials of the Grand Trunk warned investors against the new Canadian Pacific Railway Company. Experts warned that it would be impossible to fulfill the CPR plan of building along the northern shore of Lake Superior. The experts were wrong. The impossible simply took a little longer and cost a lot more. A formidable American engineer, William Van Horne, managed the construction and galvanized the huge labour gangs. To cut off the Northern Pacific from future Canadian business, the company abandoned Sandford Fleming's original northerly route to the Yellowhead Pass and headed straight west across the prairie, through the Palliser Triangle. Again experts snorted that the CPR would never sell the arid land. They knew nothing of a more frightening risk. As Van Horne's crews raced westwards across the flat prairie, and Andrew Onderdonk's Chinese labourers struggled eastwards through the coastal mountains, surveyors had yet to discover a pass through the difficult Selkirk Range. Only in August 1882 did reports come that a way had finally been found.

In the mood of that year, Canadians might have forgiven such colossal risk-taking. A little prosperity had returned with the new decade and the adventure of nation-building was again in style. The Liberals, now led by the high-principled but ponderous Edward Blake, offered crushing condemnation of each Macdonald policy. His "voluble virtue" could not bury the suspicion that, back in office, Liberals would either do the same as the

Tories or nothing at all. Meanwhile, the government could claim credit for each new factory and job. There were many.

An unconscious victim of the National Policy was Canada's merchant fleet, the fourth largest in the world in 1867. Ottawa worried about railways, manufacturers, and farmers; shipping policy was limited to a penurious attempt to make coastal navigation a little safer. Not even the Maritime region's powerful political spokesmen, Charles Tupper, John Thompson, and William Fielding, crusaded for the kind of laws which Britain had used to foster her own merchant marine. In the 1870s and 1880s Canadian shipping grew impressively in vessel size and efficiency; "Down-East" skippers and crew won a high reputation. It made no difference. Falling shipping rates persuaded owners to put their money elsewhere. A great industry was dying and few Canadians even mourned its passing.

In the Maritimes, new fortunes were being made. Manufacturers regularly complained that they got no protection from "Upper Canada"; in fact, they prospered. Along the line of the Intercolonial, factories sprouted in towns like Moncton and Amherst. Coal from Pictou and Cape Breton promised to fuel the new Canadian industrial revolution. Certainly growth was fastest where markets were already largest—in southern Quebec and Ontario. Railways confirmed the favourites—Montreal, Toronto, Hamilton—but they also fostered smaller cities where cheap labour could be drawn from over-sized farm families. The flow of *Canadiens* to New England mills could be diverted to Scugog, Valleyfield, and other new textile towns.

In time, Canadians would learn to condemn the new factories and the squalid houses and streets that grew up around them. Governments had cast-iron economic principles as well as political friendships to deter them from meddling with long hours, unsafe machinery, and harsh factory discipline. Factory safety laws, adopted by Ontario and Quebec by 1887, were ill-enforced and were mainly concerned with discouraging the employment of women and children. The few trade unions organized skilled workers in construction jobs, the railways, and a few old crafts like printing. The Knights of Labor, a radical and idealistic working-class movement that swept into Canada from the United States in the 1880s, won short-lived political influence for workers in Ontario and Quebec and left a residue of radical ideas and leaders, but it was almost dead by the end of the decade.

Middle-class humanitarians did as much as workers to ease some of the worst consequences of urban and industrial growth in the wake of the National Policy. Defending the sanctity of the family from drunkenness, prostitution, and bad sanitation gave the wives and daughters of the middle class their first excuse to demand a political voice. Dr. Emily Stowe, Canada's first woman doctor, mustered a variety of reforming forces in the 1880s when she helped launch a campaign for women's suffrage. Some clergy cautiously added their weight to reform causes but the intractable problems of urban life in themselves forced city councils to create more efficient police forces, recruit health inspectors, and develop water and sewage systems. Private investors also learned that monopoly franchises to provide street cars, electricity, and telephone service could be highly profitable. A little easy-going corruption among the city fathers helped confirm the deals. In 1886, reform mayors in both Montreal and Toronto waged angry, short-lived crusades against assorted municipal evils from prostitution to pit privies. The horror of contemporary American cities such as Chicago or Philadelphia spurred on their righteous followers.

In the early 1880s, most Canadians were too pleased with themselves to be critical. Benjamin Disraeli had taught British Conservatives that imperialism could win working-class votes. Canadians too were "British" and shared vicariously in the thrill of distant wars. They were flattered when Queen Victoria spared her fourth daughter, Princess Louise, to accompany her husband the Marquis of Lorne to what Disraeli affably described as "one of our great vice-royalties." But their pleasure was spiced with a determination to prove a sturdy indifference to snobbish affectation. As head of the clan Campbell, Lorne was shocked to find Canadian Campbells reluctant to doff their caps to their feudal chief.

In 1881, when the Marquis, as Canada's new Governor General, launched the Royal Society of Canada to honour the Dominion's scientific and literary achievements, the *Globe* dismissed it as "a mutual admiration society for nincompoops." The *Canadiens,* less ill at ease with intellectual distinction, rejoiced without reserve when their poet, Louis Fréchette, won the French Academy's Prix Montyon in 1880. In the same year, as part of homecoming festivities to entice *Canadiens* home from New England, Calixte Lavallée composed *Ô Canada*, a future national anthem.

By 1882, when Macdonald sought re-election, he could count on an easy victory. He took no chances, rigging the boundaries of Ontario constituencies just in case farmers really did deplore the tariff, and supporting Home Rule for Ireland to consolidate his Irish-Catholic support. The British were not amused. Nor did they welcome the creation of a powerful High Commission in London as a quasi-embassy for the Dominion. The British did not vote in Canadian elections, however, and those who did gave Macdonald 139 seats to Blake's 71. It was hard to quarrel with prosperity.

That prosperity depended on the West. In 1881, a record number of immigrants poured into Canada, and many of them headed for Manitoba. By 1883, the postage-stamp province had filled its best farmland, largely with the sons of Ontario. Winnipeg had grown from a few shacks to a town of ten thousand people— ugly, flat, but dotted with churches and schools and vacant lots that sold for an incredible $750 a running foot. Lord Lorne, travelling west in 1881, dutifully inspected the Mounted Police, two thousand loyal Blackfoot warriors, and the Rockies. His entourage of British newspapermen was properly impressed by the prospects for farming and ranching.

Suddenly, in the summer of 1883, the bubble burst. Land prices tumbled. Fortunes invested in land along the expected northerly CPR line vanished when the railway took the southern route. Almost everyone blamed Ottawa. Farmers, furious at the failure of their speculations, met to share grievances over freight rates and elevator monopolies and created the first of many prairie protest movements. Métis, who had sold the land grants received as part of the 1870 agreement and had moved west to the valley of the South Saskatchewan, again met the surveyors and saw in them the vanguard of white settlement. The buffalo hunt was gone; the railway and river steamboats threatened their livelihood as teamsters. Métis settlers wanted title to river-front lots they had staked out. Ottawa hesitated. How could the Métis be discouraged from selling their land again as so many had in Manitoba? The suggestion from Catholic missionaries—giving Métis reserves like Indians, was not helpful.

Indian reserves were not a very encouraging model. Perhaps there was no better solution for native people, once the buffalo were gone, than to form reserves and teach Indians to be farmers. More realistic answers are still hard to find. What is certain was that no one anticipated the patience or resources necessary to turn nomadic hunters into peasants. The government expected the job to be done in a generation. In 1879, when the buffalo finally vanished, Ottawa authorized government rations for starving, destitute Indian bands. Food was used as a lever to force the last roving bands to choose reserves and to pay attention to white farm instructors. After 1883, shrinking federal revenue and official impatience coalesced. To compel Indians to tend their herds and their fields, rations were cut. Ottawa stubbornly discounted police warnings that the Indian reserves were seething with resentment.

Ottawa was not wholly unreasonable though it was certainly remote. Macdonald, who kept personal control of Indian policy, understood that transition would be painful whether it was quick or slow, and that it was wiser to strengthen the police than to allow Indians to fantasize about alternatives to their agricultural future. Moreover, the government had more immediate worries as an economic slump returned. By the end of 1883, the CPR was floundering toward bankruptcy. The immigrant flow had stopped. Land sales had not provided revenue. The Grand Trunk's warnings to British and European investors had finally begun to work. In London, Sir Alexander Galt, Canada's new High Commissioner, could not get the British either to invest in the CPR or to assist emigration.

Macdonald himself was ready to retire, but so were too many of his trusted contemporaries. Tupper, urged by his wife to seek the bright lights of London, followed Galt as High Commissioner. Tilley, worn out, withdrew to Fredericton as lieutenant-governor. Macdonald's preferred successor, D'Alton McCarthy, a young Irish-born Protestant, needed his Toronto law practice to pay his debts. John Thompson, a solid, sensible Nova Scotian who had served briefly as provincial premier, came reluctantly to Ottawa in 1885. An age of religious bigotry saw in him a fatal flaw. Protestant-born, he had converted to Catholicism at his marriage, to become, in the vicious language of the day, a "pervert." From Quebec, there had come no successor to Cartier, dead from Bright's disease in 1873. Sir Hector Langevin, the portly, dignified guardian of the alliance with the clergy was, Macdonald curtly admitted, "lath painted to look like steel." Langevin was also enmeshed in the tangled corruption of his Department of Public Works. His rival was Joseph Chapleau, bold, arrogant, and opportunistic. Chapleau spoke for the old pragmatic *bleu* tradition. He despised the *Castors* or Catholic ultramontanes who mustered so many forces in his fiefdom of Montreal. Neither man could unite Quebec; either would destroy the other if he could.

After so much easy success, Macdonald found himself adrift on a sea of troubles. The grievances of Indians, Métis, or settlers were lost in the waves. In 1883, with the unfinished CPR foundering, Macdonald faced a bitter struggle with his own caucus to approve a loan. French-Canadian members, resentful that CPR spending had not helped their province enough, refused to vote until Macdonald pledged funds for the ailing, corruptly-managed North Shore Railway from Montreal to Quebec City. New Brunswickers bargained their support for a "short line" that would take the CPR from Montreal through Maine to Saint John. In a single year Canada's national debt rose by fifty per cent. By the winter of 1884–85, the CPR loan was spent, gaps remained north of Lake Superior and in the Rockies, and unpaid employees struck. The paycar sat at Montreal, empty.

Like a kind of *deus ex machina,* on March 16, 1885, came dramatic news. Police and Métis had clashed at Duck Lake, not far from Prince Albert. Twelve police and volunteers lay dead in the snow. The rest had fled. The Dominion faced its first great crisis. The peace and order which were Macdonald's prime goals for protecting and settling the West lay shattered.

The explanations were already in Ottawa, in sheaves of settler and Métis petitions and long, worried reports from police and officials. One of the petitions was the work of Louis Riel, summoned back from self-imposed exile in Montana by a Métis deputation financed by Prince Albert's white settlers. To them, Riel was the man of 1870 who had forced a distant Ottawa to do his bidding. Fifteen years, some of them in the terrible Beauport lunatic asylum outside Quebec, had transformed Riel from a young excitable politician to a moody religious visionary, bitter at his own poverty and failure. At times he now seemed content to draft petitions for land claims and more elected members in the territorial assembly at Regina and in Ottawa, underlining his own professed financial claims on the government. "My name is Riel and I want material," he told a local politician. In other moods, he created *l'Union Métisse de St-Joseph,* dreamed of a Métis empire of the South Saskatchewan and proposed that Bishop Bourget of Montreal should become the pope of the New World. Missionaries and Métis grew alarmed at sacrilege. Indians, summoned to join the new movement, listened and kept their own counsel. In Regina, Lieutenant-Governor Edgar Dewdney sent police reinforcements to the district and planned to go north later in the spring to negotiate face-to-face.

Riel did not wait. On March 18 he seized power, arresting clergy, local officials, and any who disagreed with him. Next day, he proclaimed his new provisional government, an odd theocracy he called the Exovedate. It became his preoccupation during the weeks he expected to wait while the distant government sent negotiators, as it had in 1870. At Duck Lake, he had hoped to capture the police as hostages. The bloodshed appalled him, and he allowed the battered force to escape. At the Cut Knife and Frog Lake reserves, young Cree warriors took the police defeat as a signal for war. Two whites died near Battleford and nine more at Frog Lake, two of them Catholic missionaries. Across the Northwest, panic-stricken white settlers crowded into police forts and wired Ottawa for troops and weapons.

Though caught by surprise, the government had no intention of negotiating. Instead, it improvised brilliantly. The CPR's promise that it would somehow get troops and equipment over its unfinished track was argument enough for a further loan. Within a month, an army of five thousand regulars, militia, and local volunteers had spread across the Northwest. The militia commander, Major General Fred Middleton, was old and a little pompous, but he was also able, clear-headed, and an expert in the kind of mobile warfare the 1885 campaign demanded. Within two months of Riel's proclamation of the Exovedate, Middleton's untrained, ill-armed militiamen had captured Batoche, Riel's stronghold. A few days later, Riel himself surrendered. Though Indians had fought more successfully than Riel's divided followers, their resistance collapsed with the fall of Batoche.

The 1885 Rebellion is a thicket of self-serving mythology. The CPR could pretend that it had saved the Northwest from Riel. In fact Riel saved the CPR from ruin. Canadian troops could have as easily passed through the United States: many did. The Americans were eager to help stop a dangerous threat north of their border. If any corporation made a difference, it was the Hudson's Bay Company. Without its supplies and transport, Middleton could hardly have stirred beyond the CPR track. Middleton's reputation suffered at the hands of subordinates who wanted all the credit. He set out sooner and marched faster than the experts thought prudent, split his forces only at Ottawa's insistence, and did his utmost to protect his raw troops from surprise or heavy casualties. In both purposes, he succeeded. Middleton's greatest ally was Louis Riel. Having launched his Métis and Indian followers in open revolt, Riel retreated into mystical fantasy, inhibiting every intelligent effort at self-defence. The tragedy of 1885 was not the fate of Riel but that of the people he had led. A Half-Breed Claims Commission, established before the outbreak, settled Métis land claims, but Riel's failure ended any real pressure to reassess Indian policy or the destiny of the New Nation. The rebellion of 1885 was disastrous to Indians and Métis alike.

Riel's egoism remained unquenched. At Regina, where he was allowed to use the police commissioner's office, he wrote to Macdonald to ask for a state trial in Ottawa. Once acquitted, he would like to be Premier of Manitoba. Macdonald had other plans. Those who had plotted the outbreak would be punished as a warning to anyone else who might fish in troubled waters. Investigation found no widespread conspiracy, only Riel. He was tried for high treason. Lawyers despatched by the Quebec *rouges* sought to prove that Riel was insane. A Protestant jury might agree, but when Riel spoke on his own behalf he was rational and persuasive, if long-winded. Only one verdict was possible but a jury of westerners understood Riel's grievances well enough to add their own plea for mercy. The judge condemned him to hang.

A later generation, using a later definition of "treason," sometimes insists that Riel never betrayed anyone. This is undoubtedly true. However, the language of law and that of popular parlance sometimes differs. Since no one had denied that he "levied war upon Her Majesty," it is worth remembering that it was for this kind of treason that he was condemned. Egomania, folly, and religious eccentricity also had nothing to do with the law.

Riel's sentence split Canadian opinion. Orangemen demanded vengeance for Tom Scott though Ontario opinion was far from united. *Canadiens* were as shocked by rebellion as anyone and even more horrified by the murder of missionaries, but they shifted ground as they had in 1870 and closed ranks before the Orange onslaught. Riel became the pathetic madman, alone in his Regina cell. French Canadians had refused to join the flood of western settlement, but the Métis remained their proxies and their grievances were real enough. J. Israel Tarte, a veteran *bleu* organizer, warned: "At the moment when the corpse of Riel falls through the trap and twists in convulsions of agony, at that moment an abyss will be dug that will separate Quebec from English-speaking Canada...." The decision rested with Macdonald, and it had been made long before controversy broke out. Few politicians had more contempt for public opinion—"mere newspapers" he called it—or for the Orange Lodge. Macdonald was a patient man and if Quebec colleagues insisted on allowing appeals or on more medical examinations of Riel's sanity, he would wait. His three Quebec colleagues finally gave their consent. "Old Tomorrow" had learned that political fires sooner or later die down. On November 16, 1885, Riel was hanged.

Macdonald was right. The fires would die, but not soon. On November 22, huge crowds packed Montreal's Champ de Mars. "If I had been on the banks of the Saskatchewan," shouted Wilfrid Laurier, "I too would have shouldered my musket." Even more heard Honoré Mercier, the former *bleu,* now Quebec Liberal leader and emerging as the leader of the *Parti Nationale,* a strange new alliance of *Castors* and *rouges.* "Riel, our brother, is dead," cried Mercier, "victim of his devotion to the cause of the Métis, of whom he was the leader, victim of fanaticism and treason—of the fanaticism of Sir John and some of his friends, of the treason of three of our people who sold their brother to keep their portfolios." In Ottawa, Conservative strategists manoeuvred to control the damage. On a key vote, condemning the government, sixteen French Canadians abandoned the government, but twenty-three English-speaking Liberals deserted Edward Blake's party.

In much of Canada, the scars of the Riel Rebellion soon vanished. In the West, settlers were too busy struggling with homesteads and a serious drought cycle to care very much. The notion of a Protestant Ontario ravening for Riel's blood is an ugly myth perpetuated by lazy historians. Violent editorials from the Orange *Sentinel* or the radical Toronto *News* might be set against a Liberal press which condemned Macdonald as much as Riel for the tragedy. Blake's defence of Riel in 1886 and his insistence on Laurier as his successor in 1887 were two of the decisive steps in determining the future dominance of the Liberal party, but they came from a party whose electorate was still firmly in Ontario.

It was Quebec that was transformed by the Riel affair. Anger forced politics to catch up with reality. To all appearances, Quebec had gained all that Cartier had promised from Confederation. The reward was an almost uninterrupted *bleu* dominance in provincial politics and even the luxury of internal controversy among the factions of *bleus, rouges,* and *Castor* ultramontanes. Economically, Quebec appeared to be a major beneficiary of the National Policy, with dozens of new factories. Montreal, confirmed as terminus for both of Canada's major railways, was more than ever a commercial and financial metropolis.

Yet, apart from lawyers, politicians, and a few exceptional businessmen, few *Canadiens* shared the new wealth or opportunities. The factories drew people from rural parishes into cities and towns often dominated by English-speaking Protestant elites. Slums and low-paid jobs were the French-Canadian share. Macdonald's federalism guaranteed Quebec its own cultural and religious institutions, but provinces had little money of their own to spend on projects that might not be a national priority, such as railways north and south of Quebec City or the dreams of colonization urged by the persuasive Curé Antoine Labelle. If children of the *habitants* were not to be lost to New England or the Montreal slums, huge sums were needed to settle them in the "New Quebec" of Lac St-Jean and the Saguenay or on the hilly fields of the Eastern Townships. Churches, schools, and employment must be available from the outset if settlers would accept the brutally hard work of the frontier. It all required money that *bleu* regimes at Quebec City would not or could not collect.

These were mostly dull problems, grinding below the surface. Riel's execution was an explosion. Mercier, eager for power and at odds since 1865 with the Cartier view of Confederation, seized on the feelings of isolation and impotence of French Canadians when their clear, collective desire to save the Métis leader had been ignored. Earlier, when Macdonald had deposed a Liberal-appointed lieutenant-governor at the insistence of Quebec City *bleus,* Judge Thomas Loranger had offered as part of an indignant protest a new view of Confederation as a "compact" or contract between the two founding nations of French and English. Provinces, not Ottawa, were the sovereign powers in Confederation. Growing numbers of Quebeckers absorbed Loranger's legal fiction as though it were historical truth. If it were, Quebec had been betrayed by the English and for that matter, by their own representatives in the government. An embattled people, Honoré Mercier now insisted, could not afford the luxury of political divisions. It must also abandon false dreams of sharing the great Canadian patrimony. Surely Riel had tried and now he was dead. From ultramontanes to *rouges,* French Canadians must unite. Only corrupt *bleu* opportunists would refuse.

The arguments, honed and perfected by Mercier and his lieutenants, recalled the old tradition of the compact colony of New France, the ruralism of the post-conquest clergy, the cultural separatism of Papineau. They challenged a rival tradition, reinforced by pragmatism and represented by the memory of Lafontaine and Cartier and by the very real practical power of the *bleus* in Macdonald's government. There was no monolith but there was movement. On October 14, 1886, after a provincial election in which Mercier had ridden the corpse of Riel across Quebec, his *Parti National* won a convincing victory. The Conservative stronghold was cracked. With Ontario's help, it might crumble.

That help seemed likely. Since 1873, Oliver Mowat as Liberal premier of Ontario had cemented his provincial power as Blake never could have. The little bespectacled lawyer rejoiced in the title of "the Christian Statesman," and he delegated the sordid side of politics to trusty but remote agents. It was Mowat who discovered and satisfied an Ontario appetite for moralizing and an equal taste for tiny but incessant reforms. The provincial legislature was constantly busy. The Ontario premier had also discovered a new way to fight the old Upper Canadian battles with Lower Canada. As a Father of Confederation, Mowat had been rare among the Reformers in urging true federalism and greater provincial powers. He had lost in 1867, but as an insider in the British North America Act negotiations Mowat had a shrewd idea of how to attack. The Judicial Committee of the Privy Council in London, the appeal court for a world-wide empire, reveled in its assumed expertise in everything from Roman-Dutch law to Tamil marriage customs. Of the politics and history of Canadian federalism, British judges knew nothing; of classical federalism they knew all they wanted to know. An able lawyer could do the rest.

Mowat's first major triumph had established Ontario's western boundary at considerable cost to Manitoba. No one had really cared very much about the line until rumours were heard of gold at Rat Portage, (now Kenora). Macdonald backed Manitoba's Premier John Norquay against Mowat and the Grits. The courts ruled otherwise, and Premier Mowat had the added bonus of showing that the Tories had refused to defend Ontario interests. The rumours of gold soon faded and the remote region lapsed into neglect. Mowat moved on to fresh issues. A long-drawn but victorious struggle for control over the licensing of taverns elevated the provincial responsibility for "property and civil rights" over the newly limited federal role in "peace, order, and good government." It also transferred a rich opportunity for patronage from federal Tory to provincial Liberal hands. Tavern-keepers would now be "Grits." Liquor, the best known solvent for a vote, would be dispensed by Liberals.

Thanks to Mowat, it was Ontario, not Quebec, that began the steady erosion of the strong central government Sir John A. Macdonald had hoped to entrench in 1867. When Mercier's *Parti National* took power in 1887 Mowat found an ally. He soon had others. In Nova Scotia, the anti-Confederate cause, under a Liberal label, had slowly mellowed as the old slogans lost their potency and people readjusted. A Conservative provincial government was perversely defeated on the same day in 1882 that Nova Scotians gave most of their federal seats to Macdonald's Tories. As boom turned to bust and the time for re-election approached, Premier W. S. Fielding and his Liberals returned to their old anti-Ottawa program. At the end of the 1886 session, J. W. Longley, Fielding's Attorney General, moved to repeal Nova Scotia's membership in Confederation. After speeches of passionate provincial patriotism, the motion passed, fifteen to seven with numerous abstentions. Armed with such proof of their devotion to Nova Scotia, the Liberals won twenty-eight of the thirty-eight seats. For the first and almost the only time, a provincial legislature had voted against Confederation.

The trend to provincialism was catching. In 1887, Honoré Mercier summoned his fellow premiers to Quebec City. Mowat, Fielding, Blair of New Brunswick, all Liberals, and a lonely Tory, John Norquay of Manitoba, appeared. Norquay's grievances were notorious. Once completed in November 1885, the CPR had set out to recoup its investment with all deliberate speed. Freight rates were as high as any profitable monopoly would set them. Being a monopoly was a cherished part of the CPR's contract, secured by Act of Parliament. A procession of Norquay's laws permitting rival railways were solemnly disallowed by his fellow Tories in Ottawa. Norquay, Manitoba's first Métis premier, must have known that his political career would be in danger when he consorted in Quebec with the Liberal enemy. A year later it would end.

In any case, the 1887 premiers' meeting accomplished nothing. It was a symbol. The unity of Confederation, so easily taken for granted in 1878, was splitting only a decade later. The second round of nation-building was in trouble. So was Canada.

# 4 / Political Revolution

By now the elements of Macdonald's National Policy were in place. On November 7, 1885, a white-bearded Donald Smith pounded home the last iron spike of the CPR. Passengers could soon travel the three thousand miles from Montreal to Burrard Inlet in a week. On the way, they could see the world's largest nickel deposit, accidentally discovered at Sudbury by CPR survey crews. Settlers, coming west on the CPR's colonist cars, would find land offices ready to help them locate and prove up their quarter-section grants in the vast checkerboard pattern the surveyors had laid on the prairie. At Indian Head, a government experimental farm would soon begin to wrestle with the problems of prairie agriculture. In the East, Macdonald's 1882 victory had convinced even timid investors that protective tariffs would last. New factories opened and old ones expanded, despite the return of hard times.

In Parliament, newspaper editorials, and countless country stores, the merits of the "NP" had been endlessly debated. Riel's execution, symbolically as important as the CPR in showing that the West was open for peaceful white settlement, had helped hand Quebec to Honoré Mercier. By the end of 1887, the CPR's monopoly clause had undermined Norquay and the Conservatives in Manitoba. In British Columbia, the choice of Vancouver as CPR terminus had infuriated both Victoria and New Westminster. When Onderdonk's Chinese labour stayed on as cheap labour for the province's mines and forest industry, white workers got a solid economic basis for their racial prejudices. The result was a durable, radical labour movement, toe-to-toe with powerful employers.

Eastern workers might owe their jobs to the NP's tariffs but they had little else in common with their increasingly wealthy and powerful bosses. Worried commentators warned that Canada would soon see the labour violence of the United States or the class warfare of Europe. A royal commission on the relations of capital and labour, designed to glorify the achievements of the National Policy, collected endless testimony of employer tyranny and greed. "To obtain a very large percentage of work with the smallest possible outlay of wages," a commissioner concluded, "appears to be the one fixed and dominant idea." Such scolding did not lead the Commission to suggest any significant reforms.

Farmers were even more resentful than workers. No policy could have protected them from a cycle of drought, poor yields, and low world prices, but the NP included nothing specific to please them. Western settlers complained that CPR freight rates and policies reflected all the evils of monopoly. Farmers everywhere condemned a tariff that forced them to pay more for their balers, binders, and hay rakes and, for that matter, for the boots, ribbons, and corsets their wives wanted for their Sunday best. In the 1870s, joining organizations like the Grange had helped make some farmers class-conscious but unpolitical. Now the Grange was supplanted by the militant Patrons of Industry, an American-based organization which soon had thousands of members across Ontario and the West, denouncing tariffs, monopolies, and the corruption of traditional politics.

Caught between Mercier and Mowat, with his policies under attack and the country plainly in trouble, Macdonald should have lost the 1887 election. Edward Blake wore out himself and his audiences with thoroughly documented evidence of blunders, failures, and maladministration. In Quebec, the ghost of Riel stalked every *bleu*. It was all in vain. Macdonald emerged with 126 seats to 89 and even a tiny majority in French Canada. Sick and humiliated, Blake quit.

Every problem remained and some of them grew worse as Canada followed the world deeper into the depression. Macdonald had won because Blake had been too honest to offer any panaceas. For all his denunciations, the Liberal leader could see no fundamental alternative to the NP—except, of course, his own incorruptible management.

Others insisted that Canadians had alternatives to both the NP and to the shapeless, corrupt compromises of Macdonald's pluralist politics. Since 1884, when Torontonians had formed a branch of the British-born Imperial Federation League, their rising star had been the handsome, gifted young Tory politician named D'Alton McCarthy. His arguments had a powerful appeal for those English-speaking Canadians who believed that their country would be a simpler, happier place if the battle on the Plains of Abraham had represented a final solution. The Riel affair, with Quebec's apparent insistence that the Métis leader go free because he was French, struck McCarthy's followers as a case in point. McCarthy's cold, logical mind rejected the florid excesses of Orange bigotry; it bored through to even more dangerous doctrines. Nations, he insisted, grew from common experiences and language. Canada must be British or French, Protestant or Catholic. The decision must be made firmly and soon. His audiences uproariously agreed.

McCarthy's version of British-Canadian nationalism was a perfect foil for Mercier. In his own way, McCarthy echoed all of Mercier's criticisms of the *bleus*. As premier, Mercier was scrupulously fair to his English Protestant minority, but he displayed himself as the flamboyant champion of a French, Catholic Quebec as no *bleu* premier would ever have dared. He defied anti-clerical opinion by making Curé Labelle Deputy Minister for Colonization. He visited Paris and Rome and returned bedecked with French and papal decorations. He launched railways and public works Quebec could not afford but which it badly wanted. Above all, Mercier settled the tiresome old Jesuit estates issue in a way deliberately designed to tease the Equal Righters and to win more French and Catholic votes.

So far, the Jesuit estates issue had only divided Catholics. Confiscated in 1800 when the last Jesuit in Lower Canada had died, the rich estates had helped finance both Catholic and Protestant schools. When the Jesuits had returned to Canada in 1843, they asked for their land back. Rival Catholic orders had jealously guarded their share of revenue from the land and the quarrel had poisoned Church relations for decades. Mercier's trip to Rome gave him a solution: Protestants were happy with $60,000 in compensation, another $400,000 would be shared among Catholic groups. The Pope would serve as final arbiter of the distribution of public funds. The Jesuits would regain their land.

Mercier knew perfectly well that any reference to the Pope and Jesuits would draw out Protestant militants and they rose to the bait. Across Ontario and in English-speaking Quebec, protest meetings denounced papal meddling, appealed for "equal rights for all," and demanded that Ottawa disallow the Jesuit Estates Act. Horrified at the bigotry and even more by the political folly of followers like McCarthy who had joined the campaign, Macdonald refused. By a margin of 188 to 13, Parliament agreed with the Prime Minister. Across the country, newly-created Equal Rights Associations hailed the dissenters as the "Noble Thirteen." In the rag-tag of Liberals and Tories, D'Alton McCarthy shone as a leader. Had McCarthy not preferred principle over ambition he might have succeeded Sir John A. Macdonald. In Canadian politics that made him a dangerous man.

In Manitoba, Norquay had been beaten by a lacklustre Liberal named Thomas Greenway. Within two years, Greenway's government was mired in failure and minor scandal. In the summer of 1889, McCarthy visited the West, drawing throngs to the parks and picnic grounds of raw prairie towns. In two decades, immigration had transformed the Red River colony into a little Ontario. Crowds cheered themselves hoarse at McCarthy's assault on separate schools and French. Westerners, he claimed, had the power "to make this a British country in fact as in name." Greenway Liberals, bereft of policy, heard the cheers and took the hint. In 1890, a new law gave the little province its first "national school" system, non-denominational, English-speaking, and publicly financed. Greenway's party won a new and bigger majority. The guarantees that missionaries and Métis had won in the Manitoba Act of 1870 had apparently vanished under majority assault. Now it was up to Ottawa to provide remedies.

Between them, Mercier and McCarthy severely damaged the *bleu*-Tory alliance that had effectively held power since 1854. In Manitoba, McCarthy's views had been seized on by Liberals. For the party's untried new federal leader, that was acutely embarrassing. In retiring, Blake had insisted that Wilfrid Laurier must be his successor. The young Quebec politician hesitated. He had neither the health nor the private wealth for the job. Even worse, in the mood of the times, could a French-speaking Catholic ever be accepted by the Grit strongholds of Ontario? Party elders agreed with the reservations but Laurier would do in the interim while a real decision was deferred. The interim leader lasted thirty-two years.

Party strategists agreed on one point: Blake had lost in 1887 because he failed to provide the "heroic remedy" Canadians wanted. One was now available. Erastus Wiman, a New York millionaire and Canadian expatriate, and Samuel Ritchie, the American who had developed Sudbury's nickel, urged a "Continental Union" of Canada and the United States with a common customs wall against the world. If full annexation followed, so be it. Massive Canadian emigration to the United States and the failure of the National Policy already marked Confederation as a failure. "CU," as the scheme was abbreviated, delighted inveterate free-traders like Sir Richard Cartwright. Ned Farrer, the lively journalist who now edited the *Globe,* took up the idea. So did Goldwin Smith, the former Oxford professor who had moved to Toronto, married a rich widow, and appointed himself Canada's resident intellectual. Annexation, Smith believed, was only a logical first step to an entire English-speaking union. Americans would accomplish what timid Canadians had failed to do: the full assimilation and reform of the French-Canadian Catholics.

For Laurier, annexation was repugnant; even a customs union was too heroic. A more moderate version—unrestricted reciprocity—was ideal. Tariff barriers between the two countries would vanish but each would set its own tariffs against the world. The economic details never bothered Laurier; it was politics that mattered. Unrestricted reciprocity satisfied party veterans like Cartwright. It gave the Liberals a compact slogan to match "NP." Above all, it captivated Ontario farmers, distracting them from Laurier's race and religion and his accented, if eloquent, English. Even loyal Canadians still pined for the old Reciprocity Agreement. The flood of emigrants depopulating Ontario as well as Quebec farms confirmed what visitors reported: the United States was booming while Canada stagnated. Friedrich Engels, Karl Marx's partner, finally had a good word for capitalism when he visited Canada in 1888. After three days of seeing decaying towns and ruined farmsteads, he realized "how necessary the feverish speculative spirit of the Americans is for the rapid development of a new country...." Canadians who agreed could make their choice between CU and unrestricted reciprocity.

Either policy threatened an end to an independent Canada. Did anyone care? By the end of the 1880s, many agreed with Laurier himself: "We have come to a period in the history of this

110

young country when premature dissolution seems to be at hand." In Winnipeg, the *Free Press* warned Newfoundland, bankrupt and considering Confederation, to give the Dominion a wide berth. "There are few provinces, if any, in it today that would not rejoice to be out of it." J. W. Longley, the Liberal who had tried in 1887 to repeal Nova Scotia's membership in Confederation, now travelled the United States as Wiman's agent promoting Continental Union.

Yet envy of the Americans mingled with fear and resentment. In 1890, Canadians had plenty of reason to see the harsh as well as the prosperous side of their neighbours. On both coasts, fisheries agreements had proved costly and painful. In the Bering Sea, American warships seized Canadian sealing vessels in the name of conservation while American sealers went undisturbed. James Blaine, the new Secretary of State, had made his name with Irish voters as an enemy of Britain and Canada. In Congress, the new McKinley tariff promised to end Canada's important grain trade across the border. In his speaking tours in 1890, Macdonald found that farmers could talk of little else.

The Old Chieftain's first notion was to outflank Laurier. He would seek a modest new reciprocity agreement and unveil it for the inevitable 1891 election. But Blaine refused to see an official delegation from a mere British colony. He then told a curious congressman that he knew of no Canadian negotiations, and the scheme blew up.

Macdonald was forced into another strategy—bolder, more dangerous, and yet far closer to his heart. The talk of dissolution and annexation and continental union disgusted him. In 1887, he had fought a winter campaign with draughty meeting halls, icy sleigh-rides, and long hours in unheated railway cars; he did not want another, but time was not on his side. On February 2, 1891, Macdonald called the election. Experts foresaw defeat. Yet, as long as he lived, the old Conservative alliance would survive. Business would fill the party coffers to protect the NP, and William Van Horne could promise that every CPR employee was "a circumcised Tory." And one issue might again pull weary voters back to the Conservatives: loyalty. Louis Kribs, a German-Canadian journalist, coined the slogan: "The Old Man, the Old Flag, the Old Policy."

Across Canada, even in Quebec, Macdonald could summon personal loyalty. There was more. "A British subject I was born, a

British subject I will die," he told his audiences. "With my utmost effort, with my latest breath, will I oppose the 'veiled treason' which attempts with sordid means and mercenary proffers to lure our people from their allegiance." Posters, more elaborate than in any earlier elections, depicted Laurier and Cartwright negotiating with Americans behind the Old Chieftain's back. Two weeks into the campaign, Macdonald revealed the "treason": printers' proofs of a pamphlet by Edward Farrer not just arguing for annexation but showing precisely how America could squeeze Canadians into surrender. Since Ned Farrer edited the leading Liberal newspaper, the link to Laurier hardly needed to be made.

Laurier was not helpless. In Quebec, Mercier gave his full support. In Ontario, Mowat was staunch and as unquestionably pro-British as Macdonald. The Grit farmers liked the Liberal trade policy. So did Quebec farmers, for all the warnings from their bishops that annexation might result. On March 5, the great loyalty campaign ended. In Quebec, Laurier took 37 seats to 28; in Ontario, Macdonald emerged with a mere 4-seat margin. It was the rest of Canada—the "shreds and patches," as Cartwright called them—that settled the outcome: for Macdonald, 121 seats, for Laurier, 94. The margin came not only from the CPR-dominated regions but also from the Maritimes, where the call of British loyalty had worked.

Three months later, Macdonald was dead. The campaign had killed him. He died believing that he had saved the country he had created. Many of the nation's three-quarters of a million voters felt that they knew him, with his huge nose and his flying hair, his wit and his patient cynicism. "You'll never die, John A.," the crowds had shouted and now that he was suddenly gone, without an obvious successor, it seemed possible that the young Dominion might die with him. It dismayed his contemporaries and later generations that the undoubted first Father of Confederation could never provide uplifting moral lessons for the young. In fact, Macdonald had shown how Canada could be managed; with infinite cunning and patience, by bold visions and an infinity of small compromises, and by remembering that every enemy might someday be needed as a friend.

Macdonald had also taught patience. "A week is a long time in politics," said a later British prime minister. Macdonald knew it well. Riel, equal rights, Jesuit estates, had barely mattered in 1891,

112

and with luck they might vanish forever. The census of that year furnished all the statistical evidence of depopulation critics of the NP desired, but the election was over when the figures appeared, and a new boom was building. British markets absorbed the wheat excluded by the McKinley tariff and asked for more. In the Kootenays of British Columbia, a mining boom began to roar, worrying only because it was American-financed. Talk was heard of a new railway through the Crowsnest Pass.

As Canadian self-confidence recovered, the Liberals could question themselves and their new leader. The 1891 session brought some comfort. J. Israel Tarte, the Quebec Tory organizer and Chapleau's ally, had slowly exposed the corrupt tangle of contracts and kickbacks in Langevin's Department of Public Works. Now, as a Liberal convert, Tarte forced the new Parliament into a session of scandals. One MP and a cluster of officials went to jail. Langevin might well have joined them but for a timely resignation. Liberal rejoicing was premature. Suddenly, Honoré Mercier's own corruption lay exposed in the scandalous finances of the Baie des Chaleurs Railway. All Canada could know how his luxurious journeys to Paris and Rome had been financed. Provincial Conservatives swept the discredited regime from office and then settled down to the dry, unpopular business of restoring Quebec's financial credit. Mercier countered Langevin. All politicians were tarred with the same brush.

Liberal troubles were not over. Blake and even Mowat had seen the annexationist implications of Laurier's policy of unrestricted reciprocity. Both men had loyally kept silent, but now, with the election over, Blake explained in a public letter why he had not stood again in West Durham. His letter virtually accused his fellow Liberals of plotting treason. It was all that Macdonald could have wished.

Blake himself never expected the devastating consequences of his letter. After every general election, the parties laid a host of challenges for electoral malpractice. Always, party managers had met, traded off cases and settled on a few to be fought through the courts and in by-elections. This time, with their coffers bulging, the Tories insisted on trying every charge. The Liberals, penniless, had no means to defend themselves. In a flood of by-elections, the West Durham letter sent the party to defeat. By 1895, the Tory majority had climbed from thirty-one to sixty-three. To many

Liberals, it was proof enough that Laurier's leadership had been a sad mistake. Even without the Old Chieftain, the Tories seemed unbeatable.

Appearances deceived. One small nagging issue slowly tore the government apart: the Manitoba schools.

Macdonald had put off the issue, as he had so much else. A strong successor could have made a decision, confident that the inevitable turbulence would have settled in the four or five years before another election. No competent lawyer could question the issues. As a province, it was obvious that Manitoba could enact its Schools Act. Under the remedial sections of the Manitoba Act, Ottawa was equally obliged to take action to restore the rights of the French and Catholic minority. The questions of majority rights, Protestantism, or a mythical compact of founding nations were not at stake: the only issue was the political will to enforce the law.

Macdonald had no strong successor. Instead, a cabinet of feeble ministers chose old Sir John Abbott, the one-time annexationist of 1849, because he was "not particularly obnoxious to anybody." If Abbott had then promoted the ambitious Joseph Chapleau to be his lieutenant he might have found himself a new Cartier, but he would also have hurt poor Sir Hector Langevin's feelings. Abbott did nothing, and by November 1892 he was gone, fed up with politics.

Abbott's successor was inevitable: Sir John Thompson. Rarely had a more decent or honourable man come to Ottawa. His wisdom and ability were apparent in the Criminal Code and his other reforms as Minister of Justice. Dignified, an able debater, widely knowledgeable, Thompson had one political affliction, his conversion to Catholicism. As Prime Minister, he could never rise up and flatten the bigots who called him "pervert." He would not promote Chapleau because the Orangemen would have protested, so the last great *bleu* left for gilded retirement as Lieutenant Governor of Quebec. Thompson was left with the extremes, F. A. Angers, an ultramontane *Castor* whom Chapleau had despised, and N. Clarke Wallace, past grand master of the Orange Lodge.

For all his sober virtues, Thompson was not the man to solve the Manitoba issue. Instead, he sent it back to the courts for two more years, forcing the Manitoba minorities to wait and showing even the most patient French Canadian that Ottawa would do almost anything to avoid upholding equality of language and religion in the West. Only a month before the Judicial Committee decided the obvious—that Ottawa had the right to impose remedial legislation—Thompson suddenly died at Windsor Castle while visiting Queen Victoria.

By rights, Sir Charles Tupper should have become Prime Minister but in the cabinet some ministers shuddered at the thought of the decisive, bullying "War Horse of the Cumberland." They were saved by an unexpected ally. Lord Aberdeen, a Scottish Liberal, now was Governor General, but it was the formidable Lady Aberdeen who was in charge. Like many others, though for obscure reasons, she detested Tupper. Left to herself, she might have summoned Laurier, but her husband compromised. Another ancient veteran, Senator Mackenzie Bowell, an honest but indecisive Orangeman, followed Thompson. All hope of firm action on Manitoba faded. First Angers and then Wallace left the cabinet. Canadians, once again in a state of gloom after a new world-wide economic crash in 1893, could divert themselves with the government's fumbling.

First, Bowell politely asked Manitoba to mend its ways. Clifford Sifton, the province's able Attorney General, waited eight months before saying no. Seven federal cabinet ministers, in January 1896, resigned in a body to force the hopeless Bowell to quit. First Bowell branded them a "Nest of Traitors"; then he took them back. Parliament, nearing the end of its five-year term, set out to debate remedial legislation for the Manitoba minority while the Liberals held up proceedings with endless speeches. In May, the session expired.

Manitoba was as dangerous to Laurier as it was to the Tories. The Liberal leader had fumbled his first test; the second seemed even harder. In 1893, the Liberals met in Ottawa in their first national convention, buried "unrestricted reciprocity" and came up with a compromise. They did not resolve the Manitoba issue. Laurier was caught between the Protestant Liberals of Ontario and Manitoba and the pledge, brought by the great missionary from the Northwest, Father Lacombe, that Quebec's bishops would rise as one man to support remedial legislation.

Canada in the 1890s seemed aflame with religious conflict. The fires set by the Equal Rights Association had not gone out. In 1894, a Protestant Protective Association in Ontario had elected fourteen members against Oliver Mowat. In Quebec, the old Holy War against the Liberals was being fanned into life. What could a French-Canadian Catholic with a following in Protestant Canada do?

The answer was that he would do nothing. It was the first proof that Laurier was Sir John A's true disciple. Israel Tarte, the ex-*bleu*, was now his closest confidant. In Quebec, where the turncoat had applied his remarkable talents to building a Laurier machine, Tarte made a crucial discovery: ordinary French Canadians knew little and cared less about Manitoba. They did not intend to go there. They did not care much for the few who had. On the other hand, with both Macdonald and Mercier gone, and a colourless Conservative government in Quebec City, *Canadiens* yearned for a real political leader. Wilfrid Laurier was the only candidate.

Faced with this shrewd analysis, Laurier's course was clear: silence and inaction. It was, after all, the ultimate privilege of an opposition leader. Forced to speak, Laurier recalled the old French fable of the man who had shed his coat for the sun, not the wind. Coercion, he warned, would never work: "If it were in my power, I would try the sunny way." It was a message that Tarte could sell on Laurier's behalf; he believed in it himself. Outside Quebec, Laurier could preach provincial rights. It was now a safe doctrine everywhere.

On April 23, the 1896 election campaign began. By prior agreement, Tupper took over as Prime Minister, the fifth in five years. Everywhere in Tory ranks, he found division and defection. Chapleau refused to help the party that had ignored him; secretly he sent *bleu* supporters to Laurier. In Ontario, Tory candidates preached hostility to the remedial legislation they had supposedly spent months trying to push through Parliament; in Quebec, the Conservatives proclaimed their devotion to minority rights. Above all, they counted on the bishops. When the bishops met, they proclaimed it "a great wrong" to back any candidate who refused to back remedial action. Promptly, all but eight of Laurier's Quebec candidates swore their support for remedial legislation. Only Bourget's disciple, Bishop Laflèche, issued his customary flaming denunciation of the Liberals. He was echoed by some Ontario Protestants. A Liberal vote, warned one Methodist preacher, "would stare the voter in the face at Judgement Day and condemn him to eternal perdition."

116

Despite the air of religious intolerance, clerical threats had surprisingly little effect in 1896. In fact, it was Sir Charles Tupper who was his party's chief asset. The dogged old man, tirelessly bullying his worn-out party machine into action, could not deliver a victory; he certainly prevented a rout. Though both D'Alton McCarthy and N. Clarke Wallace campaigned as hard for Laurier as they did for themselves, Tupper revived the old issues of industry and tariff protection. When the polls closed, Laurier's Liberals had won 118 seats to Tupper's 88. The Patrons of Industry, rustic pioneers for the third parties of the future, elected three members from Ontario.

In an election full of ironies and reversals, the greatest was in Manitoba. Only with great difficulty could the two Protestant champions, Sifton and McCarthy, get themselves elected. Manitobans voted forty-seven per cent for the party of remedial legislation, and only thirty-five per cent for the Liberals.

A political revolution was complete. Canadians in 1896 could not know it, but the Liberals would prove even more durable in office than the Conservatives. Neither period of hegemony was unbroken. Macdonald had lost to Mackenzie; Laurier would lose to Robert Borden. Yet both parties would regain power and cling to it because Macdonald and Laurier each mastered the compromises that made Canada possible.

Like most revolutions, the political upheaval that occurred in Canada between 1886 and 1896 changed symbols, not substance. The Liberals had won and would continue to win if they remembered their core of support in Quebec, the firm guidance of the business community, and the scattered, contradictory grievances of the rest of Canada. Sir John A. Macdonald had found his successor at last.

# PART III

# "The Century of Canada"

# 1 / Flourishing

Later, Canadians would know that 1896 was one of the decisive years of their history. At the time, they barely noticed. Of course politics and the election were national preoccupations. On the other hand, few Canadians were bothered by a dispute between Venezuela and British Guiana that almost brought Britain and the United States into war—with Canada as the inevitable battleground. Apart from buying a few rifles and machine guns for her ill-equipped militia, the Dominion did nothing. In Britain, as we shall see, the consequences were much more profound. History rarely shows its significance all at once.

Canadians also ignored other vital events of the year. Washington announced the end of homesteading on public lands. Manitoba offered William Mackenzie and his burly partner Donald Mann $7000 a mile to build a line from Gladstone to Dauphin. They agreed. In August, a man known as "Lying George" Carmack, with two Indian companions, Skookum Jim and Tagish Charlie, discovered a little gold near the Klondike River.

All three developments were probably as important to Canadians as Laurier's 1896 election victory. So were others. Gold, pouring out of South African mines by the 1890s, would send prices for food and other natural products climbing. Shipping rates stayed low, continuing the slow strangulation of an old Maritime industry but making it feasible again to pour wheat into the European market. At Niagara Falls in 1895, workmen began the first hydro-electric installation. When Canadian engineers had solved the problem of winter freeze-up, "white coal" would provide a basis for dramatic industrial growth.

Instead of hope, most Canadians in 1896 shared a durable gloom. The Bank of Commerce reported in June on a year "of constant anxiety and almost unexampled difficulty in making profits and avoiding losses." Farmers grumbled at the McKinley tariff. Worse would come when the Republicans, as now seemed inevitable, returned to power. A promising cattle trade with Britain ended abruptly with severe quarantine regulations.

Meanwhile, Laurier's victorious Liberals took power. The hand-over was graceless. Tupper had made a post-election bid to cram every vacant judgeship and Senate seat with a Tory. The Aberdeens refused to sign the appointments, and the old man resigned in a snarling constitutional fury. Most Canadians were amused at Tupper's failure to fill jobs before voting day, when the patronage might have won him votes or campaign funds.

The new Prime Minister would make no such errors. Laurier looked frail, but he had grown tougher with age. Voters and even colleagues knew him as an elegant, courtly man, with an aura that could inspire love but never familiarity. Laurier had no taste for laborious detail; he could be captivated by ideas and he had the language to captivate others. His ministers sometimes came to believe that Laurier was a charming lightweight, to be used for their purposes. Such men were dismissed with swift, icy ruthlessness; they found themselves so isolated that they could not even avenge themselves. On the low road of politics as on the high, Laurier was a consummate expert.

He showed his skills immediately. The new cabinet was the ablest Canada had yet seen. William Fielding, one of three provincial premiers brought to Ottawa, took finance. Cartwright, still the unrepentant free trader, was relegated to trade and commerce. The tariff would be safe with Fielding. Old *rouge* comrades were set aside. Tarte, the link with the *bleus,* would wield the immense patronage of public works. To settle Manitoba, Laurier adopted more than "sunny ways." To earn his cabinet post, Clifford Sifton helped talk Thomas Greenway into a compromise. Manitoba's minorities could go to school in their own language if they could form classes of ten or more students. Religious instruction would occur at the end of the day. Catholic bishops threatened new holy wars at the inadequacy of the settlement, but a papal envoy insisted on restraint. The old, dangerous issue vanished and the bishops found some pleasure in dealing with a French and Catholic Prime Minister.

Laurier took office with no real policies. He simply inherited the old NP. History played into his hands. Essentially, the National

120

Policy had rested on false assumptions. In the 1880s, Canada was not yet an east-west economy. Her products went to Britain, the United States, or stayed home unsold. Immigrants would never go to the Northwest while good American land remained. Macdonald's policy flew in the face of facts. Suddenly, the facts changed. American public land was closed in 1896. The Canadian prairies became the "Last Best West." Rising world prices and cheap shipping created a world market for the hard spring wheat from Canada. It was now Laurier who could claim that "this scientific tariff of ours" safeguarded a booming western market for Canadian manufacturers.

Laurier's good fortune was as much an accident as was Carmack's discovery of gold with the resulting fever that summoned swarms of prospectors to the Yukon. The Klondike made few durable fortunes and established no permanent industry. By 1899 the bonanza was over. The gold rush poured a brief but dramatic economic stimulus into British Columbia and Alberta, and it drew a flood of attention to Canada. The photographs of sourdoughs and the Chilkoot Pass did not dispel the Dominion's image of "Our Lady of the Snows" but they did replace the impression of stagnant decay absorbed by Engels in 1888 with a vision of dynamism and wealth and of firm law and order enforced by scarlet-coated policemen.

As Macdonald's heir, Laurier responded to the Klondike discovery much as the Old Chieftain might have. Mounted Police, then troops, were sent because order was vital, not merely for its own sake but to give Americans in nearby Alaska no pretext for intervention. A railway link was considered but abandoned as too costly and slow. By 1899, when many of the thirty thousand people began thinking of leaving, a Yukon territorial government was in place.

It was probably Canada's good fortune that so many Americans had always believed that the northern prairie was as cold as the Yukon. This illusion had discouraged neighbourly covetousness. Now, with no other outlet for the younger sons who had always gone west to homestead, Americans came to see for themselves. Clifford Sifton, Minister of the Interior, had the happy historical role of presiding over the inevitable. He did so with flair. Editors and farm leaders joined guided tours. Lush prairie produce was sent to win prizes at agricultural shows. The claims of Red Fife wheat were trumpeted until it was supplanted, in 1903, by an even finer product of the Dominion's experimental farms, Charles Saunders's Marquis. Visitors revelled in Sifton's philosophy. "One of the principal ideas western men have," he boasted, "is that it is right to take anything in sight provided nobody else is ahead of them."

American homesteaders, often with an Ontario ancestor or two, made an easy transition. Most had experience in dryland farming and the backing of a family farm in Kansas or Minnesota. Sifton, however, was not content to wait. Bales of pamphlets and speakers armed with magic lantern slides set off for the traditional recruiting territory of Britain. Colonization agents waited at Hamburg and Bremen, where European immigrants would set sail for America. In his aim of populating the Canadian West, Sifton was bluntly indifferent to the old limits of race and language. Instead, he welcomed "stout, hardy peasants in sheepskin coats," who could endure pioneering hardships and make the prairie prosper. If they were Poles or Germans or Ukrainians the "national schools" he had won for Manitoba would turn their children into good Canadians.

The newcomers justified Sifton's expectations. The North West Mounted Police, whose systematic patrols and hard-headed welfare programs were as vital to prairie homesteading as railways and land offices, judged "Sifton's sheepskins" with a stern but practical eye and found them acceptable. Others did not pass their test. Keir Hardie, the Scottish socialist, was shocked to find that English labourers were among the least favoured species of settler. Employers complained that they often brought trade union ideas with them. Meanwhile Canadian labour protested immigration policies that undermined their wages with floods of cheap labour.

With or without Sifton, the Canadian West's time had come. Between 1896 and 1911, more than a million people poured into the region. Wheat production rose from 29 to 209 million bushels a year. A spider web of railway branch lines spread across the prairie, built mainly by homesteaders eager for cash between seeding and harvest time. Ten miles was as far as any settler could haul wheat in a horse-drawn wagon. Where rail lines crossed, towns grew up. In the Sifton free-enterprise spirit, land speculators were free to build costly dreams of future metropolises on local pride and cupidity. Sometimes the land speculators struck paydirt. In 1900, Saskatoon was a general store. In 1902, it was hard to find twenty houses to make it a village. Three years later it was a city, and the 1911 census found twelve thousand people, a university, and two transcontinental railways.

Prairie settlers had little in common with the self-sufficient backwoodsmen in Upper Canada or the *habitants* of New France. Beyond turf for their first leaky sod hut and a flurry of birds and small animals for the pot, the land provided nothing but a cash crop. Pioneers were consumers. To build homes, they needed lumber from British Columbia and nails, glass, and furniture from the East. Even fuel for the long prairie winter came from coal mines that Sir Alexander Galt's sons had profitably developed in the foothills of the Rockies. It was all very much as Sir John A. Macdonald would have predicted, with the infuriating exception that Liberals were in power, taking the political and (in Sifton's case) the personal profits.

In 1897, for example, it was perfectly in the NP tradition that the CPR would receive a handsome subsidy for pushing a line through the Crowsnest Pass to Vancouver. This restored a Canadian presence in a region American mining companies were treating as their own backyard. The CPR gained subsidies, a new region, and an unexpected dividend, the rich Sullivan mine at Trail. In return, the railway agreed to a perpetual freeze on the freight rates for wheat heading east and manufactured goods heading west. In an age of stable prices, the Crowsnest rate seemed like a fair deal.

Meanwhile, in 1898, unremarked by most Canadians, the Intercolonial Railway finally reached Montreal in its long struggle to become profitable. In its patronage-ridden career, the ICR had served its region as best it could. Unlike the CPR, which thirsted for profits, the ICR wanted political friends, and it had found them by cutting its rates. It did so still. Maritime producers got rates as much as fifty per cent lower than in central Canada—and even lower ones could be negotiated. While the Maritime age of wood, wind, and water was ending, industrialism had already taken its place. In 1870, New Brunswick's per-capita manufacturing had been as high as the national average, and it kept on growing. From 1900 to 1920, manufacturing grew four-fold in Nova Scotia and five-fold in New Brunswick. Two iron and steel complexes developed; so did sugar refining, clothing and shoe factories, and a host of engineering and hardware manufacturers. Thanks to the ICR's favours, even prairie residents used Simms's brushes, ate Ganong's chocolates, and spread Crosby's molasses. The Maritimes grumbled and prospered, a satisfying combination.

At times, Laurier could even improve on Macdonald. Caught among his party's protectionists and free-traders, with a rising chorus of imperialists in Toronto and English-speaking Montreal, a fumbler might have failed. Between them, Fielding and Laurier united such disparate forces by proclaiming, in the 1897 budget, a unilateral "imperial preference." The tariff reductions hurt few entrenched interests, pleased tariff cutters, and helped Laurier cut an imperial figure when he went to London for the Diamond Jubilee of the venerable Queen Victoria. British audiences delighted in the frail, eloquent French Canadian. Private sessions were a little different. The colonial secretary, Joseph Chamberlain, found the newly-knighted Sir Wilfrid obdurate in resisting British schemes to win Canadian commitments to imperial defence.

This, too, was in the Macdonald tradition. The old man had despised "over-washed Englishmen." D'Alton McCarthy's "imperial federation" Macdonald had dismissed as nonsense. British overtures for military aid in 1885 during the Sudan crisis had been politely rejected. Militia colonels "anxious for excitement or notoriety," according to Macdonald, would not speak for Canada. In 1891, when Macdonald had proclaimed "a British subject I was born, a British subject I will die," he had meant no more than had Laurier in 1897, when he declared to London audiences, "I am British to the core." Neither man could contemplate being an American; the alternative was to be British. The English were something else.

Among some English-speaking Canadians, the British connection was becoming more important. To McCarthy and imperial federationists in the 1880s, being British had also been an alternative to the shame of being merely Canadian, the people of a failing country that still refused to be American. Now, in the post-1896 prosperity, the Canadian mood was vastly more positive. British imperialism, in its sensationalist heyday, offered the vulgar conceit of racial superiority. Its American counterpart, triumphant in Cuba and the Philippines in 1898, offered the same appeal.

Sprayed by the same effusions, many Canadians accepted a flattering new kind of "imperial nationalism." If, as British and American imperialists insisted, northern races would dominate those in warmer climates, who could be more northerly than Canadians? In no distant era, Canada would dominate the British Empire. Meanwhile, in the novels of Gilbert Parker and the Rev. C. W. Gordon (writing as Ralph Connor) they could rejoice in the fictional triumphs of physical and moral courage. They could yearn for Canada to be summoned to play a heroic role.

Such dreams, fostered by an outspoken English-Canadian elite, were not universal. Imperialism was as absurd as ever to families with their roots deep in Ontario or Maritime soil and their minds preoccupied with economic realities. *Canadiens* remembered Mercier's warning that the imperialists would conscript their sons and send them to perish on the burning Sahara. On suitable occasions it was polite to attribute *la survivance* to British justice; most French Canadians naturally preferred to keep the credit themselves. The clergy might preach a dutiful allegiance, but they could not urge love. No more than English Canadians did the *Canadiens* know or care what their partners in Confederation really felt.

Sir Wilfrid was almost uniquely knowledgeable. Years before, he had given Toronto his most memorable image of Canadian duality. Recalling the waters of the Ottawa River and the Great Lakes, meeting below the island of Montreal, he had declared: "There they run parallel, separate, distinguishable, and yet are one stream, flowing within the same banks. . . ." Under Laurier, pure luck had given Liberalism an almost mystical association with prosperous times. It was Laurier himself who committed his party to the holy grail of national unity.

His test came in 1899 with the crisis in distant South Africa. Two tiny Boer republics had concluded that preservation of their Old Testament lifestyle compelled them to drive the British into the sea. In ordinary times, Britain would have met the challenge alone but her own diplomacy had isolated her from the European powers. The approaching war might even be deterred if self-governing colonies voluntarily displayed their solidarity; at the very least, Europe would be impressed. Laurier cheerfully won unanimous Canadian parliamentary approval for Britain's opposition to the Boers. An official contingent was another matter. If

Britain were in real danger, Canada would respond with utter devotion. The Boers posed no such threat. Of course the British were perfectly entitled to recruit soldiers in Canada. As well the outspoken Tory MP and imperial loyalist, Colonel Sam Hughes, promised to raise thousands of volunteers. Neither arrangement met Britain's need to display imperial solidarity to a hostile world.

Laurier's cautious policy collapsed within two weeks of the outbreak of war in October 1899. In Toronto and Montreal, concerted press campaigns by Tory and popular newspapers demanded action. Embarrassing leaks in Ottawa about a planned contingent suggested government duplicity. Some Liberal ministers pressed for an official force. On October 14, Laurier gave in. In an unexpected display of efficiency, a battalion of a thousand volunteers was recruited, equipped, and despatched to Cape Town by the end of the month. Another contingent left early in 1900. Donald A. Smith, now Lord Strathcona and Canadian High Commissioner in London, sent a mounted regiment at his own expense. Though the British paid almost the full cost of the troops in South Africa, the men served as Canadians, performed well, and incidentally, came home with a stronger sense of national identity than stay-at-homes would have expected. Under Colonel William Otter, the Canadians had been trained and disciplined like regulars, not like wild colonials. The precedent would stick.

The warlike experience might have united Canadians in a new pride, as it did Australians. In fact, it added a new cause for division. In Montreal, news of a British victory led to boisterous fights between French- and English-speaking university students. In Ontario, Tories insisted that Laurier had been controlled by the wicked J. Israel Tarte and that French Canadians had proved their disloyalty in Britain's hour of need. As usual, one extremism called forth its counterpart. Jules-Paul Tardivel, the Kentucky-born convert to Quebec ultramontane nationalism, offered his readers new and more passionate arguments against Canada in his Montreal-based journal, *La Vérité*.

Those were not the arguments of the bearded young MP for Labelle. Henri Bourassa, Papineau's grandson, was a lifelong admirer of Laurier but he was too intelligent, too logical, and too proud to be anyone's disciple. The despatch of an official contingent had shocked him and he forced Parliament to debate the issue. Had Laurier bowed to imperial coercion? Had he set a fearful precedent for future British wars? If so much had been done against two tiny, distant nations, Bourassa asked, "how many men shall we send, and how many millions shall we expend to fight a first class power or a coalition of powers?" From Laurier, there came only denials that any precedent had been set.

Bourassa was no threat—yet. As the 1900 election approached, it was Ontario that threatened Laurier's majority. Across Canada, poor Tupper's collection of government scandals and misjudgements dwindled to absurdity in such unexpected prosperity. It was no real argument to claim that the Liberals had stolen Conservative policies: political larceny was no crime. Ontario Tories, left to their own devices, could exploit only the old racial and religious hatreds. The Liberals cheerfully ensured that *Canadien* and Irish voters were listening. A phrase of Tupper's, "Laurier is too English for me," was torn from context and blazoned across Ontario by the Liberals—admittedly to little effect. Tupper took Ontario but little else. Laurier held 133 seats to the Conservatives' 80. The Tories had become what the Liberals had been, a party of outsiders, tied to the prejudices of Ontario. An Ottawa editor mourned that his party had "Francophobia on the brain."

The need for national unity had persuaded a reluctant Laurier to send troops to South Africa. So had a more pragmatic concern: British diplomatic leverage was needed for Canada's final boundary dispute. In 1898, a joint high commission had left two painful issues of Canadian-American relations unsettled: reciprocity and the Alaska boundary.

Until the Klondike discoveries, no one had bothered about the vague, straggling line down misleading maps of the Alaska Panhandle, or about the 1825 Anglo-Russian treaty that had placed the line there. Surely British pressure would help the Americans to be reasonable. Nothing was more unlikely. President Teddy Roosevelt, in the full flush of American imperialism, was in a bullying mood. Businessmen in Seattle and Tacoma were eager for northern wealth. Britain had decided its North American course in 1896: war was not an option. Moreover, three-quarters of a century of neglect had enfeebled a weak Canadian-British case. On October 17, 1903, the British delegate, Lord Alverstone, refused to cause "an international calamity." He sided with three partisan American commissioners, leaving two equally partisan Canadians to cry foul. Roosevelt's view of the

127

Alaska boundary prevailed. Canada was shut out from access to the Yukon.

More fortunate than Macdonald in 1871, Laurier was free to blame the British for the Alaska boundary fiasco. It is still hard to see Lord Alverstone's crime. He had avoided a war for which Canadians were as unprepared as the British and in which they would have suffered vastly more. Economics, not boundaries, had already condemned the Yukon to be bypassed for another forty years. That barely mattered. The Boer War had fostered Canadian military nationalism. The Alaska disappointment prodded Canadians to demand diplomatic independence and a new, purely Canadian nationalism. This was now Henri Bourassa's ideal. He was echoed and joined by John Skirving Ewart, a Winnipeg lawyer who had helped defend Riel in 1885 and Manitoba's Catholics in the 1890s. In *The Kingdom of Canada* (1908), Ewart first argued the disturbing new notion that Canada might stand on her own as a fully sovereign state. "How are we to unify Canada?" he asked, and answered himself. "Make her a nation in name as well as in fact."

Few Canadians would follow Ewart and Bourassa. Only a minority cared about such matters, and most of those felt happier with Laurier's vague bid to the British to "call us to your councils," or his insistence that Canada would not be sucked into "the vortex of European militarism." In the wake of South Africa, Joseph Chamberlain had no plans for formal military commitments. By taking over British dockyards and fortifications at Halifax and Esquimalt in 1905, Ottawa sought to preempt pressures at home or from London for more adventurous roles in imperial defence.

Imperialism and nationalism were distractions from the main business of Canadians and immigrants alike. Both were eager to get rich, and Laurier approved. Much as he had once taken up unrestricted reciprocity to distract attention from divisive issues of race and religion, the Liberal leader perceived that prosperity and national unity went together. In his first term, Laurier had simply inherited and refined the National Policy. Safely re-elected, he added a grandeur all his own.

By 1900, it was obvious that a single transcontinental rail line would not suffice for the expanding West. In 1901, bad management and lack of freight cars kept the CPR from moving more than a third of a bumper crop before freeze-up on Lake Superior. Angry farmers launched the Territorial Grain Growers' Association to protest the blockade and even took the railway to court. Expansion was the answer. "We want all the railways we can get," declared the Manitoba *Free Press*; farmers, promoters, contractors, politicians, and assorted boodlers agreed.

In the West, the CPR had a dangerous competitor in William Mackenzie and Donald Mann's Canadian Northern Railway. Its jerry-built tracks, laid by farmers in the spirit of an old-fashioned barn-raising and equipped with second-hand rolling stock, ran in a network north of the CPR line, heading west to Edmonton and east to Port Arthur to compete with the CPR terminus at Fort William. Lake ships had barely ten weeks to rush the western harvest down the lakes and canals to Montreal. In eastern Canada, the Grand Trunk was excluded from the western bonanza. Its new American-born manager, Charles Hays, finally admitted what most people had long suspected: the Chicago-to-Portland route would never pay a dividend. His long-suffering shareholders needed a true transcontinental to prosper.

The solution was obvious. The Grand Trunk and the Canadian Northern should merge. Laurier even presided over a few meetings which unfortunately failed. Confident of prairie support, Mackenzie and Mann demanded control. Hays disparaged "that little bunch of lines up around Winnipeg" and reminded Liberals of past political services. Laurier might have tried a shotgun marriage, but he had no such intentions. The visionary and the politician took over. In 1903, Laurier unveiled his program. If the Tories had boasted of the CPR, the Liberals would do even better. If Sifton was right, the West would have twelve million people within one generation. Boldness was justified. A government-built National Transcontinental would start from the Intercolonial headquarters at Moncton, cross the St. Lawrence at Quebec City, and traverse the clay-belt region of northern Quebec and Ontario on the way to Winnipeg. The Grand Trunk would lease the line for ninety-nine years and construct its own Grand Trunk Pacific line to Prince Rupert on the Pacific coast. As for Mackenzie and Mann, they were free to come east whenever they were ready.

Canadians gasped. Hardly an interest was untouched, from

bankers and contractors to Quebec clergy and *nationalistes,* guaranteed new space for their dreams of colonization. Only the Minister of Railways, A. G. Blair, was angry, partly because he had never been consulted, partly because he favoured Mackenzie and Mann. Laurier got rid of him. The opposition protested too—with little more effect. Tupper's heir was an honest, unflamboyant Halifax lawyer named Robert Borden. He was dismayed by the folly of a scheme that left taxpayers to carry nine-tenths of the cost while the Grand Trunk was almost guaranteed its profits. Canadians, if they had paused to reflect, might have agreed. Instead, Laurier cheered them on with a logic suited to a school playground. "I am aware that this plan may scare the timid and frighten the irresolute," he admitted, "but I may claim that every man who has in his bosom a stout Canadian heart will welcome it as worthy of this young nation. . . ."

Railway development pushed Canadians, for the first time, toward their northern frontier. The National Transcontinental, the Canadian Northern, and the Grand Trunk Pacific cut across the Canadian Shield and the park belt that fringed the prairies. If colonists faced a grim future farming the clay belt, a pulp and paper industry would grow up from the now-accessible forests. So would a mining industry. Its harbinger was the great complex Francis Clergue had built with American capital at Sault Ste. Marie. Ships of his Lake Superior Consolidated Corporation brought iron ore, and trains of his Algoma Central hauled timber and nickel ore to the mills and smelters Clergue housed in impressive stone factory buildings. Tourists and promoters marvelled—until 1903 when the whole grandiose enterprise collapsed. Ontario's Liberal government glumly assumed the debts and persisted in its dreams for what people called New Ontario. Later that year, as the province's Temiskaming and Northern Ontario railways pushed north, miners uncovered the richest silver deposits in the world at Cobalt. Other provinces envied and imitated their neighbour.

Never in their history had Canadians experienced such a run of prosperity. In 1904, they could re-elect the architect. Only a scheme by the bitter A. G. Blair (backed by Mackenzie and Mann) to buy up Liberal newspapers and turn them Tory briefly troubled the Liberal chieftain. Laurier disposed of the plot by threatening exposure, then he travelled the country with a message that set rafters ringing. "Let me tell you, my fellow Canadians," the Prime Minister told a packed audience in Toronto's Massey Hall, "that all the signs point this way, that the twentieth century shall be the century of Canada and of Canadian development. For the next seventy-five years, nay for the next hundred years, Canada shall be the star towards which all men who love progress and freedom shall come."

Torontonians cheered (though they voted Conservative). Even Laurier now accepted that old habit. He had rich compensations. Not since the Pacific Scandal election of 1874 had any party won such a majority of seats or votes; 138 Liberals to only 75 Conservatives. In Nova Scotia, every Tory—including Robert Borden—was beaten.

Prosperity certainly had its rewards.

# 2 / Questioning

Voters rewarded Laurier as the political designer of their prosperity, but businessmen were the real heroes. This was a novelty. Canadians had never before attributed omniscience or patriotism to their industrial and financial magnates. For the most part, business leaders had led decorous, frugal lives, working long hours and deferring gratifications for the hereafter. They and their families ate much the same monotonous meals as humbler Canadians (though even the lower middle class expected to be served by a maid). They dressed for respectability, not the climate, and suffered without complaint.

The gulf between rich and poor was now opened wide. Aristocratic visitors to Canada marvelled at the vulgarity of the wealthy, not at their seeming absence. Huge and sometimes hideous new mansions sprouted in major cities. Elegant automobiles, often worth more than the Prime Minister's annual salary, stood at the front doors. Americans referred to their post-Civil War era of corrupt and speculative wealth as "The Great Barbecue." Laurier presided over the Canadian counterpart. Some of its leading beneficiaries "helped" Liberal ministers with their investments.

Businessmen also expected their desires to be respected. The righteous might grumble about cartels and the "trusts"; no serious corrective legislation was enacted. British Columbians clamoured against Oriental immigration, but so long as Sir James Dunsmuir, the province's chief coal-mine owner, wanted cheap labour for his mines, the Chinese suffered no more than a discriminatory head tax and a ban on bringing their wives. In Ontario, small businessmen demanded publicly-owned hydroelectricity delivered at cost instead of having the power of Niagara Falls left to an avaricious Toronto-based monopoly. When provincial Liberals backed the private monopoly in 1905, their

132

scandal-ridden government lost power to the Tories. By 1907, Ontario's publicly-owned hydro system, commanded by the autocratic Adam Beck, demonstrated the blessings of business socialism. In Quebec and Manitoba, the hydro developers wisely made peace with business critics.

Business sometimes had reforming instincts. Sir Clifford Sifton, a millionaire as well as a politician, turned the Canadian Commission of Conservation into a powerful if short-lived force for environmental improvements. He opposed power exports to the United States; worried publicly about pollution, drainage, forest fires, and migratory birds; and promoted town planning. Canada's cities, slum-ridden and mortally dangerous to small children, cried out for reform. In 1901, mayors Oliver Howland of Toronto and W. D. Lighthall of Westmount formed the League of Canadian Municipalities with the devout goal of eliminating politics and making city government "a business proposition."

Even in prosperity, businessmen grumbled endlessly about unions, anti-tariff farmers, politicians, and the relentless struggle for "a living profit." The strain of competition, some feared, led to "dyspepsia of the mind." It also led to a dramatic growth in joint stock ownership to finance the expensive new machinery, and a wave of mergers and consolidations after 1909 that fully justified the fears of enemies of "trusts" and critics of unearned wealth. A young Max Aitken, fresh from New Brunswick, earned $1.5 million in common stock for organizing Canada Cement and almost as much for creating the Steel Company of Canada. The fortune launched a British publishing and political career. Aitken would live most of his life as Lord Beaverbrook.

Admiration for businessmen and the affluence they had apparently created was widespread but not universal. Whether or not business methods could reform cities, industries helped to make them grimy, overcrowded, and slum-ridden. Electricity now lighted main streets and the wealthier districts of major cities, but the poles marched past the poorer streets without connections. Herbert Ames, a Montreal businessman-reformer, explored and dutifully catalogued incomes and living conditions in working-class wards of his city. Officials, clergy, and journalists did much the same work in Toronto, Winnipeg, Halifax, and Vancouver. Perhaps it was a sign of prosperity that anyone cared, even though investigation did not usually lead to substantial action.

The plight of the poor had an old and easy explanation. Men were masters of their fate—though it troubled softer consciences that women and children usually shared a man's misfortune. The Rev. E. H. Dewart in the Methodist *Christian Guardian* offered a brisk dose of the conventional wisdom: "The best anti-poverty society is an association of men who would adopt as their governing principle in life, industry, sobriety, economy and intelligence." In so hard-drinking a society as Canada, sobriety needed extra help. Temperance, transformed slowly into total abstinence and prohibition, had been the single most powerful social reform crusade in nineteenth-century Canada. Most Protestants and even a few Catholics endorsed it like an extra gospel though it would not have been Canada if the French had not differed markedly from the English on the question. In 1898, when a national referendum favoured prohibition for Canada, Laurier had politely ignored the vote, ostensibly because less than half the population had voted, or because Quebec had been stoutly opposed.

The prohibition cause drew women into political life as defenders of the sacred institution of the family. Only rare eccentrics like Toronto's superintendent of schools, James L. Hughes, Tory, Orange, and educational reformer, insisted on the fundamental equality of men and women. More universal was a faith in "maternal feminism," the divinely sanctioned role of women as wives, mothers, and guardians of social convention against those heedless brutes, their husbands. The nurturing role grew as Victorian Canadians came to see their children not as undersized adults but as beings in a key stage of development. Nursing, teaching, perhaps even medicine, became logical extensions of the maternal role. So did social reform.

Canadian women went into politics not to win theoretical equality but to gain specific goals. The Women's Christian Temperance Union (founded at Owen Sound in 1874), in conjunction with broader organizations like the Dominion Alliance, attacked liquor. Adelaide Hunter Hoodless crusaded for pasteurization of milk and for university-based training in domestic science. Her Women's Institutes became another of the organizations which Canada has given the world. The National Council of Canadian Women, launched in 1893 by the redoubtable Lady Aberdeen, denounced liquor, divorce, prostitution, profiteering and "the modern cult of self-indulgence and its god, pleasure."

Dominated by the wives of the elite, the Council insisted that women would do more good by gentle persuasion than by thrusting themselves into the corrupt world of politics. Not all agreed. Emily Stowe, Canada's first woman doctor, had pioneered the women's suffrage issue in Toronto in the 1880s. Her daughter, Amelia Stowe-Gullen, continued the crusade, but it was characteristic of the new Canadian West that the flame burned most brightly in the prairie cities. Nellie McClung, a novelist and ingenious publicist, burlesqued Manitoba's all-male legislature and its pompous premier, Sir Rodmond Roblin. Cora Hind, a brilliant Winnipeg crop-forecaster, and Emily Murphy, later an Alberta judge and a novelist whose best-known work dealt with drug addiction, were powerful allies. So were leaders of the West's agrarian movement. E. A. Partridge of the *Grain Grower's Guide* wondered pointedly why the vote was available to "the lowest imbruted foreign hobo" but not to Canadian women.

Though the National Council grew to two hundred fifty thousand members—about half as many people as backed Laurier in 1904—the majority of Canadian women remained collectively silent. So did the mass of Canadian workers. Prosperity was by no means evenly shared. It dribbled slowly across the widening gulf between employer and employee. A powerful, if misleading, impression that the wealthy were self-made men was an effective antidote for egalitarian yearnings. The flood of immigrants, most of whom entered into direct competition with Canadian workers in factories and construction camps, was a more practical weapon against employee militancy. Devotion to the protective tariff and foreign investment coincided, in business ideology, with faith in a free labour market and abhorrence of foreign labour agitators. In 1903, a bill sponsored by Senator James Lougheed of Alberta would have sentenced such union organizers to two years in jail. It passed the Senate but the lower house was too busy to debate it.

In 1900, as a bid to win and organize workers' votes, the Liberals created a small Department of Labour. A promising and dependable young graduate student, William Lyon Mackenzie King (a grandson of the Upper-Canadian rebel) was put in charge. Among King's duties (executed by loyal Liberals in the tiny union movement) was collection of the first statistics on employment

135

and cost of living. For the first time, labour union memberships were also counted. A statistic that business leaders did not cheer during the century's first decade was union growth; from twenty thousand in 1900 to a hundred and twenty thousand by 1911— eight per cent of the entire labour force, male and female.

Organized labour was a feeble, divided critic of a prosperity that gave most Canadian workers no more than a mean and precarious subsistence. From Charlottetown to Vancouver, skilled workers joined international affiliates of the American Federation of Labour. When Ralph Smith, the Liberal president of the Trades and Labour Congress, tried to kick the internationals out of the organization, the TLC convention at Berlin, Ontario, in 1902 gave him the boot instead. Employers were left to run their own anti-AFL crusade, borrowing the approved American tools—strikebreakers, calls on the militia, and "yellow dog" contracts (solemn oaths extracted from employees never even to contemplate union membership on pain of fine and dismissal). From 1902, union growth was painfully slow; strikes grew longer and more bitter.

In Europe and even in the United States, the early twentieth century saw the emergence of powerful labour and socialist movements, strong and even violent challenges to business power. By contrast, Canada was really a backwater of radical and union activity. The small, doctrinaire Socialist Party of Canada actually won a few seats in the British Columbia legislature and an occasional municipal election across the country. A lengthy Alberta coal strike in 1906, just before the coldest winter in western memory, publicised Mackenzie King's growing talent as a conciliator and led to the Industrial Disputes Investigation Act of 1907..By publicising issues and forcing negotiation, the IDI Act was probably more useful than its labour critics have ever admitted but neither King nor business could concede that unions had a right to exist as such or that workers had a right to bargain collectively. Long, violent, often unsuccessful strikes were waged over union recognition. In 1909–1910, most of Canada's tiny regular army stood guard over Cape Breton coal mines until starvation forced miners to abandon the international union of their choice.

Distance, small numbers, and divisions, not ideology, kept labour from becoming a national force. Skilled workers in craft

136

unions had no links with the unorganized, unskilled majority. Only radical unions like the Western Federation of Miners and later, the Industrial Workers of the World, tried to organize the migrant army of "bunkhouse men" in construction, logging, and mining camps. They had meagre success. In Quebec, clergy and *nationalistes* did their best to shield *Canadiens* from socialist and materialist influences.

Where labour votes could be concentrated, they could elect populist candidates like Médéric Martin, the cigarmaker who became mayor of Montreal, or Alphonse Verville, president of the Trades and Labour Congress. In Toronto, Horatio Hocken, a Tory Orangeman, used his past leadership of a printers' strike to win labour votes. In return he gave the city parks, playgrounds, public baths, free milk for slum children, and a municipal abbatoir and cold storage to fight the meat trust. Infant mortality fell sharply, Toronto became more habitable, and its workers embraced the charms of Tory democracy.

Farmers rediscovered their political influence too. It was not easy. First the Grange of the 1870s and then the Patrons of the 1890s had collapsed in a wreckage of mismanaged co-operatives and political sell-outs. Only the grievances survived—the tariff, a weak bargaining position, rural depopulation, and jarring reminders of a disgraceful disrespect for the nation's primary producers. Canadian farmers grew sensitive to "Hey Rube" jokes and taunts.

In the West, farmers developed a heightened sense of exasperation. Eastern farms had diversified sufficiently that no climatic or market disaster was total. The western monoculture of wheat (in an unpredictable and often merciless climate) and the exactions of railways, elevator, and milling monopolies, and the Winnipeg Grain Exchange could easily reduce prairie farmers to penury. Rainfall, frost, soil conditions, and insects could not be helped, but once a farmer had hauled his grain ten miles to the only available elevator, he could hardly take it home again. The only answer to arrogant and dishonest elevator agents or to mysterious fluctuations of the commodity markets was political action and co-operation. The message might be preached by cautious Liberals like W. R. Motherwell, founder of the Territorial Grain Grower's Association, or passionate socialists like E. A. Partridge, editor of the influential *Grain Grower's Guide*.

Farmers soon understood. So did governments. Across the vast West, farmers were the only voters in sight, and, unlike workers, their minds were not easily distracted.

A federal Grains Act in 1900, imposing regulations and inspectors, proved ineffective but instructive. Partridge successfully promoted a Grain Growers' Grain Company and a reluctant Manitoba government finally coerced the Grain Exchange into granting it a seat. Farmer-owned elevator companies spread across the West. So did farm organizations and subscriptions to Partridge's *Grain Grower's Guide*. At least some readers absorbed his view that the story of the West was "a history of heartless robbery . . . by the Big 'vested' interests—so called from the size of their owners' vests."

One prairie issue was the political future of the North West Territories. By 1897, a long campaign led by a Regina lawyer, Frederick Haultain, won responsible government for the Territories. In 1904, both parties promised provincial status, and a year later Laurier was ready to act. By creating the two provinces of Alberta and Saskatchewan, split at the sixtieth meridian, he separated Haultain, the grand old man of territorial politics, from most of his supporters, and he launched both new provinces with strong Liberal governments. By keeping federal control of land and resources, Laurier also guaranteed continued free homesteads and a friendly climate for investors. A generous financial settlement, soon extended to other provinces as a "final and unalterable" resolution of old fiscal arguments, guaranteed political peace and economic prosperity for the prairies.

There was one small problem. The new provinces assumed that they would continue their Ontario-style system of schools; even Protestants were reconciled to some minority Catholic rights. Privately, however, Laurier had promised Catholic bishops a return to their full equality of 1875. In the draft autonomy bills, he had quietly inserted an appropriate guarantee. An astonished and furious Clifford Sifton resigned. Fielding threatened to follow. Bitter at the "betrayal" by his Protestant colleagues, Laurier compromised. The conflict became public. Richard Bedford Bennett, the Alberta Tory leader, tried to light the Ontario heather with speeches against Catholic-inspired coercion. More savage by far was the anger of men like Bourassa. By retreating, Bourassa insisted, Laurier had made the West "a land of refuge for the scum of all nations." Armand Lavergne, once Laurier's friend and now Bourassa's chief supporter, went farther. "In constituting the French Canadian . . . the equal in rights and privileges to the Doukhobor or the Galician who had just disembarked," he declared, "we have opened a gulf between eastern and western Canadians which nothing will fill."

One might argue, of course, that French Canadians showed little sign of wishing to share the West and that Laurier's leadership was enough evidence of their influence. The phenomenal birthrate, sustained since 1760, a provincial government, a self-confident Catholic clergy, and a proud culture should have been protection enough for the French fact in North America. Instead, French Canada in the 1900s experienced an acute crisis of self-confidence, aggravated by Liberal policies and the Laurier prosperity.

The West had few attractions for the *Canadiens* but they could see the floods of immigrants hurried through Quebec by Sifton's agents. Many of them halted in Montreal to create Jewish, Greek, and Italian ghettoes with customs and languages even stranger and more unwelcome than the English and Irish. British Canadians might grumble about foreigners but they were as confident as Sifton that assimilation would come. French Canadians saw only the menace of people who neither knew nor respected the old racial compact and compromises.

Some French Canadians, like Rodolphe Forget, J. D. Rolland, and François Béique, became millionaires in the resulting business bonanza; but most shared only the jobs created by English-speaking employers. Montreal, once half-English, now was filled with rural French Canadians. Quebeckers no longer fled to New England; instead they crowded into the slums of an alien city. As a French tourist complained, one could live for weeks in Montreal without seeing or hearing any language but English. The Quebec government, Liberal since 1897, saw its role as the fervent promoter of private development of natural resources as much as factories. Only if English and American capital expanded the provincial economy could Quebec afford the costly and futile colonization projects favoured by the Church and *nationalistes*.

Bourassa himself, fleeing the futility of federal politics to turn his fire on the provincial Liberal regime, toyed with a more progressive version of the nationalist program. Errol Bouchette, Quebec's first economist of note, pleaded with Quebeckers to regain control of their own resources and industries, by public ownership if necessary. Opinion-leaders recoiled at such socialist heresies. Bourassa recommended control of trusts, Catholic unions for *Canadien* workers, even the municipal reforms urged by Montreal's civic-conscious business leaders. No more than his grandfather Papineau could Bourassa emancipate himself from a traditional, rural view of French Canada's future. The problems of colonists tilling the thin soils of northern Quebec would be blamed on politicians. The hardships depicted in Louis Hémon's *Maria Chapdelaine* must be endured, and, like Maria, French Canadians must reject the easy life of assimilation to remain true to their traditions. "It is not necessary for us to possess industry and money," declared Jules-Paul Tardivel. "We would no longer be French Canadians but Americans like the others. Our mission is to possess the soil and to spread ideas."

Such notions might have limited impact on the hard-headed and sometimes hedonistic *Canadiens*. The preaching of clergy and intellectuals should not be confused with public opinion, but at intervals the two connect. If Bourassa and his youthful followers increasingly saw Laurier as a sell-out to imperialists, materialists, and exploiters, ordinary French Canadians had less reason than their English-speaking neighbours to revel in Laurier's economic achievements. Nor were those achievements always apparent.

By 1908, the federal Liberals looked shopworn and dirty. The country had survived a short but sharp recession in 1907, the harbinger of worse to come. Robert Borden, still the Tory leader, had chosen that year to unveil his Halifax Program, a reaffirmation of the National Policy spiced by calls for public ownership of telephones, telegraphs, and railways, an efficient and reformed civil service; and a ban on election contributions from corporations. Laurier introduced a civil service commission and waited patiently while Tories predictably denounced their leader's proposals as intolerable socialism. As voter bait, Conservatives were left with what contemporary Americans had christened "muckraking." Admittedly the scandals were rich and redolent, from Sifton's corrupt old Department of the Interior to the supply contracts for the government's Arctic voyages of explorations.

The government replied in kind and the resulting campaign in 1908 was as sordid as any Canadian election in history. On election day, the Liberals retained 135 seats to the Conservatives' 85.

The Liberals had urged voters to "let Laurier finish his work." Probably Laurier's work was done. In 1909, Mackenzie King, elected to Parliament in 1908, became minister of a full-fledged Department of Labour. A tiny Department of External Affairs opened over an Ottawa barber shop. Its task was to cope with what Laurier never quite managed, systematic replies to the relentless flow of British memoranda on diplomacy, defence, shipping, and utter esoterica. Few Canadians cared, but diplomacy had done well for them since the Alaska dispute. In 1904, the French had forsaken their old, troublesome landing rights on the Newfoundland shore. Tribunals accepted Canadian views of a controversy over the Bering Sea and the ninety-year-old fisheries disagreement with the Americans. Laurier could have left with his country prosperous and respected. Instead, he looked at his aging colleagues, found no successor, and carried on.

Old issues such as imperialism took new shapes. In Europe, Britain had ended her old hostility to France and Russia because an old friend had suddenly become a dangerous new threat. Germany's industrial power had given her the world's best army. Now battleships poured from her dockyards to challenge the Royal Navy's supremacy. Wealthy and aristocratic British taxpayers, asked to finance a modest new welfare state as well as a massive expansion of their fleet, threatened rebellion. Canada and other dominions received urgent invitations to help. Laurier saw the political trap and seized a solution. Launching a small Canadian navy would look helpful, but both control and spending would remain at home. To his delight, an appropriate Conservative-sponsored resolution passed Parliament unanimously.

Then the compromise fell apart. Within a year both imperialists and Quebec nationalists had savaged the new Naval Service Act. Laurier offered a "tin-pot navy," the imperialists argued, when Britain needed battleships. Bourassa, in his newly-launched newspaper, *Le Devoir*, insisted that the navy was a subterfuge for committing Canada to imperial wars and the conscription of young *Canadiens*. What enemy would distinguish between British and Canadian warships bearing identical White Ensigns? A symbolic by-election in rural Quebec in the autumn of 1910 showed the *nationalistes* that they had finally found a popular issue.

Laurier was unafraid. He spent that summer in a triumphal visit to the West. With his own eyes he saw the vast fields and the booming cities. The 1907 recession had been a mere hiccup in the process of endless growth. Homesteaders poured into the West in ever greater numbers. With too few misgivings, officials sent them to till the Palliser Triangle. Heavy rains in the Triangle in 1910 seemed to confirm their wisdom. Of course, there were discontents. Delegations met the Prime Minister to repeat old grievances about tariffs, freight rates, and land policies, but as ever, Laurier pursed his lips, shared his deep concern, and promised action. That fall, a thousand farmers staged the first "March on Ottawa," coming, like most of their successors, by train and not on foot. Again Laurier promised action.

Thanks to Washington, this time he delivered. By signing the Payne-Aldrich Bill, which sent American tariffs to new heights, President William Taft had finally provoked a free-trade revolt in a mid-term election year. Taft hoped that dusting off the old Canadian Reciprocity business might regain western support. With astonishing speed, an agreement was signed and despatched to both Canada and the Congress for approval. In Ottawa, a Tory politician later confessed that his heart sank to his boots. After half a century of trying for Reciprocity, it was Laurier who could claim the coup. Then politicians went home to their ridings and got another shock: Canadians were displeased. After years of prosperity and east-west trade, Canadians no longer cared about Reciprocity; in fact, for millions of them in business, factories, and transportation it represented a deadly threat to jobs. In Toronto, eighteen prominent Liberals, led by Clifford Sifton and Sir Edmund Walker of the Bank of Commerce, publicly broke with their party. In Montreal, Sir William Van Horne of the CPR brusquely commanded his business associates "to bust the damned thing."

Neither Borden nor Laurier immediately grasped their altered fortunes. Exasperated by a Tory filibuster on the Reciprocity Agreement, Laurier called an election for September 1911. In Quebec, Tory businessmen now funnelled cash to Bourassa and the *nationalistes,* leaving them to veto candidates and manage the

Conservative provincial campaign. In return, the *nationalistes* hoped, Bourassa's followers would hold the balance of power. Elsewhere, anti-Americanism and Reciprocity were the real issues, with a flood of money and smooth provincial organizations in Ontario, Manitoba, and British Columbia to support Conservative fortunes. By the end, Laurier glimpsed defeat. Rowdy mobs in Montreal drove him from his platform to seek refuge in a railway car. On the night of September 21, Conservative candidates swept 107 seats outside Quebec, 4 short of a majority. Quebec gave Borden 27 more (mostly from rural counties) for a total of 134. Laurier salvaged only 87, and most of his ministers, Mackenzie King among them, were gone.

The *nationalistes* had miscalculated. Robert Borden could now manage without them, though some secured minor portfolios. Like Laurier in 1896, Borden sought compromise and moderation. Thomas White, a defecting Liberal from the Toronto financial community, became Minister of Finance, while George Eulas Foster, scourge of the Liberals in the opposition years, had to settle, like Cartwright in 1896, for trade and commerce. Reluctantly Borden accepted Sam Hughes, the favourite of Orangemen and imperialists, as Minister of Militia, an obscure enough portfolio in normal times. With a suitably new broom, Borden set reforms afoot in the civil service, proposed a commission to set a "scientific" tariff and launched an investigation of the scandalously mismanaged and overdue National Transcontinental. Manitoba's northern border, a vexed issue for three years, climbed north to join its neighbours at the sixtieth parallel, and both Ontario and Quebec expanded to include the vast Ungava district around Hudson Bay. An exasperated Borden complained that he could have done so much more if his colleagues had not spent so much of their time with quarrels over political favours. Borden's distaste for patronage was only one of the things that distinguished him from Laurier and Macdonald.

Another was his view of empire. The Tory-*nationaliste* alliance on the naval question had been based on self-deception. Like old Joseph Howe but unlike Laurier or Macdonald, Borden believed in some form of imperial federation. Some day, colonies would sit as equals with the mother country, but they would have to earn their places by honourable sacrifice. Such an opportunity had come. After direct consultations with the British admiralty,

Borden announced that Canada would send $5 million to buy three of the most advanced battleships. At once, his Quebec lieutenant, Frederick Monk, demanded a referendum. The request refused, Monk resigned. The Liberals filibustered, dragging the debate into 1913. Then Borden's brightest recruit, Arthur Meighen, devised a closure motion to cut off debate. This first use of closure did not save Borden's naval policy. A Liberal-dominated senate bluntly rejected it, and, for good measure, his tariff commission and a federal highways law as well.

The Senate could do so cheerfully because Borden's government was now in deadly trouble. The long years of prosperity were over. By 1912, a world-wide depression was taking hold. Immigrants, arriving in greater numbers to escape economic woes at home, joined growing armies of unemployed in Canadian cities. In 1913 and 1914 the prairies suffered their first widespread crop failures in a decade. The ecological folly of farming the drought-prone Palliser Triangle was exposed. Close to completion, the new transcontinental railways found themselves in a desperate credit squeeze. Hardest hit was the Canadian Northern, its eastern route authorized by Laurier in 1908 and financed by Toronto's Bank of Commerce. Promoters who had paid lavish favours to the Liberals now had to plead for Tory sympathy. The thirst for political revenge had to be resisted by an argument as old as the Grand Trunk and the 1850s: railway bankruptcy would destroy Canadian credit with foreign investors.

Beset by problems it had not caused, Borden's government faced new problems from its Ontario stronghold. Urged on by Michael Fallon, Roman Catholic bishop of London, and by fears of French-Canadian settlement in Ontario's eastern counties, Sir James Whitney's provincial government issued Regulation 17, curtailing the education rights of Ontario's French-speaking minority. For Fallon, Regulation 17 was sweet revenge for his dismissal by French-speaking clerics at the University of Ottawa years before. Franco-Ontarians knew they were victims of raw prejudice and opportunism. In Ontario's 1914 election, Liberals vied with Tories in backing Regulation 17. The Tories won in a landslide.

For Canada as a whole, Regulation 17 was another brutal, needless confrontation between French and English at a moment when Canadian unity would be tested as never before.

# 3/National Crisis

Suddenly, Canada was at war. The crisis that bubbled out of the Balkans in the summer of 1914 had looked no worse than half a dozen predecessors. Inexorably, alliance systems and mobilization plans clicked into place. Serbia, Russia, and France ranged against the Austro-Hungarian and German empires. At midnight on August 4, the British ultimatum to Berlin expired and another empire joined the war.

In Winnipeg, J. W. Dafoe told readers of the *Free Press* that Canadians would make their own war on Prussian militarism. In Ottawa, Sir Wilfrid Laurier was more conventional. In Britain's hour of danger, Canada's only possible answer was "Ready, Aye Ready." Crowds in Montreal, Toronto, and Quebec bellowed their support.

Canada was a little better prepared than she knew. Since 1897, defence spending had grown six-fold. In 1913, sixty thousand militiamen had drilled in camps. Since 1909, most provinces, including Quebec, had imposed military training in their schools. Pre-war planning even safeguarded ports, canals, and bridges from surprise attack. A detailed scheme would have despatched a twenty-five-thousand-man Canadian Expeditionary Force within a month. Other preparations were less helpful. In 1902, at the behest of Colonel Sam Hughes, Laurier's government had adopted the Ross rifle. It was a fine target rifle, and it could be made in Canada; experience would reveal few other virtues.

The war crisis excited Canadians. When Parliament met, a Liberal insisted that Borden's emergency legislation "omit no power that the Government may need." The War Measures Act met that test. Experts universally agreed that the war would be short. If massed armies did not settle the issue, economic collapse certainly would. As Minister of Militia, Sam Hughes scrapped mobilization plans designed by his professional soldiers, summoned volunteers to a brand new camp at Valcartier, near Quebec, and went in full uniform to sort out the confusion he had caused. By early October, a vast convoy had left for England with thirty-two thousand ill-trained soldiers. Canadians marvelled.

They also poured out their patriotism in voluntary effort. A Canadian Patriotic Fund collected donations for soldiers' families. A Military Hospitals Commission created facilities for the sick and wounded veterans. The pre-war militia organization and patriotic civilians recruited close to half a million men by early 1916 with scarcely a penny of government money. Churches, charities, the Red Cross, and women's organizations found interesting and often useful ways to "do their bit," from buying machine guns to distributing white feathers as symbols of cowardice to healthy young civilian men. Patriots also forced the dismissal of Germans and Austrians from public employment, banned the teaching of German in schools and universities, and pressured the city of Berlin into renaming itself Kitchener. Miners in British Columbia went on strike to prevent the hiring of "enemy aliens," and by April of 1915, public clamour had forced the government to intern more than seven thousand largely harmless people.

From the first, the frugal practices of peacetime public finance were forgotten. At the best of times Sam Hughes was a spender and the war gave him and a growing entourage of cronies all the excuse they needed. By 1915, the militia department was swallowing more than the entire government had spent in 1913. Less public but almost as serious was the financial appetite of the transcontinental railways. Cut off from traditional money markets by the war, with facilities badly needed to ship men and supplies, the Grand Trunk and the Canadian Northern left Borden's government no choice but to support them.

As Minister of Finance, Sir Thomas White was no innovator. Only a horror of raising taxes and a faith in a short war forced him into the first heavy Canadian borrowing in New York. Financiers universally believed that Canadians would never lend money to their government. They were wrong. Desperation drove White in 1915 to seek $50 million in a special domestic war loan; Canadians gave him $100 million. Further loans in 1916 and 1917 were also over-subscribed. Victory Loans, directed at humbler citizens and backed by floods of advertising, delivered $400 million in 1917 and $600 million in 1918. While government revenue rose from $126 million to $233.7 million between 1913 and 1918, mostly due to higher tariffs, the national debt climbed from $434 million to $2463 million. By then, White and his colleagues had to argue that the cost of a war to end all wars might fairly be shared with later generations.

The burden would have been far greater without massive exports of wheat, timber, and Canadian-made munitions. At first, the war only aggravated the prevailing depression. Hunger as well as patriotism drove thousands of young men into the Canadian Expeditionary Force. Industrialists, eager for business, got Hughes's backing to form a committee to bid for British artillery shell contracts. By the summer of 1915, the Shell Committee had orders worth $170 million but greed, confusion, and the problems of learning by doing allowed them to deliver only $5.5 million's worth. The British, beset by their own comparable problems, insisted on reorganization. The solution was an Imperial Munitions Board, officially a British agency, headed by a talented and hardheaded Canadian manager, Joseph Flavelle. By 1917, Flavelle had turned his skills as a bacon exporter into making the IMB the biggest business in Canada with a quarter of a million workers and a turnover of $2 million a day. In 1917, when the British, desperate for foreign exchange, could no longer afford to buy in Canada, Flavelle neatly switched his market to a rearming United States. By the war's end, the IMB's own factories and its contractors were producing ships, aircraft, chemicals, and explosives as well as shells.

The war also ended the depression in agriculture. With huge conscript armies trapped in the trenches, and Russia's wheat exports stopped by the war, Canada's allies needed all she could produce. Nature obliged with an unprecedented fifteen million bushels of wheat in 1915. Prices soared and the caution which might have returned the prairie dry belt to grazing was forgotten in the rush for profits. Yields fell in the later war years but farm profits climbed, and consumers accepted higher prices and shortages as the cost of war. Manufacturers shared the benefits as farmers spent their new wealth on cars and furniture as well as more land and machinery. Employers and farmers soon regretted that so many men had been encouraged to go to war.

Manpower had become the crucial resource of the war effort.

By the end of 1914, the government had authorized fifty thousand men for the Canadian Expeditionary Force. By the summer of 1915, the target was a hundred and fifty thousand. A visit to England shocked Borden with both the magnitude of the struggle and the ineffectiveness of British wartime leadership. As if set them an example, he raised Canada's manpower commitment to two hundred fifty thousand, and in January 1916 he doubled it to five hundred thousand.

At the outset, Henri Bourassa had backed the war, but he added a prescient warning. The government, he suggested, should "ensure our own internal security before starting or pursuing an effort that it will perhaps not be in a state to sustain until the end." The government's own chief military advisor, Major General Willoughby Gwatkin, cautioned in 1915 that Canada might have trouble finding men for even two divisions in the trenches. Instead, by 1916, Hughes had committed the Dominion to four divisions with the promise of many more.

In fact, men were found. When the old militia had exhausted its influence, politicians, businessmen, and local patriots accepted colonelcies from Hughes and raised still more battalions. Appeals to civic pride, sporting links, and the passion for wearing Highland regalia drew recruits. Clergy preached on Christian duty and women wore badges proclaiming "Knit or Fight." Medical officers sometimes accepted the young, the old, and the physically or mentally handicapped. Barriers of racial prejudice were lowered to admit Indians and Japanese Canadians, though most black Canadians were funnelled into a construction unit.

Even when backed by acute social pressure, voluntary recruiting was highly selective. Most of the men of the early contingents were British-born recent immigrants to Canada, with close ties to their homeland and harsh experience of a country where employers often advertised "No English need apply." In cities like Winnipeg, Toronto, and English-speaking Montreal, recruiting pressure was more powerful than in rural districts or in regions like the Maritimes where roots went very deep. In French Canada, the pressures were weak indeed. No one distributed white feathers in Quebec City. The agencies that recruited in other provinces—the militia, local leaders, imperial patriots—were, in French Canada, weak or otherwise engaged. Historians often repeat a myth that a Methodist was put in charge of Quebec recruiting. In fact, no one was in charge of recruiting in Quebec or anywhere else until 1917. Lies, however widely spread and innocently believed, remain lies.

It was easy to blame Sam Hughes and the Borden government. No man was less fitted to understand French Canada than the tempestuous Minister of Militia. Though most of Borden's *nationaliste* colleagues loyally backed the war, they had won election by passionately opposing such imperial adventures. Quebec Liberals enjoyed their discomfiture and Bourassa, rapidly losing interest in the European conflict, dismissed his former colleagues as traitors. Ontario's Regulation 17 was a convenient distraction. The real enemies of French Canada were not Germans, insisted Bourassa, but "English-Canadian anglicisers, the Ontario intriguers, or Irish priests." As if to confirm the point, wartime nativism drove the western provinces to annul French and minority education rights conceded years before.

In fact, French Canadians did not need Bourassa's speeches to convince them to stay out of uniform. When Quebec's famous Twenty-second Battalion, the "Vandoos," was authorized in October 1914, it had difficulty filling its ranks. So did most of its many successors. Few Quebeckers were moved by loyalty to Britain or France; unemployment or an urge for adventure and escape were the usual goads for recruiting. For the vast majority, the ordered familiarity of the farm or home town, well-paid work in the new munitions factories and textile mills, and a comfortable sense of isolation from a dangerous world were reason enough to stay home.

Those Canadians who did enlist became part of the British army. Not even the assertively nationalistic Hughes claimed to control "his boys" in action, though he lustily condemned British tactics. Hughes's zest for chaos and croneyism complicated Canadian administration in England. By 1916, three rival Canadian generals each claimed Hughes's full authority. Hundreds of CEF battalions arrived in Britain only to be broken up for reinforcements. The embittered soldiers blamed unfeeling military bureaucrats. The staff, more knowledgeably, blamed Hughes.

No more than in 1812 or 1885 were Canadians natural-born soldiers. They learned their business in the daily misery of trench warfare and in bloody battles made more dangerous by inexperienced officers and bad equipment. After the second Battle of Ypres, where a raw First Division counted 6035 casualties, soldiers abandoned their useless Ross rifles. At the St. Eloi craters in 1916, the Second Division suffered a painful setback because its commanders could not locate their men. The remorseless test of battle eliminated the hopelessly inept and persuaded the survivors that precise staff work, painstaking preparation, and sensible but uncompromising discipline could both win battles and save lives. The clearest evidence came on the Easter weekend of 1917. After weeks of stock-piling, tunnelling, rehearsals, and bombardment, Sir Julian Byng sent forward all four divisions of the Canadian Corps to take Vimy Ridge. In five days, the seemingly impossible had been done. It was one of those great deeds, done together, which have created nations. French and English could take equal pride in the victory.

Byng was British but his ways were inherited only weeks later by his Canadian successor. Sir Arthur Currie was a pear-shaped figure with a slightly shady pre-war record as a Victoria real estate speculator. The war proved him to be a cool, methodical soldier, with a fondness for unconventional tactics and an openness to innovation. That summer, instead of squandering men in an attack on Lens, as his British superiors wanted, he captured nearby Hill 70. Then, when the Germans, as he had predicted, desperately tried to retake the position, Currie used his artillery to destroy them.

Currie's authority was all the stronger because, after 1916, Canada had assumed effective control of her overseas forces. In November of that year, after a tempest of rage and threats at his loss of power, Hughes finally resigned. Sir Robert Borden created a new Overseas Ministry in London to manage Canadian forces in England and France. The chaos and conflict that affected every branch of administration, from chaplains to veterinarians, slowly vanished. By 1918, the British retained little more than tactical control of the Canadian units in France. Brilliant soldiers like Brigadier General A. G. L. McNaughton, a chemistry professor before the war, pioneered innovations in gunnery and military engineering. In military terms, if not yet in constitutional law, the war had transformed Canada from a colony into a junior but sovereign ally. Both administrative efficiency and hard-won military prestige had achieved the change.

Canadians also won a reputation in the air. By war's end, almost a quarter of the pilots in the Royal Air Force were Canadians, many of them trained at British flying schools in Canada. Two Canadians, Major W. A. Bishop and Major Raymond Collishaw, ranked third and fifth among the air aces of the war. They and many others established a remarkable Canadian reputation in the air, in part because of superior training methods. Having deplored a distinct Canadian navy, Borden's government approved an independent Canadian air force only in the last months of the war. It never saw action. At sea, a few Canadians served with the Royal Navy but Canada's own tiny navy was allowed no greater role than patrolling for German U-boats outside Halifax harbour.

Experts have long debated alternatives to the Allies' blood-soaked strategy of seeking victory on the Western Front. Not even skill, experience, and careful preparation prevented heavy casualties. Taking Vimy Ridge cost 10,604 dead and wounded. Ordered to finish the grim British offensive at Passchendaele in October 1917, Currie protested that he would lose sixteen thousand men. The toll was 15,654. Keeping each of the four Canadian divisions in action required twenty thousand new soldiers a year. By 1917, they were no longer coming.

A year earlier, the patriotic leagues had warned that their recruiting efforts were failing. To soften Quebec's rising hostility to the war effort, prominent Torontonians launched a "Bonne Entente" movement. Banquets and speeches failed to soften the bitterness of French-English relations. Soon, many of these same men began to demand conscription. The arguments became familiar. Volunteering took too many of the bravest and best young men of English Canada. Industry suffered when skilled workers joined up. Acutely aware of its 1914 promise of voluntary recruiting, the government tried to keep faith. Borden finally put Quebec recruiting in charge of a prominent French-Canadian drug manufacturer. One of his Quebec cabinet ministers set out (vainly) to raise a battalion. Borden also launched a voluntary scheme of national registration to identify potential recruits. Though suspicious that the scheme was a mere prelude to conscription, both the Quebec Catholic hierarchy and the Trades and Labour Congress urged compliance. A fifth of the registration cards were never returned. Of the registrants who seemed eligible, almost none volunteered.

Save for his short, discouraging visit to London in 1915, Borden knew no more about British policy and strategy than he could read in the papers. Once, in January 1916, frustration and ill-health provoked him to write that Canadians would not put five hundred thousand men in the field "and willingly accept the position of having no more voice and receiving no more consideration than if we were toy automata." He tore up the letter and spent that year struggling to reform his creaking war administration and, in spare moments, urging sympathetic Americans to forsake their neutrality.

In London, December 1916 brought dramatic shifts, partly engineered by the expatriate Canadian, Max Aitken. David Lloyd George, a former Welsh radical and the only man in the British government Borden had really respected, headed a new coalition. Faced with hostile officials and a war effort sadly awry, Lloyd George summoned the dominion premiers. "We want more men from them," he bluntly explained. "We can hardly ask them to make another great recruiting effort unless it is accompanied by an invitation to come over and discuss the situation with us." On March 2, Borden and his fellow prime ministers met to hear the dreadful news. Russia was collapsing. The French army had mutinied. Germany's submarines would bring Britain to starvation. The Americans had finally entered the war, to Borden's profound delight, but years might pass before American military strength was mobilized. Lloyd George's purpose was served: Borden worked hard on developing a new consultative Imperial War Cabinet, but the manpower message sunk in.

Visits to Canadian camps confirmed the need for men. Without reinforcements, wounded men would be returned to the fighting until they were dead or too terribly mangled to be useful. Canada's honour depended on keeping her Corps at full strength, though Borden halted Hughes's former policy of expanding it. The bitter victory of Vimy Ridge in April 1917 only confirmed the Prime Minister's resolve.

Later, Liberals would pretend that Borden dreamed up conscription to save his party. This was absurd. Certainly the Tories were in trouble. A 1914 political truce had long since ended. Conservatives had lost every provincial election since then. A wartime record of fumbling and ill-concealed scandals seemed to promise Laurier's comeback at the next election. Borden was not fooled by the patriots; conscription would be unpopular across Canada. In Australia, voters had rejected it already and would do so again. But Borden saw no choice. With all the earnestness that drove him, Borden would keep faith with Britain and with Canada's own young soldiers. On May 18, 1917, he announced that men would be selectively conscripted for service overseas.

Almost inevitably, conscription became a French-English debate. Opponents in English Canada—farmers, trade unionists, pacifists—had few outlets for their views; French Canada was virtually unanimous in opposition, and Bourassa provided ready-made arguments. Borden, he insisted, was a mere imperialist, pouring out Canadian lives and money at Britain's command. Canada's front line was Canada, not France and Flanders. Canadians should use the war to get rich by supplying the food and shells the belligerents needed. Such arguments enraged English-Canadian patriots. To Borden, they were servile and unworthy. Despite their image as a cold, materialistic people, Borden wanted to lead Canadians to a higher destiny. His reputation would perish in the attempt.

On the means Borden was very flexible. He would form a coalition with Laurier. He would delay conscription until a general election. The Liberal leader refused. Sensing imminent victory over the Tories, Laurier's party would surely stay loyal. If Laurier joined Borden, he would again lose Quebec to Bourassa. Liberal party meetings in Toronto and Winnipeg trounced advocates of conscription.

Despite the evidence, Laurier was wrong. Especially in Ontario and the West, the war had become a crusade, as Dafoe had proclaimed in 1914. Out of the terrible fiery furnace of sacrifice, surely a new and purified Canada must come, purged of corruption and selfishness. It was a conviction which Liberals could share more easily than Tories. It lay behind the sudden, overwhelming triumph of reforming campaigns across the West in 1915 and 1916, such as prohibition and women's suffrage. By 1917, women in provinces from Ontario to British Columbia had won the right to vote though both sexes had also lost the right to drink. Both causes remained frankly repugnant to Laurier, Quebec Liberals, and, for that matter, to Bourassa and the *nationalistes*. Hate the Tories as they might, reforming Liberals like Newton Rowell, the party's Ontario leader, and Manitoba's J. W. Dafoe could see that Borden was in earnest about the war, and Laurier patently was not.

153

The Prime Minister was also a shrewder, abler politician than Laurier would ever admit. Reaching out to second-rank Liberals, Borden found them sympathetic but nervous. With help from Arthur Meighen, Borden gave himself two more weapons. A Military Voters' Act would enfranchise soldiers; a Wartime Elections Act gave votes to soldiers' wives, sisters, and mothers and took it away from Canadians of enemy origin naturalized since 1902. The women, Meighen explained, would speak for men who had lost their lives; disfranchised aliens would also be spared from conscription. It went without saying that they had also voted Liberal. It took closure to end the debate. Almost at once, sensing that Laurier was lost, the Liberal defections began. On October 6, Parliament dissolved, and the long-postponed election could take place. Five days later, Borden announced a coalition Union government pledged to conscription, wartime prohibition, and the elimination of political patronage. It was a pledge Borden could never have won from his own party. The man who had grown to despise partyism could finally lead a government based on talent and patriotism—as he saw it.

The brand-new Union government expected an easy victory with endorsements from eight out of nine provincial premiers (Quebec's Sir Lomer Gouin was the obvious exception) and almost every English-language newspaper. Outside Quebec the Liberal leadership was shattered. Unexpectedly, in the Maritimes and parts of the West, rank-and-file Liberals began to revive their party. Struggles to compress Tory and Liberal ambitions into a single Unionist candidacy provoked exasperating squabbles. On a western tour, Laurier drew large crowds. At Kitchener, with its German-speaking population, an anti-conscriptionist crowd howled down Borden. By late November, nervous ministers had persuaded Borden to announce that farmers' sons and soldiers' brothers would be exempt from conscription. At last the Union campaign got going. While Quebec extremists exulted at British defeats, respectable Ontarians' newspapers insisted that a vote for Laurier would allow Bourassa to rule Canada and set the German Kaiser rejoicing. By election day, English Canadians could almost believe that conscription would fall exclusively on "slackers" and French Canadians.

The result split Canada as no election ever had before: Borden took 153 seats, only 3 in Quebec, Laurier won 82, only 20 of them outside Quebec. As usual, seat totals could be deceptive. Without the military vote, Laurier had only a hundred thousand fewer supporters than Borden. The soldiers gave the government 14 more seats and two hundred thousand votes.

During the months of campaigning, from October to December, the Military Service Act had been in abeyance. Devised by Arthur Meighen, it was not a monument to his usual lucidity. Conscripts, selected on the basis of age and marital status, had three separate stages of appeal. Of 404,395 called in the first class, 380,510 appealed. When the men were called for training, less than twenty thousand appeared. "Freely denounced as an engine of oppression," one commentator observed, the Act "contained so many safeguards against oppression that it had been made in no small degree inoperative." Quebec conscription tribunals, duly composed of a Conservative and a Liberal, granted blanket exemptions to *Canadiens* but, according to the central appeal judge, "applied conscription against the English-speaking minority in Quebec with a rigour unparalleled."

The new government was soon busy with its program. Early in 1918, regulations prohibited the import, sale, and distribution of liquor for the duration of the war and one year after. On May 24, the federal franchise was open at last to women as well as men. The coalition made it a little easier to settle one part of the long, agonizing railway problem—Mackenzie and Mann's now-bankrupt Canadian Northern. In December 1917, Borden finally achieved the solution he had advocated as long ago as 1904: public ownership. In return for money to rescue the Canadian Northern's heaviest investor, the Bank of Commerce, the railway vanished into a new Canadian Government Railways system. The Grand Trunk would have to wait.

So would much else. In March of 1918, disaster struck the Allied cause. German armies, redeployed after the collapse of Russia, smashed through the British lines. The entire British Fifth Army dissolved. By coincidence, anti-conscription riots broke out in Quebec City on the Easter weekend. They ended only when soldiers, rushed from Toronto, fired on a furious crowd, killing four civilians. Future protesters, warned Ottawa, would be conscripted on the spot. To meet the likelihood of heavy losses in France, the Union government also cancelled all exemptions under the Military Service Act. At the onset of seeding time, farmers watched their sons depart to the military depots and cursed the lying Unionist politicians.

More than farmers and French Canadians were bitter now. Thousands of families mourned soldier-sons and husbands. Inflation, moderate until 1916, soared out of control in 1917. Wages could not keep pace and more workers than ever turned to unions and to strikes. Suddenly, the violence of war came home to a peaceful country. On December 6, 1917, the blast from an exploding munitions ship devastated the working-class end of Halifax, killing 1630 people. Dazed survivors faced the worst blizzards in years. In that winter, German U-boats started patrolling near Halifax, surfacing to sink and capture merchant ships.

Amateurism and voluntarism had run their course. Behind the façade of business-dominated committees like the Patriotic Fund, it was government that controlled, regulated, and provided the money. Food and fuel controllers preached conservation, sought ingenious ways to increase production, and hunted for hoarders. Called on to conscript wealth as well as men, the Finance Minister, Sir Thomas White, cautiously imposed a Business Profits Tax and a War Income Tax. In 1918, only 31,130 Canadians were paying taxes through their new T-1 forms, for a total of $8 million. An "anti-loafing" regulation threatened jail for any man, sixteen to sixty, who was not gainfully employed. For the first time, the government authorized its federal police forces to hunt for sedition. Radical unions and foreign-dominated socialist parties were ordered suppressed, and, after years of patriotic pressure, publications in "enemy" languages were at last outlawed. A wartime labour code was more permissive, at least for employers. Collective bargaining and equal pay for men and women were recommended but the right to strike was banned for the duration.

Overseas, the mood of exhaustion and despair was far heavier, but the Canadian Corps was exempt. By amazing luck, it had escaped the major German offensives, and Currie grimly insisted on holding it together. The 5th Division, held in reserve in England since 1916, was finally broken up for reinforcements despite election promises that it would serve as a formation. The extra men made the Corps the strongest organization of its size on the British front.

Borden came back to England that spring, angry at the waste of Passchendaele, furious when he learned from Currie of the sloth, mismanagement, and lack of foresight of British generals. "Let the past bury its dead," he stormed at Lloyd George and his fellow prime ministers, "but for God's sake let us get down to earnest endeavour." Through the summer Borden finally got a share in the British planning for a war which it seemed might well drag on to 1920. Somehow, the British army must be husbanded and rebuilt. Perhaps the Russian front could be revived with Canadian help. Then, in mid-August, he headed back to Ottawa, trapped by the practical dilemma of imperial federalism—Canada could not seem to manage without its Prime Minister; no one else could represent it effectively in London. If anything, the war had shown Borden the limits of Empire and the surprising convenience of dealing with wartime Washington. When the diplomats could be sidestepped, Americans talked business and made decisions as the British never would. It was a disturbing thought in what might be only the middle of an interminable war.

Then, in a sudden, unexpected development, the war rushed to a conclusion. On August 8, 1918, a Canadian and Australian attack near Amiens smashed through the German lines. Tanks, aircraft, and infantry worked with new efficiency. Before the assault bogged down, Currie insisted on switching fronts. Again and again Canadian troops attacked, suffering huge casualties but driving deeper than ever before imaginable. The conscripts were needed as the Corps rolled forward, passing still-green fields and undamaged towns. Retreating Germans fought dangerously well to the final day at Mons, where the war had begun for the British in 1914. On November 11, at 11 A.M., it ended for everybody.

The Canadians had lost 60,661 dead; as many more would return hopelessly mutilated in mind or body. During the autumn of 1918, almost as many Canadians may have died from a strange, virulent influenza epidemic. Both tolls had taken the young and the talented. For the survivors, nothing would ever be quite the same again.

# 4 / Dead Ends

Two contradictory hopes sustained most Canadians during the war years: on the one hand that they would find a new and finer world; on the other that they would return to the old one. Reformers could take heart in women's suffrage and prohibition. Reform-minded books ranged from Mackenzie King's turgid tract on labour relations, *Industry and Humanity,* to Stephen Leacock's essay, "The Unsolved Riddle of Social Justice," with its surprising conclusion that the government "ought to supply work and pay for the unemployed, maintenance for the infirm and aged and education and opportunity for the children." The conservative view was less literary: its proponents were too busy running businesses and the country to write much.

Reformers were also audible. Backed by a resolution adopted in Calgary in February 1919, a quarter of a million veterans and their supporters demanded a $2000 re-establishment bonus. It seemed a fair return for years of earning $1.10 a day while civilians prospered safely at home. Profiteers like Sir Joseph Flavelle, with embarrassing gains of $1.7 million from his bacon business, could pay the bill. The Union government offered a flinty resistance. Ministers insisted that Canada had done more than the Americans for war widows, orphans, and the disabled. Money for the able-bodied would only reinforce the paternalism of army life. Warned that "full re-establishment" would cost $1 billion, politicians, business, and even some veterans' leaders turned against the bonus. When the pressure collapsed, the government seized the moment to "tighten up" pensions and retraining as well.

Organized labour looked tougher and better organized. The war years saw union ranks grow from 143,200 in 1915 to 378,000 by 1919. The expansion concealed sharp splits. In 1918, conservatives recaptured the leadership of the Trades and Labour Congress from the radicals who had wielded it since 1912. The angry minority, mostly from the West, swore to meet in Calgary in March 1919, to plot their strategy. By the time they met, an even more militant caucus, drawn from western cities, notably Vancouver, had taken over the meeting. The excited majority called for a proletarian revolution in Canada, cheered the Bolshevik Revolution in Russia, and so frightened a timid Sir Thomas White in Ottawa that he proposed summoning a British cruiser to Vancouver harbour. Delegates dispersed to plan a "One Big Union," an industrial organization of workers, to challenge the craft-based conservatism of the Trades and Labour Congress.

None of this, beyond steaming rhetoric, had much to do with the Winnipeg General Strike. In fact Bob Russell, prime architect of the One Big Union, worked in vain to prevent the outbreak among his fellow machinists. The trouble was that a general strike in 1918 had won collective bargaining rights for Winnipeg's civic workers; now it must be tried again to help the employees of Winnipeg's obdurate factory owners. On May 15, after an overwhelming vote of support from its twelve thousand members, Winnipeg's Labour Council proclaimed a general strike. An astonishing thirty thousand Winnipeggers walked out, from waiters to telephone operators. Other general strikes spread from Vancouver to Amherst, Nova Scotia.

Strike organizers never understood that it was their angry speeches, not their cautious deeds, that Winnipeg's nervous middle class noticed. After a month without strike pay, most Winnipeg workers had had enough. Strikes elsewhere had collapsed. The words on both sides got angrier. Winnipeg's civic leaders, convinced that labour was plotting its own Bolshevik Revolution, got automatic backing from Arthur Meighen, Manitoba's cabinet representative in Ottawa. Persuaded that "enemy aliens" were behind the strike, Parliament swiftly amended the law to allow easy deportation. Dawn arrests of strike leaders promptly followed. This gave a dying strike a last, tragic rally. On Saturday, June 21, crowds filled the street in front of the city hall to protest the arrests. Mounted police charged the throng and special constables attacked with clubs. "Bloody Saturday" and the ensuing trials of the strike leaders (British or Canadian to a man) gave Winnipeg's workers a long, bitter memory of their ordeal. Driven back

159

to the city's north end, they gave their neighbourhoods a durable allegiance to labour and socialist politics.

In the wake of the strike's collapse and the trial of leaders for sedition, the attempt to create a One Big Union was doomed. Employer resistance, counter-attacks by the craft unions, and bitter disputes among the OBU's own leaders left only fragments of its bold vision. The split was also a foretaste of divisions to come. Within a few years, the TLC drove out its biggest Canadian affiliate, the Canadian Brotherhood of Railway Employees, because it rivalled an international union. A tiny Communist party, organized in a barn near Guelph in 1921, obeyed Moscow's orders to "bore from within" the labour movement with divisive consequences. By 1927, the Communists had begun to build their own labour organization, the Workers' Unity League. In Quebec, years of sermons and editorials combined with the resentments of the war years to produce a small Catholic union movement. In 1921, the Catholic "syndicates" took public shape at a congress in Hull. The dream of a strong, united, and radical Canadian labour movement was buried for the next thirty years.

Only businessmen seemed to win their post-war demands, largely because they already dominated politics, media, and opinion. Manufacturers were determined to safeguard the tariff; merchants aimed at wiping out government controls; financiers insisted on ending inflation at once. They all succeeded. Within days of the Armistice, Sir Joseph Flavelle had closed his munitions factories and put their assets on sale. That might have been sound if bankers had not clamped on their favourite weapon of deflation, high interest rates. Capital to readjust industry to peacetime purposes vanished. So did jobs. In due course, so did inflation, but not before farmers and small businesses had suffered financial disaster. Bankers and their admirers found such policies excellent. Fiscal righteousness had been profitable for them.

In 1917, the government had closed the Winnipeg Grain Exchange and created a single Wheat Board to market grain. Farmers first grumbled and then rejoiced as prices soared to a record $3.15 a bushel. After the 1919 crop, the Wheat Board dissolved and free enterprise returned. The earlier rural grumbles salved the politicians' consciences; faith in the market did the rest. Despite a serious crop failure on top of years of declining prairie productivity, wheat prices plummeted forty-five per cent in two

160

years. Farmers who had invested in land, machinery, and comforts in the confidence of high prices now had real reason for lamentation.

Unlike veterans and labour, however, they still had the strength to be influential. In the war years, farmers had confirmed the political independence of the Canadian Council of Agriculture by endorsing a Farmers' Platform in 1916. In 1918, furious at the cancellation of their sons' exemption from conscription, farmers had marched on Ottawa. Many endorsed an even stronger platform, deliberately titled a "New National Policy," loaded with familiar demands for reciprocity, lower freight rates, and bank reform, and fresh planks insisting on railway nationalization and a graduated income tax. In T. A. Crerar, Minister of Agriculture for the Unionists, the farmers had a leader who even wrote his ministerial letters on United Grain Growers' paper. When White's 1919 budget fell short of farmers' wishes, Crerar quit.

The Prime Minister seemed far removed from the domestic turbulence of 1919. Even before the Armistice, Borden had left for Europe to achieve the war aims he had set for Canada. So far as Sir Robert was concerned, his country had just won her War for Independence. Inside or outside the Empire—Borden was no longer as sure as he had once been—Canada must emerge from the war a sovereign power with her own signature on the peace treaty and her own seat in the new League of Nations. Borden's powerful patron, David Lloyd George, had no real objections. Once it was clear that the great powers would dominate both arrangements, Canada's concern could be met. It was the Americans who resisted, outraged that the devious Lloyd George would use mere colonies to win extra votes for Britain. Finally, on May 6, 1919, President Woodrow Wilson glumly withdrew his objections, but Americans on the whole did not. Canada's full membership in the League of Nations became an added argument for American isolationists, who protested British dominance in the organization. The United States stayed out, Canada remained, but the League was crippled. Borden's international dreams had reached a dead end.

Even in Canada, Borden's hard-won overseas triumphs were seen as merely symbolic and perhaps even dangerous. The Prime Minister's insistence that Parliament vote on the German peace treaty was dismissed by a leading Liberal, William Fielding, as "a colossal humbug"; Article X of the League Covenant, pledging members to mutual defence, was seen by a French-Canadian MP as putting Canada "at the beck and call of a Council not responsible to the nation." Borden's own colleagues bitterly resented his absence in the midst of so many crises and at a time when the post-war fate of his Union coalition was so obviously in doubt. For all his earnestness and sense of duty, Borden seems to have lost interest in politics. In July, he sailed down the St. Lawrence in a bold bid to win over Quebec's premier. Sir Lomer Gouin was tempted; he had been running the province for Ottawa since the 1918 riots. Electoral common sense hauled Gouin back, and Borden went home. By the autumn, the Prime Minister was too ailing and exhausted to postpone any longer a long-awaited rest cure in the United States.

Borden's colleagues, buffeted from all sides, welcomed the rest cure because they knew they could not agree on a replacement. They were not idle. A Royal Commission on Labour Relations collected a long list of useful reforms, most of which would wait a generation to be seen again. A civil service reform removed forty thousand government employees from patronage (and robbed Unionists of that much more influence). Titles of nobility, discredited by wartime profiteering and scandals, also ended (with a brief revival in the 1930s). As cynics might have expected, the income tax survived the war and grew dramatically in size and bite. One legacy of the influenza epidemic (and fears of wartime venereal disease) was a small Department of Health. Even after "tightening up," the government had to treat eight thousand sick and wounded veterans and maintain eighty thousand pensioners.

No problem had bigger economic or political impact than the railways. In 1919, the Grand Trunk followed the Canadian Northern via receivership into nationalization. This time, there was no Bank of Commerce to guard its interests; $180 million in watered shares simply evaporated, mostly at the expense of English investors. Politically, the real issue was a plan by Lord Shaughnessy of the Canadian Pacific to lease the entire national railway system, run it under the CPR, and charge its losses to the taxpayer. In this fashion, free enterprise would prevail and the CPR (with its eager partner, the Bank of Montreal) would profit immensely. Arthur Meighen bluntly rejected the scheme. Lord Shaughnessy was beside himself with rage and Montreal's powerful financial and

162

business community dutifully echoed his fury. Most Canadians came to see Meighen as an austere, even frigid exponent of free enterprise: to Montreal business, he was a rabid socialist. His party, denounced by the Quebec electorate for conscription, lost access to its richest financial sources. Henceforth, the party of the Canadian rich would verge on penury.

The government's railway policy had other consequences. In November 1918, the old, patronage-battered Intercolonial was drawn into the new system, christened the Canadian National Railways in 1919. The ICR headquarters left Moncton for Toronto and then Montreal. To meet the appalling debt charges for the system, rates were immediately raised to central Canadian levels and, in September 1920, subjected to a drastic, system-wide forty-per-cent increase. Maritime protests were dismissed as the familiar whining of a too-favoured region. In fact, Maritimers were right. The ICR was *their* railway. Its regionally-based rates were not only vital to local manufacturing, they had produced a regular profit. By 1925, the Maritimes' national market was gone. British Empire Steel Company, owner of Cape Breton's steel and coal industry, reeled towards ruin amidst wage-cuts and long, violent strikes. In half a decade, a hundred and fifty thousand Maritimers left the region. Lack of hydro-electricity, a lower coal tariff, and greedy profit-taking were all factors in the first great era of Maritime decline, but the loss of the ICR was decisive.

Perhaps, as Dafoe had predicted in 1918, no one in power in the post-war years could have made friends. In October 1919, veteran politicians got a shock even opposition parties had to heed: Ontario provincial voters handed the legislature to the United Farmers and a clutch of labour members. With a premier, Ernest Drury, who had not even run in the election, a new farmer-labour government took office. In February 1920, Crerar emerged as leader of a National Progressive party. By 1921, farmers held power in Manitoba and Alberta. In Saskatchewan, a foxy Premier C. A. Dunning made his Liberals look so much like Progressives that no one bothered to try telling the difference. Far more than veterans or labour, farmers were the force that rolled out of English-speaking Canada like a juggernaut, sweeping up more Liberals than old Tories.

On February 17, 1919, the venerable Sir Wilfrid had died, confident as ever that he would have regained power. To his

French-Canadian followers, Laurier's ghost would be their guide to a successor. Lady Laurier sensibly thought that William Fielding might be the man to reunite a shattered party but he had deserted in 1917. Young William Lyon Mackenzie King, too brash and ambitious to win the living Laurier's approval, was now the beneficiary of the ghost. Had he not run as Laurier's candidate in 1917 and lost? When Liberals gathered in a sweaty Ottawa exhibition hall in August 1919 for Canada's first leadership convention, they agreed King was a bearable alternative. His youth and his contact with modern notions like unions and management efficiency might help him. King won on the third ballot.

King's antagonist would not be Robert Borden. The old Prime Minister had returned to Ottawa in the spring of 1920 still sick and indecisive. Colleagues urged him to stay on. Meighen, bluntly, advised him to go. A weary Borden, dutifully trying to preserve Unionism, preferred Thomas White, perhaps even Sir Lomer Gouin, as his successor. Both refused. The Tory backbenchers wanted Meighen, and, on July 10, 1920, they got him. "The only unpardonable sin in politics," claimed the new Prime Minister, "is lack of courage." He had plenty. He was tough, hard-working, brilliant in speech and grasp. He was also as utterly inflexible in his political principles as the plump and prolix King was adjustable. When Progressives continued to win by-elections, Meighen ended the suspense and ordered the longest federal election campaign in history—from September 1 to December 7, 1921.

Meighen wanted time because he had a message. The tariff, he believed, could be as clear and successful an issue as it had been in 1911. While King treated Progressives as "Liberals in a hurry," Meighen flayed them with all the brilliance of his tongue. Crerar campaigned in Ontario and the West but experience had shown that farmers would organize themselves. As for King's campaign, Meighen's description was not misleading: "Protection on apples in British Columbia, Free Trade in the Prairie Provinces and rural parts of Ontario, Protection in industrial centres of Ontario, Conscription in Quebec, and Humbug in the Maritimes." In a sense, it worked. Humbug and Conscription gave King almost all his 116 seats. Outside Ontario and British Columbia, where he collected 50 seats, Meighen was routed. Farmers in Ontario and the West gave Crerar 65 seats. Winnipeg and Calgary each elected a labour member. One of these, J. S. Woodsworth, a former

Winnipeg clergyman and editor of a strike newspaper, insisted that for the first time Labour would sit as a separate party.

Canadians in 1921 had voted in distinct regional patterns, and they had elected their first minority Parliament. King now proved to have an acute and single-minded commitment to compromise. The prospect was daunting. On tariffs, railways, and much else, his conservative Quebec caucus had more in common with the Conservatives than with the Progressives with their Protestantism, their economic fancies, and their wartime espousal of conscription. Liberal ranks included both Laurierites and conscriptionists. As a labour negotiator, resolving opposite viewpoints with no visible opinions of his own, King had acquired the experience he now deployed.

King found the little that united farmers and Quebeckers and swiftly exploited it. Both *Canadiens* and farmers hated militarism. Defence would be cut to the bone. Both despised imperialism. With J. W. Dafoe and his new Under Secretary of State for External Affairs, O. D. Skelton (Laurier's biographer), King would be properly escorted to London to put Canada's blunt veto on any schemes for consultation or imperial collaboration. Nationalists and *nationalistes* might not cheer but they would take quiet comfort. Lloyd George's appeal for aid in a possible war with the Turks at Chanak in 1922 inspired Meighen to utter an instinctive "Ready, Aye Ready." From King, it drew resentful silence. The League of Nations, with its dangerous Article x, would be reminded by Senator Raoul Dandurand, president of its Assembly in 1925, that "Canada is a fire-proof house, far from the source of any conflagration." If more public gestures were needed, King sent another *Canadien,* Ernest Lapointe, to Washington in 1923 to sign the Halibut Treaty without the proffered assistance from Great Britain.

If this seemed little, at home there was less. Not until 1924 was the tariff even modestly reduced—on items that exclusively troubled Tory Ontario. The Hudson's Bay Railway, a prairie dream for thirty years, would come—but only when King got a majority. The Crowsnest Pass freight rate, suspended during the war, was restored—for wheat only—in 1923. In the Maritimes, solid for King in 1921, there was very little, for surely the region was as Liberal as it needed to be. It was the West that needed pleasing and patience.

In 1923, the Ontario farmer government was utterly defeated. Its reforms counted for little in the face of internal divisions and voters eager to sneer at rural earnestness. Those weaknesses could be exploited. Pragmatic farmer-politicians like Ernest Drury and Thomas Crerar were driven half-mad by rural ideologues, determined that farmers form a movement, not a party. Alberta's Henry Wise Wood preached that government must be based on groups like farmers, business, and labour, not on political parties. This brand of social corporatism did not fit practical politics. Nor did farmers like what their representatives were doing for them. The Progressives, on the dubious principle that they were not really "politicians," forbade Crerar from becoming leader of the opposition in 1922. Thereafter, their movement fell apart. Radicals debated freight rates and such monetary theories as Social Credit; the pragmatists plotted how they could safely make peace with King.

By 1925, some were ready for a switch. So was Meighen. In opposition, he had worked ingeniously and well. The Maritimes had risen with one voice in a Maritimes Rights movement that just happened to be managed by Tories. By 1925, all three Maritime provincial governments had fallen to Conservatives. Elsewhere, Meighen could count on the recurrence of hard times since the war and what seemed to him the transparent futility of King's government. About Quebec, Meighen could do nothing nor would he even try to buy votes in the West. If anyone really wanted the Hudson's Bay Railway, he promised $3 million and no more. The outcome of the election, on October 29, 1925, was as good a victory as Meighen could have hoped to get: forty-seven per cent of the votes to King's forty per cent, and 116 seats to 99 for the Liberals, with the Progressives cut to nine per cent and 24 seats.

Yet King did not resign. Liberals raged privately at his "vanity and pomposity," his "predilection for strange and unworthy favourites." When Meighen and King each presented the Progressives with their programs, seven switched back to King and his majority held. Defeated in his own seat, King went west to win Prince Albert, and he brought Saskatchewan's C. A. Dunning back with him to the cabinet. A new finance minister gave Canadians a "prosperity budget" of tax-cuts and give-aways, an experience few of them had had since 1906. Meighen's near-victory in 1925 forced voters to realize that the Progressives were through and that the next contest would be a Liberal-Tory run-off. J. W. Dafoe was typical. In three elections he had avoided voting Liberal; now he saw no alternative.

First, there would be an unpleasant test. Prohibition, dead in most of Canada by 1924, persisted bravely south of the border, imposing a strain on the morality of customs officers and their elected superiors that natural avarice could not resist. The result, exposed by a vigorous Tory MP, Harry Stevens, was an odorous scandal of kickbacks, cover-ups, and bribes reaching all the way to the Minister of Customs, a French Canadian. King swiftly hoisted the guilty minister to the safety of the Senate and offered no signs of repentance. Tories raged, and pure-minded Progressives squirmed. The upshot, after much uproar, was a vote of censure on King's government which it would surely lose. But first, King won a weekend adjournment. Next, he headed to the Governor General, Lord Byng of Vimy, to seek a dissolution, thus avoiding formal censure. Byng, shocked by the impropriety, refused. An equally shocked King urged him to check with London. Byng refused so colonial a gesture. King indignantly resigned. Meighen, against good advice but out of loyalty to the Governor General, an honourable British soldier, accepted office. Then, when the Liberals orchestrated their own vote of censure, Byng gave Meighen the election he had denied King.

Meighen never could understand it. His opponent, the man who perennially insisted that "Parliament would decide," had been caught trying to run away from Parliament's decision. The man of insistent legalism had defied constitutional convention. King, too, may have been nonplussed by events, but luck was with him. In English-speaking Canada, the election issue had already been settled by the prosperity budget and Meighen. The customs scandals might arouse loyal Tories, but, in good times, muck smells like fertilizer. In Quebec, Byng could easily be portrayed as a British colonial governor, bullying the great rebel's grandson. And many of the Tories' customs house villains had been *Canadiens*. Meighen added Nova Scotia to his majorities in Ontario and British Columbia but his 99 seats could still not match King's 128 nor the remnant of 20 Progressives and 3 Labourites. Meighen suffered the ultimate humiliation; defeat in his own riding.

In memory, the twenties would shine as a golden era suspended between the Great War and the Great Depression. Only the last half decade actually qualified as golden, but economic growth was steady and remarkable. American prosperity poured over the border in the form of investment in branch plants, able to serve a British Empire sheltered behind an empire-wide tariff. Automobile, rubber, chemical, and clothing factories grew up around the lower Great Lakes in industrial cities like Hamilton, Oshawa, Windsor, St. Catharines, and Montreal. To supply both Canadian and American markets there was a prodigious prodding and digging away at the minerals of the Canadian Shield, from the Noranda copper properties in Quebec to the gold of Kirkland Lake and the nickel of Sudbury. When King finally launched the promised Hudson's Bay Railway in 1927, it fulfilled an old tradition by opening up Flin Flon, Lynn Lake, and the area beyond for the exploitation of its mineral wealth.

In 1920, the CNR earned $234 million, spent $231 million, and had the balance to retire its $1311-million debt. Instead of collapsing under the impossible debt load, the CNR staggered into the new decade.

An American-born, British-seasoned railroader, Sir Henry Thornton, cheerfully accepted King's invitation to run the system. Thornton was not original in his insistence that salvation lay with expansion, but he certainly expanded with a flair. The CNR added five thousand miles of track, built new locomotives, cars, and the grandest hotels the country had seen, from the Nova Scotian in Halifax to Jasper Park Lodge in the Rockies. The CNR bought ships to service the West Indies, experimented with air service, and created a transcontinental network to send programs to "radio cars" on its luxurious passenger trains. It was the golden age of Canadian rail, and of all the potential dead ends in the decade this was the most certain.

The twenties brought American investment and American markets, and these would make Canada a north-south nation once again. British economic influence had slipped with wartime liquidation of investments; now it fell consistently. The routes of the new transportation network would be highways, barely two-lane and winding at the beginning of the decade; a spreading telephone system; and the air itself, now spotted with the frail aircraft sent out by the British after the war as a gift to an infant Canadian air force. Even before its official birth in 1923, the Royal Canadian Air Force had shown how planes could be used to spot forest fires, deliver treaty money, and even catch smugglers. By surmounting the barriers of distance and mountain ranges to deliver prospectors and supplies to the far North, bush pilots managed to make northern isolation easier to bear. To the south, cars and trucks were having an even greater economic impact. Just as Canada's costly railway system had begun to rationalize and reform itself, road traffic had arrived as its most devastating competition. Canadians with $3250 to spend on a McLaughlin roadster or $850 for a Model T hardly worried. Provincial treasurers certainly did.

Almost every development of the twenties contradicted national unity. Ottawa had always managed railways; roads had been left under provincial control as unimportant. Now they mattered. The expansion of secondary education, and new allowances for widows, the blind, and the disabled were paid for from provincial coffers. Sir John A. Macdonald had planned an east-west country; now the branch-plant factories, the mineral exploration, the floods of American films, magazines, and radio programs were switching Canada to a north-south axis. Perhaps that was why Meighen's 1911-style nationalism grew fainter and more shrill.

With new responsibilities, provinces needed more revenue. Eager for allies, Mackenzie King tried to oblige, restrained only by his concern for the national debt. In London, the Judicial Committee gave a hand. Lord Haldane, as its spokesman, administered a final kick to the once-sweeping claim that Ottawa was responsible for "peace, order and good government." In yet another decision about the regulation of booze, Haldane's Committee ruled that Ottawa's sweeping powers were restricted to periods of emergency. Otherwise, it was the provinces, with their control of "property and civil rights," which had the sweeping powers. As a further boost to provincial rights and revenues, King gave the prairie provinces full control of their natural resources.

Under duress, the federal government took a few initiatives. In 1929, over opposition from Ottawa and Quebec, the courts reinterpreted the British North America Act to say that women, as well as men, were "persons." Its responsibility for veterans had kept Ottawa slightly involved in health policies and a national employment service. In 1925, in exchange for supporting King, J. S. Woodsworth of the tiny Labour Party extorted a promise that old-age pensions would be established. The promise was kept in 1927—Ottawa would meet half the cost of a meagre, means-tested pension for those over seventy. The provinces, compelled to pay the other half, hesitated. Nova Scotia found a novel way to raise its share. It legalized liquor, sold it profitably in government-run stores, and helped its elderly. Other provinces followed suit. By ending prohibition, Ontario's new Tory government bounced from deficit to surplus budgets.

Even when Britain, through the Statute of Westminster, granted Canada and her four other dominions formal independence in the world, Canada's provinces interfered. Before the Statute could be passed, Canada needed a formula to amend her constitution, the British North America Act. Not even the euphoria brought on by the country's diamond jubilee in 1927 could bring the premiers and Ottawa to agree on such a formula. While the British waited impatiently to adopt the Statute of Westminster, premiers Howard Ferguson of Ontario and Alexandre Taschereau of Quebec imposed their conditions. Canada's constitution, they insisted, would stay in London. Independent they might be, but Canadians could not yet trust themselves to alter their own system of government fairly.

The diamond jubilee year generated some tinselly nationalism, but nothing could hide the raw racial intolerance that had flourished since the war years. A Manitoba author had tried to create a more positive image of Canada's racial diversity by describing the provinces as a mosaic of cultures, but the diversity of languages and cultures seemed to give no pleasure. Bishop G. E. Lloyd of Saskatchewan, a colourful prairie pioneer, publicly denounced the "mongrelization" of Canada. It was Lloyd who provoked an aging Sir Clifford Sifton to deliver his tolerant, if condescending comments about "peasants in sheepskin coats." Later in the decade, the white hoods and flaming crosses of the Ku Klux Klan invaded western Canada, symbols of hatred of Catholics and "foreigners." Within a year, the Klan promoters had absconded with a hundred thousand dollars in membership funds, but their ugly message remained. In 1929, Saskatchewan voters chose a Tory government headed by J. T. M. Anderson, a respected educator whose book, *The Education of New Canadi-*

*ans,* had demanded firm assimilation with "a true Canadian spirit and attachment to British institutions."

Nationalism and anxiety about alien forces had made the West a natural birthplace for the interdenominational movement that ended in 1926 with the formation of the United Church of Canada. Methodists, Congregationalists, and all but a sturdy core of Presbyterians joined the new organization. Enthusiasts had seen the new church as specifically Canadian and a challenge to a secular age. Others, with less idealism, saw it as a sensible business merger or as an answer to the numerical challenge of the Catholics. The first Moderator, George Pidgeon, firmly suppressed any vestiges of the old Methodist radicalism; wealthy contributors might be upset.

Not even Church Union could rescue Canadian Protestantism from the challenge of fundamentalists on one side or of rationalism and secularism on the other. Nothing could save the churches from paying the price of two great but divisive crusades: the War and prohibition.

Quebec had resisted both crusades and would fight until 1940 against a third: votes for women. In the post-war world, French Canada's leaders felt their people to be more isolated and endangered than ever. The conscription crisis had not been something as remote as Riel or the Ontario schools. The Canadian majority had imposed its will on Quebec; had taken Quebec's sons into an English-speaking army. Henri Bourassa, back in Parliament after 1921 as an independent, pleaded still for his bilingual, bicultural Canadian compact but he also grew conservative, abandoning forever the few radical ideas that earlier had inspired him.

In this, Bourassa was following a new intellectual fashion. The leader of the newest nationalism was Abbé Lionel Groulx, a tireless elf of a man who taught the history of Quebec to generations of students at the new University of Montreal. Only within Quebec, argued Groulx and his disciples of the *Action Française,* could a French and Catholic nationality be preserved. This preservation would demand rejection, even in the cities, of the external taints in films, books, and magazines. On Sunday, January 9, 1927, Montreal's Laurier Palace cinema burned, killing seventy-eight children. Groulx's campaign to ban youngsters from movie theatres (and thereby the influence of American and British movies) was won.

Yet the triviality of the reform underlined the mean-minded limits of the *Action Française* program. Montreal was an ugly, unhealthy city for too many of its people, and by 1931, two-thirds of the 818,377 Montrealers were *Canadiens*. But, for them, as for most Canadians, the cities seemed bright, more lively, crowded with the material rewards of the era. In good times Groulx's austere, moralistic nationalism commanded disciples, not a mass following. In the thriving twenties, Groulx himself knew that his cause had stalled.

The twenties was really the first decade of mass-produced culture. Films, magazines, gramophones with "hit" records, professional sports, all promised a lifestyle ordinary people might soon enjoy. Intellectuals could read *Canadian Forum,* debate the merits of the Toronto-based artists, the Group of Seven; they might even have heard of Emily Carr's lonely work. Others could boast of the sailing feats of the *Bluenose* or hum the songs of the Dumbells, the soldier-entertainers who sustained what little remained of wartime nostalgia.

Canada was producing respected actors, musicians, and singers, but their renown was earned in New York, Paris, or London. The country's own frail culture was shrinking before the excitement and prosperity of the United States. No cultural force broke down the international barriers more swiftly than radio. By the mid-twenties, powerful American stations carried signals into most populated parts of Canada, and the technology of a crystal set receiver was not beyond a dexterous youngster. Canada, with its frugal comforts, its low wages, its backwater vision of itself, had never been more immediately or more dangerously challenged. Perhaps the inspiration would do some good.

# 5 / The Depression

Great events have complex causes. Few now would date the Great Depression of the thirties from the Wall Street crash of October 1929. And, although the slump *was* a symptom of a much wider sickness, there are not many who would still believe those contemporary preachers who blamed it on falling morals, rising skirts, and self-indulgent insistence on living beyond one's means.

In 1929 it cost over ten thousand dollars a year to live the resplendent life depicted in the rotogravure supplements; only 13,477 Canadian families admitted to such an income. The federal Department of Labour insisted that a family needed $1200 to $1500 a year to maintain a "minimum standard of decency." Sixty per cent of working men and eighty-two per cent of working women were earning less than $1000 a year. By any definition, most people were as poor as Canadians had been for generations. Depressions did not occur because ordinary people lived beyond their means. In fact the British economist, John Maynard Keynes, would soon point out that the economy shut down because too many people had no means to buy what it could produce. Most Canadians qualified for this category.

The immediate cause of the Depression in Canada was not the Wall Street crash but the enormous 1928 wheat crop. A decade of immigration had filled the last, most infertile prairie land. As well, western farmers had forgotten politics as times improved. They listened instead to a persuasive American lawyer named Aaron Sapiro. Rather than going to the Wheat Board or the Grain Exchange, Sapiro said, why not pool the wheat harvest and sell it with the united bargaining power of any good cartel? Thousands of farmers joined the wheat pool, prospered, and added to their acreage. The idea worked brilliantly—as long as there was no glut and no serious competition. By 1928, there were both: 567

173

million bushels at a Pool-guaranteed price of $1.28 a bushel, to be sold in a world that could now buy much more cheaply from the United States, Argentina, Australia, and even the Soviet Union.

Of course, no one worried too much in 1929. Prosperity now seemed permanent, but perhaps, as brokers warned their clients, the market needed just a tiny "correction." Inventories had become too large. Capital investment was a trifle optimistic. Salesmen on the prairies confessed that orders were down. Business prophets cautiously reminded their customers that economies, like workers, needed an occasional rest. Slowly, and then irreversibly, an economic system based on credit, confidence, and massive resource exports began rolling down the cycle. Distant buyers cancelled orders for timber, fish, and base metals. Construction stopped. Industrialists checked their shrinking order books, and commanded wage cuts, half-time work, or even a temporary shutdown. There should be no astonishment; depressions had already occurred twice in that prosperous decade, in 1920 and 1923.

Politicians in Canada did not face much annoyance from economic indicators or unemployment statistics. The few available figures were collected in a somewhat haphazard system of local reports by the Department of Labour and published in its *Labour Gazette*. In 1929, the *Gazette* found about three per cent of its sample looking for jobs; a year later, the total had reached eleven per cent, or 530,000 men and women. That was alarming but not unprecedented. Provincial governments, pestering Ottawa for relief measures, were undoubtedly playing politics. They were also dodging their constitutional responsibility for social welfare. Mackenzie King, proud of his soberly balanced budget, was outraged that Tory premiers should mine votes from an unpleasant but short-lived down-turn. He would not give one cent, he told the House of Commons on April 3, 1930, "for these alleged unemployment purposes." He might confer with the more respectful and needy prairie premiers, but as for provincial governments that diametrically opposed him, "I would not give them a five-cent piece."

Such blunt comments were out of character, but the Prime Minister felt quite removed from the economic calamity that was beginning to preoccupy Canadians. He had determined on a 1930 election long before his current spiritualist added her blessing, and his new finance minister, C. A. Dunning, duly cut the federal sales tax to one per cent. The prairies could thank the Liberals for giving them control over their natural resources. Nationalists could applaud the promised Statute of Westminster, and Quebec would always remember the Tories and conscription. A royal commission on broadcasting, headed by Sir John Aird, had recommended a BBC-style safeguard for Canada's invaded airwaves, but discussion of a publicly-owned broadcasting system could safely be postponed. Who knew what Quebec sensitivities it might arouse?

King felt all the more secure because of his opposition. In 1927 the Tories had followed the Liberal example with an American-style leadership convention in Winnipeg. The winner was Richard Bedford Bennett, a New Brunswick-born corporation lawyer who had waged his party's hopeless battles in Alberta before his friendship with the heiress to the fortune of the Ottawa Valley's E. B. Eddy lumber company brought him a vast inheritance. As a youth Bennett had pledged total abstinence, and he fought temptation with candy and sugar. He was a big, plump man with a booming voice, a domineering manner, and a capacity for kindness that he kept utterly secret. Like King, a lonely bachelor, Bennett carried an aura of the business competence that the era already worshipped. King considered his opponent far inferior to Meighen. About Bennett's intellect, King was right. In electoral terms, King was wrong.

The Depression was Bennett's chance. The "five-cent piece" speech was soon burnished in memory as proof of King's callousness. "Mackenzie King promises you conferences": trumpeted Bennett, "I promise you action." Quebec farmers were told to blame their miseries on imports of New Zealand butter. Bennett would save them. The Liberals had allowed a one-sided imperial preference; Bennett would demand full reciprocity. In the crisis, the United States had led the way in hoisting tariffs. Bennett would do so too, but in his hands, protection would "blast a way into the markets of the world." Even doubters stayed to marvel. After the years of anaemic compromise and shuffling evasion, here was self-confidence and dynamism. As a businessman rich enough to finance his party's entire campaign, Bennett would resolve the Depression. On July 28, Bennett won the kind of triumph Tories had not seen since the days of Sir John A. Macdonald: 137 seats to 91 for King and a rump of only 12 for the Progressives. Among the Tories, to prove that this was the age of miracles, were sixteen French-Canadian rural members.

If vigour could have demolished the Depression, it would have vanished within a year of the election. Bennett summoned the new Parliament for September 1930, forced through the biggest tariff increases since 1879, passed $20 million in emergency relief, and boasted that added protection would guarantee twenty-five thousand industrial jobs. In London for the Imperial Conference of 1930—and to supplant King in signing the Statute of Westminster—Bennett joined his old friend, Lord Beaverbrook (the former Max Aitken) in a vain crusade for an Empire-based exclusive trading system. Two years later, after Britain's own efforts for free trade had utterly failed, an Imperial Economic Conference in Ottawa gave Bennett his belated victory. Desperate for any agreement, the British lowered their tariff barriers to Canada and received no more than Bennett's pledge not to raise his fifty per cent protection any higher. Canadian financiers and industrialists had good reason to rejoice. British politicians grumbled that Bennett had bullied them mercilessly.

While Canadians found themselves in a trade war with a steadily more protectionist United States, Bennett made a determined bid to launch the long-contemplated St. Lawrence Deep Waterway project. A treaty with President Herbert Hoover's Republican administration passed all the way to the American Senate. Senators from the Atlantic states, worried about the waterway's effect on trade in their harbours, promptly killed it. Thousands of potential jobs vanished, but Bennett poured still more money into provincial relief projects, adding close to a billion dollars to the national debt. The Wheat Pool, utterly ruined when its advance payments to farmers far exceeded the price it received for their wheat, staggered on only because Bennett provided secret subsidies. Canada's chartered banks preened themselves on surviving without a bankruptcy, but Bennett finally forced them to accept a central Bank of Canada—though the government held only a minority of the shares.

Bennett's most unexpected creation was the Canadian Radio Broadcasting Commission. Prodded by young enthusiasts in the Canadian Radio League who insisted that it would be either the State or the States, Bennett had taken up the Aird Commission

176

report with unexpected interest. A Judicial Committee decision, surprising only because of the Committee's past practices, confirmed that broadcasting was in the federal domain. Born in 1932, in the depth of the Depression, the CRBC was a sadly underfinanced compromise. It was also a Canadian stake in public broadcasting in the decade when radio became the mass medium that mattered to almost everyone.

Radio mattered because, as the Depression deepened, radio sets became the only escape from a besetting hopelessness for many people. This was no ordinary depression in which savings vanished and countless city families slipped home to the security of the farm. As J. S. Woodsworth told Parliament, "If they went out today, they would meet another army of unemployed coming back from the country to the city." People in Ottawa, he reported, took refuge in garbage dumps. Bennett's own files bulged with reports of misery. Even the aged daughter of a former prime minister was reported to be on the verge of starvation.

Unemployment insurance had been a Liberal policy in 1919. Only unions now pleaded for it: experts and politicians claimed that it would subsidize idleness. Instead, they insisted, wages must fall until everyone would find work. It took time. By 1933, the government's crude statistics reported twenty-three per cent out of work. A third of Canada's manufacturing jobs had vanished. Net farm income fell from $417 million in 1929 to $109 million in 1933.

Those with jobs found some compensations. Prices fell faster than wages until 1932–33. A fifteen-per-cent wage cut imposed on civil servants by Ottawa and imitated by most provinces and other major employers still left living standards undamaged. The prosperous few could enjoy themselves with an obliviousness to wider suffering that wealth seems to confer. Newspapers and radio helped. Media in the thirties seem to have accepted a solemn duty to trivialize or ignore the misery of millions. Lush Hollywood musicals and adventure films filled neighbourhood movie theatres. Air races, professional sports, and the exotic junketing of reporters such as Gordon Sinclair gave the public an escape. The birth of the Dionne quintuplets on May 28, 1934, at Callander, Ontario, provided some reporters, politicians, business promoters, and members of the medical profession with a special chance for fame and fortune.

The unemployed would eagerly have shared in the escape, but relief procedures, designed to force the idle to work, crushed self-respect. Relief officials insisted that cars, telephones, pets, ornaments, comfortable furniture, and all but a single bare light fixture be sacrificed. Recipients collected food vouchers, sought medical care from an over-worked contract doctor, and visited a municipal depot for issues of used clothing. Men shovelled snow, chopped wood, or pulled weeds for their relief benefits. Since women did not work, often no provision was made for their clothing or personal needs. The new social work profession sold its services as "experts" in detecting fraud and waste.

Misery on relief was deliberate public policy. Even at the depths of the Depression, editors and business leaders insisted that jobs were available if men would only hunt for them. One result of this was that single unemployed men were sent packing by relief officials. Thousands rode boxcars to British Columbia. Some froze to death or were murdered on the way. Provincial governments established work camps for single men. In 1933, Bennett's government followed suit, using the Department of National Defence to run camps behind a discreet façade of civilian administration. On paper, men hacking at bush or restoring historic fortifications cost a dollar a day. After their expenses had been deducted, twenty cents remained as their actual pay.

Those who held jobs knew that thousands were waiting for a chance to replace them. Some employers fired women because men needed work; others replaced men with women because they would accept lower pay. There were few strikes. Only the Communist-led Workers Unity League organized vigorously, and its efforts often ended in bloodshed and failure. Bred in the doctrine of self-help, individual Canadians seemed almost pathetically willing to accept responsibility for their plight. Some literally died rather than accept relief. Only slowly did guilt turn to despair and then to deep resentment as the depth and duration of the Depression exceeded every memory. When urban politicians like Montreal's Camillien Houde or Vancouver's Gerry McGeer sought votes by helping the unemployed, their cities risked bankruptcy.

Nowhere was destitution greater than across much of the prairie West. In eastern Canada, farmers suffered falling prices and occasional foreclosures, but there was food to eat, and the rural population actually increased. In the West, where Canadians had boasted of the greatest farmland in the world, the thirties brought literal starvation.

The collapse of world grain markets would have been catastrophe enough, but people would have eaten. In 1929, drought devastated much of the harvest, and not for another ten long years would weather or crop conditions give the prairies a satisfactory harvest. In 1931, the wind began lifting the topsoil in great black clouds. The next year brought the first great plague of grasshoppers, which devoured every green thing and clothing and tool handles besides. In 1933, drought, hail, rust, and frost joined the grasshoppers, as though all nature's forces had united in giving prairie settlers a notice to quit.

Thousands obeyed, fleeing the region in despair or hauling their families and remaining livestock to the parkland belt or the Peace River country. A battered remnant stayed and, in a rare collaboration of farmer and scientist, learned to fight the encroaching desert with trash cover, contour ploughing, and new strains of wheat. Huge acreages, sold for cultivation through the greed of governments and railways, were finally returned to the grazing role for which they were appropriate.

The prairie West had been Canada's proudest achievement. In 1928, only British Columbia had boasted a higher per-capita income than Alberta's $548. At $478, Saskatchewan had stood fourth. By 1933, at a mere $135 a person, Saskatchewan was the poorest province in Canada. Her government was bankrupt and her people turned gratefully to the trainloads of food and used clothing sent as charity from other regions. Even Depression-battered Newfoundland sent salt cod; the poor westerners, not knowing how to use it, soaked it, boiled it, and finally used it to plug holes in their roofs.

Bennett's bold speeches and dynamic policies provided no solutions to the spreading misery. Within the narrow available orthodoxies, no government could. By espousing protection, Canada merely added to the beggar-my-neighbour policies that deepened the world-wide depression. In opposition, the Liberals provided no alternatives. Their defeat in 1930, they soon discovered, had been another stroke of luck. The Tories were in trouble and Mackenzie King had no intention of helping them out with his own ideas. King's fourteen-point program of 1933 set high standards for vagueness and contradiction. The Liberals, King claimed, would "liberalize internal trade"; they would create "a more equitable distribution of wealth." Such phrases were almost deliberately meaningless. At heart, King seemed satisfied that the economy was working as badly as could be expected when Liberals were out of power.

Bennett would have been unlikely to take King's, or anyone else's advice. A lonely, domineering man, inhabiting an extensive suite in the Chateau Laurier, Bennett was portrayed by cartoonists as conducting cabinet meetings with himself in every chair. By now his wealth and corpulence inspired more loathing than reassurance. Goaded by his own sense of failure, Bennett's reaction was to strike out.

The labour crises of 1919 had added Section 98 to the Criminal Code: a sweeping description of sedition accompanied by savage prison terms and possible deportation. In 1931, the government seized leaders of the small Communist party. Chief Justice Sir William Mulock (a Laurier minister and King's first patron) condemned the men with every appearance of relish. Bennett's pledge to crush communism "with the iron heel of ruthlessness" was remembered. Book censorship became a duty of customs officials. The Royal Canadian Mounted Police, expanded in 1920 from the old Royal North West Mounted Police, now served Bennett as a secret service and riot police. Though Communists *were* involved in much of the unrest that accompanied the Depression, some Canadians saw the strikers, hunger marchers, and even rioters only as fellow human beings, fighting for jobs, a living wage, and a little dignity.

There had to be alternatives, but few were emerging. Among the country's intellectuals, the University of Toronto economic historian, Harold Innis, lectured his junior and more radical colleagues against venturing to mingle their ideas with contemporary politics. The United Church of Canada, heir to a reforming Methodist tradition, worried about its dwindling finances and prudently proclaimed moral depravity a greater evil than economic misery. J. W. Dafoe, editor of the influential *Winnipeg Free Press,* urged Liberals to find new ideas and then damned anything that strayed from his *laisser-faire* individualism.

The ferment came, as had almost every radical idea of the twenties, from Calgary. One doctrine was already familiar, thanks to the advocacy of William Irvine, Woodsworth's Labour partner

180

in the 1921 Parliament. Social Credit, brainchild of an English engineer, argued that the difference between the return to a producer and the final price of a product created "poverty in the midst of plenty." In the 1920s it was theory. In 1932, it was harsh reality in Alberta when a Calgary high school principal and fundamentalist radio preacher named William Aberhart took up the Social Credit message. Rarely had medium and message been better combined. A gospel-reared audience, frightened by debt, insecurity, and sudden poverty, responded to simple economics taught with the imagery of thieves, money-lenders, and social dividends. The radicalism of overthrowing the entire financial system seemed less when the temples of Canadian banking would crash in the distant east. Besides, Mr. Aberhart of the Prophetic Bible Institute was a man of God, not a politician like the corrupt opportunists in Ottawa, Toronto, and Edmonton.

Social Credit mingled radical and conservative messages in brilliant counterpoint. Another idea was less ambiguous, if more complex. Canadian socialism had shattered on the Bolshevik Revolution of 1917. The Communists had become the disciples of Lenin and Stalin and servants of Soviet policy. The remnants shared little more than a commitment to democracy. The craft unionists of the Trades and Labour Congress had fled politics in the 1920s and nothing in the 1930s would entice the TLC's aging, frightened leaders back. The wreck of the federal Progressives had left a radical remnant, the "Ginger Group," more correctly called the "co-operating independents." Among them, only the slight, bearded ex-clergyman and pacifist, J. S. Woodsworth, had both a strategy and patience. Someday, Canada would have its own version of Britain's Labour Party, complete with intellectuals, riding associations, MPs, and trade union affiliates. The Depression might be Woodsworth's opportunity to build such a party.

In 1932, a few academics ignored Innis's prudent advice and formed the League for Social Reconstruction. Woodsworth was made honourary president. That summer, at Calgary, delegates for the regular meeting of western labour parties found that the economic crisis had attracted members of farmer and socialist parties and even a solitary eastern unionist, A. R. Mosher from the nationalistic All-Canadian Congress of Labour. The result, with Woodsworth's shepherding, was the proclamation of the Co-operative Commonwealth Federation (Farmer Labour Socialist). A year later, a first national convention of the CCF met at Regina and, after laborious debates, adopted a manifesto and a constitution. Apart from a conclusion tacked on to add spice, the manifesto was an academic and sometimes technocratic document befitting its chief author, Professor Frank Underhill of the University of Toronto. The conclusion, appended at Regina, promised rather more than the body of the document would have justified: "No CCF government will rest content until it has eradicated capitalism and put into operation the full programme of socialized planning which will lead to the establishment in Canada of the co-operative commonwealth." Woodsworth, more cautiously, reminded listeners that socialism came from "the good old Latin word for 'friend,'" and promised an authentic Canadian version.

Unlike Social Credit, whose study groups and mass radio audiences swept it almost silently toward power, the CCF was exposed and embattled from birth. By 1934, it could boast hundreds of clubs and an organization in most provinces. It had also been denounced by business leaders and editors, repudiated by the TLC, and condemned as a danger to Catholicism by the coadjutor bishop of Montreal. For good measure, the disciplined militants of the Communist party were as bent on the CCF's destruction as on that of R. B. Bennett, with rather better chances of success. Social Credit, in contrast, remained within Alberta and Saskatchewan, under the sweep of Aberhart's powerful radio message.

Third parties usually look more frightening before elections than afterwards. The CCF started strong. In 1933 it could build on an old labour-socialist tradition in British Columbia to win second place behind the Liberals. T. Duff Pattullo triumphed on a slogan of "Work and Wages." The next year, the Ontario Liberals, under an engaging young onion farmer named Mitchell F. Hepburn, won that province for the first time since 1902. This time, the CCF won a single labour seat. More predictable was the Liberal victory in Saskatchewan under the former premier, Jimmy Gardiner. This time, not a single supporter of Premier Anderson's Tory government survived. The small opposition was CCF.

Not even the Depression nor Woodsworth's saintly mien could make many Canadians embrace socialism. Small businessmen and upholders of a modified status quo found their own hero in H. H. Stevens, the British Columbia Tory who had been hero of the Customs scandal. As Minister of Trade and Commerce, Stevens had turned into a crusader. A small merchant himself, Stevens had no trouble understanding how big companies controlled or shared the market. In the Depression, they had preserved their own generous profit margins by squeezing their smaller suppliers or independent retailers. The evidence was in the price spread between the primary producer and the ultimate consumer. Stevens demanded an investigation. A parliamentary committee found all the evidence it wanted of price-gouging, starvation wages, sweated labour, and predatory behaviour, with powerful names like Eaton's and Simpson's to grace the testimony. Harry Stevens and his main backer, Toronto clothier Warren K. Cook, were delighted. Bennett was not. When the Prime Minister tried to suppress Stevens's opinions and drove him from the cabinet, millions of Canadians accepted the ex-minister as a crusading hero.

Canadian heroes were scarce. Until 1932, people saw no alternative leaders. Under Herbert Hoover, Americans were faring no better. Then, in developments Canadians could follow on their radios, Franklin Delano Roosevelt swept into the White House and the long drama of the New Deal began. A generation of Canadians became instinctive Democrats. The Roosevelt radio image may have been artificial but its effectiveness transcended borders. For the first time, Canadians coveted their neighbours' political leadership. Even Bennett was not immune to Roosevelt's spell. Privately he had writhed at the sneers of shantytown "Bennettburghs" and horse-drawn automobiles called "Bennett buggies." All his life, Bennett had seen himself as a dynamic successful figure. His frustration now drove him to imitate Roosevelt. Since 1927, Canada had had a legation in Washington. Bennett had chosen his brother-in-law, W. D. Herridge, for the post. A man of ideas, Herridge now urged Bennett to adopt the style and perhaps even some of the content of the New Deal. Bennett was game. Herridge drafted speeches and Bennett demanded radio time. On January 3, 1935, he began.

Canadians listened dutifully and then with astonishment, none more so than Bennett's Tory associates. It was not the substance that was new; it was Bennett's flamboyant, uncompromising language. If the CCF's J. S. Woodsworth had seized the microphone, the words could not have been more unexpected. "There can be no permanent recovery without reform," Bennett declared. "And, to my mind, reform means Government intervention. It means Government control and regulation. It means the end of *laisser faire*." It meant unemployment insurance, minimum wages, and maximum hours of work, marketing legislation for farmers, and measures against price-fixing. The federal trade commission Stevens had sought would now become reality.

In a few days, Bennett had regained the initiative. Then he fell ill. When he recovered, he had to hurry to England for the Silver Jubilee of King George V. By the time he returned, Mackenzie King had found his line: if Bennett's New Deal was good, it was already Liberal policy; if it was not, it was typical Tory dictatorship. In either case, King declared, most of the new program was plainly beyond Ottawa's constitutional powers. Old Tories and business interests orchestrated their opposition. By the time the Dominion Trade and Industry Commission Act appeared, Stevens had left his party. On July 7, 1935, he announced the formation of a new one. Within five days he had a program and a title: the Reconstruction party. Its target would be those thousands of Canadians who still hoped for a reformed capitalism.

By summer, Canadians wondered whether Bennett even remembered his January cry for reform. In May, Communist organizers pulled men out of the shabby, demoralizing relief camps in British Columbia. The men came eagerly. Surely there had to be more to life than labouring under army discipline for twenty cents a day. Soon, more than a thousand had piled on boxcars for an "On-to-Ottawa" trek. At Regina, Bennett ordered the march halted. He would meet the leaders. The result was a cascade of insults between a plump Prime Minister and the trek leader, Arthur "Slim" Evans. On Dominion Day, RCMP and city police in Regina broke up a trekkers' public meeting. A policeman was beaten to death. Even so, sympathy lay with the trekkers.

On August 22, Aberhart's Social Crediters annihilated Alberta's farmer government. The simple certainties of two-party politics had dissolved. CCFers, Reconstructionists, Communists, and Social Crediters vied with Liberals and Conservatives for votes. Bennett, pounding out the old verities of tariff and Empire, pouring his own money into the Tory campaign, seemed oblivious to all that had happened in five of the worst years his audiences had experienced. It was Mackenzie King who caught the frightened mood with his slogan, "King or Chaos." The hysteria easily captured Quebec's Premier Alexandre Taschereau. In 1930, he had admitted that Bennett might be "a safe man"; now Taschereau raged that the Tory leader had "launched into a Socialistic venture bordering on Communism."

King was confident enough not to make promises. He was right. No Parliament had ever been so lop-sided: 173 Liberals were voted in, a mere 40 Tories, and 17 Social Crediters to reflect Aberhart's provincial sweep. In contrast, with over twice the Social Credit national vote, but spread across Canada, Woodsworth led only 6 CCFers, and Stevens led only himself. In the Canadian system, third parties could mean stronger governments and bigger majorities.

Afterwards, Canadians would be accused of excessive caution in choosing King. The Liberal majority is deceiving: King gained a smaller percentage of votes in 1935 than in 1930. Canadians had so many choices they could not make up their minds.

King's luck had worked twice, with defeat in 1930 and victory in 1935. It worked yet again. In the months before the election, Bennett and the Americans had finally negotiated the Reciprocity Treaty both countries had toyed with since 1866. Within weeks of the Liberal victory, King could go to Washington to collect the prize. Its Tory origins were conveniently forgotten.

King's new government was more positive than its program. In 1937, the Bank of Canada was made a purely public institution without private shareholders. The feeble CRBC, which had enraged King by allowing Tory election propaganda, was replaced by a stronger Canadian Broadcasting Corporation. King's transport minister, C. D. Howe, launched the government-owned Trans-Canada Airlines.

Across North America, the Depression had reached bottom in 1932. Slowly, painfully, the economy was climbing from the trough. Perhaps Bennett's policies had helped. They had certainly rewarded the business and financial backers of his party. Their sectors of the economy suffered less enduring pain; it was humbler Canadians who suffered too much. After 1933, as the statistics of recovery climbed to their peak in 1937, incomes and employment lagged far behind. In the United States, more by accident than by guidance from economists like John Maynard

Keynes, Roosevelt had discovered that purchasing power might be the key to recovery. In Alberta, if the British North America Act had not been used to checkmate his monetary ideas, the new Premier Aberhart might have fallen on the same solution. Social Credit's twenty-five-dollar "prosperity certificates," were, after all, an eccentric form of purchasing power. Hidden among the better-educated young mandarins in Ottawa, similarly heterodox notions were percolating, though clad in wholly conventional language. A combination of sympathetic and unknowing Liberal ministers and the relapse of the economy in 1938 would give Canada its first Keynesian budget in 1939. Cautiously, young officials actually talked of a "stimulative deficit." Their experiment was soon obscured by a far greater event: war.

King's opposition now came from provincial premiers, not Parliament. Men like Pattullo, Hepburn, and Aberhart had broken the tradition of grey, invisible provincial leadership. In 1936, they were joined by another premier, Maurice Duplessis. Not since 1897 had the Liberal hold on Quebec been broken. On his own, as leader of the tiny provincial Conservative party, Duplessis could never have managed it, but, like Mercier, he had united the extremes. The pretext this time was not Riel but the grim, exhausting economic crisis and a provincial government too corruptly linked to the English-dominated "trusts." For Quebec, the Depression was a national as well as an economic issue. Young, nationalistic Liberals had abandoned their party. Duplessis had scooped them up in a *Union Nationale*, pledged to social reform and nationalization of the worst oppressors, such as the electricity trust. Once Duplessis was in power, the younger Liberals were set aside. Duplessis would govern in his own style, courting the Church, persecuting Communists, unionists, and even the Jehovahs' Witnesses with an ingenious application of "property and civil rights." A "Padlock Law" allowed police to lock up premises used for "Communist" purposes. As for business, Duplessis was open to friendship, and Montreal's English-speaking leaders knew how to respond.

Duplessis's style was a variant of a new pattern. The Depression had shown the constitutional and fiscal weaknesses of the provinces. If Canada was to be a modern industrial society, drastic constitutional changes were needed. None of the new premiers agreed. They had captured the hopes of voters by arguing that style, not fresh ideas, would suffice to cure the Depression. None obliged the voters more than Ontario's Mitch Hepburn. He auctioned off government limousines in a football stadium to show that he was a man of the people. He summoned the press to watch him fire senior career officials. At the same time, Hepburn was also discovering sensual pleasures vouchsafed to few Elgin county onion farmers. Now he was the guest and confidant of financiers, speculators, and the handsome mining promoter, George McCullagh, new owner of an amalgamated *Globe and Mail*.

In 1937 General Motors employees at Oshawa contrasted soaring company profits with their own latest pay-cut and decided to organize. By summoning organizers from the bold new Congress of Industrial Organizations in the United States, the workers made Ontario that much less comfortable for American investors. When they struck General Motors, Hepburn did his best to beat the workers. In the end, it was the company that buckled. The little bridgehead of industrial unionism at Oshawa held, but Hepburn had the arguments and the money to win a smashing re-election that same year. Other premiers could take note. So could the Tories, some of whom had backed the Oshawa strikers.

The Depression forced thoughtful Canadians to realize that feeble central government had crippled their country's power to meet the crisis. Most of Bennett's five belated New Deal laws fell before the courts. Provincial premiers like Hepburn, Pattullo, Duplessis, Aberhart, and Nova Scotia's charismatic Angus L. Macdonald represented effective barriers to reform. Years of judicial reinterpretation, allied to Ottawa's fiscal caution, had left neither federal nor provincial governments with the strength to revive the economy in peacetime. Politics and the British North America Act locked Canadians into their Depression misery.

In time, Canada might have recovered. Instead, a world-wide tragedy became Canada's salvation.

# PART IV

# Middle Age, Middle Power

# 1 / Mr. King's War

With passage of the Statute of Westminster in 1931, Canada could claim her full voice in the world. The 1917 experiment of a common imperial foreign policy had proved hopeless. Its major accomplishment was the end of the Anglo-Japanese alliance, demanded by Canada to placate American opinion. The British had no further appetite for sharing vital decisions; the dominions had even less taste for imperial burdens. By 1926, Lord Balfour's proposal for a "British Commonwealth of Nations," linked by no more than sentiment, tradition, and a common monarch, seemed to be the only acceptable survivor of the imperial dream. Three centuries of colonial rule ended without rancor.

Post-war Canada fled commitments in the Empire or the League of Nations. Like their American neighbours, Canadians rejoiced that the Atlantic separated them from the sordid diplomacy and quarrelsome politics of the old world. They could enjoy the luxury of near-disarmament. Under King and his isolationist under secretary, O. D. Skelton, Canada did little more than preach to the delegates who assembled regularly at Geneva for what Skelton termed "The League of European Victors." Few Canadians needed to be persuaded that the Versailles settlement had been short-sighted; even fewer wished to die to uphold its terms. Long before he re-wrote economics, John Maynard Keynes had convinced a generation that the harsh, punitive treaty would lead to a new war. He was, of course, right. Sir Robert Borden, as much as Mackenzie King, disapproved of the League's mutual security provision, Article x.

Canadians in the twenties and thirties were isolationists, indifferent to the old world. Even Canadians with strong British loyalties halted their allegiance at the English Channel. The conservative, Catholic leaders of French Canada found everything to abhor in Soviet communism and German and French socialism but much to admire in Mussolini's fascism or Franco's Spanish Falange. Both purported to be bulwarks of the Vatican. Among Canadians of neither French nor British origins, European conflicts had their own reverberations. A tiny Communist party recruited its cadre from Finns, Ukrainians, and Jews with memories of tsarist Russia. Nazi and fascist organizations sought recruits among German and Italian Canadians. Old-world divisions were too easy to import.

In the twenties, King had found that his eternal "no" in external relations and defence had provided useful common ground for his awkward coalition of prairie and Quebec supporters. He needed no reminder of the experience when he returned to power in the far more dangerous world of 1935. In 1931, Japan had invaded Manchuria; in 1933, Hitler's Germany had defied the arms limitations imposed at Versailles, and the direction, if not the horrifying extent, of Nazi policies was becoming apparent. As King took office, nervous diplomats at Geneva were devising sanctions to try to deter Mussolini from invading a helpless Ethiopia. Left on his own by the change of government, Canada's permanent official at the League, W. A. Riddell, took his chance to add oil to the list; no other commodity would more surely affect the Italian war machine

Journalists hailed Riddell's initiative as the "Canadian Resolution." In Ottawa, Mackenzie King was horrified. Riddell had apparently committed Canada to defying Italy. He had offended influential French Canadians who saw no harm in Mussolini's imperial adventure. The "Canadian Resolution" was withdrawn; so was Riddell. Instead, the League was treated to a homily from King on the virtues of conciliation and a reminder of the Dominion's interests: "Canada's first duty to the League and to the British Empire," King explained in 1936, ". . . is, if possible, to keep this country united."

Canada's attitude did not cause the Second World War. Like that of New Zealand, which valiantly upheld the cause of collective security in the League, Canada's influence was tiny. It was, however, also clear. The twelve hundred Canadians who went to Spain to fight Franco were threatened with a two-year jail sentence. (A third of them did not survive service in the International Brigade's Mackenzie-Papineau battalion.) Refugees fleeing Hitler's concentration camps were rejected by Canada. Jewish immigrants were unwelcome to King's lieutenant, the Minister of Justice, Ernest Lapointe, or to influential anti-Semites across Canada. In the autumn of 1938, King rejoiced as much as most Canadians when Neville Chamberlain, the British Prime Minister, returned from Munich with the promise of "peace in our time." The crusty J. W. Dafoe of the Winnipeg *Free Press* sounded curmudgeonly when he headed his editorial, "What's the Cheering For?"

If Britain had gone to war over Czechoslovakia that autumn, King knew that even his divided country would have followed. Reluctantly, he had begun to prepare Canada for the ordeal. Fifteen years of military neglect during major change in the weapons of war had left her virtually defenceless. Rearmament might also be designed to avoid the heavy casualties that had led to conscription in the First World War. Building up the young Royal Canadian Air Force and the Royal Canadian Navy would strengthen coastal defences and avert charges of imperial subservience. The army, Canada's pride in the earlier war, would have lowest priority.

Rearmament reflected a new dimension in Canadian policy: defence links with the United States. The flood of American tourists, investment, and mass culture had accelerated the trend of Americanization, but until Roosevelt's inauguration in 1933, nothing had altered Washington's traditional indifference to Canada. As much as the dynamism of the New Deal, Roosevelt's "Good Neighbour" policy transformed Canadian-American relations. Economic links had strengthened in 1935 with a sweeping trade agreement, but more was to come. By the 1930s, it was no longer science fiction to believe that enemy bombers, refuelled at some hidden Arctic base, could sweep down on the United States. American security was affected by Canada's vast, undefended territory. Subtly, Canada now found herself sheltered behind the 120-year-old Monroe doctrine and subjected to Washington's anxieties.

At Kingston in 1938 to receive an honorary degree from Queen's University, Roosevelt assured his Canadian audience that ". . . the people of the United States will not stand idly by if domination of Canadian soil is threatened by any other empire." A delighted Mackenzie King promptly promised that Canada, too, understood her obligations: invaders must not be able to use her soil to attack the United States. It was a firmer guarantee than King had ever given Britain.

The American commitment was comforting. By early 1939, war was inevitable. Appeasement had failed. King's French-Canadian followers were sternly brought into line by Ernest Lapointe. King's adamant promise about conscription helped: "So long as this government may be in power, no such measure shall be enacted." The pledge was promptly echoed by Bennett's Tory successor, Robert Manion. In a further brilliant stroke to unite Canada, King stage-managed the country's first royal visit. In 1937, the monarchy had been shaken by the abdication of Edward VIII. In June 1939, Edward's successor, a shy, stammering George VI and his radiant queen crossed the Dominion twice. A whiff of glamour suddenly excited a Depression-weary country. The glow was still there in September, when German tanks rumbled across the Polish frontier.

By September 3, 1939, Britain was at war. Unofficially, so was Canada. Before politicians could assemble in Ottawa, the War Measures Act had been proclaimed and meagre forces had moved to war stations. King fulfilled his promise that "Parliament would decide" on the war. Only two Quebec nationalists and the CCF leader, J. S. Woodsworth, dissented. When Canada officially entered the war on September 10, she was more united than anyone could have imagined only a year before. In Montreal, a young nationalist, André Laurendeau, hunted for allies to protest the war; he found too few to matter. Across Canada the unemployed flocked to militia armouries to enlist. Montreal regiments filled their ranks first.

It was by no means apparent what should come next. A 1st Canadian Infantry Division was approved and sailed in December, but the Army's war plans suffered drastic cuts. French and British troops settled down to the "phoney war" on the French frontier. In Ottawa, the government considered how war orders might pull the economy out of a depression that was still claiming half a million unemployed. Unexpectedly, the British offered a solution. Canada's vast spaces and secure skies had been used to train flyers in the earlier war; now Canadians should contribute to a far more massive program. By December 1939, after much ill-natured haggling, King and British negotiators could announce a British Commonwealth Air Training Plan designed to train twenty thousand pilots a year. Canada would pay $350 million of the $600 million cost and provide most of the trainees. At King's insistence, the British reluctantly defined the BCATP as Canada's major contribution to the allied effort. The government could rejoice: its money would be spent in Canada. Britain would pay for the airmen once they reached England, and it seemed inconceivable that aircrew casualties could ever lead to conscription. Other countries would provide the cannon fodder.

Ordinary Canadians were also satisfied. That was the evidence of the polls. In October, Duplessis sought a new mandate from Quebec voters, offering himself as national saviour against Ottawa centralizers and conscription. Lapointe and other federal ministers criss-crossed the province, repeating pledges against conscription and swearing they would resign and leave Quebec voiceless if Duplessis won. Liberals, under Adélard Godbout, swept the province. In Ontario, Mitch Hepburn pursued his old vendetta with King by denouncing the half-hearted national war effort. Mackenzie King seized on Hepburn's attack to call a snap election. He summoned MPs to Ottawa, forced them to listen to a throne speech, and dissolved Parliament before they could reply. "Fighting Bob" Manion, out-manoeuvred and floundering, got no help by rechristening his Tories the National Government party. The CCF, divided on the war and the pacifism of their venerable leader, did no better. Voters gave the Liberals their most one-sided margin in history: fifty-one and a half per cent of the popular vote and 181 seats to only 40 for the Tories, 10 for Social Credit, and 8 for the CCF. King had a mandate for his kind of war. Manion, personally beaten, resigned.

It would be a war waged with one guiding light: avoid the errors that had destroyed the Tories in 1914–18. A Wartime Prices and Trade Board stood guard against profiteering and inflation. Organized labour, through the cautious Trades and Labour Congress, would be consulted. Every policy would be scrutinized for any possible threat of conscription. Above all, King would avoid Borden's fatal mistake of sacrificing himself and his party to the cause of allied victory. The interests of national unity and Liberalism prevented any talk of the last man or the last dollar.

Suddenly, such a negative philosophy seemed inappropriate. On April 9, 1940, Hitler struck at Norway. By June 4, the British had abandoned Dunkirk. Eight days later, France sought an armistice with Germany. Britain and her dominions stood alone against the might of Hitler and Mussolini. In Britain, the raw Canadian troops under Major-General A. G. L. McNaughton stood in the front lines against a German invasion. Behind them, a shattered British army struggled to re-arm.

Every feature of Canada's war effort was transformed. Instead of a single division, Canada's overseas army would expand to five divisions, maybe more. To combat German submarines, now free to use French and Norwegian ports, Canada must build and man scores of escort vessels to guard the Atlantic convoys. She must also build her own aircraft for the air training plan. All this had to be done with desperate haste and without experience or training.

As a measure of urgency, Parliament passed a National Resources Mobilization Act—conscription for home defence. When Montreal's tempestuous Mayor Camillien Houde denounced the national registration which followed, not even Quebeckers opposed his prompt internment. Canada was in danger. Even Americans would help. On August 18, 1940, Roosevelt summoned an excited Mackenzie King to Ogdensburg, New York. A scribbled memorandum recorded their agreement: a Permanent Joint Board of Defence would "consider in the broad sense the defense of the north half of the western hemisphere." A rapturous King rejoiced that he had perhaps brought the two great English-speaking powers together. Winston Churchill, the new British Prime Minister, did not rejoice. He recognized that Ogdensburg represented Canada's ultimate transfer from one empire to another.

Few Canadians had the detachment or historical grasp for such reflections. The crisis of 1940 created a mood of total war, at least on the home front. Its symbol was not King but the dynamic new Minister of Munitions and Supply, C. D. Howe. At once Howe had seen that almost anything Canada produced would be needed somewhere. An engineer and a businessman, Howe gradually won the confidence and then the devotion of able industrial leaders and businessmen. Some worked for a symbolic dollar a year, running crown corporations, controlling scarce commodities, scouring the United States for machine tools and aircraft engines. Tax concessions, credit, and $1.5 billion in direct investment unleashed the huge industrial potential that had lain idle in the thirties, and then added to it at a rate few countries have experienced in peace or war. By 1943, 1.2 million Canadians

194

worked in war industries, mostly in factories that had not existed in 1939.

Howe and his officials worried little about costs or consequences. J. L. Ilsley, a dour Nova Scotian and King's finance minister after 1940, found the money. His own frugality coincided with the Keynesian principles of his younger officials. Remembering the deliberate borrowing of the First World War, this time Canada would pay its way with direct taxes and individual borrowing. The Rowell-Sirois report, published in 1940, recommended a sweeping rearrangement of federal-provincial fiscal arrangements. Premiers from the richer provinces bluntly rejected the proposals, but the war gave Ottawa all the power it needed to take over direct taxes. Provincial governments could choose between grants equal to pre-war revenue or having Ottawa absorb their debt burden.

In five years, federal revenue from income, corporation, and inheritance taxes rose six-fold. Within six years, Ottawa had borrowed $12 billion, half of it from individuals. Over the first two years of the war, prices climbed fifteen per cent, but then Ottawa imposed sweeping wage and price controls, enforced by the Wartime Prices and Trade Board, and for the rest of the war, inflation was held to a mere three per cent. Donald Gordon, the hard-drinking Scot who ran the Wartime Prices and Trade Board, got much of the credit, but Ilsley's tough fiscal policies made the real difference.

Howe's massive production program helped defray the costs of war. Two-thirds of Canadian war production went to the Allies. As in the earlier war, there was a catch. By the end of 1940, Britain's reserves of gold and American dollars were gone. Not only could she not afford to buy from Canada; she could not provide the currency Canadians needed to buy vital components from the United States. For the British, Roosevelt's solution was "lend-lease," with repayment at the end of the war. For Canada, lend-lease would have meant post-war economic paralysis. Officials found an answer from the 1917 experience. On April 20, 1941, King met Roosevelt at his Hudson River estate, Hyde Park, and signed an agreement integrating the Canadian and American economies. Orders for Britain would be charged to the British lend-lease account. With E. P. Taylor, a youthful beer magnate, as his salesman, Howe soon exceeded the $250-million ceiling the

Hyde Park agreement had set on Canadian munitions sales to the United States. There were no protests from Washington.

As for Britain's debt to Canada, not even the take-over of almost a billion dollars of British direct investment could meet it. By war's end, the Canadian government had approved $4 billion in direct aid and forgiven massive loans to Britain and her allies. Since almost all the money was spent in Canada, charity stayed profitably at home.

Wartime prosperity was tangible. Wages might be frozen but they were certain. More and more women joined the work force and this time the social barriers against working wives and mothers collapsed. Governments even experimented nervously with day nurseries. Full employment gave Canadians money to spend but war needs absorbed scarce raw materials, foreign exchange, and factory space. Regulations under the War Measures Act imposed exchange controls, banned non-essential imports, and ended production of civilian cars, toys, jewellery, silk stockings, and a host of hotly-desired items. In January 1942, Canadians had their first experience of rationing for basic food items. By European standards, hardships and sacrifices were slight. For many Canadians, the war years were a bright contrast with the grim Depression. Discomfort and disruption contributed to the atmosphere of a common purpose and a sense that Canada had rediscovered its youth and vigour. Boring jobs or military routine had at least lifted people from pre-war ruts.

On December 7, 1941, the Japanese attack on Pearl Harbour brought the war suddenly closer. Canada declared war on Japan. Two battalions of infantry, sent to the hopeless defence of Hong Kong, were the first significant Canadian casualties of the war. Frightened British Columbians clamoured for defences. Ottawa sent thirty-four thousand soldiers, most of them conscripted under the National Resources Mobilization Act. Under the shabby pretext that Japanese Canadians needed protection from their angry neighbours, the government also interned nineteen thousand men, women, and children, auctioning off their property for derisory prices. It was an inexcusable act, born out of half a century of racial prejudice. Generals, admirals, and the RCMP protested that there was no military justification for the act. Politics sufficed.

The war with Japan demonstrated some of the realities of

Canada's role in continental defence. With Alaska threatened, the United States poured men and equipment into the task of reaching the remote territory by road and of piping oil from Norman Wells to a refinery at Whitehorse to support a prospective theatre of war. Together, the Alaska Highway and the Canol project cost $270 million. At the height of construction thirty-three thousand Americans were at work in Canada, blithely indifferent to the minor details of Canadian sovereignty. Warned by an alarmed British official, Ottawa asserted its authority by despatching a "Special Commissioner" with his own aircraft. Nervously, Ottawa paid the Americans, even for airfields and bases that were never needed. Not until the fifties did Washington concede Canada's claims to its vast arctic domain.

By bringing the United States into the war against all of the Axis powers, Japan had ensured an eventual victory for the Allies. So had Hitler, when he invaded the Soviet Union in the summer of 1941. The strength of the two superpowers was not yet apparent in 1942, while Britain was experiencing the most stunning disasters of her war, the fall of Singapore and the loss of Tobruk.

Amidst defeats and inexplicable catastrophes, many Canadians felt that they had done too little in the war. By transferring most of the British Commonwealth Air Training Plan's graduates to the RAF, King's government had deliberately sacrificed any claim to a strong, autonomous Canadian air force. Until that decision was reversed, most Canadian flyers served happily enough with the British but their contribution was buried in RAF news releases. The navy's dreary, arduous, and dangerous role of escorting Atlantic convoys attracted little publicity. King himself had refused to allow troops to be sent to the most active British theatre, the North African desert. Guilt about that decision had prodded the government into the tragic Hong Hong commitment. Contrasted with their First World War experience, in this war Canadians felt themselves on the sidelines.

In 1940, Canadians had endorsed a lacklustre war effort. By 1942, supporters of total war sensed fresh support for their views. One symbolic but fatal word summed up a Canada utterly committed to victory: *conscription*. By its own appeals for greater sacrifice, the government unconsciously fuelled a public sense that everything possible must be done for victory. Newspaper headlines, news broadcasts, and propaganda warning of the horrors of a Nazi or Japanese victory added their impact. Conservatives and anti-Mackenzie King Liberals like Hepburn seized the issue. Arthur Meighen, summoned from retirement to lead his party once again, proclaimed that he would make conscription his cause.

With deft opportunism, King acted. The issue, he announced, would be put to the people in a plebiscite. They could release the government from its pledge. Robbed of his issue, Meighen went down to defeat at the hands of the CCF in a Toronto by-election. It was a warning that although old-fashioned patriotism was the strongest political current in wartime Canada, it was not the only one. In the April plebiscite, sixty-four per cent of Canadians voted to free the government: eighty per cent of Manitobans, eighty-two per cent of Ontarians, and twenty-eight per cent of Quebeckers, the people to whom the pledge had really been made. It was the betrayal Duplessis and the nationalists had warned about. To fight conscription, a host of nationalists, young and allied, had rallied opinion. Lawyers and journalists like André Laurendeau and Jean Drapeau (a future mayor of Montreal), even a youngster named Pierre Elliott Trudeau, had joined the campaign and shared the defeat. For Quebec, another bitter memory was preserved for a people whose motto was *Je me souviens*.

King had not finished, of course. The National Resources Mobilization Act would be amended but Parliament would have to vote again before conscripts went overseas. It was, he explained, "not necessarily conscription, but conscription if necessary. . . ." Lapointe was dead by now, but for Pierre Cardin, the ranking Quebec cabinet minister in Ottawa, it was conscription enough to bring his resignation. For J. L. Ralston, the dogged, honest Minister of National Defence, King's act was a needless obfuscation and he, too, resigned. Then he relented, and the resignation remained in King's desk.

The conscription issue of 1942 was one of those savagely divisive symbolic distractions from reality which Canadian politics so often generates. Manpower was already an issue, as a population so uselessly surplus in the thirties proved desperately inadequate to meet both military and industrial needs. A succession of councils and committees wrestled with labour shortages. By the summer of 1941, all three armed services had cautiously established women's branches. National Selective Service, established in October 1941, steadily extended its authority. By September, no employer could hire or fire without giving notice to NSS. Men and young women were compelled to register; even those considered "underemployed" could be compelled to take a designated job.

Industrial or military conscription could allocate manpower in Canada; it could not solve recruiting problems for the armed forces. The RCAF was the favoured service for young men eager for the adventure. The needs of the Royal Canadian Navy were easily met, though there was a sometimes crippling shortage of qualified technicians. The army was the Cinderella service. Talk of a new, mechanized army fooled no one. Bitter experience had proved that front-line infantry needed high mental and physical standards to survive. To King, evidence of high rejection rates only proved that the generals were sabotaging voluntary recruiting. But the generals were doing their best. The NRMA men were encouraged by every strategem the army could devise to "go active." Many agreed, but others refused, and eventually, a tough core of NRMA men, proof against any threat or promise, gloried in the abusive term of "zombie." Fully trained and fit, they remained in uniform because coastal communities demanded their presence and because Ralston knew they were his only reserve of infantry reinforcements.

A mixture of policy and luck had so far saved Canadians from heavy war casualties. While other Allies, including Australia and New Zealand, had borne the brunt of fighting, Canada's overseas army remained on guard in England. Air and naval losses so far were small, as King had expected, in part because it took years before trained aircrew could enter operations in strength. Canadians took enormous pride in the dramatic expansion of their fleet of corvettes, frigates, and other small warships. They did not notice that the ships were often too ill-equipped and the crews too ill-trained to defend convoys effectively. Since German U-boats concentrated on merchant ships, not on their escorts, it was civilian seamen who paid the price while the RCN learned its job. Though long-range aircraft proved to be decisive weapons against submarines, the RCAF gave low priority to coastal patrols. Canadian admirals resented British criticism and Canadian officials usually insisted on installing inferior Canadian-made radar and rejecting other costly electronic gear as unproven.

In the winter of 1942–43, at the crisis of the Battle of the Atlantic, failure in convoy battles forced the withdrawal of Canadian escort groups for training and re-equipment. Canadian naval authorities never acknowledged that humiliation, but all three Allied partners learned from it. In March 1943, Canada was assigned its own sector of the Atlantic under Rear Admiral L. W. Murray. The RCAF finally acquired long-range aircraft, and Canadian ships returned to battle fit to match a wily, courageous, underwater enemy. By war's end, Canadians could take pride in the third largest navy in the world—373 warships and ninety thousand men and women.

Winning the Battle of the Atlantic meant only that a massive Allied build-up in England was possible. Allied military and political leaders differed sharply over the next step. Canadians found no role in such decisions, and neither Churchill nor Roosevelt sought King's advice. Unlike Sir Robert Borden, King was content to be photographed with Allied leaders on the terrace of the Chateau Frontenac in Quebec City and to leave the fate of Canadian soldiers and airmen to their decisions. With the exception of the stubbornly independent General McNaughton, few Canadian senior officers had their own thoughts to offer. Trained between the wars in British military schools, veterans of the tiny permanent force accepted British leadership, even if they often resented an unmistakable British air of superiority.

Senior RCAF officers, for example, fully shared the Royal Air Force's faith in the bomber offensive against Germany. Belated "Canadianization" eventually produced forty-five RCAF squadrons overseas, flying everything from Spitfires to transport planes, but the largest RCAF formation was 6 Bomber Group. Its eleven squadrons included only some of the thousands of Canadians who flew and died in the most controversial major operation of the war. Even Canadianization was controversial as 6 Group struggled with its problems of inferior aircraft, morale, and inexperience. Like the navy's, the RCAF's eventual achievements were won at a heavy price. Part of the cost was 9980 young men who died in the bomber offensive (more Canadians than fell in the long advance from Normandy to the Hochwald Forest). It was an ironic comment on King's expectation that air war could never lead to heavy casualties. In all, the RCAF lost 17,101 men. It also became the fourth largest air force in the world.

Many Canadians avoided the army because their fathers remembered the First World War. Nonetheless, it became the largest of the services, with 730,000 men and women. General McNaughton eventually won his battle for a highly mechanized force. Mackenzie King had recognized the old general's passionate opposition to conscription and his conviction, inherited from the earlier war, that science and preparation could save lives. Mustering five infantry and armoured divisions in England, the army trained for long years, but still it lacked the final, vital preparation of battle experience. To the government, land operations entailed the risk of conscription. At the same time, the army's inactivity was the evidence every critic used to show that Canada was not playing her part.

The years of waiting made it virtually impossible for Canadian generals to reject or even to criticize the Dieppe operation. The raid, on August 19, 1942, was the most conspicuous Canadian disaster of the war. Of 4963 troops who set out for Dieppe, 907 lay dead; 1946 remained as prisoners. Canadians have never ceased finding scapegoats, from McNaughton to the debonair Lord Louis Mountbatten. A less innocent nation might have recognized that amphibious operations are the riskiest form of war and that inexperience doubles the risk. Common sense might have argued for the kind of equipment and fire support that could have brought success. Only bloody experience at Dieppe helped convince generals and politicians that costly new resources would be needed for a real invasion of Europe.

Pressure soon resumed for further operations. To gain battle experience, the 1st Division shared in the Sicily landing in July 1943. A month of fighting turned green soldiers into effective fighting units. It also brought such public acclaim that Mackenzie King insisted on sending an additional formation—the 5th Armoured Division—and a corps headquarters, to join the ensuing Italian campaign. Angrily opposed to the destruction of his army, mistrusted by Ralston and his British superiors, General McNaughton was removed. The symbolism of a Canadian army in the field was preserved by the promise of other Allied formations. Meanwhile, British, American, and Canadian troops crossed to the Italian mainland, ran into relentless German resistance and discovered that the war of mud, trenches, and bloody offensives had not vanished in 1918.

On June 6, 1944, Canadian sailors, airmen, and soldiers shared in the D-Day landings. The 3rd Division was one of five Allied assault formations. The Canadian price for the day was 1074 casualties. It was only a down payment. Weeks of bitter fighting followed to defend the beachhead, capture Caen, and hold the bulk of the German armies so that the Americans could break out. Savage battles in the hedgerows, aggravated by a seemingly inevitable time lag of experience, cost the 2nd and 3rd Canadian Divisions the heaviest losses of any of the formations under British command. The 4th Armoured Division, spearhead in closing the Falaise Gap, was almost as hard-hit. As the Canadians fought in Normandy, their comrades in Italy fought two brutal offensives, breaking the Hitler Line in June and the Gothic Line in the autumn. In two separate theatres, Canadians had lost twenty-three thousand men, most of them trained infantry. They would have to be replaced.

It was the crisis King had feared throughout the war. Everyone could be blamed, from staff officers who failed to anticipate casualty rates and allowed too many men to remain in support units, to generals who demanded victories, regardless of cost, to enhance their own careers. By splitting the Canadians and sending unneeded troops to Italy, King himself had aggravated the manpower problem, creating a double system of administration and reinforcements. The fact remained, as J. L. Ralston saw for himself, that the infantry reinforcement pools were empty. Canadians knew it too. Major Conn Smythe, a popular Toronto sportsman wounded in Normandy, made it his business to tell a sensational story of untrained replacements stumbling into German fire. To Ralston, there was only one answer. Conscription was now necessary. The NRMA men must be sent.

For King, conscription was quite unthinkable. The war had virtually been won. Surely, a few thousand volunteers could be found from so huge an army. There must be a plot by the generals, he reasoned, or even by his own more conservative ministers, to destroy him. Resourceful as ever, he recalled both Ralston's earlier resignation and Ralston's enemy, General McNaughton. On November 14, an astonished cabinet learned that McNaughton would be the new minister. Ministers sat dumbfounded as Ralston rose, shook hands with colleagues, and silently left.

The rest was nervous anticlimax. McNaughton's charisma had

no impact on hardened "zombies." They still did not volunteer. In British Columbia, Major-General George Pearkes, who commanded most of them, sent in his resignation. In Ottawa, McNaughton's senior staff officers insisted that volunteers could not be found. To the ingenious King, this represented an opportune "general's mutiny," enough to frighten wavering ministers and Quebec backbenchers. A shaken, discredited McNaughton confessed failure. It was left to King himself to tell a divided Parliament that fifteen thousand NRMA conscripts would be sent to Europe. He was upheld 143 to 70, with 34 Quebec Liberals dissenting.

Neither the crisis nor the irony was over. In Montreal, there were riots. At Terrace, British Columbia, a brigade of NRMA men mutinied for almost a week before senior officers persuaded them to submit. On February 5, McNaughton lost a by-election in Ontario. The irony was that, in the end, the conscripts were hardly needed. After the brutal battle for the Scheldt estuary in October, Canadians went into winter quarters in Holland and Belgium. At Canadian insistence, the two divisions in Italy were brought to the Netherlands in a long, needless journey that nonetheless kept them from harm. The final offensives that drove into Germany and the flooded Netherlands cost six thousand casualties but very few of them were conscripts. On May 6, Germany surrendered. Japan followed suit on August 14. As it had in 1918, pure accident had made the bitter political crisis unnecessary.

# 2 / Prosperity

Canada benefited richly from the war. The costs were high: forty-three thousand men and women had died; the national debt had quadrupled. Yet casualties were far lower than they had been in the First World War and they came from a larger population. Most of the money, including virtually all of the mutual aid, had been spent in Canada, doubling the gross national product and creating industries that would have a durable role in the post-war economy. Ordinary Canadians lived hard, frugal, wartime lives, but most of them always had. Wartime incomes and savings had created reserves of spending power which a previous generation could hardly have imagined. Despite wartime shortages, Canadian consumer spending rose forty per cent between 1938 and 1944.

Most Canadians both yearned for and feared the end of the war. The astonishing growth in support for the CCF was the clearest symptom of the apprehension that peace would restore the unemployment and hopelessness of the Depression. The remarkable wartime government feat of ending unemployment, stopping inflation, and redistributing income made the Depression era seem all the more unnecessary, but only the CCF promised to carry wartime planning, controls, and massive public spending into the post-war world. In 1943, Ontario voters had narrowly favoured George Drew and the Conservatives as their new government, but the CCF had come from nowhere into second place. A few months later, a Gallup Poll claimed that the CCF edged out both traditional parties in public support. In June 1944, the CCF under Tommy Douglas swept Saskatchewan to become the first socialist government anywhere in North America.

Liberals and Conservatives felt the wartime mood. It was evident as much in innumerable earnest evening forums and debates, in journalism and radio commentaries, as in electoral movements or the new opinion polls. In their latest bid for electoral support, the Tories had turned for leadership to the dry but respected Manitoba Premier, John Bracken. Part of his price was the addition of the word "Progressive" to the party name. Becoming "Progressive Conservative" was also at least a cosmetic concession to the public demand for change. Even the Communists profited from the ground-swell. Earlier in the war the party had been banned for dutifully supporting Moscow's alliance with Hitler, but the line switched the instant the Nazis invaded Russia. Re-emerging as the Labour Progressive party, the Communists basked in the reflected glory of the powerful Red Army. They also used their considerable influence in the labour movement to ban wartime strikes and to attack the hated CCF. In turn, the CCF fought back, winning over union militants.

The real initiative lay, as always, with the government. Even in 1940, the overdue adoption of unemployment insurance had promised at least one difference in post-war Canada. By mid-1942, an Allied victory seemed certain. Citizens and their government could begin to think seriously about post-war reconstruction, but the right direction was by no means clear. One approach, represented by a committee of distinguished academics, urged the adoption of a comprehensive system of social insurance for health, income, and old age, and a massive program of public works. This initiative, embodied in a 1943 report by Leonard Marsh, a McGill University professor, was deftly gutted by the brilliant team of civil servants that Clifford Clark, Deputy Minister of Finance, had gathered around him in his department.

Clark's approach was fiscally more cautious but conceptually more radical. While Marsh had ignored constitutional obstacles, Clark urged a restructuring of federalism to give Ottawa the fiscal power to manage the national economy in proper Keynesian fashion. Provinces would be financed so that the richest and the poorest could each provide a comparable level of services, avoiding the terrible inequities made apparent by the Depression. The influence of the abandoned Rowell-Sirois report was no coincidence. W. A. Mackintosh, a major Rowell-Sirois contributor, had become Clark's alter-ego. Louis St. Laurent, an eminent Quebec City lawyer and the commission's counsel, had entered King's cabinet in 1941 as successor to Ernest Lapointe. Another contributor, Brooke Claxton, became the minister of a new Department of Health and Welfare in 1944.

The "mandarins," as Clark and his able team of civil servants soon were called, gained immense influence and prestige yet their power depended entirely on the Prime Minister. When labour problems that had seethed for years finally burst forth in 1943, costing the economy a million days in strikes, it was King himself who engineered the government response. The problem, as Mr. Justice Charles McTague of the National War Labour Board had no trouble proving, lay with Canada's lack of procedures for union recognition and orderly bargaining. Reluctantly impressed by the argument and even more by defection of labour votes to the CCF, King approved P.C. 1003, the Wartime Labour Relations Order, in early 1944. This order-in-council gave Canadian unionists the rights to organize enjoyed by their American counterparts since 1935. It formed the basis for federal and for most provincial labour legislation when the war ended. Its immediate success was demonstrated by a dramatic drop in strikes during the balance of the war.

Another wartime measure, urged by Ian Mackenzie, the Minister of Pensions, by Leonard Marsh, and by McTague's board, was family allowances. For decades reformers had urged that such allowances were the only effective way to cope with the most obvious cause of family poverty, low incomes among parents. King had been horrified by the cost and the threat to individualism. He was converted by the growth of CCF support, by the desire to burnish his own self-image as a reformer, and by the arguments of his secretary, J. W. Pickersgill, that growing up as a war widow's son on a government pension had not sapped his initiative. Characteristically, King's resolve was strengthened by discovering that the same ministers and backbenchers who demanded conscription were often as fervent in opposing family allowances. Some Progressive Conservatives tactlessly underlined another Liberal party argument for family allowances by complaining that the allowance would be a massive subsidy to the huge families of French Canada.

By 1945, King's government had acquired all the enemies ten years of power and six years of bitterly controversial decisions could have earned. If the opposition parties needed encouragement, they found it in Britain, where voters had decisively rejected their powerful wartime leader, Winston Churchill, for the untried Labour party of Clement Attlee. John Bracken and the

CCF's M. J. Coldwell could each take comfort from the example. In Quebec, conscription and loyalty to Ottawa had destroyed Godbout's Liberals; since 1944, Maurice Duplessis and the *Union Nationale* had been back in power.

Yet King's infinite caution and flexibility had their rewards. Even the Quebec anti-conscriptionists who ran as independents preferred him to any other leader, especially after Bracken promised to send conscripts to fight the Japanese. King's pledge of a "New Social Order," adorned by family allowances (delivered in mid-campaign) and the promise of a health insurance plan, offered security without CCF socialism. For the first time, leaders of the Trades and Labour Congress endorsed the Liberals. In more private and effective ways, so did the Communists, splitting industrial constituencies which the CCF had smugly taken for granted. An unscrupulous but effective scare-mongering campaign, financed by business, administered the *coup de grace* to the CCF. On June 4, George Drew swept to a one-sided Conservative victory in Ontario; a week later, King led Liberals to a much narrower federal success with 125 seats against 67 for Bracken and 28 for Coldwell's CCF (almost all of them from the West). Social Credit held 13 seats, and 12 independents, mostly from Quebec, gave King his margin of safety. With symbolic fitness, soldier-voters defeated the Prime Minister in his Prince Albert riding. It was only a minor humiliation.

The Liberals now faced a divided opposition and the post-war challenge. It was not necessarily an easy inheritance. Whatever their promised plans and programs, cabinet members could easily recall the painful aftermath of the earlier war.

On May 6, 1945, jubilant sailors wrecked downtown Halifax. At home and overseas, soldiers and airmen demanded prompt demobilization. Britain, a major trading partner, was bankrupt. American generosity had shrivelled as the war's end approached. Roosevelt was dead; isolationist Republicans were rampant in Congress. Even by 1944, Canadian war production had eased off and some industries had switched back to civilian purposes, but the task was daunting and costly. Canadians, in their comfortable oasis, were impatient and demanding, but the rest of the world was shattered—perhaps beyond recovery—and Canada had to trade to live.

In the war with Japan, Canada played as modest a role as she could manage. Insistence that Canadian servicemen must volunteer for the Pacific led to some embarrassment when the only major Canadian unit in the war, a cruiser, effectively voted itself out of action and sailed for home. On the other hand, as long as the war continued, so did the government's limitless emergency powers. When King summoned provincial premiers to Ottawa on August 6, 1945, federal authority loomed over the meeting. Neither Drew nor Duplessis was impressed. When King, nervous enough at the radicalism of Clifford Clark's fiscal proposals, promised co-operation, not coercion, the premiers found their weapon: delay. Almost a year would pass before the finance department mandarins conceded defeat for economic centralism, but the basic rules of federal-provincial antagonism survived.

Ottawa's power and prestige remained for a time. So did its hold on tax revenue. Clark's elaborate scheme disappeared but the goal of relative equalization was soon built into complicated formulas and agreements by which all the provinces but Quebec and, for a time, Ontario, "rented" their direct tax fields to Ottawa in return for compensation. The unpopularity of being tax collector to the nation had been somewhat eased by the wartime invention of payroll deductions.

One minister at least had been utterly sanguine about Canada's post-war prospects. C. D. Howe had despised the moanings of what he called "the Security Brigade." That made him the logical choice to head a vague co-ordinating department of reconstruction. Howe accepted, but only when he retained the sweeping powers of his wartime role. Canada needed "reconversion," not reconstruction, Howe insisted. His weapons were generous credits for investment and exports, a minimum of regulations, and an ingenious tax device, "accelerated depreciation," which protected investors from loss if the economy turned sour and allowed them to turn a quick buck if it thrived. Meanwhile, Howe unashamedly cherished the crown corporations he had launched before and during the war. An aircraft industry would back up his earliest public venture in 1937, Trans-Canada Airlines. Polymer Corporation at Sarnia and Eldorado Nuclear at Port Hope would show that Canadians could work at the frontiers of science and technology. Meanwhile, as "Howe's Boys" left their dollar-a-year jobs to return to the seats of private power, they remained a loyal network and a source of funds that Howe alone could tap.

Even Howe was prudent. A government white paper by W. A. Mackintosh in 1945 had promised full employment; Howe substituted a vaguer "high and stable level of employment." Either commitment had seemed bold. It was soon apparent, though, that the post-war depression would not happen. Instead, Canada was booming. Wartime forces melted away, their transition to civilian life eased by the gratuities, grants, and educational opportunities their fathers had yearned for after the First World War. By the summer of 1947, Canada's armed forces had dwindled from a million people to only forty thousand. Barely fifteen thousand veterans were collecting out-of-work benefits. Even a limping housing industry was infected by Howe's dynamism, the insatiable post-war demand, and a National Housing Act that made mortgages available to families that would never have dared apply for them before. By 1947, builders were producing houses faster than couples were marrying, making up for years when families had been forced to double up. Three-quarters of the new buildings were individual homes, monotonous boxes scattered across cheerless suburban developments to fulfil the durable pioneer expectation that a Canadian was entitled to land and individuality.

One by-product of prosperity brought no joy to Howe and his friends, but it was as vital to continued growth as their tax concessions. In 1945, workers at the Ford Motor Company in Windsor won the Rand Formula, a uniquely Canadian basis for union security. Employees need not join a union but they had to "pay the freight" for its benefits. In 1946, the brash new industrial unions tested their wartime gains with a co-ordinated nation-wide bid for higher wages. Strikes in the British Columbia forests and in eastern Canada's basic steel, electrical, and rubber industries cost more working days than in any year since 1919, but this time there was little violence, and most unions won modest concessions. Instead of eliminating unions, employers learned to live with them. Most workers kept enough purchasing power to sustain the post-war economic boom.

More than dollars were needed. Canadians could not escape their battered world or even the disorders of their own economy. Pressed by business, the government hurried its "orderly decontrol," but meat and butter rationing returned in the post-war months. Gas and tire rationing ended, but liquor remained not only diluted (as it still is) but controlled. Farmers, harvesting bumper crops since the summer of 1939, had prospered beyond their dreams in the war years. Now a hungry Europe could no longer afford the scarce dollars to buy Canadian products. James Gardiner, the Minister of Agriculture, preened himself on selling a huge wheat deal to the British. Other British orders were possible only with a $1.5 billion Canadian loan, fully a third as much as Washington provided. Even this was no solution to Canada's real problem, a lack of American exchange. By 1947, King's government was reduced to drastic measures to save its dollar reserves: exchange controls, a ban on luxury imports, licensing of major purchases, and a limit on the cash tourists could take south.

Economic arguments made little impact on Washington. Congress had gone solidly Republican in 1946. Business was business again. It was another, far more frightening crisis that now seized American opinion.

Even before the Allied armies had met at the Elbe in May 1945, the wartime alliance was falling apart. Canada knew little of the details: only that even more than the First World War, this one had been a war between the world's great powers. Canadian voters in 1945 were assured that Mackenzie King had enormous influence in the world. If so, he did not use it. Canadian diplomats, as able a team of officials as would ever serve her, struggled for the "functional principle"—Canada would demand a voice only when she had a major role to play. Occasionally, when they were asked to feed refugees or provide raw material, Canadians were actually consulted. At Bretton Woods in 1944, when bankers had launched the International Monetary Fund and the World Bank to reform the currency crises of the thirties, a Canadian delegation under Louis Rasminsky was found useful and constructive. At Dumbarton Oaks and San Francisco, where the United Nations was shaped and launched, Canadians also won approval. Unlike the bumptious Australians, Mackenzie King's delegation made no trouble for the major powers and kept its disquiet to itself.

Only two world powers now seemed to matter: the United States and the Soviet Union. Canada, to her acute discomfort, lay between them. Her allegiance was clear. Stalin's Russia was a tyranny as atrocious as Hitler's, tolerable only to the self-deceived or the would-be totalitarian. Russia was also a deeply wounded and profoundly frightened power. No nation had lost more in the war, but its huge armies would be no safeguard against the kind of bombs that had annihilated Hiroshima and Nagasaki and driven Japan from the war. Canadian officials were among the first to know of the desperate Russian bid to equal the nuclear balance. In September 1945, a Soviet embassy cypher clerk shared secrets of a Communist spy ring that reached into King's own office. Official Ottawa's shock was almost matched by its revulsion at having to deal with the problem. Eventually the revelations sent officials, professors, and the single Communist MP to prison. Neither King nor most of his advisers were convinced that Stalin was really bent on world conquest. The seizure of eastern European countries with all the brutal apparatus of terror and repression, they believed, merely established a vast buffer zone for a nervous but inward-looking Soviet empire.

Others did not agree. Americans had been as eager as Canadians to demobilize. Now Washington insisted that Russia posed a continental threat. The arrangements made at Ogdensburg, as Roosevelt had insisted, were permanent. Canadians found that if they were to preserve sovereignty, they would have to defend themselves or take the risk of having America do it for them. "If we do enough to assure the United States," confessed one of King's trusted advisers, "we shall have done a good deal more than a cold assessment of the risk would indicate to be necessary." On February 13, 1947, a bilateral defence agreement promised that Canadian forces would henceforth use American arms, equipment, and tactics, share facilities, and co-operate with the United States. Continentalism now had a military dimension. Another British link had withered.

In 1946, the continental threat was remote—a bogey to promote American rearmament. Western Europe was another matter. Only Britain maintained respectable military strength; her continental neighbours were now virtually defenceless against invasion or subversion. Canada's foreign exchange crisis, with its threat to peacetime reconversion, was a tenth as serious as those of western European countries. Without American credit, European recovery was hopeless. In Washington, business was business, but not if Europe fell to the Communists. Action was needed. The European Recovery Program or the Marshall Plan, launched in 1948, was a vast outpouring of American material and financial aid. To Canadian delight, American congressmen allowed Europe's Marshall Plan credits to be applied in other

"American" countries. Canada's 1947 exchange crisis was over.

Europe's security crisis was not. In February 1948, Czech Communists, backed by the Soviet garrison, seized power. Days later, Jan Masaryk, symbol of Czech resistance to Hitler, fell from a window. It was "suicide," claimed the new regime in Prague. To the West, the fall of Czech democracy was a bitter reminder of the tragedy of pre-war appeasement. Next, Soviet troops blockaded the British, American, and French zones of Berlin. Stalin must be answered as Hitler had not been: by Allied unity. In western Europe, politicians struggled to fashion a defence alliance but it was a union of the weak. Canada might join; even Mackenzie King had now been shaken from his habitual caution. Not even Duplessis's Quebec could condemn resistance to communism. First, though, Canada would await the decision of the Americans. In June 1948, Congress was finally willing. Ten months later, in April 1949, the North Atlantic Treaty Organization was proclaimed. Its twelve members had pledged, at Canada's insistence, to be more than a defence league; in fact, they wanted rearmament on the cheap. Committed to buy American-style weapons, Canada, for example, could generously spare the British equipment she had stockpiled in 1945.

Canadian post-war diplomacy might be moralizing and self-important but it had finally escaped from King's management. In 1947, the old Prime Minister had handed external affairs to the trusted Louis St. Laurent. A conservative corporation lawyer, St. Laurent was Quebecker enough to be unimpressed by the symbols and sentiment of the British connection, but he was no provincialist. In the controversy over Clark's federal proposals, he had bluntly backed the centralizing scheme. Quebec would always complain, he explained, but Quebeckers would also admire the government that did most for them. St. Laurent was fascinated by Canada's potential role in the world. He backed officials such as his new under secretary, Lester Pearson, who insisted that Canada was now a "middle power," with influence in the United Nations, NATO, and the emerging multiracial Commonwealth. St. Laurent earned credit for persuading India to remain in the Commonwealth after 1947 when its instincts were to break all the old imperial ties. Other emerging colonies would follow that lead.

Of all Canada's connections, Washington obviously mattered

most. Wartime experience had shown Canadian officials how insensitive a great democracy could be when its own interests were concerned. Moreover, rebuffs and criticism could easily drive Americans back to their old isolationism. Not only would Europe be left vulnerable; Canadians would be left alone with their huge and often heedless neighbour. Diplomatic skill was no luxury in post-war Canada.

In June 1950, North Korean tanks rolled deep into South Korea. Canadians had little knowledge of the small peninsula with its history as a Japanese colony and its post-war partition. They saw it as a test of collective security in a Cold War turned hot. A dying session of Parliament approved the despatch of three destroyers, and, when the war went badly for troops under UN colours, the government approved a special infantry brigade recruited from veterans. Three years of fighting cost Canada 1642 casualties, 309 of them fatal. The United States and South Korea bore the heavy brunt of costs and losses.

If Korea brought the kind of response democracies should have offered Hitler, it also raised a terrifying thought: was the invasion a Soviet-ordered diversion, leaving western Europe defenceless? The fear spurred NATO rearmament. No longer could it be cheap and leisurely. Early in 1951, Ottawa announced substantial new military commitments: twelve fighter squadrons and an infantry brigade for Europe; two more brigades available as immediate support; a fleet of Canadian-built destroyer-escorts to withstand any new Battle of the Atlantic. Armed forces would grow to a hundred twenty thousand men; new weapons and equipment would cost $5 billion. C. D. Howe received fresh economic powers as Canada undertook its first serious peacetime military effort.

It was no longer Mackenzie King's Canada. At seventy-four, having served as Prime Minister longer than anyone in British history, he was content to go. A Liberal convention in August 1948 chose his only possible successor: Louis St. Laurent. King had been the architect of modern Canadian Liberalism, with its seemingly permanent hold on power. He retired, as he had served, with little love from Canadians and far less respect than he deserved. St. Laurent was instantly more popular: a courtly, dignified man, a permissive autocrat who left ministers to manage their departments but whose will could be inflexible. He was conservative, too, and the unfulfilled promises of King's 1945 program remained safely unused.

St. Laurent began with a bonus. In the war years, Canada had staked her claim to Newfoundland, posting thousands of troops on the island to match the American garrison. Between them, the wartime visitors had brought a brief, unfamiliar prosperity to the island, but it was the islanders themselves who would choose their fate. The British commission of government, established in 1934, was about to end. The logical choice, to almost everyone but a small, bespectacled ex-broadcaster named Joey Smallwood, was a return to responsible government. It was Smallwood, reaching past the island's merchant elite by means of the broadcast proceedings of the constitutional convention, who helped persuade Newfoundlanders to make Confederation an option. Next, after two 1948 referenda, Smallwood finally emerged with a narrow majority for union with Canada. On March 31, 1949, Newfoundland entered Confederation. Her 350,000 people had been won by social benefits, fiscal guarantees, and, above all, by the hope that prosperous, expanding Canada would haul Newfoundland from its historic poverty. The merchants and lawyers of St. John's were unpersuaded.

The details would be left for time to take care of. Proud of the overdue completion of Canada, Liberals could now seek a new mandate. The Conservatives had a new leader, their fifth in a decade. George Drew was handsome, articulate, and had won Ontario three times. Though his government had been more progressive than Hepburn's, Drew was an unabashed Tory and pro-conscriptionist. That gave Liberals in Quebec ample ammunition. When Drew sought an electoral alliance with Duplessis in the name of their anti-Ottawa axis, he inspired an even less scrupulous Liberal campaign in Ontario. The image of a Drew-Duplessis alliance, with Camillien Houde in the background, exploited anti-Quebec feelings. For his part, Drew played indelicately on the kind of neurotic anti-communism that was winning votes for Senator Joe McCarthy in the United States. Communism, liberalism, and the CCF were lumped in a socialist stew. Over the grubby politics of 1949 floated the avuncular image of Louis St. Laurent, addressing his audiences through their children, offering benign platitudes fit for a summer campaign in a country fully aware of its good fortune. The result was a landslide—193 Liberals to a mere 41 Tories, 13 CCFers and 10 Social Credit. In Newfoundland, only a resentful St. John's bucked the Liberal trend.

Canadians had voted for prosperity. The Cold War rearmament and Korea had restored an economy that had begun to flag slightly in 1949. American investment had fallen off in the early post-war years, leaving Canadians to finance their own boom, but now capital poured into Canada. While corporations built or expanded branch plants to supply Canadians with the cars, radios, refrigerators, and, after 1952, the television sets they could now afford, much more foreign investment was directed at unlocking Canadian resources. Oil and gas in the Turner Valley had given Alberta a modest role in a pre-war petroleum industry, but nothing prepared the province for the huge strikes at Leduc, outside Edmonton, in 1948. By 1956, Alberta was supplying three-quarters of Canadian needs, though as much as possible was exported to the United States and Arab oil was still much cheaper. At Chalk River, Ontario, in 1952, Canadian scientists began preliminary work on an even newer energy source: the CANDU, or Canadian Deuterium Uranium, reactor. Rearmament and the American development of nuclear weapons were creating a demand for uranium and a long list of non-ferrous metals.

Transportation had always been a major Canadian industry. New railways reached north to Lynn Lake, Manitoba, for nickel; to Pine Point in the Northwest Territories, and to Labrador's Knob Lake to reach one of the richest iron ore deposits in the world. Since the Wisconsin deposits that had sustained American heavy industry were close to depletion, Labrador's became the only alternative. The long argument over the St. Lawrence Seaway came to an end just as Canada had decided to proceed on its own with a hydro-electric development. By 1959, after five years of building, the billion-dollar project was completed. In 1948, Ottawa had promised $150 million to the provinces to help develop a Trans-Canada Highway for an increasingly road-bound population. (It was only finished in 1965 at a cost of almost a billion dollars.) Meanwhile a new transportation technology, pipelines, carried Alberta crude oil east to the Lakehead at Superior, Wisconsin, and west over the mountains to British Columbia. Engineers were now ready to tackle two of the great remaining hydro-electric projects of the country, Churchill Falls in Labrador and the Columbia River in British Columbia.

215

Critics might complain that the huge new developments fostered a continental more than a purely Canadian economy. New railways and pipelines reached into the North but their termini were often in the United States. Trade, like investment, was increasingly a bilateral affair; efforts to improve Canadian exports to Britain were dismissed as imperial echoes. As in the twenties, a few querulous academic voices complained that key sectors of Canada's economy had fallen under foreign control and that more would follow. Most Canadians were too delighted with their new prosperity to echo such worries. They certainly had no place in the minds of C. D. Howe or his associates. Even in Quebec, where Duplessis's regime was entrenched in an old-fashioned alliance of Catholicism and conservative nationalism, foreign investors formed a silent partnership. Like Liberal premiers before him, Duplessis welcomed the revenue and the jobs and let wages look after themselves. When Catholic unionists at Asbestos struck their American employers in 1949, provincial police provided management with strong-armed support. The resulting violence shocked Catholic leaders and pulled unions across Canada into unprecedented solidarity with the Quebec-based syndicates.

Later, the Asbestos strike would be interpreted by an observer, Pierre Elliott Trudeau, as the symbolic beginning of a new kind of Quebec nationalism. At the time, it was much more a reflection of a common Canadian demand to share in the new prosperity and a North American standard of living. No more than Cape Bretoners or Ontarians would Quebec workers accept deprivation for themselves and their families as the price of distinctiveness. Nor, given the cornucopia of apparently limitless Canadian wealth, did they have to. Maurice Duplessis might win votes by such symbolic acts as giving Quebec her own flag in 1948—a blue and white emblem mythically linked to the 1758 victory over the English at Carillon. In daily life, *Canadiens* became more North American.

The 1951 census found fourteen million Canadians. It quietly revealed another fact: by the usual definitions of poverty at the time, a third of Canadians qualified, most of them elderly, rural, or tied to the have-not regions; too many of them native people and Métis. What passed without comment is that censuses from 1921 to 1941 had found that two-thirds of Canadians were poor. For the first time, the poor were a minority. Like all the best social revolutions, this one passed unnoticed. The explanation was simple: family allowances, unionization, and, above all, fulfilment of the promise of "high and stable rates of employment." Families with steady incomes and a little to spare could now break out of slum housing, find a home in the suburbs, buy a second-hand car, live healthier lives, and see their children continue a few years farther in school. They could enjoy the one- or two-week holidays that union contracts won for members and non-unionists alike. The spread of a consumer society created new sectors of service and white-collar employment. So did the growth of government.

Canadians celebrated their better life with a baby boom. During the Depression years, immigration and birth rates had both tumbled. Not since the 1880s had Canada's population grown more slowly. But by 1947, natural increase alone was adding two per cent a year. Women were leaving the work force not through coercion—that had been tried in 1919–20 and the numbers of working women had actually climbed—but through choice. The reason was apparent in maternity wards, and, by the 1950s, in a frantic demand for new schools, teachers, and, in due course, expanded colleges and universities. Prosperity not only allowed more children; it allowed them to be fed and educated to a standard no generation of Canadians had experienced.

Natural growth was supplemented by the largest flood of immigration since Sir Clifford Sifton's day. Between 1945 and 1957, a million and a half people came to Canada, including war brides, concentration camp victims, even thirty-five thousand refugees from the 1956 Hungarian uprising. Many brought industrial skills; very few came to farm. They fitted well into a Canada that was now overwhelmingly urban. By 1956, half the people of British Columbia lived in Vancouver or Victoria; a third of Quebeckers clustered in Montreal and its sprawling suburbs. While five hundred thousand of the newcomers came from the British Isles and a hundred thousand came from the United States, many of these immigrants had no links with either founding culture or even with the eastern European roots of Sifton-era arrivals. Yet prosperity and economic growth brought racial acceptance with astonishingly little friction or cultural antagonism. On the contrary, the newcomers often made their own demands on Canada for a more sophisticated, culturally varied life. The puritan conformity of Canada began to crack as immigrants and the Canadian-born alike chafed at drinking laws, "blue" Sundays, and restaurants that served bad food and no wine. Canadian family attitudes, in turn, strained old-world traditions of parental authority and female roles.

Change was always controversial. The United Church, still dominant among Protestants but threatened by a largely Catholic influx of immigrants, defended the Sabbath and opposed liquor. Roman Catholics fought to keep birth control as an offence under the Criminal Code and deplored a soaring divorce rate. In the 1930s, the number of divorces in Canada hovered between one hundred to two hundred a year; by the 1950s, six to seven thousand marriages a year were ending in divorce. As they usually had, Canadians blamed the United States for the invasion of loose morals and permissiveness. Films, radio, and television were the obvious culprits. The Canadian Broadcasting Corporation, earnest but under-financed, developed two excellent radio networks only to be outflanked by the newer medium. By 1952, it had bravely launched Canadian television in French and English. The enormous costs of TV production compelled the CBC to buy most of its programs from American networks and to concentrate resources on a coast-to-coast microwave link-up that might unite viewers for special national occasions such as *Hockey Night in Canada*.

In 1949, a reluctant St. Laurent approved a Royal Commission on the Arts and Letters in Canada. While St. Laurent had few qualms about meddling with provincial concerns for culture, he had robust doubts about "subsidising ballet dancers." The commission's report in 1951, under the heavy imprint of its chairman, Vincent Massey, argued forcefully that the government must do just that if Canadians were to share in performing and creative arts and to develop universities worthy of the name. The report lay where it landed, and the arts struggled on. Vancouver's symphony orchestra played in an arena. Canada's art treasures could be found behind the dinosaurs in the dusty National Museum.

Prosperity and immigration slowly built pressures politicians had to notice. In 1953, Stratford's Shakespearean Festival opened in a tent. The *Théâtre du Nouveau Monde* opened in Montreal. Suddenly, as a matter of civic pride, cities began erecting theatres. What may have been the nadir of the arts in Canada, the late

218

1940s, began to pass. At least some people in an affluent Canada, far from being horror-struck at the thought of subsidizing ballet dancers, began to wonder why they had not done so before. In 1957, the adventitious death of a couple of millionaires, Sir James Dunn and Isaac Killam, gave such a windfall of inheritance taxes that the federal government launched the Canada Council and endowed it with $100 million, half for capital grants to universities, the rest for scholarships, loans, and grants. Nervously, Canada had made itself a patron of the arts; now it awaited the critics.

Most Canadians did not seem to care. Later, they might complain that the fifties were boring, marked only by the successive fads of American popular culture. Politics too were predictable and routine, grey and repetitive. In a 1953 national election, the sober competence of St. Laurent and Howe, the regular government surpluses, and a discreet trickle of pre-election goodies made the Liberals proof against George Drew's bluster and evidence of scandal in the expanding defence department. The opposition parties gained a little in the election—the government lost twenty seats but the popular vote was hardly altered from 1949. Thoughtful observers assessed the results and wondered whether constitutional reforms might be desirable. Canada seemed bound for permanent one-party government.

Still, few Canadians gave any sign of caring.

# 3 / Recession

In the fifties, Canadians could believe that they lived in a permanently prosperous, internationally esteemed, and increasingly united country. Ottawa's mandarins, their prestige undimmed from the war, skillfully applied the approved doctrines of macroeconomic management. Nationalists could be pleased that the ambitious, aristocratic Vincent Massey, was the first native son to be Governor General. Abroad, talented Canadian diplomats pursued a modest but moral path as confidants of both the Third World and the West. Even social and regional tensions seemed to be fading. The CCF was in decline. Canada's two largest labour organizations, worried by stagnant membership and the costs of rivalry, merged in 1956 as the Canadian Labour Congress. Federal-provincial conferences were decorous affairs. If few provincial premiers were now Liberals, most followed Ontario's affable Leslie Frost in a spirit of "live and let live." Only Maurice Duplessis made public war on Ottawa; privately, even he preferred compromise.

Yet problems persisted, although few of the fifteen million affluent Canadians hunted for them. Keynesian economic principles amounted to no more than Joseph's advice to the Egyptian pharaoh: run a surplus in good times to cover the deficit in bad times. In 1949 and 1953, economic down-turns had coincided with pre-election budgets. Liberal politicians and mandarins congratulated each other when re-election coincided with recovery. Yet the pharaoh had not had to manage a federal democracy. By the mid-fifties, it was the provinces, not Ottawa, that were big spenders. A baby boom, urbanization, and prosperity demanded hospitals, water and sewer systems, and highways for the two-thirds of Canadians who now owned cars. The rich provinces, Ontario and British Columbia, clamoured for money as loudly as their poorer neighbours, for they were the ones doing the most expensive growing.

Canada's post-war international role had been another Liberal bonus. Tories (and Duplessis) deplored foreign aid, and the CCF harboured a pacifist wing and condemned German rearmament. Neither approach won many votes. Most Canadians, even in Quebec, accepted commitments to NATO, Korea, and rearmament. Brooke Claxton, Minister of National Defence, even believed that conscription could have been possible with St. Laurent as Prime Minister.

But Canadian intellectuals deplored Communist-hunting by American politicians, and Canadian diplomats worried at the populist violence of American foreign policies. NATO had seemed like a way of curbing Washington's rashness, but the Republican administration elected in 1952 began to switch from reliance on costly, conscripted conventional forces to a so-called "massive deterrent" of strategic bombers. American taxpayers might like "a bigger bang for the buck"; allies like Canada worried increasingly about their power to restrain an American trigger finger. Anxiety grew as American policymakers found it necessary to persuade allies and enemies that they would, indeed, risk a nuclear holocaust to defend the United States' interests.

It was, however, two older allies who turned Canada's external policy into a Liberal embarrassment. The Anglo-French invasion of Egypt in October 1956 split the Commonwealth. Canada lined up with the newer, non-white members and, more gratefully, with the United States in deploring the Anglo-French move. At the United Nations, Lester Pearson performed diplomatic miracles in securing the UN's first peacekeeping force to cover the Anglo-French (and a simultaneous Israeli) withdrawal. His reward was a Nobel Peace Prize.

Some Canadians were not pleased. Opinion polls in 1956 showed a small majority of support for Britain. Perhaps these were the same Canadians who had grumbled as St. Laurent created a distinct Canadian citizenship, abolished appeals to the Privy Council in London, and firmly if discreetly removed crowns, Union Jacks, and other historic symbolism from the public scene. Now the Suez affair gave British sympathizers a focus for their discontent.

So did another event in an unusually active year. Bent on

linking Alberta natural gas with Quebec and Ontario markets, C. D. Howe had sought fast parliamentary approval for giving a pipeline contract to a Canadian-American consortium. The project fitted national and nationalistic goals, but Tory tacticians decided that obstruction would drive Howe into one of his increasingly explosive rages. The tactics succeeded. Using their majority, the Liberals imposed closure and indiscreetly jeered when the opposition protested. A hitherto respected Speaker collapsed into partisan subservience. The ensuing parliamentary struggle lasted long enough for most Canadians to take notice. The issue itself was unimportant: the pipeline was built without further controversy. It was the arrogance of politicians like C. D. Howe that people noticed. Liberals had been too long in power.

George Drew's own public arrogance might have saved the Liberals, but, in December 1956, his ill health forced the Tories to find a successor. John Diefenbaker was quite unlike any previous Canadian party leader. First elected in 1940, Diefenbaker had held a lonely Saskatchewan seat by dint of preacher-style rhetoric and a well-publicised devotion to the underdog. He had as little in common with Tory financiers as he did with Ottawa civil servants, but his backers believed that he could find supporters in places where no one had ever voted Conservative. They were right. The Liberals also knew Diefenbaker and they dismissed him.

June 1957 was early to hold an election, but St. Laurent was now seventy-six and he could be used only one more time. This time, economic wisdom called for tight restraint on pre-election bonuses. Old-age pensioners would have to be satisfied by a six-dollar increase. Western farmers were grumbling about huge unsold stocks of grain, but surely the blame lay with the Americans' give-away export programs, not with Ottawa. Besides, the West had never voted Tory. A Liberal victory seemed a foregone conclusion. The experts and the polls agreed. The experts also agreed that Diefenbaker was impressive, reaching past prosperous Tories to voters who had missed out on wealth and power. For the first time, a Conservative leader was rallying Canadians against the smug officials with their taxes and "tight money." Even the pension increase was scorned as the work of the "six-buck" boys. Still, had voters ever shot Santa Claus?

Many Canadians went to bed on June 10 convinced, as some

premature magazine headlines claimed, that St. Laurent would be returned by a reduced majority. Instead, voters had elected 112 Conservatives and only 105 Liberals. Twenty-five per cent of voters had shifted from the Liberals to Diefenbaker, incidentally boosting the CCF to 25 seats and Social Credit to 19. In Port Arthur, one of those CCFers, Douglas Fisher, defeated C. D. Howe himself.

The Liberals did not cling to power. By June 21, John Diefenbaker headed a new, hopelessly inexperienced government. The change suddenly seemed refreshing. Civil servants recalled their neutrality and dutifully faced their new masters. Suspicions were mutual and, for Diefenbaker and some of his associates, never fully alleviated. The Liberal strategy was plain. St. Laurent resigned the party leadership and his decimated caucus sat demurely silent, giving Diefenbaker time to hang himself. In January, a Liberal convention gave the succession to the Nobel Prize-winner, Lester Pearson. A world-famous diplomat with the misleading public image of a folksy, uncomplicated baseball fan seemed like a sure winner. Pearson seems to have thought so himself. Fresh from his convention victory, he demanded that Diefenbaker resign and return power to the Liberals. Even some Liberals blanched.

To his credit, Pearson saw at once that he had made a dumb move. So did Diefenbaker. Promptly he called an election. Unconsciously, Pearson had demonstrated the Liberals' unrepentant arrogance. His flood of election promises sounded phoney from politicians who had held office for twenty-two years. When Liberals tried to campaign on the harsh recession which gripped Canada by 1958, Diefenbaker presented damning evidence that the previous government had forseen the crisis. Radio, television, and brilliantly organized public meetings, as well as Diefenbaker's spectacular theatrical skill, allowed the new Prime Minister to dominate the campaign. Audiences hushed as he summoned them to "catch the vision of the kind of Canada this can be." Pearson and intellectual critics could fume that it was all humbug—it worked.

Indeed, Diefenbaker's speeches were hardly necessary. Before the election, the Tory support stood at fifty per cent in the polls. Canadians were captivated by their new government. The Liberals disintegrated. Minor parties vanished in irrelevance. Waverers could scramble aboard a certain winner. Diefenbaker had paid no court to Quebec either in seeking the leadership or in the 1957 campaign. The 1958 Tory strategy was simple: *"n'isolons pas Quebec,"* said the advertisements, and Quebec would not be isolated. In 1957, Frost had ended his neutrality and delivered Ontario to the Tories. This time Duplessis released the *Union Nationale* machine. Quebec Liberal MPs who had scarcely campaigned in their careers never knew what hit them. On March 31, 1958, fifty Conservatives, many of them Duplessis nominees, swept the province's seventy-five seats. Across Canada, Diefenbaker won 53.6% of the popular vote. Only Borden in 1917 had ever done better. The Conservatives held 208 seats, the Liberals held 49 (not one of them in western Canada), the CCF had dwindled to 8, and Social Credit had vanished.

The 1958 landslide was more a referendum than an election, with Diefenbaker the triumphant issue and almost no national divisions. Only Newfoundland stayed Liberal. In 1957, the four western provinces had elected more CCFers than Conservatives: nine months later they were solid for Diefenbaker—Conservative votes literally doubled. It was the kind of majority that Diefenbaker's hero, Sir John A. Macdonald, once claimed "could corrupt a committee of archangels." It evoked automatic sympathy for a tiny opposition, and it persuaded journalists, self-important by nature, to assume the role of critic. It was not hard to find things to condemn. Ministers were inexperienced and sometimes inept. Some civil servants were disloyal and many more resented that their loyalty was plainly suspect. Above all, the Prime Minister himself seemed nervous about his majority and eager to prove his record as a defender of Parliament even if it meant endless debate. The mere volume of sound from Parliament, liberated from the cavalier condescension of St. Laurent's ministers, persuaded Canadians that there must be much to criticize.

So there was, but much was accomplished too. Diefenbaker's "vision" had been conceived by an adviser as a development plan for Canada's northern frontier; it became a catch-all for miscellaneous but useful projects like the South Saskatchewan dam, the railway to lead-zinc deposits at Pine Point on Great Slave Lake, or the development of Frobisher Bay on Baffin Island. A procession of royal commissions, headed by impeccable Tories, produced some uncomfortably radical reports. Mr. Justice Emmett Hall provided unanswerable arguments for Medicare as well as over-

224

optimistic statistics on its costs. Kenneth Carter's commission on tax reform would infuriate the wealthy a decade later with its claim that income from capital gains should be as taxable as a paycheque. Grattan O'Leary, a veteran Tory editor, embarrassed Canadian governments and annoyed Washington with a report that proposed banning American magazines that competed for Canadian advertising.

For the first time in memory, the West was in power in Ottawa. The flood of Quebeckers who arrived in 1958 were too late for major cabinet posts. It never occurred to Diefenbaker that Tory election prospects depended on making room for them. Donald Fleming, finance minister and voice of traditional eastern Toryism, carried little weight. He had run against Diefenbaker for the party leadership in 1956. Western ministers like Alvin Hamilton, Howard Green, and George Pearkes had the Prime Minister's ear. So had the voices of prairie populism. Old-age pensions rose sharply. Despite free-enterprise rhetoric, the government adopted costly price supports for twenty-four farm products and kept the Wheat Board. An Agricultural Rehabilitation and Development Act (ARDA) was designed to help some farmers to prosper and others to leave the land. In 1960, Diefenbaker seized the chance to sell the huge western wheat surplus to China. Washington grumbled at Canada giving aid to the Communists, but western farm incomes tripled. With advice from a royal commission and from a new National Energy Board, the government forced Ontario to be a market for Alberta's high-priced oil. Only Quebec and the Maritimes could still profit from cheap imports.

Diefenbaker's most cherished project, a Canadian Bill of Rights, grew out of his own prairie experience and memories of the discrimination he himself had suffered, even in Tory circles, for his foreign-sounding name. Passed by Parliament in 1960 with copies immediately distributed to millions of Canadians by a sympathetic toothpaste manufacturer, the bill promised too much. It was powerless to bind provinces or even a later Parliament. It also ignored the kinds of rights French Canadians had sought for generations. To Diefenbaker, fervently preaching an "unhyphenated Canadianism," cultural and language rights were irrelevant or divisive. It was a widespread western view. Quebeckers, Diefenbaker felt, should be satisfied now that Ottawa issued them bilingual cheques.

225

Even with a huge majority, power gave traditional Tories far less pleasure than they had hoped. Their one major partisan bonus was the outcome of a Liberal-appointed royal commission. A 1957 report satisfied the old demand of private broadcasters that the CBC be stripped of its regulating powers. In 1958 the Conservatives established and staffed a new Board of Broadcast Governors. Among its early decisions was approval of a private network (CTV) to rival the CBC's national television coverage. John Bassett, an energetic Toronto Conservative and part-owner of the CTV network, was the chief beneficiary.

Opposition parties have always championed provincial rights. In power, Diefenbaker had costly promises to fulfil. In 1957, with the tax rental agreements ended, St. Laurent had bluntly told the provinces that, like Quebec, they could have ten per cent of federal income and corporation taxes. Ottawa would collect more, but provincial taxpayers would feel it. More was needed because by now hospital insurance had become the latest and most costly of over a dozen shared programs. Under Diefenbaker, Ottawa's share of income taxes fell from ninety to eighty-four per cent by 1962. Federal-provincial relations grew more acrimonious. A long-awaited constitutional amending formula almost won approval until Quebec backed out—her demand to run unemployment insurance had been rejected. British Columbia's Premier W. A. C. Bennett repudiated a Canadian-American agreement to develop Columbia River power and then demanded control of off-shore resources. Joey Smallwood cried betrayal when Ottawa insisted on the letter of Newfoundland's terms of Confederation in 1949 instead of Smallwood's more generous interpretation. He was furious too when Diefenbaker refused RCMP reinforcements to crush a loggers' strike in 1959.

Such battles were a reassertion of history. It was Ottawa's immense post-war power and the harmony of federal-provincial relations which had been unusual. So, too, was Canada's post-war industrial strength. A clear economic strategy with tough priorities, heavy investment, and conscious sacrifice of inefficient industrial sectors might have given Canada a durable, if specialized, industrial future. Instead, it was her defeated enemies who chose that route while Canadians prospered from a flood of foreign investment. Simply being North American had seemed guarantee enough of permanent prosperity.

226

It was not. Brief recessions in 1949 and 1953–54 gave warnings. Canada's return to the vulnerability of a resource-exporter was concealed by pride in her new hydro-electric projects and pipelines and in the Seaway. With the conservatism of wealth, the Liberals had reverted to the older monetarist techniques of high interest rates to curb inflation. The new governor of the Bank of Canada, James Coyne, was an ardent fan of the policy. His strategies of "tight money" provided Tories with a campaign issue in 1957, but, though recession deepened and modest inflation rates vanished, Coyne's policies persisted. Canadians, he insisted, must tighten their belts and pay their way. A professed nationalist, Coyne found arguments from the warnings in another Liberal royal commission report on Canada's economic prospects, headed by a wealthy Toronto accountant, Walter Gordon. Foreign investors now controlled key Canadian industries and resources, Gordon warned, threatening Canada's sovereignty. Yet the Bank's high interest rates attracted foreign money while they dampened Canadian business and industrial expansion. As a nationalist, Coyne did more harm than good.

Diefenbaker's government had inherited far worse problems from the Liberals than it or most Canadians realized, and its huge majority left it no alibis. In Europe, the new Common Market threatened old Canadian markets. Giant supertankers, developed when the Suez Canal was blocked in 1956, cut the price of oil and threatened Alberta's favourite industry. The government solution, banning imported oil west of the Ottawa river, angered Ontario. Another problem was $6.4 billion in Victory Bonds, maturing fifteen years after the war. Reconversion of the bonds at higher interest cost money. James Coyne claimed that bondholders should have had even higher rates. Canadians, believing the expert, felt cheated and blamed Diefenbaker. The Prime Minister blamed Coyne. The outcome was an ugly public row. Conservative politicians tried to blacken Coyne for arranging a $25,000 pension for himself, not for his policies which neither they nor most Canadians probably understood. In the end, Coyne went, but not without damaging the Tory regime with the voters and even with the mutually protective band of Ottawa mandarins.

Despite Coyne and a substantial ignorance of economic mysteries, Diefenbaker's policies were far more effective against the recession than contemporaries recognized. His spending proclivi-

227

ties were the despair of Donald Fleming. Regularly the finance minister promised surpluses, squeezed civil service salaries, demanded restraint, and froze hiring, only to have to confess yet another deficit. Government spending between 1957 and 1961 rose thirty-two per cent. A winter works program taught the construction industry to work year-round. Grants to universities doubled and a federal technical and vocational training program not only expanded schools but kept hundreds of thousands of students from the overcrowded labour market. Grim unemployment figures hid the fact that employment and output had both grown. Yet Diefenbaker's own political approach encouraged Canadians to look at appearances, not facts, and the image was a damning contrast to the Liberal's apparent record of efficiency and success.

Economic disorder was matched by Canada's relations with the world. With a rhetorical flourish, Diefenbaker had pledged a fifteen-per-cent shift of Canadian trade from the United States to Britain. The figure, taken from the air, was absurd. While the British took up the proposal, the new government raised tariffs instead. Diefenbaker toured the world, seeking the prestige Pearson had garnered. He revelled in the links with Britain and the monarchy. To his initial embarrassment and later pride, Canada played a major role in excluding South Africa from the Commonwealth in 1961. Alone among the innumerable repugnant policies of Commonwealth members, apartheid was deemed intolerable. Having condemned Canada's Suez role in 1956, the Conservatives took their own share of UN peacekeeping in the Congo in 1960. Through no Canadian fault, it was not a happy experience as soldiers were beaten and abused without the right of self-defence.

Whatever the dangers and attractions of the world, economics and defence had bound Canada steadily closer to the United States. China, and later the Soviet Union, might buy Canadian wheat but the bilateral trend was steady. Each year, Canadian-American trade grew while manufactured exports to other countries declined. Walter Gordon's report had helped push the Conservatives toward economic nationalism. A new law required corporations and labour unions to report their affairs so that the degree of foreign influence might at least be public.

American dependence on the deterrent and Soviet development of both nuclear weapons and the means to deliver them to

American cities made continental defence a major priority. Late in the forties, the Liberals had approved a Canadian-designed fighter plane, the CF-100, and, later a Canadian share in building three radar warning lines. Next, developing a newer, supersonic fighter, the Avro-Arrow CF-105, became essential, exciting, and so costly that it would probably not have survived a Liberal victory in 1957. Even plans for a unified North American Air Defence Command (NORAD) had been too touchy to be settled before the 1957 election.

Once in power and with the aged Major-General George Pearkes as defence minister, Diefenbaker acted decisively. The North American Air Defence Command agreement was signed before officials could even warn of its dangers. The Arrow was a tougher problem. Suspicious of Liberal contractors, certain that costs would rise and that no other buyers could be found, Diefenbaker finally cancelled the project on February 20, 1959. In a day, fourteen thousand engineers, scientists, and skilled workers became unemployed. In a week, all five prototypes were demolished. Amid the bitter outcry, Diefenbaker added to the confusion. The age of the missile had arrived, he claimed, and both bombers and fighters were obsolete. The Arrow's replacement was indeed a Bomarc missile, but it was useful only against manned bombers. It had to be supplemented by F-101 fighters which the Americans had relegated to their reserves. National pride was doubly hurt. So was national security and Diefenbaker's credibility.

The Bomarcs were dubious weapons, useful only with nuclear warheads. An anti-nuclear crusade, begun in Britain, had spread to Canada to be endorsed by women's groups, professors, and by both the Liberals and the CCF. More seriously, it appealed to the rigid moralism and anti-Americanism of Howard Green, Diefenbaker's latest Secretary of State for External Affairs. Canada, the government announced, would not acquire nuclear weapons. Or perhaps it would. Or did it know? Every major weapon system the government had ordered for its NATO and NORAD commitments, from Bomarcs and F-101s to Honest John rockets, depended on nuclear warheads. Diefenbaker insisted otherwise: the weapons were non-nuclear. Only the innocent and the resolutely unmilitary could believe him. In Canada, such people were numerous.

Cancelling the Arrow was the last tough defence decision Diefenbaker was willing to make. The aftermath of confusion and deception undermined his reputation with allies and Canadian opinion-makers alike. Not even the nuclear disarmers could trust him. In Washington, Diefenbaker's contradictions and Green's increasingly evident hostility might have been tolerated by an aging, complacent Republican administration, but a dynamic new president, John F. Kennedy, viewed them differently. Diefenbaker instinctively disliked Kennedy. It was mutual. As in the 1930s with Roosevelt and Bennett, many Canadians contrasted their own leader with the handsome, articulate American and were embarrassed. The image of Camelot persuaded younger members of the Canadian elite that they were too sophisticated for the fire and brimstone or the crude evasions of their own national leader.

There were now alternatives, though none was as charismatic as Kennedy. Under Pearson, the Liberals had shed most of the veterans of the St. Laurent era. Reassured by Conservative fumbling that Liberalism was still the way to power, ambitious younger politicians emerged to rebuild party organizations, notably in the major cities. Newer Canadians, angry at sharp Tory restrictions against immigration imposed in 1957, remembered which party had brought them to Canada. Business leaders recalled the old competence of the St. Laurent-Howe era. Newer policies, some of them proposed but unnoticed during the 1958 debacle, brightened the Liberal image.

A competitor was a regenerated and retitled CCF. The post-merger Canadian Labour Congress had settled its differences about endorsing the CCF by agreeing to form a new left-wing party. A battered CCF agreed, and, by 1961, a New Party movement was under way. With the CCF's guiding genius, David Lewis, in control, two thousand delegates met in Ottawa for a steaming August convention. It was an amalgam of new and old politics. Veteran CCF and labour organizers managed the business and delivered the leadership to the CCF premier of Saskatchewan, Tommy Douglas. A surprise delegation of left-wing Quebec nationalists committed the excited convention to a "two-nations" version of Canada. Rank-and-filers ignored their leaders' pleas for a title that could never be abbreviated. The "New Democratic Party," the delegates' choice, at once became the NDP.

230

Liberals and New Democrats seemed more fearsome than they were. Under Pearson, the Liberals had forgotten the rural ridings where King had patiently hunted supporters. Some CCFers warned that the NDP's labour image would be hard to sell to prairie farmers. Both parties seemed designed to split a sophisticated urban electorate that had been the most fragile and flighty element of the 1958 Tory coalition. More dangerous but unnoticed was Social Credit, not in the West anymore but in rural Quebec. A spellbinding used-car dealer named Réal Caouette had quietly created a mass hinterland movement of people angry at governments, taxes, and change. No one much cared, for there was much more exciting news from Quebec City.

In 1959, Duplessis had died. His *Union Nationale* had been a personal regime, a tight, authoritarian machine with which *Le Chef* could guard his endangered people. Even the Church, for all its seeming influence, depended utterly on Duplessis for money to run its imposing empire of hospitals, schools, and orphanages. Beyond ruthless use of patronage and an electoral machine that did not shrink from violence and fraud, Duplessis had depended on his wars with Ottawa to harvest votes. Successive Liberal leaders were dismissed as "travelling salesmen" of federalism. Now *Le Chef* was gone. Soon, so was his able and reforming successor, Paul Sauvé. By backing Diefenbaker, the *Union Nationale* had gained patronage and lost independence. The initiative now lay with Jean Lesage, once Pearson's parliamentary assistant and a man whose aloof dignity contrasted with the vulgarity of the Duplessis era.

*Il faut que ça change*, proclaimed the Liberal slogans, to be echoed by younger, better-educated Quebec voters, shaped by the 1950s to demand more of life and of government than the Church or Duplessis had allowed them. When Lesage won the 1960 election, most Canadians welcomed the message and saw it take shape as a superbly talented new team—Paul Gerin-Lajoie, René Lévesque, Georges Lapalme—began attracting comparable talent to the task of reform. Canadians were slower to overhear the other slogan of the 1960 victory, *maîtres chez-nous*. The state would replace the Church and the land as the fundamental instrument of *Canadien* survival. Unless something dramatic happened in Ottawa, that state would be *Québécois*; its logical direction was independence.

On June 10, 1962, Diefenbaker faced the electorate. The experts had predicted a Liberal victory, guided by polls and a mid-campaign economic crisis in which the dollar had been sharply devalued. Economists might approve, but Liberals issued a "Diefenbuck" as a triumphant reminder of Tory mismanagement and despatched a "truth squad" to report Diefenbaker's lies. The tactics backfired. It was the Liberals' own campaign that sagged. Even with warm backing, Lester Pearson did not excite Canadians. To be fair, he had a huge margin to trim. Voters elected 112 Conservatives, 100 Liberals, 19 New Democrats, and an astonishing 30 Social Crediters, all but 4 of them from Réal Caouette's grass-roots Quebec campaign. With their help, Diefenbaker could still govern. He did so now with deeper suspicions of officials and even of colleagues. Only the West had remained true and solid.

The defence issue should have gone away. After all, peacetime governments had always let politics rule military decisions. Diefenbaker listened to Howard Green and believed his anti-nuclear mail. The Bomarcs, finally inserted in their silos at North Bay and La Macaza, were armed with sandbags. The F-101s were safer unarmed. Decisions could wait.

The Cuban missile crisis ended the delay. For a few tense days in October 1962, President Kennedy waged a war of nuclear bluff against Soviet strategic will. Canada did not play. NORAD in the United States moved to readiness; its Canadian element, covering New York and Pittsburgh as well as Toronto and Montreal, did not. Whatever they might have felt later, most Canadians at the time were appalled. The polls reflected a dramatic switch in favour of acquiring nuclear warheads. Lester Pearson switched with the polls. In January 1963, a single speech in Scarborough reversed the Liberal anti-nuclear stand. George Pearkes's successor in the defence portfolio, Douglas Harkness, resigned, humiliated by his Prime Minister's evasions. A series of American statements, deliberate or accidental, refuted Diefenbaker's speeches. A blunt State Department release summarized American opinion and the plain facts: Canada had proposed no arrangement "sufficiently practical to contribute effectively to North American defence." It was a bomb-shell.

Even modest overtures to Caouette's *Créditistes* might have kept their loyalty. Diefenbaker saw no need. On February 5, they abandoned the sinking government. So did more Tory ministers. The government sank. An election followed.

Within days, the nuclear weapons issue vanished. Diefenbaker promised a full statement on defence. It never appeared. Instead, he denounced the White House for engineering his downfall. Almost no newspapers backed Diefenbaker or his Tories. In much of urban Canada, Conservatives sat out the campaign. Pearson's campaign, programmed carefully on the Kennedy victory of 1960, stumbled and backfired but this time it did not fail—quite. On April 8, Pearson won 129 seats to Diefenbaker's 95. The NDP won 17, Social Credit 24. For the first time since 1925, Liberals would face a minority government. The Mackenzie King alliance of Quebec and the prairies against Tory Ontario was gone. Of 48 prairie seats, Diefenbaker's Tories held all but 7. The two central provinces had given Pearson all but 30 of his supporters. In Quebec, two elections had cut Progressive Conservative voter support from fifty to nineteen per cent.

In five years the great national consensus of 1958 had dissolved. The old rivalries and frustrations had found new shapes, but they had all the old virulence. Once again, Canadians were face to face with their history.

# 4/Confusion

It had been the elite more than the ordinary Canadians who had abandoned Diefenbaker. They yearned for the effortless competence of post-war governments, the smooth relations with Washington. Some humbler voters, frightened by the recession, recalled the ancestral wisdom that "Liberal times are good times." Only in the West had Diefenbaker's times been good.

Like other Canadians, Pearson took Liberal efficiency and prosperity for granted. Few guessed his own priority: French Canada. Outside Quebec, most Canadians rejoiced at the so-called "Quiet Revolution." In 1962, René Lévesque had bullied a reluctant Jean Lesage into making hydro nationalization a provincial election issue. The outcome was a rout for the *Union Nationale*. Much of the rest of Canada approved: publicly-owned electricity would make Quebec more like other provinces. So would displacement of church control of the schools by a new department of education in 1964. Now Quebec would have a high-school system like other provinces. Surely Canada would be more united.

Diefenbaker had ignored Quebec ministers when they tried to explain the significance of such developments. In 1961 the NDP had encountered the radical new Quebec nationalism, absorbed the catch-phrases, and continued on its own familiar, centralizing way. It never regained its chance in French Canada. Only Pearson, unilingual, indecisive, and unpolitical, had a diplomat's ears. In 1962, in a speech unnoticed outside Quebec, Pearson had recognized that *Canadiens* would control their economic and cultural destiny; they must also play a full and equal role in Ottawa. In power, he launched a powerful Royal Commission on Bilingualism and Biculturalism, as much to educate as to find answers. André Laurendeau, now the cool, reflective editor of *Le Devoir*, and Davidson Dunton, a former head of the CBC, were joint chairmen. For a start, French would become a language heard in the Liberal cabinet and caucus.

Bereft of any powerful Quebec Liberals, Pearson chose his own Quebeckers: able, decent men, often with his own lack of gut political instinct. In vengeful opposition, Diefenbaker was now in his element. Too often it was Quebec ministers who were bloodied or humiliated by his shafts. An irresolute Prime Minister and a minority government seemed helpless in their defence.

However, Quebeckers were not alone in their humiliation. Walter Gordon, inspiration of economic nationalism in the fifties, had been Pearson's ally and financial advisor in rebuilding the party. As finance minister, he was important to Pearson's pledge that Liberals would begin with "Sixty Days of Decision." Gordon's contribution was a confused, ill-argued budget. Never before in Canadian experience had parts of a budget been hauled back for revision. Opposition parties had tasted Liberal blood, and the procession of scandals provided a national spectacle.

Pearson's insistence on a simple maple leaf flag as national emblem in place of the traditional red ensign had provoked indignant protests from the Royal Canadian Legion convention where it was unveiled in 1964. Diefenbaker's caucus rallied against the so-called "Pearson pennant." For months, Parliament was trapped in the uproar until the bland compromise emerged: red on white with a single stylized leaf. National unity was not one of the by-products.

Liberals had not restored efficiency; few people watching the parliamentary cacophony gave them credit for reviving prosperity. Economic recovery was real enough but it had begun in 1961 as Chinese and then Soviet wheat sales spread their impact. Thanks to wheat as a leading staple, Canada entered a new era of export surpluses. Liberals took credit for implementing an old and controversial solution to Canada's fading branch-plant automotive industry. The Auto Trade pact of January 1965 erased the border for firms in Canada and the United States making cars and parts. The immediate outcome was an impressive boom in Ontario's manufacturing towns.

By the mid-sixties it was rare for Ottawa to get much credit for economic achievements. The Conservatives' success with the Agricultural Rehabilitation and Development Act (ARDA) inspired a procession of acronymic programs from the Liberals. Canadians absorbed the latest American faith that costly agencies with well-paid officials could somehow lift neglected regions from poverty.

In the new decade, provinces aspired to grandeur. Quebec's huge Manicouagan hydro dam satisfied René Lévesque's claim to the obvious—that Québécois could be brilliant engineers. Toronto had acquired its first subway line in 1954 and a second by 1960; Montreal must follow suit in time for a grandiose world's fair in 1967. Nova Scotia boasted a Volvo assembly plant; Quebec matched it with Peugeot. To finish the education of the baby boom, every province expanded old universities and most added new ones. In a single announcement, Ontario created a collection of twenty-two community colleges exclusively for skills training. In British Columbia, where Premier W. A. C. Bennett's government seemed more eager to develop mountains than people, cheap Columbia power was given to the Americans so that Bennett could develop his own hydro-electric scheme on the Peace River. To the despair of General A. G. L. McNaughton, ending his career as co-chairman of the International Joint Commission, the Pearson government limply acquiesced.

The pendulum of power had swung back to the provinces as it had before, but it would swing even farther if they could get more money. The need was clear enough. The baby boom grew more costly with age. Post-secondary education, experts now claimed, was the key to economic growth and social justice. Both seemed desirable. So was Medicare. In 1962, Saskatchewan's CCF government braved financial risks and a doctors' strike to introduce comprehensive medical insurance. Liberals had promised such a plan since 1919 but had not hurried: it was a provincial matter. Some premiers, like Ontario's John Robarts, latest in an endless Tory dynasty, professed philosophical objections. Others merely shuddered at the cost.

In their campaign, the Liberals had promised a new era of "co-operative federalism" to waft away the familiar jurisdictional quarrels. Words made no difference when money and power were at stake. A major federal Liberal promise was a national scheme of contributory portable old-age pensions. Who cared that the plan invaded provincial jurisdiction? Premiers did. They also saw that a contributory plan would create a huge capital fund for years before big pay-outs began. While Ontario's John Robarts, as a Conservative, had no love for the scheme, it was actually the Liberal premier of Quebec, Jean Lesage, who was most awkward. The politics of grandeur cost money. Surpluses, squirreled away by the frugal Duplessis, had vanished. Buying private electricity companies had used up Quebec's credit and there were still universities and secondary schools to build. Provincial voters grumbled that the Liberals were taxing too heavily. In fact, Lesage was running a staggering deficit. Rural Quebec threatened one flank; radical nationalists even in Lesage's own government used revolutionary bomb blasts and holdups to press their case. A magazine poll in 1964 showed thirteen per cent of Quebeckers ready for independence.

When Pearson and the premiers met in Quebec City in 1964 to discuss the pension plan, the old tradition of affable federal-provincial relations ended. Behind police guards, amid bomb threats, Canadian politicians shared a revelation. The normally cool, dignified Lesage was angry and defiant (and drunk). Even more significant, the Quebec Pension Plan his officials unveiled was plainly better conceived and better argued than the federal version. Ottawa's mystic expertise had vanished. Paradoxically, the humiliation helped save the federal plan. A far-sighted John Robarts sensed that Confederation might crumble if Ottawa's plan collapsed. Ontario backed Ottawa—at a price. A new Canada Pension Plan would imitate the Quebec version. Quebec would still opt out, but the other provinces would get the CPP's funds to invest as they chose against the day when pensions would be paid. A crisis had passed but neither Pearson nor his officials would easily recover their prestige.

At least Canada's external standing should have been safe with the Liberals. With Kennedy, Pearson had already found an easy rapport; he resembled the tweedy, liberal-minded academics with whom the young president surrounded himself. As Pearson had promised, Canada at once accepted nuclear warheads for its weapons with all the safeguards Washington had promised. A white paper by Paul Hellyer, the new defence minister, reassured anti-war activists that first priority for Canadian armed forces would be peacekeeping. New equipment would be non-nuclear and military strength would be trimmed to pay for it. Allies were content. Few readers noticed a discreet but explicit promise: the armed forces would also be unified.

237

All was not serene. Gordon's ill-fated budget had initially included a take-over tax on foreign purchases of Canadian businesses. The O'Leary Report, postponed by Diefenbaker, led to a law discouraging Canadian advertising in foreign periodicals in order to promote the sale of Canadian magazines. Pressure from Washington persuaded the Liberals to exempt *Time* and *Reader's Digest*. More friction came from the government's reluctant decision to put the corrupt Seafarers' International Union under trusteeship and to prosecute its American ex-gangster leader, Hal Banks. When Banks jumped bail to the United States and his parent union showed no repentance for its corruption, federal officials were forced to seek help in Washington. President Kennedy, however, seemed to prefer union blandishments to Ottawa's appeals.

On the whole, though, Canadian-American relations improved. Pearson's own policies imitated the programs of Kennedy's "New Frontier." A "Company of Young Canadians" was a strife-ridden imitation of the Peace Corps. An overdue concern for Canada's blacks and Indians was a guilty reflection that Canada, too, had civil rights problems. Kennedy's assassination on November 22, 1963, was a blow an entire generation of Canadians would not forget.

Kennedy's successor, Lyndon Johnson, offered no such human rapport. At the time, few Canadians recognized the sterility of Kennedy's record or the practical idealism of Lyndon Johnson's "War on Poverty," although privately Pearson had questioned the wisdom of Kennedy's policies on Cuba and the Far East. Merely by continuing his predecessor's Vietnam entanglement, Johnson had taken the United States into a real war by February 1965. Vietnam was not Korea. Canadians, full of moral righteousness, condemned the war, and Pearson took their disapproval to Philadelphia in April 1965. It was a deed few Canadians would have welcomed from an American leader, and President Johnson was not a tolerant man. "Lester," he told the Canadian, "you peed on my carpet." His rage forced an apology from the Canadian Prime Minister but the era of special relationships was over.

Often, in 1965, leading Liberals reviewed opinion polls, a fractious Parliament, and their own achievements—chiefly the flag and the Canada Pension Plan—and pondered how pleasant life would be with a majority. It seemed easy. The Conservatives were preoccupied with plots against Diefenbaker. Social Credit split into English- and French-speaking factions. A July announcement of Medicare by 1968 would silence the NDP. Canada was unmistakably prosperous, and even the West would be won by the latest wheat sales to Russia. Only Pearson was reluctant, but his friend, Walter Gordon, was persuasive. On September 7, uncertainty faintly sounding in his voice, Pearson made his public case for an election.

While Diefenbaker was being annihilated by Liberal voters, the Prime Minister decided that he would remain in Ottawa, bearing the burdens of state, safe from the electorate. It did not work out. Electioneering was Diefenbaker's delight. Reluctant Tories, dragooned to old loyalties by the party's brightest organizer, Edwin Goodman, found funds and candidates to save the party. Their leader campaigned joyfully, gleefully throwing Liberals on the defensive to the ecstasy of rural and small-town audiences. The Liberal campaign floundered and even ran short of money. As in the past, Pearson could not help it much. On November 8, voters returned a virtually identical House of Commons—131 Liberals, 97 Conservatives, 21 New Democrats, 9 of Caouette's *Créditistes*, and a rump of 5 Social Crediters. Only Tommy Douglas found comfort from the campaign: his NDP had finally profited from disillusion to reach a new plateau of eighteen per cent of the vote. A dynamic Quebec New Democrat, Robert Cliche, had helped win support but no seats.

Cliche might have done even better without the only significant Liberal coup of the campaign. More than ever, Pearson wanted a powerful Quebec lieutenant. His choice fell on Jean Marchand, leader of Quebec's formerly Catholic unions and the man who had steered them away from both the Canadian Labour Congress and the NDP. Marchand refused to come alone. One partner, Gerard Pelletier, editor of *La Presse*, was welcome. The other, Pierre Elliott Trudeau, was not. Ostensibly a law professor, Trudeau had the reputation of being a wealthy intellectual dilettante who had edited a radical magazine and had denounced Pearson for adopting nuclear weapons in 1963. But Marchand insisted, and safe seats were found for all the "three wise men."

Marchand was indeed influential. Ever since the Conservatives had frozen civil service salaries in the struggle to balance

239

their budget, federal employees had demanded collective bargaining. All three major federal parties had agreed. By 1965, many civil servants also insisted on the right to strike. As an ex-civil servant, Pearson was appalled. Marchand, his Minister of Manpower, was not. Quebec had granted that right to its provincial employees without disaster, and his own union had profited; Ottawa must follow suit. The Public Service Staff Relations Act in 1967 gave federal employees a free choice and a chance to change their minds between compulsory arbitration and going on strike.

Marchand was too sanguine. A younger generation of workers, free of Depression memories, demanded more even than their leaders recommended. A violent wildcat strike at Hamilton in the summer of 1966 was part of a year of labour turmoil. Canadians survived the first railway strike since 1950 and an illegal postal strike that drew unexpected sympathy for ill-paid sorters and letter carriers. Public opinion forced a generous settlement. For the first time, hospital workers and even teachers joined picket lines. Buying labour peace was costly. To forestall a crippling St. Lawrence Seaway strike, a government arbitrator approved a thirty-per-cent increase in wages. Without remotely considering the arguments, editorials called the settlement "the Pearson Formula" and raged at the government's folly.

Peace was needed because Montreal was about to become an international showplace. Preparing for Canada's centennial had become a sour joke. To some Canadians, part of the national identity was an aloofness to windy boosterism and flag-waving. The eager opportunism of communities, folk groups, and publishers jostling for the cornucopia of centennial grants made easy satire. One town would burn its outhouses; another would build a pad for flying saucers. No centennial project could match the magnitude of Montreal's. Almost single-handed, Mayor Jean Drapeau had dreamed up the idea of a world-class exposition, sold it to the international community, and virtually blackmailed Ottawa and Quebec City into underwriting his efforts. Despite Canada's vast empty spaces, the fair would be staged on islands in the St. Lawrence, built with earth excavated for the city's new subway line. Of all the absurdities of centennial year, Expo '67 easily took the prize. For a city with crowded slums and without even proper sewage treatment, it was an extravagance beyond excuse.

In 1966, Quebec voters rejected the Lesage version of the

240

politics of grandeur. Under Daniel Johnson, the *Union Nationale* had recovered from 1962, shed some of its conservatism, and burnished its nationalism. Johnson's slogan was *Québec d'abord* or "Quebec first," discreetly translated for English-speaking supporters as "A better Quebec for all Quebeckers." The French was more precise. Johnson won because rural voters resented the cost of Liberal reforms, but the new government changed very little. Instead, Johnson presented Ottawa with new, uncompromising demands for fiscal transfers. He also set out to assert Quebec's role in the world. In France's President Charles de Gaulle, Johnson had an eager patron. Since the war, de Gaulle had sought vengeance for humiliations he felt he had suffered at the hands of his Anglo-Saxon allies, and it was irrelevant to him that most Quebec opinion had favoured his wartime enemies in Vichy.

Financial demands were one thing; seeking an international role was another. Pearson was furious. As usual, he also felt helpless. Even the Lesage government had argued that Quebec had a right to be involved in treaties that affected such constitutional responsibilities as education or culture, but for Daniel Johnson, external aggrandisement offered a cheap and a popular issue. The French cheerfully made life miserable for Canada's ambassador and bluntly refused to welcome General Georges Vanier, Canada's Governor General.

Meanwhile, Pearson had discovered unsuspected virtues in the most dubious member of the "three wise men." As a parliamentary assistant, Pierre Elliott Trudeau had offered Pearson unexpected and welcome advice about Quebec. As Minister of Justice from April 1967, he showed a quite untraditional zeal for reform and an astonishing flair for handling critics. It was hardly in the tradition of Ernest Lapointe that a Quebec Liberal would proclaim that the state had no business in the bedrooms of the nation, or that divorce reform was overdue.

Even more valuable was Trudeau's hard distinction between the national and the provincial rights of French Canadians. Like Pearson, Trudeau was committed to having the federal government—and as much of Canada as could be managed—provide equal opportunities for French and English. Unlike Pearson, he had a firm, perhaps an unrealistic, idea that the functions of a federal government could be clearly defined. Years before he had lectured the infant NDP on the dangers of centralization. Yet,

241

where the federal role was clear, he felt, provinces had no business. Trudeau felt liberated from the ancestral tribalism of Quebec nationalism and scornful of those who remained in self-imposed bondage in what he called "the wigwam." Talent, boldness, and inherited wealth had taken him to Harvard, the Sorbonne, and the London School of Economics. He had travelled the globe. If St. Laurent, Laurier, and Cartier had burst the limits of Quebec to see themselves as Canadians, Trudeau's limits were the world.

Suddenly and quite unexpectedly, Canadians too seemed liberated from parochialism. When centennial year came, the sneers and the cynicism died away. To their own astonishment, a host of Canadians looked about themselves and felt proud of their achievements. Celebrating turned out to be fun, and the organization of the celebration proved more efficient than most people had expected. To national surprise and then delight, Montreal's Expo '67 opened on schedule. Then came a suffusing glow of pride as Canadians realized that they had even helped sponsor an artistic and innovative success. For once, Canadians felt smugly superior to their American neighbours, torn with urban riots and sinking deeper in the morass of Vietnam. Boosterism was in fashion. Mordecai Richler, an expatriate Montrealer who had deplored Canada's feeble cultural nationalism, now confessed that he no longer yearned for the day when the border would vanish. "Vietnam and Ronald Reagan," he wrote in 1967, ". . . have tempered my enthusiasm. Looked at another way, yes, we are nicer. And suddenly that's important."

Obviously, not everyone agreed. Still angry at Canadian criticism of his Vietnam policies, President Johnson paid a cold, perfunctory centennial visit. Quebec separatists fashioned license plate tags proclaiming *100 ans d'injustice*. The violent student riots which had greeted a 1964 royal visit to Quebec were not repeated when the Queen opened Expo, but massive police precautions were unsettling reminders. The visit of Charles de Gaulle was a carefully orchestrated contrast. Ottawa was virtually excluded from the arrangements by Daniel Johnson and by Paris. The French President landed at Quebec and rode in a triumphal motorcade up the valley of the St. Lawrence. It was the glittering welcome Johnson had promised. At Montreal on July 14, the old general strode to the city hall balcony to deliver his regal greeting and concluded, arms outstretched, *"Vive Montreal! Vive le Quebec! Vive le Quebec libre!"*

Had vanity, mischief, or calculation led de Gaulle to shout the slogan of Quebec independence? It hardly mattered. He had had his vengeance on the Anglo Saxons. The euphoria of 1967 dissolved. "Canadians do not need to be liberated," sputtered a furious Pearson, and De Gaulle promptly returned to France. English Canada echoed the Prime Minister. As ever, Quebec responded defensively and angrily. *Le Devoir*'s Claude Ryan scolded Pearson for hysteria and fear; sixty per cent of Quebeckers condemned the Prime Minister's counterblast. The Saint-Jean Baptiste Society summoned the ranks of local worthies to a grandly-named *Estates General* and solemnly demanded associate statehood for Quebec, on a basis of full equality with the rest of Canada. René Lévesque, whom years of television commentary had made the best-known of Lesage's ministers, issued *Option Québec* in September, a clear demand for Quebec independence. When fellow Liberals hesitantly rejected the Lévesque program, he left the party. On November 18, 1967, Lévesque launched his *Mouvement souveraineté-association*.

In Canada's hundredth year, the forces of disintegration had finally found a compelling leader and a program. The logic and the example of a world of liberation movements had come to Quebec. The long tiresome arguments about language and powers and money could end if it was Québécois who were the majority and it was the English who could suffer the humiliations of a minority. It was the logic of Papineau, Mercier, and Duplessis, carried to its modern conclusion. For young, ambitious *Québécois*, frustrated by the persistent dominance of Montreal's English-speaking commercial elite, resentful of the burden of mastering a second language, independence was irresistibly seductive. For a decade, English Canadians had bored Quebeckers with the question "What does Quebec want?" René Lévesque had furnished a clear, disturbing answer.

The next question was what Canada would do about it. For a start, she would change, testing whether centennial euphoria really meant a new willingness to live on as a transcontinental nation. The armed forces, usually scorned or ignored in peacetime, became a controversial symbol of change. A stubborn, ambitious Paul Hellyer had been entirely in earnest about unification. A unified force in a single green uniform would not only win him renown for its originality and efficiency; it would break the last British links of uniform and tradition. The protests of admirals, generals, and air marshals were dismissed as mutinous threats to civil supremacy. On Canada's hundredth birthday, her three armed forces reluctantly became one. Other changes came even harder. At the end of 1967, the Royal Commission on Bilingualism and Biculturalism delivered its first report. The recommendations were predictable, sweeping and now inescapable: the federal government must not only provide services in both official languages, it must provide a working environment where French as well as English Canadians could work in equal comfort.

More than language, uniforms, and symbols needed changing. The revolution in the status of women began hesitantly in the wake of Enovid, the first apparently safe oral contraceptive. Now it gathered momentum. The political response sought by Pearson's sole woman minister, Judy LaMarsh, was a Royal Commission on the Status of Women. Other problems, smaller or more urgent, were subjected to mere task forces. Embarrassment at the "Pearson Formula" led, in 1966, to a study of labour relations. To ease his political demotion, Walter Gordon sponsored a task force on foreign ownership, headed by a sympathetic but hitherto antinationalist economist, Melville Watkins.

If Canadians had given any message in 1965, it was that most of them wanted new political leaders. By 1967, New Democrats ranked with their rivals in the polls, but John Diefenbaker rejected the hint. The outcome was a harsh, year-long battle between his loyalists and the party's youth, financiers, and urban supporters. Dalton Camp, the Toronto advertising executive who engineered Diefenbaker's overthrow, was also sponsor of Robert Stanfield, his successor, an accident that preserved disunity in the party. Robert Stanfield, the premier of Nova Scotia, was a man of wit, integrity, and painfully cautious speech, and he deserved better. Diefenbaker fought to the end. His final bid for leadership, he insisted, was inspired by a convention resolution endorsing a Canada of two nations.

Lester Pearson, on the other hand, went quietly, content with his achievements and painfully aware that even the untried Stanfield had soared in the opinion polls as Canadians welcomed any new face. The Liberal inheritance drew half a dozen cabinet ministers, from the nakedly ambitious Paul Hellyer to aging veterans of the St. Laurent era such as Robert Winters and Paul Martin. All aspirants went against two Liberal traditions: the alternation of leaders from Ontario and Quebec and the preference for inexperience. Laurier, King, and even St. Laurent had served far briefer apprenticeships than had the more obvious claimants.

In November 1967, Ontario's Premier John Robarts summoned premiers to Toronto for a "Confederation of Tomorrow" conference, fulfilling an election promise, and expressing his own profound desire to save the country. Canadians watched Daniel Johnson dominate proceedings with a vision of a divisive future few of them welcomed. A few months later, in February 1968, the premiers came to Ottawa. This time, television watchers saw the new Minister of Justice answer Johnson with a blunt severity few of them could remember ever hearing from a federal spokesman. Pierre Elliott Trudeau's campaign for the leadership of the Liberal party was launched. By April 4, when Liberals met in Ottawa, he was the clear favourite. He won on the fourth ballot.

Pearson had expected the chance to say farewell to Parliament, but Trudeau dissolved it at once. Like Diefenbaker, he ran against his own party as much as against the opposition, but his style was utterly different from "the Chief's." Trudeau teased and challenged audiences and invested them with his own sophistication and style. The pride and self-satisfaction of 1967 revived and found fulfilment in a leader who seemed literate, eloquent, and adventurous. In a contest of images judged by the media, neither Stanfield nor the NDP's Tommy Douglas stood a chance. In the sole television debate they gave as good as they got, but journalists eagerly covered for their new hero. In Quebec, separatists and conservatives grumbled about Trudeau, but Stanfield's complex remedies, rendered in painful French, were no substitute for local pride. Even the rural, small-town base of conservatism was shaken by Diefenbaker's departure. Diefenbaker loyalists now voted NDP as once they had voted CCF. On June 25, Trudeau won the majority that Canadians had denied Pearson, with 155 seats to Stanfield's 72, and 22 for the NDP. Even the West had relented: the four western provinces had given 27 of its seats to Trudeau, 25 to the Conservatives, and 16 to the NDP.

It was a new era and Canadians had given a national mandate to a new leader.

# PART V

# A Country Shared

# 1 / Liberation

Ever since Confederation, Canadians had usually been more eager than Americans to use the power of governments to finance and administer great national undertakings, from the CPR of the 1880s to the nationwide health insurance program that finally took shape in 1968. On the other hand, Canadians believed that they were socially more conservative, law-abiding, and moral than their neighbours. Sir Wilfrid Laurier, for one, proudly pointed to comparative crime and divorce statistics to prove the happier state of Canadian society.

By 1968 the contrasts were blurred and, for some Canadians, even a source of embarrassment. Personal liberation had become a watchword, cherished as fiercely by separatist terrorists as by drop-outs in the drug culture. Liberation ranged from long hair and blue jeans to unblushing acceptance of premarital sex and unmarried cohabitation. Members of religious orders demanded freedom from their vows. Censorship became intolerable. So did the burdens of marriage, child-rearing, and family. Homosexuals emerged to defy the "straight" majority for the sake of "gay rights." A dependable and seemingly safe birth-control pill had ended the baby boom early in the sixties. Maternity, once defended by feminists as the highest role of womanhood, became an interlude that could be avoided at will. The consequences were unexpected. Quebec's birthrate fell from the highest to the lowest in Canada, raising alarm over French-Canadian survival. Traditional barriers to the employment of women, even in mines and construction sites, crumbled. The composition of the Canadian labour force changed from being one-quarter female to being almost one-half female within one generation.

In itself, liberation was not new; the young had regularly challenged their elders. But never had the defenders of authority and tradition collapsed so abjectly. Clergy, educators, editors, and politicians hastened to meet demands for change. Claude Bissell, president of the University of Toronto, hurried home from a traumatic year at Harvard to impose drastic changes on his elderly institution. Radicals abused him soundly for his pains. Electronic media disseminated a world-wide youth culture. Terrorists, innovators, and rioters could share the psychic thrill of seeing themselves on television. Post-secondary education now embraced almost as large a share of the young as had the armed forces in two world wars. Colleges and universities became centres for the new culture of drugs, popular music, and protest. Superficial exposure to the social sciences bred faith in Marx, in pop gurus like Charles Reich of Consciousness III or Timothy Leary, prophet of LSD, and in the pseudo-science offered by groups like the Club of Rome. It was flattering to find a Canadian, Marshall MacLuhan, among the new Delphic oracles. Most ideas, from feminism to "participatory democracy," were imported from the United States and, more rarely, from Europe.

Fashions are never universal. Most Canadians avoided drugs, stayed married, and, for that matter, never voted for Pierre Elliott Trudeau. As a fashion, liberation was more conspicuous in British Columbia, big cities, and among the middle class than in Newfoundland, small towns, or among the poor. The unfashionable majority might wonder why priests urged secularism in education, or why governments financed the counter-culture through Opportunities for Youth and the Company of Young Canadians. Others took comfort in more enlightened fads. Roland Michener, the third Canadian-born Governor General, made himself a model of physical fitness for a sedentary nation by promoting jogging.

Environmental concerns could also unite young and old, radical and conservative. Rage at polluting industries and the alleged hazards of nuclear power generation went hand-in-hand with an elitist disdain for the vulgarity and waste of mass affluence. The limits of growth would be reached more slowly if only the wealthy enjoyed nature's non-renewable resources of gasoline or silver. What united environmentalists with other crusaders of the age was a humourless intensity, often incapable of recognizing its own paradoxes. Legalization of marijuana could be urged by people who wanted to ban smoking. A passionate concern for baby seals coincided with a desire to preserve the folkways of

248

Newfoundland outports. Native people must be protected from white meddling, but not if they continued their traditional discrimination against women.

In Pierre Elliott Trudeau, the Liberals offered Canadians a symbol of the liberation generation. As Minister of Justice, he had liberalized laws on divorce, abortion, birth control, and homosexuality. In his debates with Daniel Johnson, he had stressed individual rights over the group rights urged by the Quebec premier. By promising "no more free stuff," Trudeau condemned social programs which shared burdens collectively. Since liberation was largely a matter of style, its disciples adored a Prime Minister who wore sandals in the House of Commons, slid down a banister at a Commonwealth conference, and told a political opponent (in Trudeau's own sanitized version), to "fuddle duddle."

At forty-nine, Trudeau was not the youngest Prime Minister Canada had had, but he was the most inexperienced. Like most of the comfortable young Canadians who made him their hero in 1968, his wealth and success had been more the result of inheritance than of struggle. Whether as a world traveller, an outdoorsman, or as a critic of Duplessis in the 1950s, Trudeau had enjoyed the privilege of choosing his own challenges. So far, he had been spared the setbacks, frustrations, and personal financial insecurity that had taught caution and compromise to King, Laurier, or Macdonald.

As Prime Minister, Trudeau handled power with a firm and sometimes naïve confidence. Pearson, the ex-bureaucrat, knew the power of deputy ministers and circumvented them. Trudeau simply switched them so frequently to new departments that they soon knew as little as their ministers. Cabinet meetings became seminars in which ministers were compelled to defend their own policies and programs without officials to protect them. Verbal agility mattered more than dull common sense. The Prime Minister's own office expanded dramatically. Youthful aides took over the regional responsibilities of cabinet ministers. Trudeau and his confidants insisted that the change guaranteed a rationalization of the political process.

Eager for a capsule phrase to sum up their leader's goals, Liberals had promised the "Just Society." But "justice" was not easily defined, and the phrase raised more hopes than it could satisfy. A 1969 white paper on Indian policy promised to abolish the Indian Act, a perennial focus for native grievances, replacing it with "full, free and nondiscriminatory participation of the Indian people in Canadian society." An embarrassed minister, Jean Chrétien, had to flee before cries of "cultural genocide." Indians wanted special status, not equality with whites. By 1974, native people had become a vocal, federally financed pressure group. White Canadians, who had imagined that land claims were ancient history, discovered that Indians and Inuit were claiming the North and much else besides.

The new Prime Minister had more success in imposing his views in external affairs and defence, if only because his opinions were closer to a familiar Canadian political tradition. Trudeau had publicly wondered whether defence dollars would be better spent on foreign aid. Canadian armed forces had endured the trauma of unification as the price for modern equipment. With Trudeau, that commitment died. Military manpower was slashed by a fifth, and Canada's NATO contingent was cut to half-strength—five thousand men. Obsolete ships, tanks, and aircraft remained. True to the new spirit of self-interest, allies were not consulted. Trudeau had had no respect for the pompous, English-speaking diplomats who had lived in Pearson's shadow. The new priority for Canada's missions abroad would be trade, not diplomacy. A collection of little booklets on Canada's new foreign policy insisted that self-interest, not self-importance, would be the guide. Even some of Trudeau's admirers were dismayed when he bluntly refused to engage himself in moderating the miseries of Nigeria's civil war. Aides reminded them that the Prime Minister was a man of contradictions.

Canada's relations with the United States were now more important and more complicated than ever. The rhetoric of special relations and undefended borders had worn thin. By criticising American actions in Vietnam, even Lester Pearson had ignored the prudent doctrine that neighbourly differences were best discussed quietly. In Canada, anti-Americanism was a noisy feature of the youth culture, fed by draft dodgers and emigré academics. The simple-minded envy of the Kennedy years had become an equally simple-minded antagonism. Often the issues, the arguments, and the tactics echoed those in the strife-torn United States. Without the *Wall Street Journal* and the American Freedom of Information Act, it would, for example, have been difficult to document the alleged misdeeds of multinational corporations.

The most vociferous young nationalists (with Melville Watkins, formerly of Walter Gordon's task force on foreign ownership, at their head), migrated from Trudeaumania to the NDP in a bid to capture it for the newly fashionable academic Marxism. Enough nationalism remained in the older parties and in an elite-studded Committee for an Independent Canada to exercise a powerful influence on government. While Canada's external policies and foreign takeovers of Canadian companies were prime targets for the Committee, it was performers, publishers, and film producers who were the main beneficiaries of its lobbying. Canada was made safe for *Maclean's* magazine by the belated elimination of *Time*'s Canadian edition. A new regulatory agency for broadcasting, the Canadian Radio and Telecommunications Commission, imposed Canadian quotas for television programs and broadcast music. Anne Murray and Gordon Lightfoot led a flood of suddenly popularized entertainers.

The issues raised by economic nationalists like Walter Gordon, Mel Watkins, and later by an outspoken Liberal minister, Herb Gray, went to the heart of Canada's industrial weaknesses. Inefficient branch plants would be vulnerable to the first serious economic down-turn. Head offices kept research and development at home, charged artificial prices for their services, and discouraged export efforts that might compete with the parent company. Yet millions of Canadians depended on foreign companies for their jobs, most Canadian business leaders fervently defended foreign investment (it guaranteed a market if they ever sold out), and economists had no trouble proving that Canada's prosperity depended on a regular "fix" of foreign capital.

Canada's vulnerability was driven home in 1971. European prosperity and the policy of borrowing to finance its Vietnam war effort drove the United States into intolerable financial difficulties. The 1944 world of Bretton Woods, with an almighty dollar and gold at $35 an ounce, suddenly ended. President Richard Nixon abandoned convertibility, sent gold prices soaring, and clamped down on exports of capital and imports of goods. With two-thirds of her exports bound for the United States, Canada was in a desperate plight: Nixon had forgotten to exempt her. By dint of much humble pleading, Canada finally got Washington partially to relent, but the price was Canadian acquiescence in American programs to repatriate capital and increase industrial exports.

For all their prosperity, the sixties had changed the balance of power among western nations. As an American economic dependent, Canada was on the losing side. Europe offered no alternative market. Neither did China. Trudeau had fulfilled an election commitment to recognize the Peking government, but the mainland Chinese took that as their due, and any brief economic advantage was promptly capped by President Nixon's unexpected overtures to China in 1971. Canadians, like Americans, began to lose interest in a world that seemed ungrateful and increasingly hostile. Affluence and cheap airfares allowed them to travel farther and more often, but they did so as tourists, not as world citizens. A few Canadians, secular missionaries from development agencies like CIDA and CUSO, returned to lobby for the needs of less-developed countries, but Canadians kept most of their sympathy and charity at home.

There was enough there to occupy them. Trudeau's single most substantive claim to power in 1968 was his strategy for keeping Canada united. In the euphoria of the election campaign his policies might be forgotten but they had been repeated—even in the interior of British Columbia—in both French and English. Recognition of a "two nations" version of Canada and of special status for Quebec, long buried in the NDP's program and later endorsed by Robert Stanfield of the Conservatives, Trudeau angrily dismissed. Canada must become a truly federal state with equality for all of its ten provinces. Canada must be a homeland for both French and English, without sacrifice of language or culture. The keystone of Trudeau's policy was the Official Languages Act of 1969, with its provision for bilingual districts and for the transformation of the federal government and its agencies into institutions where Canadians of either official language could find service and employment. It was a law solemnly endorsed by all parties and most MPs with the exception of John Diefenbaker and a small rump of Tory supporters.

It was part of the faith of the liberation generation that history could be ignored or overturned. The Official Languages Act defined a vision of Canada which Cartier, Laurier, and the younger Henri Bourassa had sought but consistently failed to achieve. It was an attempt to annul novelist Hugh MacLennan's description of Canada as "two solitudes." To a Prime Minister with a superb cosmopolitan education and easy fluency in both languages, it seemed simple enough. It was not. In French Canada, nationalists now saw English as a deadly threat to French and demanded its repression in Quebec. In the West, Clifford Sifton's "national schools" had done their work. Generations of new-comers had sacrificed their linguistic heritage for English; nothing in their perception of Canada established special significance for French. In schools across Canada, the new fashion of student-selected courses drove second languages from the curriculum. It was "oppressive" to compel students to learn what they found difficult or unrewarding.

Yet the alternative to Trudeau's vision was far more threaten-ing to national unity. If French Canadians were to be at home only in Quebec, there would be no logical destiny for them but national independence, with instalments of "special status" eas-ing the process. The compromise of "associate statehood," now urged by the *Union Nationale*, was a reversion to the double majorities of the 1860s, this time with thirty per cent dictating to the other seventy per cent of the population. For all the grumbling about French on cereal boxes and the extravagance of making senior civil servants feebly bilingual, Trudeau was determined that his official languages program would persist.

The urgency was underlined by events in Quebec. In Mon-treal, nationalist riots became endemic. Trudeau's election vic-tory had been enhanced by his coolness in the face of a bottle-throwing mob at the Saint-Jean Baptiste day parade in 1968; in the following year, rioters simply demolished the proces-sion. In March 1969, massed demonstrators marched on Montre-al's venerable McGill University, demanding its conversion to French. In October, police and firemen struck, leaving Montreal to looters and rioting taxi drivers. The underlying grievances in post-Expo Montreal were economic, but the inspiration came from revolutionary nationalists armed with a cause that drew grudging sympathy even from conservative Québécois.

Quebec Liberals had been leaderless since the retirement of Jean Lesage. They might have chosen a tough ex-judge, Claude Wagner, if Trudeau had not intervened. His choice was Robert Bourassa, a youthful economist who had married into wealth and who possessed a computer-age image of competence. Bourassa's opposition would not be the crumbling *Union Nationale* but the new *Parti Québécois*, René Lévesque's masterful welding of the disparate, quarrelsome independence movements. To meet their fiery appeals for an independent Quebec, Bourassa offered a vision of a "profitable Confederation" and firm promises of a hundred thousand new jobs. The outcome, in April 1970, was an easy Liberal victory, but the PQ, with a fifth of the votes, was in second place, with followers bitterly chagrined by failure and by Lévesque's personal defeat in a partly English-speaking constituency.

The victory was no prize. Quebec needed an economic wizard. The province was deep in debt. Too big a share of Quebec's industries—footwear, textiles, clothing—were obsolete and survived only because of mountainous federal tariffs. These were threatened by each step toward world trade liberalization. Quebec's hurriedly-built, costly education system seemed to be staffed by teachers who were as orthodox in Marxism as they had once been in Catholicism. Their graduates were well indoctrinated but unemployable. Foreign investment, needed to keep Bourassa's promise, would be frightened off by social turbulence and whispers of revolution.

The challenge came quickly and unexpectedly. On October 5, 1970, James Cross, the British Trade Commissioner in Montreal, was kidnapped. It was a police matter, though a manifesto from the kidnappers, a pretentiously-titled *"Front de Liberation du Québec,"* was solemnly broadcast. It was the FLQ's kidnapping, five days later, of Pierre Laporte, Bourassa's labour minister, that unleashed panic and confusion. Radicals, labour leaders, and French-speaking students sympathized deliriously and publicly with the kidnappers. A mass rally chanted "FLQ, FLQ," in a downtown arena, and a purported lawyer for the kidnappers held court before the admiring media. Claude Ryan of *Le Devoir* and René Lévesque of the PQ mustered prominent nationalists to provide Bourassa with their wisdom. Ottawa, they insisted, must not get involved. It was too late, a nervous Bourassa confessed, he had already asked for the army.

Troops were needed to relieve the strain on the competing and inexpert municipal, provincial, and federal police organizations. In Ottawa, the Prime Minister went much farther than "aid to the civil power." Before dawn on October 16, the government declared that an apprehended insurrection existed in Quebec and proclaimed the War Measures Act. As ten thousand soldiers in battle order swept into Montreal, Quebec, and Ottawa, police spread out to seize a total of 468 people. Some were cases of mistaken identity; most of them had merely enjoyed the heady thrill of preaching and promoting revolution.

A few days later, Laporte's strangled body was found, and terrorists were no longer heroes.

The man who had been elected as the embodiment of liberation in 1968 was the same man who dissolved that dream in 1970. The fun went out of revolution and, overwhelmingly, Canadians approved—eighty-eight per cent across Canada, eighty-six per cent in Quebec. Trudeau's victims would not forget their humiliation; neither would erstwhile liberal admirers, horrified by so naked a use of force. They mistook his purpose. Trudeau's target was never the obscure terrorists of the FLQ, but the "self-appointed dictators," "the emergence of a parallel power which sets itself against the elected power in this country." To Trudeau, it was the chanting crowds, the coffee-table conspirators, and even men like Ryan and Lévesque who constituted the "apprehended insurrection." Bourassa's government might be feeble and frightened, but it had been elected democratically. By December the troops were gone. The police rescued Cross and found Laporte's murderers. Dismayed by its lack of information, the Trudeau government ordered the RCMP to spy on subversives and discreetly averted its eyes from the amateurish consequences. Terrorism passed from fashion.

Trudeau's critics also had a point. The War Measures Act created martyrs. It furnished ugly precedents. It casually shattered safeguards Canadians had taken for granted. Nor could Trudeau or his colleagues, Jean Marchand and Gerard Pelletier, publicly justify their role in the October crisis without explaining the intuitions gained in a lifetime of Montreal intellectual politics or without further damaging the frail credibility of Robert Bourassa's government.

Within a year, Trudeau's new Quebec enemies had their first revenge. While confessing that he was opening Pandora's box, Trudeau had returned to the old chore of constitutional reform. Perhaps to his surprise, he found that the provincial premiers agreed on a long list of issues, from shared-cost programs to a provincial role in choosing Supreme Court judges. At Victoria in June 1971, he and the premiers wrapped up trade-offs and compromises and an amending formula that limited veto rights to Ontario and Quebec. Together, they proclaimed a Victoria Charter. Even Bourassa agreed. But by the time Bourassa's plane had landed at Montreal, he had changed his mind. A storm of protest, much of it inspired by Ryan and *Le Devoir*, greeted him. Bourassa had won none of the constitutional panaceas that Ryan touted. There was no special status, equal status, or associate status for Quebec. On June 23, Bourassa declared that the deal was off.

Constitutional reform had a low priority for most Canadians; economic management held no great interest for the Prime Minister. The mismatch was unfortunate. For Canada, as for the United States, the easy post-war years were over. Confidence that Keynes had unlocked the secret of macroeconomic management was undermined by the co-existence of unacceptable levels of both inflation and unemployment. Keynesians like the Canadian-born economist, John Kenneth Galbraith, blamed the phenomenon on the price-setting power of great corporations and the wage-fixing influence of strong unions. The remedy, as in wartime, lay with selective wage and price controls. In Canada, both the problem and any solution was complicated by the split of federal and provincial powers and by the conviction that economic trends inevitably were determined by the American economy.

If economics mattered to the Trudeau government, it was because national unity or regional problems took on an economic dimension. Trudeau's version of federalism would have pushed Ottawa out of provincial fields like health, education, and welfare: provinces protested that Ottawa pressure and money had propelled them into costly programs in post-secondary education and Medicare. Retreat was not easy. Meanwhile, in the Trudeau view, Ottawa had a clear responsibility for economic equalization among regions and even among individuals. In 1969, the government's array of development agencies and programs had been clustered in a new Department of Regional Economic Expansion (DREE) under Jean Marchand. By 1979, DREE was pumping half a billion dollars a year into Atlantic Canada and eastern Quebec with no conspicuous growth in local prosperity or contentment.

Unemployment insurance, devised as a benefit for jobless factory workers, had been transformed through the seasonal benefits invented in the Diefenbaker and Pearson years into an income subsidy for fishermen and loggers. In 1971, unemployment insurance was changed again into a vast income maintenance program for a wide range of Canadians, from artists to expectant mothers. Higher-income employees were brought into the scheme. Benefits were improved to guarantee "individual development" as well as survival. Suspicious citizens complained that government was subsidizing the idle. Reporters duly uncovered "welfare bums."

The 1968 slogan of a "Just Society" implied progress on a long list of overdue reforms. Kenneth Carter, appointed by Diefenbaker in 1962 to study Canada's tax laws, delivered 2600 pages of expert opinion and a simple proposition: a dollar of income should be taxed as a dollar however earned. Wage earners cheerfully agreed, but they carried no weight. By the time tax reform became law in 1971, lobbyists had done their work. A dollar earned by sweat was still taxed at full value; a dollar added from a windfall was taxed as fifty cents; gambling winnings were still tax-free. The moral lesson was clear. By 1975, lotteries in Canada had become a billion-dollar government enterprise.

Business had gutted tax reform. It buried legislation threatening time-honoured price-fixing and monopoly practices. It stalled the schemes of economic nationalists and channelled the government's anti-inflation efforts into a verbal assault on wages. Even having to struggle with Ottawa was tiresome. The Conservatives, bereft of business support since Diefenbaker, began to look more attractive.

In the West, Trudeau proved to have a gift for making enemies. He could not be blamed for sagging world sales of grain in 1969 and 1970, but his bad-tempered response to unhappy farmers—"Why should I sell your wheat?"—ignored the fact that the Wheat Board was a federal agency. Ottawa's response to surplus, a program designed to take wheat fields out of production, coincided with crop failures in China and the Soviet Union. Incomes soared with grain prices but not for those farmers who had taken Ottawa's advice. Western Canada might have tolerated Trudeau's concerns for bilingualism and constitutional reform if he had shown genuine concern for their preoccupations. He did not.

Liberals in 1968 had secured the foundation for a western

revival. It vanished like a May snowstorm. In June 1969, New Democrats under Ed Schreyer accomplished the apparently impossible by winning a narrow victory in Manitoba. The extra votes came from provincial Liberals. In Saskatchewan, Ross Thatcher's Liberals had beaten a weary CCF in 1964, and won again in 1967. Not even the well-publicized coldness between Thatcher and Trudeau could save Saskatchewan Liberals in 1971, and Allan Blakeney became the province's second NDP premier. Within three years Saskatchewan Liberalism, the oldest and solidest branch of the party in western Canada, had virtually ceased to exist. In Alberta, the conservatism of Social Credit was replaced in 1971 by the younger but more authentic Conservatism of Peter Lougheed. In British Columbia, removed from the peculiar fervor of prairie grievances, Liberalism survived longest, helping to attract enough affluent votes in 1972 to aid Dave Barrett's NDP to win power. That trauma was sufficient to send British Columbia Liberals into Social Credit ranks by 1975, when the NDP fell before a right-wing phalanx.

The responsibility was more than Trudeau's. Polarization may have been inevitable in the western provinces with the growth of NDP support; resource-based economies were as unstable in their politics as they were in their markets. The crucial fact remained that the Prime Minister had inherited a national following and a commitment to national unity. By 1972, both Liberalism and Trudeau's party were in disarray.

Of this, Trudeau seems to have been blandly unaware. His advisors, appropriately influenced by Marshall MacLuhan, proposed that Trudeau's re-election would be a "dialogue with Canadians," under the slogan, "the land is strong." His squabbling rivals could be dismissed. Diefenbaker loyalists, dominant in the Tory caucus, had never ceased making what misery they could for Robert Stanfield. The NDP had replaced Tommy Douglas with David Lewis, a brilliant labour lawyer who had been chief architect of the CCF-labour marriage. It seemed a sad inheritance: the NDP had become the residual heir of the stormy, internecine politics of the liberation generation. Western victories were small compensation for civil war in the Ontario NDP and a Marxist-separatist takeover in Quebec. With broken enemies, the Trudeau magic, and so much expertise, the Liberals could not lose.

They got a surprise. For the NDP, Lewis turned the unpromising topic of tax reform into sensation by showing how huge firms—"corporate welfare bums"—deferred their taxes for years while ordinary citizens paid up. The facts won few converts, but the issue came as an overdue stimulus to troubled New Democrats. Tories translated Lewis's theme into an assault on more conventional "welfare bums," allegedly prospering under the costly new unemployment insurance scheme. On election night, a lacklustre election campaign became a cliffhanger. On October 30, Liberals emerged with only 109 seats, Conservatives with 107, and Lewis's NDP with 31. Réal Caouette's *Créditistes* kept 15 and independents, 2.

In 1972, the media had portrayed Trudeau as a spoiled brat, telling unemployed mail drivers to "*mange de la merde*" and dismissing journalists with icy aloofness. Perhaps he would now leave. Certainly there was a petulant edge to his explanation for the outcome: "Nine-tenths of politics appeals to emotions rather than to reason. I am a bit sorry about that, but this is the world we're living in, and therefore I've had to change."

Change he would. Quebeckers were informed that it was Trudeau's devotion to their interests that had cost the Liberals votes elsewhere in Canada. Inspectors were hired to hunt (in vain) for welfare bums. Since the Conservatives offered him no terms, David Lewis was compelled to take what Trudeau offered or force an early and possibly fatal election. Armed with budget surpluses, the government spent its way back to modest popularity, with bread and milk subsidies to offset inflation, and a Food Prices Review Board which, surprisingly, denounced the government's marketing boards, not the supermarkets. That, of course, was a cue for the new agriculture minister, Eugene Whalen, to champion farmers and their right to a good price.

By 1973, European and American economies had recovered from mild recession. The long ordeal in Vietnam was approaching its painful conclusion, and optimists boasted that the world would benefit from a "peace dividend." In Canada, unemployment fell to under six per cent by 1973 and Liberal popularity climbed perceptibly, even in the West. In the summer of 1973, David Lewis tried to persuade his party to force an election, but the New Democrats were not interested.

Few Canadians even noticed that the major oil-exporting countries had met to consider their pricing policies. Even fewer recognized that petroleum had become virtually the only significant commodity whose price was immune to inflation. Ontarians grumbled that Alberta crude cost $3 a barrel while Iranian oil sold for fifty cents. Suddenly, those days were memories. OPEC (Organization of Petroleum Exporting Countries) became a household acronym. By August, world prices of oil had risen fifty per cent in three months. In October 1973, when Egypt launched a massive and initially triumphant assault on Israel, Arab countries backed the war with an oil boycott of Israel's allies. By the end of the year, oil prices had quadrupled. A world economy based on cheap energy struggled desperately to readjust.

Canada was both a supplier and an importer. The Borden Line had given Alberta oil a protected market in Ontario. The American West imported about as much Canadian oil as the eastern provinces took from the world market. Oil company forecasts, devised to justify exports, had claimed in 1971 that Canada had enough reserves for hundreds of years. By odd coincidence, in 1973 the estimates suddenly shrank. Far from a happy immunity to the world crisis, Canadians were told that their energy reserves might vanish in a decade. It was also true that few sectors of the Canadian economy were more thoroughly dominated by multinational corporations and even more sadly true that the large oil companies had not enjoyed high public regard.

An economic crisis brought a political response. Alberta and Saskatchewan felt strongly that they had a right to the best available price for a non-renewable resource which, since 1930, they had undoubtedly controlled. Depression memories of poverty and dependence haunted people in both provinces. Without oil wealth, those days could return. The western provinces would be accommodating, but, as Allan Blakeney reminded Canadians, no one had ever suggested that Ontario sell its resources to western provinces at less than the world price. In Ottawa, the Trudeau government was unmoved. So was the NDP. Its pressure for economic nationalism had already won the promise of a Foreign Investment Review Agency. The oil crisis was a new opportunity to show what the New Democrats could do. Liberals swallowed hard and largely accepted the NDP's terms: a freeze on domestic prices; an export tax to subsidize eastern oil imports; a pipeline to carry Alberta oil to Montreal and, at long last, a crown corporation, Petro Canada, to give Canada a stake in the oil industry. It was also time to begin, in earnest, development of the Alberta tar sands and a Mackenzie Valley pipeline to connect with expected Arctic oil deposits.

The program made political sense. Alberta would grumble but it now had no Liberal seats. Canadian consumers would see Ottawa protecting them from an artificial crisis contrived by foreigners and the oil companies. Americans would pay the export tax, and eastern Canadians, particularly Quebeckers, would see the benefits of Confederation. Even the West could hardly grumble, for it was now getting far more than it had ever expected for its oil, and salting away the proceeds in bulging "Heritage" funds. Economists took a different view. The "hidden hand" must rule. World prices would be painful but nothing less would shock Canadians into genuine conservation. It was too bad that the National Energy Board had never checked the exaggerated estimates of reserves, but the gloomy truth had to be faced. New oil finds would be remote, heavy, and very costly. Synthetic crude from the tar sands depended on expensive, environmentally questionable processes.

Politics prevailed. Alberta got more money, but not a world price. Most Canadians seemed pleased.

Liberal fortunes revived. In Newfoundland in 1972, Joey Smallwood had finally fallen to the Conservatives but Nova Scotia Liberals were back in power. In Quebec, Robert Bourassa tested his popularity with an electorate sick of public sector strikes, labour violence, and militant speeches. The result, in October 1973, was a Liberal landslide of 102 seats out of 110. The margin concealed a more disturbing statistic: *Parti Québécois* electoral support had climbed to thirty per cent.

As Liberal popularity revived, it seemed a good time for a federal election. It was not hard to arrange. An April budget distributed a gentle rain of tax cuts and a dollop of corporate welfare which Lewis and the NDP felt compelled to oppose. On May 8, 1974, to its complete satisfaction, the Liberal government fell, and the blame lay squarely with the NDP. For his campaign, the Conservative leader, Robert Stanfield, had consulted the experts and the newspapers, concluded that inflation was approaching a crisis, and promised a sixty-day wage and price freeze. Whatever its validity, neither the policy nor Stanfield made much impact. Good times and warm weather made Trudeau's audiences almost as forgiving as in 1968. He had changed, he admitted to whistle-stop audiences across Canada: "I have a train, and I have Margaret." A beautiful young wife, gushing with adoration, was the definitive answer to those who had depicted the Prime Minister as cold and unfeeling.

On July 8, 1974, urban Ontario and the working-class ridings of British Columbia deserted the Conservatives and the NDP to give Trudeau back his majority: 141 seats to only 95 for the Conservatives and a humiliating 16 for the NDP. The West gave Trudeau only 5 seats. In York South, a seat the CCF had first won in 1942, David Lewis was defeated. The Italian Canadians who now dominated his district voted Liberal. So, for the first time, did their wives. A growing "Right to Life" movement had persuaded them that Lewis favoured abortion.

The age of liberation was over. The counter-offensive had begun.

# 2 / Affirmation

More than in 1968, Pierre Elliott Trudeau believed that his new majority gave him a mandate for his own approach to government. Ministers would now focus on long-term planning. A trusted friend, Michael Pitfield, took charge of the federal bureaucracy. A new jargon of policies and priorities permeated Ottawa. Rationality would surely follow.

Instead, Trudeau and his colleagues rediscovered that life in politics is lived in short gasps. Two old enemies, inflation and unemployment, would not wait for the bureaucratic seminar to end. In the minority interlude, the Liberals had echoed the theory that Canadian inflation was largely imported and beyond Ottawa's control. Quadrupled oil prices affected more than gasoline at the pump; tomatoes cost more because greenhouses were heated by oil, so did plastic gadgets since they came from an oil-based feedstock. Almost everything in Canada was transported by road or rail. In Atlantic Canada, oil-fired generators produced most of the electricity. Prices were passed on to the consumers at each stage.

The minority Liberal government's answer to inflation had been to tie wages, pensions, and many of its other payments to the consumer price index. At the same time, stealing a 1972 election promise from Robert Stanfield, John Turner, the finance minister, linked income tax deductions to the price index. This was even more popular, though it slashed Ottawa's revenue at a time when its expenses were certain to rise with inflation. Massive spending on housing programs delighted the construction and real estate industries and pleased young families eager for their own homes. Once again, spending set house prices soaring. OPEC may have started an inflationary cycle but Ottawa's policies did nothing to hinder it.

Next to OPEC, oil companies, and Alberta's Premier Peter Lougheed, the most obvious scapegoat for inflation was labour. Unionized workers usually get their chance to raise their wages near the end of the inflation cycle. Fixed contract periods had been a proud feature of the Canadian industrial relations system, locking workers and employers into two- and three-year agreements, while prices rose resolutely but discreetly. Angry union members, bent on catching up and protecting themselves from future inflation, demanded settlements ranging from thirty to eighty per cent. Once editors and politicians admitted that inflation was a problem, unions presented themselves as a convenient and familiar villain. Since the public was the employer for some of the most militant unionists, notably in the post office, resentment was more easily mobilized than ever.

In his first term of inflation fighting, Trudeau had preferred lecturing business and labour: Canada had not imitated the short-lived American experience with controls. In the 1974 election campaign, Trudeau had delighted audiences by sneering at the folly of Robert Stanfield's proposed wage and price freeze. After the Liberal victory John Turner applied his undoubted charm to urging restraint on business and labour. Union leaders were tempted. The failure of the NDP in the 1974 campaign had been disillusioning, and never had Liberal politicians been more charming. What the Liberals could not seem to understand, however, was that it was union members, not leaders, who set bargaining demands. Officials of the Canadian Labour Congress might yearn to be statesmen but their jobs depended on votes from union militants and from younger members who expected fast results.

The pressures for controls grew. Elderly government officials remembered the triumph of the Wartime Prices and Trade Board. In the United States, John Kenneth Galbraith lent his credentials to the cause, and President Nixon's 1971 experiment with price controls looked better in retrospect than it had at the time. Turner's failure to win voluntary restraint deepened his personal antagonism to the Prime Minister; in 1974 he left the government and Parliament. On October 13, Canadians could rush out and buy copies of *Maclean's* citing the Prime Minister's firm opposition to controls. They could then rush home to their radios and hear him outlining a policy of mandatory wage and price guidelines of ten, eight, and six per cent in successive years, enforced by an Anti-Inflation Board (AIB). The further details were complex and they grew in complexity as their impact filtered through the economy.

Organized labour professed outrage. The brief flirtation with Liberalism ended. Unionists who had signed agreements before October 13 could pocket their gains; those who were too late were caught empty-handed. The AIB's officials showed no sensitivity to their plight. Serious collective bargaining had been suspended for the duration of controls; the Canadian Labour Congress devoted itself to demonstrations, a court challenge, and a "Day of Protest" involving a million workers on the anniversary of the Trudeau announcement. The experience was chastening. While business slowly came to share some of the union resentment at controls and their bureaucratic application, most Canadians (including union members) welcomed anything that promised to curb inflation.

Still faithful to the dream of long-range planning, the Prime Minister invited Canadians to contemplate a post-controls period when a kind of "social corporatism" might prevail. Labour leaders surpassed business in their initial horror at the notion. Then some of them were intrigued. For a few months, echoes of Mackenzie King's tripartism of government, business, and labour, and Henry Wise Wood's theory of "group government" wafted through the thinking of Canadian Labour Congress leaders and Liberal politicians, only to vanish. By 1978, a more aggressive CLC leadership had reaffirmed its commitment to the NDP, and notions of industrial democracy returned to the files.

Nowhere was labour protest louder or angrier than in Quebec. The era when Taschereau or Duplessis could promote the attractions of a cheap and docile labour force were gone. Industrial conflict took on political overtones, with *Parti Québécois* sympathizers in unions and the media eager to embarrass the Bourassa government. The centrepiece of Robert Bourassa's economic strategy was a vast hydro-electricity project on rivers leading into James Bay. Inflation and the price exacted by native bands for their land sent the costs of the project soaring. A scheme to win labour peace on the project by handing workers to one of Quebec's rival labour federations exploded in destructive riots in the winter of 1975. For all his huge majority, by 1976 Bourassa's government seemed to be in a state of siege with no relief in sight.

265

Beyond a faltering provincial economy, Bourassa's most serious problem was the language issue. Between them, the Laurendeau-Dunton commission and the 1971 census provided evidence that suggested that French was in deadly danger. Immigrants to Montreal learned English, not French. They also earned more than *Canadiens*. In 1951, French Canadians had formed eighty-three per cent of Quebec's population; by 1971 they had dropped to eighty per cent. Riots had exploded in the Montreal suburb of St-Leonard in 1969 because Italian immigrants had insisted on sending their children to English schools. Alarmists warned that Montreal would soon become an English-speaking city where the French would feel like foreigners. Nationalists blamed the 1970 defeat of the *Union Nationale* on its refusal to abolish the freedom of parents to choose the language in which their child would be educated. At a time when Trudeau urged bilingualism for Canada, nationalists demanded unilingualism for Quebec, and no one doubted that the demand was popular.

Bourassa had bought time with a commission of inquiry. The commission's report was moderate; its evidence should have been reassuring. It was not the French who were dwindling but the Anglo-Quebeckers. The huge investment in French education in the 1960s was already paying off in higher incomes and better jobs. Passions were not reduced. In 1974, Bourassa's Bill 22 proclaimed French the sole official language of Quebec and abolished the tradition of parental choice between French- and English-language schooling. To force immigrant children into French schools, toddlers would be subjected to a language test. No one, from the *Parti Québécois* to an English-speaking minority that had always voted solidly Liberal, seemed pleased. Foes of bilingualism elsewhere in Canada had new arguments to add to their case.

In 1970, Jean Drapeau followed his Expo triumph with a fresh announcement: in 1976 Montreal would be host to the Olympic Games. There was no echo of joy beyond the mayor's circle of admirers, nor did many believe Drapeau's boast that the Games could no more show a deficit than he could become pregnant. By the time the Games opened, the Expo miracle had not recurred. A grandiose eighty-thousand-seat stadium was unfinished, and not even a new Canadian appetite for buying lottery tickets could cover the sky-high costs for it and for other facilities. Federal sports subsidies and a vivacious sports minister, Iona Campagnolo, did not overcome Canada's mediocre record in most Olympic events, and the Montreal Games left debts, unemployment, and none of the euphoria of 1967. Instead, there was the sour awareness of corruption and incompetence.

Quebeckers yearned for a change of government; they did not want independence. On both points, the polls were unequivocal. René Lévesque was a realist; so were such key advisers as Claude Morin and Jacques Pariseau, both of them prominent veterans of the Quiet Revolution. The *Parti Québécois* would now proceed step by step, first winning power and then submitting the independence issue to a referendum. Voting PQ would get rid of the Liberals, not Confederation.

It was a shrewd idea and the PQ prospered in the opinion polls. It needed a little bit more, soon provided by a few hundred pilots and air traffic controllers. As federal Minister of Transport, Jean Marchand used his new authority to order that French as well as English could be used in the Quebec skies. Pilots and controllers, predominantly English-speaking, insisted that English was the international language of the air and, in June 1976, went on strike to support their opinion. A flood of support from English-Canadian editors, politicians, and ordinary citizens sent the government into retreat. The long, heaving flood of resentment at bilingualism suddenly burst, and just as suddenly was gone. English Canadians promptly forgot the issue and barely noticed a few years later when the arguments about safety had been demolished and bilingualism was in place. But French Canadians did not forget, and on November 15, 1976, they took their resentment to the polls. That night, René Lévesque stood triumphant amidst a huge, ecstatic crowd. From six seats, the PQ had soared to seventy-one. Bourassa was personally beaten; his Liberals kept only twenty-six seats, a mere twenty-three per cent of the popular vote, only half the *Parti Québécois* share.

Outside Quebec, Lévesque's victory was traumatic. The impossible had happened, and Canadians desperately wanted a leader.

Since 1974, the earlier hostility to Trudeau had revived. In 1975, a fifth of the delegates at a Liberal policy conference wanted a leadership review. In February 1976, after Robert Stanfield had gracefully resigned, the Tories had their chance to choose a new

267

leader. Despite a strange, unpredicted bid by Diefenbaker to deliver the convention to an ex-Liberal from Quebec, Claude Wagner, delegates preferred an untried young Albertan named Joe Clark. The rest of Canada did not know him, but by that summer only twenty-nine per cent wanted Trudeau. The Lévesque victory changed that. "I say to you with all the certainty I can command," Trudeau reassured them, "that Canada's unity will not be fractured." By February 1977, half the electorate would have voted Liberal. In the spring, when Trudeau's wife left him for the role of flower child to the media, most Canadians sympathized with a lonely father left to raise three sons.

Almost as quickly as it had materialized, support dissipated. Separatism now seemed to be no threat. In power, the *Parti Québécois* was more talented than the Liberals and no more radical than one of the prairie NDP governments. Government auto insurance and the take-over of the troubled asbestos industry were hardly revolutionary. Bill 101, the PQ's language legislation, might be absurd or oppressive in imposing French as the language of work, government, and even the signs of English bookshops, but Canadians outside Quebec were unaffected, and they never had shown much sympathy for Quebec's English-speaking minority. The minority itself was confused, divided, and largely silent. Its younger members packed their bags. So did many of Montreal's head offices. Even Ottawa pleaded with businesses to stay. Separatists quietly rejoiced at the exodus.

In time, there would be a referendum. Meanwhile, both Trudeau and Lévesque competed vigorously for friends in New York and Washington—an uncomfortable reminder of where Canadian decisions were now appealed. A new federal task force, headed by Jean Luc Pepin of the Anti-Inflation Board and John Robarts, Ontario's retired premier, travelled the country, hunting for grievances in the name of national unity. Canadians returned, uncomforted, to their economic preoccupations.

In 1973, politicians had promised energy self-sufficiency. It was harder to attain than it looked. Private oil companies had been discredited by their role in the oil price crisis, but they were in full control of the industry. Most western Canadians preferred the wisdom of the Calgary "Oil Patch," the cluster of petroleum companies and their admirers to the policies of a Liberal Ottawa. Their provincial governments also controlled the resources. Only huge public investment helped the new Syncrude plant at Fort McMurray to turn tar sands into oil and two other vast projects stumbled through their planning stages as their private backers waited for the right price. Ottawa's promised participant in the oil business, Petrocan, had been too obviously a concession to the NDP. Its mere existence was an insult to the robust, American-style mood of the oil industry.

Beyond the provinces lay the fabled energy resources of the North West Territories, but the fable was unconfirmed and testing it would be enormously costly. Canadians had complacently viewed the Territories as a remote, uninhabited wilderness, to be exploited at future convenience. Belatedly, they were reminded that the Territories had a fragile ecology and a newly outspoken native population, as eager as any to profit from the energy crisis. An inquiry by Mr. Justice Tom Berger, a former NDP leader in British Columbia, publicized the problems of the proposed Mackenzie Valley pipeline, designed to carry Arctic gas to southern markets. His report neatly aligned native leaders, their white allies, and a largely sympathetic Canadian public. By 1977, the pipeline was dead.

It was all part of a leisurely, sometimes fatuous pursuit of energy self-sufficiency. Spared much economic urgency, Canadians could debate the merits of bio-mass and windmills, denounce the one substantive achievement of Canadian post-war technology, the CANDU reactor, and enjoy lower gasoline prices than Americans. In 1975, Ottawa and Edmonton had come to a reluctant agreement that Canadian oil prices would rise by 1979 almost to the rate set by the OPEC cartel, $14.75 a barrel. Thanks to the Iranian Revolution, OPEC chose that year to send prices zooming again. By the end of 1979, the world price had tripled and Canada's oil subsidy bill had climbed to $2.5 billion. With renewed fervor, the producing provinces demanded more money and the consuming provinces insisted on protection.

Oil prices were only one of many factors creating the combination of inflation and unemployment that infected most of the western industrialized nations. The analysis of the modern Keynesians was now discarded; their main policy—controls—offended labour and, in time, business. Older economic fashions fitted an increasingly conservative mood. Inflation, said the traditional textbooks, was due to too much money chasing too few goods. Monetarists promised that high interest rates would shrink a money supply inflated by excessive credit. "Supply-siders" insisted that lower taxes for the rich would give them an incentive to provide more investment capital. Money spent by governments was unproductive. Both doctrines delighted bankers and the wealthy; less influential folk went along with them since nothing else had worked.

In 1979, British voters gave Margaret Thatcher a mandate to test the old wisdom; American voters gave the same opportunity to Ronald Reagan and the Republicans in 1980. In Canada, Pierre Elliott Trudeau had not waited for an election to join the experiment. Sharing a summit with leaders of six other industrialized countries in 1978 provided the stimulus. On his return, he unceremoniously scrapped the Anti-Inflation Board, announced cuts in federal spending and programs, and promised tax reductions.

The impact on the economy and the government's fortunes was slight. A cluster of by-elections in the autumn of 1978 proved disastrous for the Liberals. Workers freed from wage controls discovered that their bargaining power had virtually vanished in an ensuing recession. Canadian industrial incomes, second highest in the world in 1970, had fallen to seventh by 1979 and would be fourteenth by 1982. Purchasing power had been out-paced by inflation since 1975, but economists unrepentantly insisted that wages had not been squeezed enough. Meanwhile, true to the tradition of James Coyne, the Bank of Canada returned to its old faith in tight money. Ottawa, to its own dismay, began to have to finance budgets that headed dramatically into the red.

Canadians had assumed since the war that the federal government could manage the economy effectively if it only chose to do so. The ingenious arrangement that allowed Ottawa to collect direct taxes for all but Quebec had been a guarantee of fiscal leverage. That leverage had dramatically dwindled. Instead of the ten per cent of federal income tax revenue they got in 1947, wealthier provinces like Ontario were taking forty-four per cent by 1977. Ottawa now insisted on limiting increases in its share of the costs of post-secondary education and Medicare to no more than the growth of the gross national product. In return, provinces could spend the money as they chose. Fiscal decentralization would again result in local standards of health care and education.

Ottawa's fiscal plight was not understood. By 1978, earlier modest surpluses had turned into an annual deficit of almost $12 billion. Opposition critics complained of extravagance. Joe Clark, seizing a figure from the air, promised to eliminate sixty thousand government jobs. He also promised to let home-buyers deduct mortgage payments from their taxable income (a revenue give-away of $3.5 billion), and to increase the size of Canada's admittedly under-strength armed forces. Ottawa could have eliminated the deficit by cutting its direct spending—if it could pay every federal expense, from the RCMP to lighthouse keepers, with $600 million. Thanks to a series of statutory programs no politician dared touch, Ottawa in 1978 paid out $14.6 billion to individuals, $10.5 billion to provinces, and $4 billion to businesses. Real federal spending was only a third of the budget.

The problem was not insoluble. In contrast to the hopeless dilemmas facing other nations in a decade of harsh economic shocks, Canadians were as fortunate as they ever had been. Problems might have been aggressively tackled. Instead, a sour, resentful mood developed. The underlying philosophy of the new economic dogmas was a conservative selfishness imported, like so much of Canada's intellectual climate, from the United States. The new mood was also a response to the disappointments of liberation. Freedom had brought pain and death. Between 1971 and 1978, the abortion rate in Canada doubled. So did murder convictions. Urban parents, once terrified by the drug culture, now worried that their offspring would be swept into exotic religious cults. Older churches, eager for "relevance" in liturgy and theology, saw the faithful depart for fundamentalist or charismatic sects. More than a third of all marriages now ended in divorce and the advance of feminism coincided with the spread of pornography and sexual assault.

Most Canadians remained in an amoral wasteland, cool to ideals or ideas. The old puritanism survived, but only when it stayed out of the line of fire. Lotteries, once illegal, had became a billion-dollar business for governments seeking funds for political favours. Liquor consumption tripled in the decade. Montreal and Toronto completed the cycle of spectator sports by acquiring major league baseball teams. Ontario politicians, guided by opinion surveys, banned beer from the ball parks. When opinion switched, in 1982, so did the regulations.

Social commentators spoke of the "me generation," or worried about a selfish narcissism. Pierre Elliott Trudeau might have claimed the credit for such developments. He had written and spoken eloquently of individualism as an ideal far higher than tribal or national loyalties. Canadians had not bothered to study his philosophy nor to absorb the stoic demands of individual freedom. Young people, as in any age, wanted dreams greater than themselves, but they could not create them and none were provided. They wanted leadership, too. How badly, they would soon discover.

Outside Quebec, which now marched to a different political rhythm, Canadians were disillusioned by Trudeau and unimpressed by Clark. A pitiless media had picked on Clark's appearance, his apparent clumsiness, and his lack of small talk. A world tour, designed to expose Clark to international leaders, was transformed by journalists into a saga of lost baggage, minor accidents, and the Tory leader's ignorance. Party strategists, sensing victory and aware that Clark was the only leader they had, cautiously programmed him to avoid "uncontrolled situations."

Leadership had decided the 1974 election. Liberals believed it would work again. When Trudeau finally called an election for May 22, 1979, he offered another new image—the statesman backed by a huge maple leaf flag, addressing high-school students stagestruck with a celebrity. Clark, in contrast, spoke only to the faithful, behind an entourage of aides. If leadership had mattered, Ed Broadbent might have won. Chosen in 1975, the new NDP leader was an autoworker's son, a politics professor with the look of a game prize-fighter. Voters said they liked him but they did not want a socialist. What they wanted was change and, narrowly, they got it. The Liberals got more individual votes than the Tories, and they won all but 8 seats in Quebec. Otherwise, they were trounced. Only the NDP stopped a western Tory sweep and a Clark majority. The new Parliament would have 136 Conservatives, 114 Liberals, 26 New Democrats, and 6 Créditistes.

Clark had thought hard about being Prime Minister—perhaps too hard. Despite his painful efforts to become bilingual, Quebec had ignored him, but he could appoint Quebec ministers from the Senate. The Diefenbaker loyalists were bypassed and the new cabinet was at least as good as its Liberal predecessor. Trudeau had filled the civil service with his appointees. Some must go.

Michael Pitfield, in tears, departed for Harvard; when the Deputy Minister of Finance followed, the sound of bureaucratic rumbling brought the decapitation process to a halt. Though a promise to move Canada's embassy in Israel from Tel Aviv to Jerusalem had not swayed Jewish voters, it had upset Arabs and their Canadian business partners. Once again, Clark's apparent toughness crumbled. Robert Stanfield was despatched to the Middle East to save the government's face.

A favourite election slogan, "community of communities," had depicted a Canada free of Liberal-induced regional strife. That seemed easier to accomplish. The Yukon would become a province. Newfoundland's Tory government would control its offshore oil. Arthur Tremblay, Duplessis's old constitutional adviser, would provide similar wisdom to Clark. In the forthcoming Quebec referendum, explained Clark, the Prime Minister would not intervene.

For a western-leaning government, energy issues were crucial. Clark had promised the abolition of Petrocan and effective bargaining with Alberta. In power, both promises looked more awkward. To eastern Canada, Petrocan looked like a lonely saviour against Arabs and Alberta. During a long, leisurely summer, Clark and his ministers met interminably, planned strategy, studied their departments, and negotiated, with no more evident success than Trudeau, with the Alberta government. The government, Clark explained, would act as though it had a majority. The figures showed that it did not; far from a honeymoon with gratified Canadians, the polls began to show a growing Liberal lead. Worried Tory MPs relaxed only on November 21 when, as expected, the former Prime Minister announced his departure from politics. At sixty, with three young children, Pierre Elliott Trudeau's political career was over. Relieved Tories could surpass Liberals in the warmth of their testimonials. A joyful finance minister, John Crosbie, could deliver a far tougher budget than he had originally planned. Indeed, he would revel in toughness to the delight of bankers, monetarists, and his own party's noisy right wing.

The outcome was utterly unexpected. Liberal members adjourned to a Christmas party, absorbed substantial courage, and accepted the advice of their house leader, Allan MacEachen, that they should vote with the NDP, beat the government, and win the next election. Conservatives, equally confident, scorned to win over *Créditiste* votes, sailed blithely into defeat, and promised themselves that they would repeat Diefenbaker's landslide of 1958. There were two modest differences. Their leader was Joe Clark, and the polls placed the leaderless Liberals twenty points ahead.

After a few days' wait had revealed which Liberals preferred his detested rival, John Turner, Trudeau modestly resumed the leadership. Liberals could almost have campaigned without him. In Ontario, where the real campaign was fought, Premier William Davis had already denounced the Clark government's budget. In time, Canadians would find out how modest that budget's eighteen-cent-per-gallon excise tax on gas at the pump (or about eighty-five per cent of world level oil prices) was. In the winter of 1980, Liberals portrayed such costs as intolerable. Caught un-awares, the parties recycled speeches, candidates, and old election signs and privately rejoiced that since 1974 the taxpayer had met much of the cost of campaigning. The opinion polls remained rock-like from beginning to end. On February 18, Ontario, Quebec, and Maritime voters restored the Trudeau majority. By the time the polls closed in Manitoba, the election was over and so were Liberal victories. It did not matter. Trudeau would have 147 seats, Clark 103, Broadbent 32. In Quebec, the *Créditistes* had vanished with the death of Réal Caouette; the Conservatives had a single member. In the West, so had the Liberals. It was no national mandate.

"Welcome to the eighties," Trudeau greeted his triumphant followers. This time, there would be no leisurely reflections on priorities. He had gained his third majority government and he had promised it would be his last.

At gatherings of world leaders, Trudeau was now a survivor, longer in power than almost anyone. The leader of 1968, con-temptuous of pompous diplomats and militarism, had learned painful lessons. Not security but European trade had forced re-equipment of Canada's NATO contingent. If Canada kept refusing to buy adequate aircraft to patrol her shores or guard her skies, Americans would do it for her. The aircraft orders were placed, even if the prime criteria was job-creation, not suitability for service. Canadians in 1969 had been told to forget the idealism of the Pearson years and they had done so. Now, an older Trudeau had different ambitions. In a globe divided between a developed north and a hungry south, Trudeau claimed intermediary nations and leaders were needed. He would volunteer. If Canadians had remembered their world responsibilities, the Prime Minister suggested, would they have fallen into the mean-minded regionalism of the seventies?

In Quebec, there would be none of Clark's professed indifference to the referendum. It was all the more urgent that Jean Chrétien, now the Minister of Justice, take charge, because, to Trudeau's dismay, Claude Ryan was now provincial Liberal leader. The man who had done as much as anyone to bring down Robert Bourassa was now his successor. Ryan's nationalism and his independence from Ottawa would be an asset against Lévesque but his alternative to Quebec sovereignty dismayed Trudeau. A feeble federal government would be the creature of all-powerful provinces, with a provincially appointed "federal council" as trustee.

Lévesque's referendum strategy was clear: he would give Quebeckers a question to which they could not possibly say no. Market testing perfected the wording. It was deliberately complicated and innocuous. Would voters give their government a mandate to negotiate sovereignty-association with Ottawa? Any outcome would be put to a new referendum. *Oui* supporters could be mustered by the superb political machine of the *Parti Québécois*. The *non* campaign would have to be managed by a similar committee in which Liberals would quarrel with lesser allies and the stubborn, uncharismatic Ryan would argue with just about everyone.

History is full of surprises. The *non* campaign was smoother and more persuasive than Lévesque had expected, and the *oui* campaign was more fervid than planned. Lise Payette, a PQ minister, inadvertently prodded female *non* supporters into action by christening them "Yvettes," the French-Canadian "goody two-shoes" image of female submission. All the ingenious working of the question could not conceal the significance of the vote and no poll had ever found a separatist majority. On referendum day, May 20, 1980, 88% of Quebeckers voted. The *oui* side won 40.5%; 59.5% voted *non*, a victory for federalism even if all the Anglophones' votes were deducted.

During the campaign, Trudeau and Jean Chrétien had promised that a *non* vote would launch immediate constitutional reform. Quebeckers might be excused for believing that such reform would reflect Claude Ryan's proposals for a divided, regionalized Canada as echoed by the 1979 report of the Robarts-Pepin task force. Trudeau had no such intention. He would resume where the Victoria Charter had stopped in 1971.

With Quebec secure, most provincial premiers now believed that they could dictate whatever their province or ego demanded. Since unanimity seemed to be the rule, each premier believed he had a veto. By 1980, few of them had much sympathy for Pierre Elliott Trudeau. Ed Schreyer, the New Democrat from Manitoba, had been closest in philosophy but he was defeated in 1977. A year later, Trudeau made him Governor General. Only Richard Hatfield of New Brunswick and William Davis of Ontario, Conservatives both, backed the Prime Minister. Allan Blakeney, Saskatchewan's scholarly NDP premier, was a possible bridge to the region Trudeau had ignored for too long. Saskatchewan's Attorney General, Roy Romanow, joined Chrétien as negotiator, devising, promoting, and revising a shrinking list of constitutional proposals, from equalization to Senate reform. By September, the momentum was gone. A week-long conference, televised across Canada, showed that federal-provincial unanimity on a constitutional amending formula and reforms, so narrowly missed in 1971, was now out of the question.

The constitutional issue seemed dead but Trudeau would not bury it. It had become a personal crusade, the achievement that he wished to mark his long and seemingly futile period of national leadership. In October 1980, Trudeau astounded the experts. On three issues: "patriation" of Canada's constitution, an amending formula, and a charter of rights and freedoms, Parliament would act on its own. A Liberal majority would guarantee approval and the British could reject the package at their peril when it came to them for confirmation. Ontario and New Brunswick approved; the other eight provinces vociferously did not. While Broadbent and more New Democrats backed the government, Joe Clark prodded his uncertain Tory caucus into opposition. Manitoba and Quebec challenged Trudeau's procedure in their courts and lost; Newfoundland's judges ruled differently, forcing the issue to the Supreme Court of Canada.

On September 18, 1981, a majority of the Supreme Court's

justices declared that the government's procedure might be strictly legal but it defied the "conventions" or customs of the past. Provincial unanimity, they added, was not necessary. (What the "correct" convention might be was left unsaid since, as Chief Justice Bora Laskin shrewdly noted in his dissent, it could not be found. The majority had simply rewritten history!)

In the spring of 1981, dissenting premiers (including René Lévesque) had finally offered their own meagre constitutional package, including an amending formula that allowed no province a veto. The proposal soon haunted its authors. In the wake of the Supreme Court decision, the NDP insisted on a final federal-provincial meeting. Before dawn on November 5, 1981, the logjam broke. Chrétien, Romanow, and all the premiers but Lévesque (asleep in his hotel room in Hull, across the river) found a compromise. Trudeau would have his Charter, the premiers would have their preferred amending formula and the right to opt out of the Charter's less basic provisions. Surely René Lévesque could have no complaints.

But he did. To the weary and triumphant premiers, Lévesque's denunciations of the compromise and his outrage at betrayal by his fellow premiers sounded forced. What the other politicians had forgotten was the situation that had revived the constitutional debate: Quebec's referendum. Now, revised and perhaps to be repented, the drafting was over. Canada would have a complicated amending process and a vast, rambling Charter of Rights which the judiciary would have enormous powers to define. Last-minute pressure from women and native organizations brought a few changes, but not many Canadians cared. Nor did most of the British politicians who wrestled briefly with the residue of colonialism as Indian demonstrators took their grievances to London. The British North America Act was dead; on April 17, 1982, the Queen proclaimed the Constitution Act. At the cold, rainy Ottawa ceremony, Quebec was not represented.

# 3 / Futures

The swift restoration to power of the Liberals in 1980 left the West profoundly dissatisfied. Electronics aggravated the sense of injury, proclaiming the Trudeau triumph before prairie votes had even been counted. At the same time, westerners had done less than they might have. Lougheed's open disdain for his former assistant and public uncertainty over whether an oil-pricing agreement had ever been reached with Alberta undermined Clark's frail image as a leader. The least Lougheed could now do was to disprove the Liberals' boast that they could get a better deal from the West than Clark. For their part, the victorious Liberals believed that the West would simply have to come to terms. The accidents of Middle East politics gave Alberta no right to an absurdly inflated world price for her oil.

In his 1980 campaign, seeking NDP votes, Trudeau had promised sweeping tax reforms, economic nationalism, and a comprehensive plan to Canadianize the oil industry. Ten months later, his energy minister, Marc Lalonde, unveiled a National Energy Program designed simultaneously to cut foreign ownership of Canadian oil to fifty per cent and to win Canadian self-sufficiency by 1990. Instead of a complicated array of tax deductions, a petroleum incentives program would let Ottawa decide who got money for exploration and how much. A year later, in November 1981, the promised package of tax reforms formed the centre-piece of Allan MacEachen's first budget as Minister of Finance.

The timing was not ideal. A decade before, Lalonde's National Energy Program would have found an underpriced, stagnant industry. It would have spared Canada some of the economic mishaps of the seventies. If tax loopholes had been plugged in 1971, not 1981, business lobbyists would have moaned as loudly but the Carter royal commission report had provided the arguments. The seventies had changed both Canada and North America. In Washington, Ronald Reagan's new administration slashed taxes, not tax breaks, for the wealthy. In the right-wing mood of Congress, environmentalists scattered before oil company lobbyists. If exploration companies felt uncomfortable in Canada, their rigs were welcome south of the border. Canadian companies, intended as the beneficiaries of Lalonde's policies, sank in the undertow of a collapsing Canadian oil industry. Even Peter Lougheed's Alberta government, bent on cutting oil shipments to the East as a bargaining weapon, was condemned by the petroleum industry.

Good times make reform easier; times in the early 1980s were not good. The monetarist treatment, begun by President Jimmy Carter, intensified by Reagan, drove the United States into its deepest recession since the thirties. Canada followed, slowly at first, then plunging deeper than its neighbour. Interest rates in 1979 had soared to record highs, hurting the Clark government when mortgaged homeowners turned their resentment into votes. Now they climbed even higher. By the end of 1980, prime rates had reached nineteen per cent. Canadians had always bought cars, refrigerators, and washing machines, as well as their homes, on credit. Now they stopped buying. Farmers made old machinery last another year. As in the thirties, an industrial economy slowly began to grind to a halt. Mass layoffs, bankruptcies, reduced hours—this time subsidized by the Unemployment Insurance Commission—were reminders from the past. By the end of 1982, one and a half million Canadians were hunting for work; many more had abandoned a futile search.

The Canadian economy might have been stronger, more diversified, and more integrated if Canadians had used their postwar prosperity to achieve more than simply a comfortable standard of living. That was not their choice. Successive generations had agreed that Canada would remain a branch-plant economy with a stake in a continental automotive industry and an export role as resource producer to the world. Prairie wheat farmers could profit from the failures of Soviet and Chinese agriculture. British Columbia would be strip-mined to fuel Japanese industry. Mineral wealth would finance Canadian imports from the United States. Canadians who wanted more could take their talent elsewhere.

By the eighties, the price of such policies had become more apparent, more difficult to pay, and much harder to avoid. Though few Canadians recognized the problem and even fewer sympathized, central Canada was in grave economic difficulties. The industries of the St. Lawrence-Great Lakes corridor had thrived on cheap energy, a steady flow of immigrant craftsmen, and proximity to the industrial heartland of the United States. By the seventies, energy was no longer cheap; skilled workers earned more if they stayed in Europe, and American industry had fled south and west, leaving behind sullen slums and ravaged landscapes. Even northern lakes lost their attraction to tourists as sulphur dioxide, transformed into "acid rain," threatened fish and vegetation.

For a time, it was the Canadian West that grew. Only Alberta and British Columbia gained significantly in population in the seventies. Though Toronto now surpassed Montreal as Canada's largest city, Calgary and Edmonton were the boom towns of the decade. Head offices, fleeing Montreal for linguistic and political reasons, bypassed Toronto for the entrepreneurial climate of Calgary. Edmonton, metropolis of the richest Canadian province, acquired the customary attributes of subway, theatres, and successful major league sports teams.

In western cities, neither tax reform nor the National Energy Program could find many allies. Despite Lalonde's claims that multinational companies would still have a better deal in Canada than in Mexico, Australia, or the North Sea countries, the oil giants went on strike and transmitted their outrage to a sympathetic Washington. To protest Lalonde's policy, Lougheed ordered a series of cutbacks in oil shipments to eastern Canada and, on the eve of the third cut, finally signed a new pricing agreement with Ottawa. By 1986, it was agreed, Canadians would pay $4 a gallon for gas, and a greater percentage of the proceeds would be absorbed by governments. Oil companies, left out of the negotiations, renewed their complaints and kept on dismantling their Alberta operations. Paradoxically, by 1982, the world oil combine had cracked and prices outside Canada fell. Two vast tar-sands projects collapsed from a combination of delays, recession, and soaring interest rates. By 1983, the western boom had once again become bust. To keep up oil and gas sales, Canada slashed prices like her rivals.

Separatism, emerging now in western Canada, survived in Quebec. In April 1981, René Lévesque won an easy re-election on a record of honest reform and subdued nationalism. The career of Claude Ryan, his austere critic, ended. In Newfoundland, a youthful Brian Peckford demonstrated to fellow Tories that a floundering, bankrupt government could win a landslide by running against Ottawa policies. Several other provincial premiers followed suit. Blakeney, the exception, was flattened by a 1982 Conservative victory in Saskatchewan—the first since 1929. Neo-conservatism—the philosophy and economics of Ronald Reagan—had crossed the Canadian border.

In the eighties, Canadians are older on average than in any decade since the thirties. They are also more diverse. Immigration in the seventies finally discarded the old restrictions against non-white races. Indians, Chinese, and West Indians joined the population mosaic. European countries surpassed Canada in the seventies in incomes and living standards. In the thirty years since 1950, income distribution between rich and poor has scarcely altered. Still, most Canadians were richer than their parents had been, and they enjoyed freedoms their parents could not have imagined. More Canadians than ever before attended schools, colleges, and universities. Cynics might complain that the expansion of knowledge had not kept pace, although, without educational growth, it seems unlikely that Canadian music, writing, and theatre would have flourished as they did in the seventies, nor would the legal and accounting professions.

The application of knowledge to government was more controversial. The social-scientific rationality of Trudeau and his followers which permeated every aspect of public policy from defence to postal administration, had not demonstrably added to the sum of national happiness. The main beneficiaries were senior officials, consultants, and experts in the newer techniques of information management; to non-admirers, they resembled the people who had sold the Emperor his non-existent new clothes.

In a world of systems, it might seem appropriate that Canadians, in common with all humanity, shared a vulnerability to nuclear annihilation. Beyond that awesome technology, spreading slowly from great powers to mere power-seekers, lay the prospect of further weapons of mass destruction, from chemical agents to biological toxins. The limitation of intellect in managing

Canada's political and economic concerns was a troubling counterpoint to the utter dependence of Canadians on the intellect of
strategists and military technologists. Understandably, there were
some Canadians who fled such horrors into fantasies of escapist
pacifism. In the 1980s, a renewed campaign for unilateral disarmament focused on new weapons and the old anti-Americanism.

By 1983, Canadians were again out of love with Pierre Elliott
Trudeau. More than half of them told the polls that they would
vote Progressive Conservative, less from conservatism than simple frustration. NDP support slipped, chiefly because it seemed a
temporary distraction from political change. The Tories had a
special yearning for change. The decent, luckless Joe Clark sought
confirmation of his leadership. Instead, on June 11, his party
chose a Montreal lawyer and executive who had never tried his
chances at the polls. Brian Mulroney, handsome, smooth-voiced,
colloquial in French, a barefoot boy from Baie Comeau, was an
image-maker's delight. Tories, desperate for victory, left Mulroney's substance to the test of time.

Canada would share that test. Years before, an American
named George Ball predicted that Canadians would collapse into
the United States when they grew tired of a lower standard of
living. The new conservatism of the Mulroney era seemed to offer
body to that claim. The "limited identities" of race, religion, and
region, defined by the historian, Maurice Careless, seemed to
leave Canada with only limited loyalties.

History is another word for experience; it is not a form of
prophecy. History tells Canadians only that they live in a tough
old country with a habit of compromise and a gift for survival.
Only Switzerland and the United States are older federal systems.
Twenty-four million Canadians have a hundred and twenty years'
experience. They have mastered the self-restraint of democracy,
learned to live in peace with each other, and, on the whole,
adapted to an environment their ancestors considered harsh and
unforgiving.

Canadians live in the only homeland they will ever know.
Beneath their shell of self-deprecation and cynicism, Canadians
are as proud of their land as any people on earth. Make no mistake
about it.

# Index

Abbott, Sir John, 46, 114
abdication crisis, 192
Abenaki Indians, 53
Aberdeen, Lady, 115, 120, 134
Aberdeen, Lord, 115, 120
Aberhart, William, 181–82, 184, 186, 187
abortion, 249, 262, 271
Acadians, 53, 60; expulsion, 53–54
"accelerated depreciation," 208
acid rain, 280
Act of Union of 1840, 41, 46
*Action Française*, 171, 172
advertising, 225, 238
Agricultural Rehabilitation and Development Act, 225, 235
agriculture, 121–22
Agriculture, Minister of, 210, 259
"aid to the civil power," 254
air training, 192–93, 199
Aird, Sir John, 175, 176
Aitken, Max (Lord Beaverbrook), 133, 152, 176
Alaska, 67, 81, 121, 197; boundary, 127–28, 141; highway, 197
Albany, 17, 63
Albany River, 63
Alberta, 135, 136, 163, 166, 179, 181, 215, 225, 258, 260, 264, 268, 273, 279, 280; creation, 139; oil prices, 259–60, 261, 278; and Social Credit, 184, 186
Algoma Central Railway, 130
Algonquins, 17, 18, 61
All-Canadian Congress of Labour, 181
Allan, Sir Hugh, 85, 87, 91
Alverstone, Lord, 127
American Civil War, 50, 71, 72, 75, 77, 132
American Federation of Labor, 136
American Revolution, 15, 23–24, 29, 54
Americans, 13, 23, 24, 32, 33, 46, 57–58, 67, 84–85, 152, 207, 211, 212, 221; and Canada, 32–36, 45, 75, 80–82, 85–87, 124–25, 158, 168–69, 185, 189, 194, 212–13, 218, 222–23, 236; immigrants, 121–22; investment, 187, 215; labour, 136, 206; imperialism, 124–25, 127–28
Ames, Herbert, 133
Amiens, 157
amnesty issue, 83–84
Ancaster assizes, 34
Anderson, J. T. M., 170–71, 182

Angers, F. A., 114, 115
Anglicans, 34, 36, 211–15
Anglo-Japanese alliance, 189
Anglo-Quebeckers, 266, 268
Anglo-Russian Treaty, 127
Annexation Manifesto, 46
Anti-Inflation Board, 264–65, 270
anti-inflation policies, 256–57, 264–65
anti-nuclear movement, 229, 232, 282
anti-semitism, 190–91
Arabs, 273
Arctic, 140, 261, 269; sovereignty over, 92, 197
Arctic Ocean, 65
Argentina, 174
armed forces, Canadian, 209, 213, 237, 243, 250, 271, 274; and unification, 237, 243–44; and October crisis, 254–55
Armistice (1918), 157, 161
Army, Canadian, 191, 192, 194, 201–3
Aroostook War, 78
asbestos industry, 268; strike, 216
Assembly, Legislative, Lower Canada, 23–27; Upper Canada, 37, 48; United Provinces, 41–42
Assiniboine River, 66, 69
associate statehood, 253, 256
Astor, John Jacob, 65, 67
Astoria, 67
Atlantic Ocean, 9, 189; Battle of, 194, 197, 199–200, 213
Attlee, Clement, 206
Australia, 42, 126, 174, 199, 210, 280
Australians, 157
Austria-Hungary, 145
Auto Trade Pact, 235
automobiles, 147, 168, 169, 279; industry, 235, 279; insurance, 168
autonomy bills, 138
Avro-Arrow, 229–30

baby boom, 217, 220, 236
Baffin Island, 224
Baie des Chaleurs, 16, 113
Baldwin, Robert, 36, 37, 38, 40, 43, 46
Baldwin, William, 145
Balkans, 145
Ball, George, 282
ballet, 218–19
Bank of Canada, 176, 185, 227, 270
Bank of Commerce, 119, 142, 144, 155
Bank of Montreal, 92, 162

Bank of Upper Canada, 36
banking, 27, 160, 161, 176, 181, 270, 273
Banks, Hal, 238
Barrett, Dave, 258
baseball, 223, 271
Basques, 16, 52
Bassett, John, 226
Batoche, 99
Battleford, 99
battleships, 141, 143–44
Bay of Fundy, 17, 76
Beauport asylum, 98
beaver, 15, 62
Beaver Club, 66
Beaverbrook, Lord, *see* Aitken
Beck, Sir Adam, 133
Bedard, Etienne, 25, 42
Begbie, Matthew Baillie, 68
Béique, François, 139
Belgium, 203
"Bennett buggies," 183
Bennett, Richard Bedford, 138, 175, 192, 226, 230; as Prime Minister, 176–77, 180, 182, 183, 184–85
Bennett, W. A. C., 236
"Bennettburghs," 183
Bentham, Jeremy, 44
Berger, Thomas, 269
Bering Sea controversy, 111, 141
Berlin blockade, 212
Berlin (Ont.), 136, 146; *see also* Kitchener
Bermuda, 40
Bernard, Hewitt, 74
Bigot, François, 22
bilingualism, 171, 225, 241–42, 252–53, 266–67; bilingual districts, 252
Bill of Rights Act, 225
birth control, 218, 244, 247, 249
Bishop, Major W. A., 151
Bissell, Claude, 248
Blackfoot Indians, 96
blacks in Canada, 50, 54, 148, 238
Blaine, James, 111
Blair, A. G., 104, 130
Blake, Edward, 87–88, 83–94, 96, 101–3, 107–8, 110, 113
Blakeney, Allan, 258, 260, 276, 281
*bleus*, 47, 73, 75, 80, 85, 86, 102, 107, 109, 114, 116, 120
Blodgett, Lorin, 69
"Bloody Saturday," 159
*Bluenose*, 172
Board of Broadcast Governors, 226
Boer War, 125–28
Bolshevik Revolution, 159
Bomarc, 229, 232

Bond Head (Ont.), 12
Bond Head, Sir Francis, 37–39, 47
"Bonne Entente" movement, 151
Borden Line, 225, 260
Borden, Sir Robert, 130, 131, 140, 142–43, 189, 193, 200, 224; and war, 145, 148, 149, 150–54; and external relations, 148, 151–52, 156–57, 171; and retirement, 162, 164
"Botheration Letters," 76
Bouchette, Errol, 140
Boulton, C. A., 83
boundaries, 67
Bourassa, Henri, 126–27, 128, 138–39, 140–43, 171, 252; and First World War, 148–49, 153–54
Bourassa, Robert, 253–55, 256, 261, 265–66, 267, 275
Bourget, Ignace, 45, 90, 99, 116
Bowell, Sir Mackenzie, 115
Bowmanville, 12
Bracken, John, 205, 206, 207
Braddock, Maj.-Gen. George, 21
branch plants, 169, 215, 235, 251, 279
Bremen, 122
Bretons, 16
Bretton Woods, conference, 210, 257
Bright, John, 90
Bristol, 11
British army, 28, 29, 32–33, 35, 57, 68–69, 77–78, 128; withdrawal from Canada, 86; in world wars, 149–55, 201
British Columbia, 68, 71, 84, 87, 92, 113, 123, 136, 143, 146, 164, 178–79, 183–84, 196, 203, 209, 215, 217, 220, 226, 248, 258, 262, 269, 279; and Confederation, 84, 89
British Commonwealth Air Training Plan, 192–93, 194, 197
British Empire, 168, 187, 189, 213; and defence, 124–25; attitudes to, 124–25
British Empire Steel Co., 163
British North America, 14, 40, 50–51, 69, 71, 72, 74–75; Act, 78–79, 102–4, 169, 186–87, 277; amendments, 170
Broadbent, Edward, 272, 274
broadcasting, 176–77, 226
Brock, Sir Isaac, 33

Brown, Anne, 74
Brown, George, 9, 10, 12, 13, 47–49, 69, 72–74, 75, 80, 87, 88–90
budgets, federal, 166, 174, 235, 237, 273–74, 278–79
buffalo, 45, 65–66, 84–85, 96–97
Burrard Inlet, 106
business, 25, 132–33, 135, 136–37, 142–43, 166, 174, 175, 194, 251, 257, 264–65, 271; and politics, 92, 111, 117, 132, 160, 183–84, 207, 235–36, 257, 273, 278–79
Business Profits Tax, 156
Butler, Capt. William, 84
Byng, Sir Julian, 150, 167
Bytown, 49; *see also* Ottawa

CTV network, 226
Cabot, John, 16, 29, 52
cadet movement, 145
Caen, 202
Calgary, 158, 159, 164, 180, 181, 182, 268, 280
California, 46, 71; gold rush, 68
Camp, Dalton, 244
Campagnolo, Iona, 267
Campbell, clan, 95
Campobello Island, 78
Canada, area, 9; population, 9, 10
Canada Cement, 133
Canada Company, 36
Canada Council, 219
Canada East, 44, 47, 72, 74–76
Canada, United Provinces of, 54, 66
Canada West, 9, 44, 47, 75
Canadian International Development Agency, 252
Canadian-American relations, 86, 127–28, 157, 185, 191–92, 194, 196–97, 210, 230, 238, 247, 250–52
Canadian Army, First, 201–3
Canadian Broadcasting Corporation, 183, 218
Canadian Brotherhood of Railway Employees, 160
Canadian Corps, 150–51
Canadian Council of Agriculture, 161
Canadian Deuterium Uranium reactor, 215, 269
Canadian Expeditionary Force, 145, 148, 149, 150–51, 152, 156–57
*Canadian Forum*, 172
Canadian Government Railways, 155
Canadian Labour Congress, 220, 230, 239, 265

284

Canadian National Railways, 163, 168
Canadian Northern Railway, 129, 130, 144, 146, 155, 162
Canadian Pacific Railway, 87, 93, 96, 98–100, 105–7, 111–12, 123, 128–29, 142, 162–63
Canadian Patriotic Fund, 146, 156
Canadian Pension Plan, 236–37
Canadian Radio League, 176
Canadian Radio and Telecommunications Commission, 251
Canadians, 6, 282; citizenship, 221
Canadian Shield, 11, 130
Canadian Canadian University Service Overseas, 252
canals, 25, 43
canoes, 17, 61
Caouette, Réal, 231, 232, 239, 259, 274
Cape Breton Island, 21–22, 54, 55, 94, 136, 163, 216
capital, 160, 182–84, 225, 251
capital city, choice of, 49
Cardin, Pierre, 198
Careless, Maurice, 282
Carillon, battle of, 22, 216
Carleton, Sir Guy, 22–23, 24
Carmack, George, 119
Carr, Emily, 172
Carter, Jimmy, 279
Carter, Kenneth, 225, 257, 278
Cartier, George-Etienne, 14, 16, 26–28, 40, 47, 50, 72, 74, 75, 79, 80–82, 84, 85, 87, 242, 257; and Macdonald, 47–49
Cartier, Jacques, 16
Cartwright, Sir Richard, 90, 110, 112, 120, 143
Castors, 98, 102, 114
casualties, Canadian, First World War, 149, 151, 152, 156–57; Second World War, 196, 201–3, 204; South Korea, 213
Cataraqui, 20
Catholic Program, 86, 90
Catholics, 14, 16, 23, 42–43, 49, 52, 57, 61, 76, 80, 108–9, 114, 139, 151, 160, 170–71, 189–90, 215, 218, 221, 254; conflict, 59, 82, 108–9, 120, 138, 144, 182; trade unions, 160, 212, 239
censorship, 180, 247
census, 123, 216
centennial, Confederation, 240–41, 243–44
Chalk River, 215

Chamberlain, Joseph, 124, 128
Chamberlain, Neville, 191
Champlain, Samuel de, 16–18, 31, 61
Champs de Mars rally, 101
Charles II, 63
Charter of Rights and Freedoms, 276–77
Chateau Clique, 26
Château Frontenac, 200
Chateauguay, battle of, 34
Château Laurier, 180
Chauveau, Pierre, 11
Chicago, 95, 129
Chilkoot Pass, 120
China, 225, 228, 235, 252, 257, 279
Chiniquy, Charles, 49
cholera, 27, 43–44
Chrétien, Jean, 250, 275, 276–77
Christian Guardian, 134
Church Union, 171
Churchill Falls, 215
Churchill River, 63
Churchill, Winston S., 194, 200, 206
civil service, 11, 177, 222, 223, 224, 228, 239–40, 271–73; reform, 140, 143, 162; unions, 240
Clark, Clifford, 205, 208, 212
Clark, Joe, 268, 271–74, 275, 276, 278
class, social, 13, 132, 159–60; conflict, 107
Claxton, Brooke, 205, 221
Clay, Henry, 33
Clergue, Francis, 130
clergy, 19, 23, 133, 137, 148, 247–48
Clergy Reserves, 31
Cliche, Robert, 239
closure, 144, 222
Cobalt (Ont), 130
Colbert, Jean-Baptiste, 19, 24
Colborne, Sir John, 27–28, 37, 42, 46
Cold War, 212, 213, 215
Coldwell, M. J., 207
Collingwood, 12
Collishaw, Raymond, 151
Colonial Advocate, 35
Colonial Office, 68
colonial union, 71–72
Columbia River, 67, 215, 226; power, 236
Commission of Conservation, 133
Commission of Government, Newfoundland, 214
Committee for an Independent Canada, 251
Commonwealth of Nations, 189, 212, 228, 249

communism, 184, 212, 214
Communist Party of Canada, 160, 180–82, 205, 211; and Liberals, 207
Company of Young Canadians, 235, 248
Confederate States, 50, 71
Confederation, Canadian, 9–10, 13–15, 31, 40, 50–51, 60, 71–79, 80, 87, 92, 102–5, 237, 261, 282; and Newfoundland, 214; compact theory of, 79, 102–3
Confederation of Tomorrow conference, 245
Congress of Industrial Organizations, 187
Congress, United States, 171, 207, 210
Connor, Ralph, see Gordon, Rev. C. W.
conscription, 164–65, 171, 206, 207, 221, 267; and First World War, 151–53, 155–56, 161; and Second World War, 192–94, 197–99, 201–3
conservation, 227, 261
conservatism, 158, 181, 245, 247, 269–71
Conservative Party, British, 95
Conservative Party of Canada, 59, 85–87, 88, 91, 92, 109, 111–13, 116–17, 127, 131, 140–41, 142–43, 162–63, 175–80, 186, 192, 193; and leaders, 114–15, 175, 183–84; see also Progressive Conservatives
Constitution Act, 1982, 277
Constitution, Canadian, 38, 102, 103–4; reform, 59–60, 186, 255–56, 257, 275–77
Constitutional Act, 1791, 24, 31
continental defence, 228–29
Continental Union, 110
controls, wage and price, 195, 256, 269
conventions, political, 164, 175, 244, 267
Cook, Warren K., 183
co-operating Independents, see Ginger Group
Co-operative Commonwealth Federation, 181–82, 183–85, 192–93, 214–15, 220, 224, 229, 236, 245, 258, 262; growth, 198, 204–5, 206–7; and NDP, 230
Coppermine River, 65
"corporate welfare bums," 259
Cosmos, Amor de, 84
coureurs de bois, 20

Coyne, James B., 227, 270
Craig, Sir James, 25
*Créditistes*, 231–33, 239, 259, 272, 274
Cree Indians, 63, 69, 99
Crerar, T. A., 161, 163, 164, 166
Criminal Code, 114, 218
Crosbie, John, 273
Crosby's Molasses, 124
Cross, James, 254–55
Crowsnest Pass, 113, 123, 165
Cuba, 124, 238; missile crisis, 232
culture, 172, 217–18, 248, 251, 280–81; in Quebec, 171, 241
Cumberland House, 65
Cunard, Samuel, 57
Currie, Sir Arthur, 150, 151, 156
Cut Knife reserve, 99
Cypress Hills massacre, 85
Czechoslovakia, 212

D-Day, 202
Dafoe, J. W., 145, 153, 165, 191
Dalhousie University, 57
Dandurand, Raoul, 165
Davis, William G., 274, 276
Dawson, Sir William, 15
Day of Protest, 265
Dean Channel, 65
Declaration of Independence, American, 23
defence, Canadian, 50, 58, 190, 191, 219, 228–29, 232, 250, 281–82
De Gaulle, Charles, 241–43
demobilization, 158, 207, 209
Depressions; 1837, 38; 1870s, 89, 91; 1880s, 96–97, 107–8; 1890s, 119–20; 1912–1915, 144; 1930s, 173–89, 209. *See also* Great Depression
Detroit, 20, 23, 45
Dewart, Rev. E. H., 134
Dewdney, Edgar, 99
Diamond Jubilee, Queen Victoria's, 124; Canada's, 170
Diefenbaker, John G., 222, 223–24, 235, 238, 239, 244–45, 252, 257, 268, 274; as Prime Minister, 222–24, 225–29, 230, 232, 234; loyalists, 245, 258, 272
Dieppe, 201
Dionne quintuplets, 177
diplomacy, Canadian, 210, 213, 250, 274
disarmament, 282
Disraeli, Benjamin, 95
Dollard, Adam, 17

domestic science, 134
Dominion, 9, 78
Dominion Alliance, 134
Dominion Day, 9–10, 13, 15, 184
Donnellys, Black, 11
Dorchester, Lord, *see* Carleton, Sir Guy
Doric Legion, 27
Dorion, A. A., 48, 49, 75
Douglas, Sir James, 68
Douglas, T. C., 204, 230, 239, 245, 258
Doukhobors, 139
Drapeau, Jean, 198; and Expo '67, 240, 242; and Olympics, 266
Drew, George, 204, 205, 207, 214, 219, 222
drought, 144, 179
Drury, E. C., 163, 166
Duck Lake, 98, 99
Dufferin, Lord, 88
Dumbarton Oaks, conference, 210
Dumbells, 172
Dundas Street, 31
Dunkin, Christopher, 75
Dunkirk, 193
Dunn, Sir James, 219
Dunning, C. A., 163, 166, 175
Dunsmuir, Sir James, 132
Dunton, Davidson, 235
Duplessis, Maurice, 186, 187, 193, 198, 207, 208, 214–15, 220, 224, 231, 235, 237, 243, 249, 265, 273
Durham, Lord, 40, 41–42; Report, 41, 59, 72

Eastern Townships, 11, 102
Eaton's, 183
economy, Canadian, 12–14, 43, 57–58. 89, 145, 173–74, 194–95, 209, 215, 220, 235–36, 251, 254, 256, 259, 261, 263–71, 279–80; *see also* Depressions
Edmonton, 129, 181, 215, 269, 280
education, 11, 45, 57, 134, 149, 169, 217, 236, 253, 256, 281; in Quebec, 234, 241, 254, 260
Edward viii, 192
Egypt, 221, 260
Eldorado Nuclear Ltd., 208
Elections, federal, general; 1867, 80; 1872, 87; 1874, 85; 1878, 91; 1882, 96; 1887, 107; 1891, 111–12; 1896, 115–17; 1900, 127; 1904, 130–31; 1908, 140–41; 1911, 142–43; 1917, 154–55; 1921,

164–65; 1925, 166; 1926, 167; 1930, 175–76; 1935, 184–85; 1940, 193; 1945, 207; 1949, 214–15; 1953, 219; 1957, 222; 1958, 223–24, 274; 1962, 231–32; 1963, 232–33; 1965, 239–40, 245; 1968, 245, 253; 1972, 258–59, 263; 1974, 261–62; 1979, 272; 1980, 274–75
Elgin, Lord, 45, 46
Elizabeth ii, 242, 277
enemy aliens, 146, 154, 156
energy crisis, 259–61, 268–69, 273
Engels, Friedrich, 110, 121
English-speaking Canadians, 20–21, 25, 29, 35, 108, 266–67; in Quebec, 75, 186, 243–44, 254; *see also* Anglo-Quebeckers
Equal Rights Association, 109, 112, 115
Eramosa River, 30
Erie Canal, 45
Esquimalt, 68, 128
Estates General, 243
Ethiopia, 190
Europe, 15, 21, 125, 136, 141, 201, 210, 211–13, 227, 280, 281
European Recovery Program, *see* Marshall Plan
Ewart, John Skirving, 128
Exovedate, 99
Expo '67, 236, 240, 242, 266
exports, 11–12, 210, 235, 251
External Affairs, Department of, 141
external relations, Canadian, 141, 161, 165, 189–90, 212, 220–21, 228, 237, 241, 250–51

Falaise Gap, 202
Fallon, Michael, 144
family allowance, 206–7, 217
Family Compact, 34–35, 36, 41, 47
Far East, 238
farmer-owned elevators, 138
farmers; and farming, 10–11, 12, 24, 58–59, 107, 147, 153–56, 173–74, 175, 176, 178–79, 187, 209–10, 279; and politics, 129, 137–38, 142, 160–61, 163, 241
Farrer, Edward, 110, 112
fascism, 190
Fathers of Confederation, 15, 78–79, 103
federalism, 51, 71–73, 74–75, 102–4, 205, 220, 241–42, 270–71, 282

286

federal-provincial relations, 169, 186–87, 195, 208, 220, 226, 236–37, 245, 255–56, 270–71
feminism, 134, 247–48, 271
Fenian Brotherhood, 77–78, 80, 86
Ferguson, Howard, 170
Fielding, William, 94, 104, 120, 125, 138, 161–62, 164
fighter aircraft, 229, 232
Finance, Department of, 143, 205, 278
finances, war, 146–47, 195
Finns, 190
fiscal arrangements, federal-provincial, 138, 195, 205, 220–21, 256, 270
Fisher, Douglas, 223
fisheries, 11–12, 52, 58, 59, 86, 141, 174, 247–48
Fitzgibbon, Col. James, 34, 37, 39
"five-cent piece" speech, 174, 175
flag, Canadian, 240–41, 272; Quebec, 216
Flavelle, Sir Joseph, 158, 160
Fleming, Donald, 225, 226
Fleming, Sir Sandford, 87, 93
Flin Flon, 168
Food Prices Review Board, 254
Ford Motor Co., 209
foreign aid, 220, 252
foreign exchange, 147, 196
foreign investment, 227, 237, 244, 251, 254, 279
Foreign Investment Review Agency, 260
Forget, Rodolphe, 139
Fort Churchill, 67
Fort Duquesne, 21
Fort Erie, 77
Fort Garry, 82–83
Fort McMurray, 269
Fort William, 66, 129
fortification loan, 1865, 76, 77
Foster, George Eulas, 143
France, 16–20, 21–22, 23, 141, 145, 149, 153, 155, 192–94, 241, 242; and New France, 19–22; Napoleonic wars, 24, 56
franchise, 35, 155
Francis I, 16
Franco, Francisco, 190
Fraser, Simon, 65, 67
Fréchette, Louis, 95
Fredericton, 55, 60, 97
free trade, 44–45, 89–90, 91
freight rates, 123–24, 166
French Canadians, 10, 14, 17, 21, 22–23, 24–27, 34, 42, 44–45, 50, 90, 95–96, 98,

127, 140, 162, 167, 171–72, 206, 216, 239–40; and 1837, 25–28; and Confederation, 72, 74–75, 83–84, 94, 100–3, 138–39, 144, 242–43, 245, 247, 258; and external relations, 125–26, 141–42, 148–49, 154, 189, 192, 198; national identity, 16, 103, 139, 171, 234–35, 275–76
French-English relations, 49, 79, 139, 144, 151, 241–44, 252–53, 267
French language, 25, 266, 267
Frobisher Bay, 224
Frog Lake reserve, 99
Front de Libération du Québec, 254–55
Frontenac, Louis de Buade, Count, 20
Frost, Leslie, 220, 224
fundamentalism, religious, 171, 271
fur trade, 6, 17, 19, 20–21, 22–23, 29–30, 34, 62–66

Galbraith, John Kenneth, 256, 264
Galt, Sir Alexander Tilloch, 46, 72, 74, 78, 97, 123
Ganong's Chocolates, 124
Gardiner, James, 182, 210
Garneau, François-Xavier, 42
Gavazzi riots, 49
General Motors, 187
Geneva, 189, 190
Gérin-Lajoie, Paul, 231
German-Canadians, 14, 122, 146, 150, 155–56
Germany, 141, 145, 149, 154, 157, 192–94, 199, 201–2, 203
"Ginger Group," 181
Gladstone, William, 86, 90
Globe, The, 9, 10, 47, 80, 83, 92, 95, 110, 112
Globe and Mail, The, 187
Goderich (Ont.), 36
gold, 119, 168; gold rushes, 68, 71, 84, 104, 119
"Good Neighbour" policy, 191
Goodman, Edwin, 239
Gordon, Arthur, 73, 76, 77
Gordon, Rev. C. W., 125
Gordon, Donald, 195
Gordon, Walter, 227–28, 235, 237, 239, 244, 251
Gosford, Lord, 27
Gothic Line, 202
Gouin, Sir Lomer, 154, 162, 164
Gourlay, Robert, 36
government, federal, 84, 85,

98–99, 109, 114–15, 155, 159, 169, 174, 177, 220, 230, 235–36, 240, 243, 254, 269
Grain Growers' Guide, 135, 137–38
Grains Act, 138
Grand Côteau, battle of, 69
Grand Portage, 64
Grand River, 30
Grand Trunk Pacific Railway, 129–30, 144, 146
Grand Trunk Railway, 10, 12, 48, 51, 78, 84, 85, 93, 97, 129, 155, 162–63
Grange, The, 107, 137
Grant, Cuthbert, 65–66
Gray, Herb, 251
Great Britain, 10, 22–23, 24–25, 35, 40, 53–54, 63–68, 67, 69, 149, 152, 197, 206, 228, 270; and Canada, 42, 46, 50, 74–79, 86, 96, 111, 124–25, 141, 143–44, 165, 189, 195–96, 221, 244, 276–77; and trade, 46, 113, 176, 207; and United States, 86, 119, 127–28; and Europe, 141, 147, 148, 192, 227
Great Depression, 168, 173–87, 192, 196, 204, 205; causes, 173–74; impact, 176–77
Great Lakes, 9, 17, 32, 52, 61, 67, 133
Great Plains, 61, 67
Great Slave Lake, 224
Great Western Railway, 12, 48
Greek Canadians, 139
Green, Howard, 229, 230, 232
Greenway, Thomas, 109, 120
Grits, 47, 69
Groseillers, Médart Chouart de, 20, 63
Grosse Ile, 43
Groulx, Lionel, 171, 172
Group of Seven, 172
Guelph (Ont.), 36, 160
Gwatkin, Sir Willoughby, 148

habitants, 18, 19, 23, 24; and rebellion, 27–29
Haldane, Lord, 169
Half-Breed Claims Commission, 100
Halibut Treaty, 165
Halifax, 12, 47, 53, 57, 59, 74, 86, 88, 128, 133, 168; explosion, 156; riot, 207
Halifax Chronicle, 76
Halifax Program, 140
Halifax Witness, 13
Hall, Emmett, 224
Hamburg, 122

Hamilton, (Ont.), 13, 31, 39, 94, 168
Hamilton, Alvin, 225
Hardie, Keir, 122
Harkness, Douglas, 232
Harvard University, 242, 248, 273
Harvey, Sir John, 59
Hatfield, Richard, 276
Haultain, Frederick, 138
Hays, Charles, 129
Head, Sir Edmund, 46, 72
Health and Welfare, Department of, 162, 205
health insurance, 207, 224–25, 226, 236–37, 256, 270
Hearne, Samuel, 65
Hellyer, Paul, 237, 244
Hémon, Louis, 140
Hepburn, Mitchell F., 182, 186–87, 193, 198, 214
Heritage funds, 261
Herridge, W. D., 183
High Commission, Canadian, 96, 126
Highlanders, 55, 65–66
highways, 168, 169, 220
Hill, J. J., 93
Hill, 70, 150
Hincks, Francis, 47, 48, 60
Hind, Cora, 135
Hind, Henry Youle, 69
Hiroshima, 211
history, Canadian, 6, 15, 29, 148–49, 221, 252–53, 282; and Indians, 61–62
Hitler, Adolf, 193, 194, 197, 210, 213
Hitler Line, 203
Hochwald Forest, 200
Hocken, Horatio, 137
Holland, 203
Holland, Samuel, 55
Home Rule, Irish, 96; see also Fenian Brotherhood
homesteading, 119, 121–23, 142
homosexuality, 247, 249
Honest John missiles, 229
Hong Kong, 196, 197
Hoodless, Adelaide, 134
Hoover, Herbert, 176, 183
Houde, Camillien, 178, 194, 214
housing, 209, 217, 263, 279
Howe, C. D., 185, 194, 208–9, 213, 215, 219, 222, 223; "Howe's Boys," 208
Howe, Joseph, 59, 60, 72, 76, 81, 82, 143
Howland, Oliver, 133
Hudson Bay, 63, 67, 143
Hudson River, 17, 45, 195
Hudson's Bay Company, 20–21, 48, 63–69, 81, 100

Hudson's Bay Railway, 165–66, 168
Hughes, James L., 134
Hughes, Sir Sam, 126, 143, 145–49, 150
Hull, (Que.), 160, 276
Hungarian uprising, 217
Hunters' Lodges, 42
Huron Indians, 17, 18
hydro-electricity, 119, 132–33, 215, 227, 236, 265

Iberville, Pierre le Moyne, 63
Ile Royale, 53; see also Cape Breton Island
Ilsley, J. L., 195
immigration, 19, 26–27, 35, 38, 43–44, 58, 61, 96–97, 121–23, 132, 139, 148, 217, 230, 266, 280; opposition to, 132, 135, 266
imperial conferences, 152, 156, 176
imperial defence, 125–26, 128
imperial federation, 124, 143–44, 157
Imperial Federation League, 108
Imperial Munitions Board, 147
imperial preference, 124, 168, 175
imperialism, 124, 128, 140–41, 142–44, 149, 165, 189
income, Canadian, 13, 172–74, 177, 179, 257, 270, 281–82
income tax, 156, 161, 226, 257, 263, 270
independence movement, Quebec, 6, 237, 243–44, 254, 267
Indian Act, 250
Indians, Canadian, 16, 17, 21, 23, 29, 61, 62–64, 84, 99–100, 148, 216, 238, 249, 265; claims, 96–97, 269, 277; policy, 96–97, 100–1, 250
Industrial Disputes Investigation Act, 136
industrial strategy, 226–27, 229, 251, 280
industrial unions, 209
Industrial Workers of the World, 137
industry, 12, 94, 176, 186, 194–95, 226–27, 280
Industry and Humanity, 158
inflation, 156, 160, 195, 261, 263–65, 269–70
influenza epidemic, 157, 162
Innis, Harold, 180, 181
Intercolonial Railway, 75, 78, 85, 87–89, 123–24, 129, 163

Interior, Department of the, 121, 140
International Brigade, 190
International Joint Commission, 236
International Monetary Fund, 210
international unions, 159–60
Inuit, 16, 61, 250
investment in Canada, 78, 162, 168, 194, 269–70; American, 168, 187, 215, 226
Iran, 260, 269
Irish-Canadians, 14, 35, 96, 127, 149; immigration of, 43–44, 45
Iroquois Indians, 17, 18, 30, 63
Irvine, William, 180–81
isolationism, Canadian, 190; American, 213
Israel, 221, 260
Italian Canadians, 139, 262
Italy, 190, 201–3

Jackson, Andrew, 27
James Bay, 63; development, 265
Japan, 190, 196, 197, 203, 207–8, 279
Japanese Canadians, 196
Jasper Park Lodge, 168
Jehovah's Witnesses, 186
Jerusalem, 273
Jervois, Col. W. F. D., 74, 86
Jesuit Order, 18, 45, 69; Estates issue, 108–9, 112; Rélations, 18, 69
Jewish Canadians, 14, 139, 190, 191
Johnson, Daniel, 29, 240–43, 245, 249
Johnson, James W., 72, 76
Johnson, Sir John, 30, 31
Johnson, Lyndon B., 238, 242
Johnson, Sir William, 62
Judicial Committee of the Privy Council, 103–4, 115, 169, 177, 221
"Just Society," 249, 257
Justice, Minister of, 114, 191, 245, 249, 274–75

Kansas, 11, 122
Kennedy, John F., 230, 232, 237–38, 250
Kenora, 240
Kentucky, 33, 126
Keynes, John Maynard, 173, 185–86, 189, 256; Keynesian economics, 195, 205, 220, 256, 269
Kilbourn, William, 39
Killam, Isaac Walton, 219
King, William Lyon Macken-

288

zie, 135, 136, 141, 143, 158, 164, 166, 167, 168, 174–76, 178–79, 184–85, 206, 233, 245, 249, 265; and external relations, 165, 189–90, 191–92, 210–11; and war, 191–95, 198–200, 202–3; contribution, 212–13
Kingston, 20, 31, 34, 36, 42, 45, 47, 91, 191
Kirke brothers, 18
Kirkland Lake, 168
Kitchener, 146, 154; see also Berlin
Klondike, 119, 121
Knights of Labor, 94–95
Knob Lake, 215
Kootenays, 113
Korean War, 213, 215, 221, 238
Kribs, Louis, 111
Ku Klux Klan, 170

Labelle, Curé Antoine, 102
labour, Canadian, 90, 135, 156, 161, 163, 166, 264, 265; organizations, 135–37, 146–47, 156, 158–60, 193, 216, 231, 240, 244, 261; and politics, 87, 106–7, 136–37, 160, 164–65, 182, 230, 265; and Quebec, 265; and women, 247
Labour, Department of, 135, 141, 173–74
Labour Gazette, 174
labour market, 135, 198–99, 228
Labour Party, British, 181
Labour Party, Independent, 163, 167, 170, 180–81
Labour Progressive Party, 205; see also Communists
Labrador, 16, 56, 62, 215
Lachine rapids, 45
Lacombe, Father Albert, 115
Laflèche, Bishop, 116
La Fontaine, Louis-Hippolyte, 28, 42–43, 45–46, 47; La Fontaine–Baldwin ministry, 43–45
Lake Athabaska, 64
Lake Erie, 32
Lake Huron, 12, 32
Lake Ontario, 20, 32
Lake St-Jean, 102
Lake Simcoe, 31
Lake Superior, 81, 98, 128
Lake Superior Consolidated Corporation, 130
Lake Winnipeg, 63, 66
Lalonde, Marc, 280; and National Energy Program, 278–79
La Macaza, 232

LaMarsh, Judy, 244
land claims, aboriginal, 250
land policy, 31–32, 35–36
Langevin, Sir Hector, 75, 97–98, 113–14
languages, 15, 25, 45, 139, 154, 225, 243–44, 252–53; conflict, 144, 266; laws, Bill 22, 266; Bill 101, 268; Official Languages Act, 252–53
Lapalme, Georges, 231
Lapointe, Ernest, 165, 190–91, 193, 198, 205, 241
Laporte, Pierre, 254–55
La Presse, 239
Laskin, Bora, 277
Laurendeau, André, 192, 198, 234–35
Laurier, Lady, 164
Laurier Palace fire, 171
Laurier, Sir Wilfrid, 90, 101, 109, 110, 115, 190, 242, 245, 247, 249, 252; in opposition, 109, 110–12, 113; as Prime Minister, 116, 120–21, 124–27, 128–31, 134, 138–39, 141–43; and First World War, 145, 153–55; character, 117, 120, 153, 163
Laval, Bishop François Montmorency de, 19
Lavallée, Calixte, 96
La Vérendrye, Pierre Gaultier de, 63
Lavergne, Armand, 139
La Vérité, 126
Leacock, Stephen, 158
leadership, political, 164, 175, 248–49, 267, 272
League for Social Reconstruction, 181
League of Nations, 161, 165, 189, 190; Convention, 162
Le Canadien, 145
Le Devoir, 141, 234, 243, 252, 256
Leduc (Alta.), 215
Lens, 150
Lesage, Jean, 231, 234, 236–37, 240, 243, 253
Lévesque, René, 231, 234, 236, 243, 254–55, 267–68, 277, 281
Lewis, David, 230, 258–59, 262
Liberal-Conservative Party, 47, 49; see also Conservative Party
Liberal Party (British), 90
Liberal Party of Canada, 76, 86–87, 88–91, 93–94, 109, 117, 120, 143, 144, 152, 163, 165, 182, 193–94, 204–5, 222, 230, 231, 264;

elections, 91, 113, 127, 140–41, 185, 193, 214–15, 222–23, 232–33, 261, 270, 272, 280; leaders, 164, 166–67, 213, 245, 267; policies, 92, 93, 115, 125, 137–38, 145–46, 179, 186, 206–7, 221–22, 229, 236, 239; and labour, 135–36, 258, 264–65; and Quebec, 90, 101–2, 139, 239–40, 243; and West, 115–16, 123, 257–58
Liberal Party of Ontario, 103–4, 130, 182
Liberal Party of Quebec, 149, 153, 186, 207, 231, 234–35, 253–54, 266–67
liberation, 242, 247–49, 252, 262, 271; and French Canada, 243
Lighthall, W. D., 133
Lightfoot, Gordon, 251
Lincoln, Abraham, 50
liquor, 104, 169, 209, 271
Lloyd, Bishop G. E., 170
Lloyd George, David, 152, 156–57, 161
loans to Britain, 196, 210
London (England), 27, 37, 47, 76–77, 79, 97, 103, 146, 165, 170, 172, 177
London (Ont.), 31, 144
London School of Economics, 242
Longley, J. W., 104, 111
Longueil, 24, 41
Loranger, Judge Thomas, 102–3
Lorne, Marquis of, 95–96
lotteries, 257, 271
Lougheed, Sir James, 135
Lougheed, Peter, 258, 264, 278–79
Louis XIV, 18, 19, 21
Louisbourg, 20–22, 53
Louise, Princess, 95
Lower Canada, 24–26, 41, 42, 43, 108
Loyalists, 24, 29, 20–22, 55–56, 61; late, 32, 35; in Maritimes, 54–55, 56
Lucan (Ont.), 11
Lundy's Lane, battle of, 34
Lunenburg, 9
Lynn Lake, 165, 215

McCarthy, D'Alton, 93, 108, 109, 117, 125
McCarthy, Joseph, 214
McClung, Nellie, 135
McCullagh, George, 187
McCulloch, Thomas, 59
Macdonald, Angus L., 187
Macdonald, Sir John A., 6, 40,

289

47–49, 50, 72–75, 79, 85–87, 88, 91–93, 96, 104, 107, 109, 111–13, 117, 120, 123–24, 169, 175–76, 224, 249; nation-building, 80–88, 91–93, 106; and the West, 81–84, 97, 101; contribution, 112, 114
Macdonald, John Sandfield, 51, 72–73, 80
MacDougall, William, 81–82
MacEachen, Allan, 273, 278
McGee, D'Arcy, 71, 75, 80
McGeer, Gerry, 178
McGill University, 15, 205, 253
Mackenzie, Alexander, 87, 117; as Prime Minister, 88, 91
Mackenzie, Sir Alexander, 64
Mackenzie, Ian, 206
Mackenzie-Papineau Battalion, 190
Mackenzie River, 65
Mackenzie Valley Pipe Line, 261, 269
Mackenzie, William, 119, 129, 130, 155
Mackenzie, William Lyon, 35–39, 40, 42, 43, 59, 72, 84, 135
McKinley, William, 111, 113, 120
Mackintosh, W. A., 205, 209
*Maclean's*, 251, 264
MacLennan, Hugh, 252–53
MacLuhan, Marshall, 248, 258
MacNab, Sir Allan, 39, 47, 48
McNaughton, Brig. Gen. A. G. L., 150, 194, 200–3, 236
Macpherson, Senator David, 85
McTague, Charles, 206
Madison, James, 57
magazine industry, 171, 238
Maine, 78, 98
Maisonneuve, Paul de Chomédy de, 17, 18
Manchuria, 190
"mandarins," Ottawa, 186, 206, 208, 227
Manicouagan dam, 236
Manion, Robert, 192, 193
Manitoba, 87, 88, 96, 100, 104, 106, 116, 117, 119, 133, 135, 138, 143, 153, 159, 160, 170, 198, 205, 215, 258, 274, 276; created, 83–84; grievances, 104–5; school issue, 109, 114–16, 120, 122
Manitoba Act, 109, 114
Manitoba *Free Press*, 129
Mann, Donald, 119, 129, 130, 155

manpower, 147–48, 198–99
Manpower, Minister of, 240
manufacturing, 12, 91, 94, 147, 160, 168, 177, 254; and Maritimes, 123–24
"March on Ottawa," 142
Marchand, Jean, 239, 240, 255, 256, 257, 267
*Maria Chapdelaine*, 140
Maritime Rights movement, 166
Maritimes, 9–10, 47–48, 52–60, 87, 94, 112, 125, 148, 154, 165, 225, 256, 279; Union, 73; economy, 123–24, 163
Marsh, Leonard, 205–6
Marshall Plan, 211–12
Martin, Méderic, 137
Martin, Paul, 244
Marx, Karl, 110, 248; marxism, 254, 258
Masaryk, Jan, 212
Massey, Daniel, 12
Massey, Vincent, 218, 220
Masson, Joseph, 44
*Matthew*, the, 52
media, communications, 172, 177, 245
Megantic County, 11
Meighen, Arthur, 144, 154–55, 159, 162–63, 164, 166, 167, 169, 175, 198
merchants, 23, 25, 46, 90
merchant shipping, 12, 94
Mercier, Honoré, 75, 101–3, 106, 108–9, 113, 186, 243
Merritt, William Hamilton, 36
Metcalfe, Sir Charles, 43
Methodism, 14, 30, 34, 45, 116, 134, 148–49, 171, 180; and recruiting, 148–49
Métis, 64–69, 81, 84, 96–97, 100–1, 105, 109, 216
Mexico, 67, 280
Michener, Roland, 248
Michilimackinac, 33
Micmac Indians, 53
Middle East, 273, 278
Middleton, Maj.-Gen. Fred, 99–100
militarism, 128, 165, 274
Military Hospitals Commission, 146
military policy, Canadian, 191, 200, 237, 281–82
Military Service Act, 153, 155
Military Voters' Act, 154
militia, Canadian, 30, 33, 39, 49, 50, 86, 119, 124, 136, 145; and Fenians, 77–78; and Northwest Campaign, 84, 99–100, 121; *see also* armed forces Militia and Defence, Department of, 143,

145–46; *see also* Department of National Defence
Minas Basin, 53
minimum wages, 184
mining, 123, 130, 168, 169, 187, 235, 279
Minnesota, 71, 122
Miramichi River, 53, 56
missionaries, 17–19, 20, 68–69
Mississippi River, 20, 21
Molson, William, 46
Moncton, 163
monetarism, 166, 186, 227, 270, 273, 279
Monk, Frederick, 144
monopoly, 132, 137, 183, 257
Monroe Doctrine, 191
Mons, 157
Montcalm, Marquis de, 22
Montgomery's Tavern, 37, 39
Montreal, 10, 12, 14, 17, 18, 22, 23, 27, 33, 40, 44, 45, 46, 49, 66, 71, 72, 75, 78, 80, 82, 83, 85, 87, 90, 94, 95, 98, 99, 102, 106, 126, 133, 137, 140, 142, 143, 162–63, 168, 171–72, 178, 186, 194, 217, 218, 240, 242, 253–55, 260, 266–67, 268, 271, 280; and Expo '67, 236
Moose River, 63
Morin, Claude, 267
Morrison, Donald, 11
Mosher, A. R., 181
Motherwell, W. R., 137
Mountain, Jacob, 24–25
Mountbatten, Earl, 201
*Mouvement souveraineté association*, 243
Mowat, Oliver, 75, 103–4, 107, 113, 116
Mulock, Sir William, 180
Munitions and Supply, Department of, 194
munitions production, 147, 160, 194
Murphy, Emily, 138
Murray, Anne, 251
Murray, Sir James, 22–23
Murray, Rear Admiral L. W., 200
Mussolini, Benito, 190, 194

Naskapi Indians, 62
National Council of Canadian Women, 134–35
national debt, 146–47, 169, 176, 195
National Defence, Department of, 178, 198, 221
National Employment Service, 169–70
National Energy Board, 225, 261

National Energy Program, 279, 280
National Government party, 193
National Housing Act, 209
National Policy, 91–105, 106, 107, 110, 120–21, 128, 140; New National Policy, 161
National Progressive party, 163
national registration, 151, 194
National Resources Mobilization Act, 194, 196, 198, 199, 203
"national schools," 122, 253
National Selective Service, 198–99
National Transcontinental Railway, 129, 130, 143
national unity, 125, 169, 193, 235, 252, 253, 256, 268, 282
National War Labour Board, 206
nationalism, Canadian, 14–15, 108–9, 128, 149, 153, 165, 170–71, 172, 242; economic, 227, 228, 235, 250–51; French-Canadian, 19, 171, 216, 236–37, 243–45, 252
nationalistes, 137, 139–43, 149, 153, 165, 171, 192
native people, 269, 277; see also Indians and Inuit
natural gas, 215, 222
natural resources, 226–27, 258, 260, 268; provincial control of, 169, 175
naval policy, 56, 141–42, 144
Naval Service Act, 141–42
Nazis, 190, 198
Nelson, Robert, 26
Nelson, Wolfred, 26, 28
Netherlands, 17, 20, 63, 203
New Brunswick, 9, 44, 54–55, 60–61, 80, 104, 123–24, 133, 175, 276; and Confederation, 73, 76–78; and school issue, 85–86
New Deal, 183, 191
New Democratic Party, 230–32, 233–34, 239, 241, 244–45, 251, 258–59, 260–62, 268, 269, 272, 273–74, 276–77; and Quebec, 234, 239, 252; and labour, 264–65
New England, 10, 16, 29, 53, 57, 64, 94, 96
Newfoundland, 16, 22, 29, 52, 56–59, 141, 179, 215, 226, 248–49, 261, 273, 276; and Confederation, 74, 76, 81, 111, 214
New France, 16–19, 21, 103;

government, 19–20; fall of, 21–22, 29
New Orleans, 24, 34, 130
New Party movement, 230
New Westminster, 68, 106
New York, city, 54, 55, 110, 146, 172, 268; state, 30, 110
New Zealand, 175, 190, 100
Niagara escarpment, 30; Niagara Falls, 41, 119, 132; peninsula, 45; River, 33; town, 48
"Ninety-Two Resolutions," 27
Nixon, Richard M., 251, 252, 264
Nobel Peace Prize, 221, 223
Nootka Sound, 67
Noranda, 168
Norfolk (Ont.), 34
Norman Wells, 197
Normandy, 200, 201
Norquay, John, 104–6, 109
North, the, 168–69, 216, 250
North American Air Defence Command, 229, 232
North Atlantic Treaty Organization, 212, 213, 220, 229, 250
North Bay, 232
Northern Railway, 12, 48
Northern Pacific Railroad, 93
North Saskatchewan River, 69
North Sea, 280
North Shore Railway, 98
Northwest Campaign, 1885, 98–102
North West Company, 64–66
North West Mounted Police, 85, 96, 97, 98, 99, 100, 121, 122; see also Royal Northwest Mounted Police and Royal Canadian Mounted Police
Northwest Territories, 84–5, 92, 96–102, 137–39, 215, 250, 269
Norway, 193, 194
Nova Scotia, 9, 53–54, 56, 58, 59–61, 72, 80, 88, 97, 104, 111, 123–24, 131, 167, 170, 187, 195, 236, 244–45, 261; and Confederation, 73, 75–78, 83, 104
Nova Scotian Hotel, 168
nuclear research, 215, 248; weapons, 211, 221, 228–29, 232–33, 237, 239, 281–82

Ô Canada, 96
October Crisis, 254–55
Ogdensburg agreement, 194, 211
Ohio River, 20–21, 62
oil industry, 215, 260–61, 263, 269, 278–79, 280; prices,

225, 227, 261, 263, 268–69, 274, 278
O'Leary, Grattan, 225;
O'Leary Report, 238
oligarchies, 36, 58–59
Olympic Games, 266–67
Onderdonk, Andrew, 93, 106
One Big Union, 159–60
Ontario, 9, 10, 11, 14, 80, 85, 91, 94, 103–4, 107, 109, 110, 115, 116, 122, 125, 130, 143, 144, 149, 164, 167, 170, 182, 186, 204, 214, 215, 217, 220, 222, 225, 236, 245, 256, 258, 260, 262, 268, 274, 276; and war, 153–55, 198; boundaries, 104, 143; politics, 83, 87, 101–2, 103, 127, 163, 165, 166, 187, 203–4, 207, 270; school system, 86, 138, 171
"On-to-Ottawa Trek," 184
Opportunities for Youth, 248
Option Québec, 243
Orange Lodge, 14, 38, 49, 83, 90, 100–1, 114, 137, 143
Oregon, 45, 67, 68
Organization of Petroleum Exporting Countries, 260, 263, 264, 269, 280
Oshawa, 168, 187
Ottawa, 9, 80, 82, 92, 115, 126, 157, 164, 181, 186, 239, 245, 277; choice as capital, 49; see also government, federal
Ottawa River, 125, 227
Otter, Sir William, 126
Overseas Military Forces of Canada, Ministry of, 150
Owen Sound, 134

Pacific Ocean, 9, 45, 62, 65
Pacific Scandal, 87–88, 131
Padlock Law, 186
Palliser, John, 69
Palliser Triangle, 93, 142, 144
Papineau, Louis-Joseph, 25–28, 37–39, 40, 42, 46, 84, 126, 140, 243
Parent, Etienne, 42
Paris, 108, 113, 172; Exposition, 12
Pariseau, Jacques, 267
Parker, Sir Gilbert, 125
Parliament, British, 78
Parliament, United Canadas, 42–43, 45–46; Canadian, 109, 113, 126–27, 161–62, 167, 171, 174, 177, 182, 192, 203, 222, 224–25, 249, 264–65
Parr, John, 54
Parti National, 103–4

*Parti Québécois*, 254, 261, 265–68, 275
Partridge, E. A., 135, 137–38
patriation, 276–77
*patriotes*, 26-27, 28, 37, 42, 43, 46, 47
patronage, political, 43, 60, 113, 120, 143, 162, 226, 231
Patrons of Industry, 107, 117, 137
Pattullo, T. Duff, 182, 186, 187
Payette, Lise, 275
Payne-Aldrich Tariff, 142
Peace Corps, 238
Peace River, 179, 236
peacekeeping operations, 228, 237
Pearkes, Maj.-Gen. George, 203, 225, 232
Pearson Formula, 240, 244
Pearson, Lester B., 212, 221, 223, 230, 231, 244, 245, 249, 250, 274; in opposition, 232–33; as Prime Minister, 234–39, 241, 243–45
Peckford, Brian, 281
Pelletier, Gerard, 239, 255
pemmican, 61
Pensions, Minister of, 206
pensions, old-age, 170, 222, 225, 236–37, 263; veterans, 158, 206
Pepin, Jean-Luc, 268
Pepin-Robarts task force, 276
Permanent Joint Board of Defence, 194
"persons" case, 169
Peto, Brassey, Jackson & Betts, 48
Petro Canada, 260–61, 269, 273
Philadelphia, 95, 238
Philippines, 124
Pickersgill, J. W., 206
Pictou, 94; Academy, 59
Pigeon Hill, battle of, 77
Pine Point, 215, 224
pipeline, 215–16, 260; debate, 222
Pitfield, Michael, 263, 273
Plains of Abraham, 20, 22, 108
police, 11, 29, 184, 186, 216, 243, 253–55
Polish Canadians, 122
politics, Canadian, 30–31, 39, 88, 112–13, 174–75, 196, 219, 258–59, 263, 282
polls, opinion, 204, 221, 223, 237, 245, 267, 268, 271
Polymer Corporation, 208
Pond, Peter, 64
Pope, 108–9
Portage la Prairie, 167
Port Arthur, 83, 129, 223

Port Hope, 208
Portland, Maine, 10, 48, 129
post-secondary education, 236, 270
potash, 25
poverty, Canadian, 134, 173, 181, 206, 216, 235–36, 281
prairies, 147, 179, 225, 232–33
Presbyterians, 14, 171
Prévost, Sir George, 25
prices, 177, 183, 184, 195, 225; price-fixing, 184, 257
Prince Albert (Sask.), 98, 166, 207
Prince Edward Island, 53, 54–55, 57, 65; and Confederation, 73, 74, 76, 81
Prince Rupert (B.C.), 129
profiteering, 158, 162
Progressive Conservatives, 204–6, 214–15, 219, 221, 222–23, 227, 232–33, 235–36, 239, 245, 252, 258–59, 261–62; and civil service, 240; Ontario, 236–37; and leaders, 225, 232–33, 244, 267–68, 272–74; and business, 257; and power, 222–26, 272–74, 281; *see also* Conservatives Progressive Party, 165–67
prohibition, 134, 153, 154, 155, 170; in United States, 167, 171
prosperity, 96, 133, 174, 186, 196, 209, 214, 216, 217, 220, 276–77
Protestant Protective Association, 115–16
Protestants 14, 22, 47, 52, 83, 100–2, 108–9, 116, 138; and Church Union, 171
provincial responsibilities, 169, 170, 174, 186–87, 220, 236
public ownership, 140, 155, 236–37, 240
Public Service Staff Relations Act, 240
public works, 11, 35, 38, 43
Public Works, Department of, 98, 113, 120
puritanism, 217–18, 271

Quebec Act, 23, 29, 75
Quebec City, 12, 22, 23, 28, 29, 49, 53, 74, 76, 80, 90, 98, 102, 104, 129–30, 145, 148, 200, 205, 231, 237, 240, 255; riots in, 155, 162
Quebec Conference, 74–75, 76
Quebec Pension Plan, 237

Quebec, province, 6, 9, 10–11, 30–31, 44, 80, 86, 94, 104, 110–12, 115, 116, 133, 134, 137, 139, 142–43, 145, 148, 154, 171–72, 184, 186, 214, 217, 222, 225, 226, 231, 234, 236, 240, 253, 256, 272, 277; boundaries, 143; and women, 153, 169; and flag, 169; as a colony, 22–24; and politics, 103, 113, 117, 140, 142–43, 167, 207, 224, 230, 231, 234, 239, 254, 261, 271, 281; and economy, 129–30, 160, 168, 265; and Canada, 101–2, 107, 116, 130, 138, 142–43, 151, 164, 175–76, 189–90, 193–94, 198, 212, 221, 233, 234, 235, 239, 241, 242–44, 245, 249, 253, 276–77
Quebec Resolutions, 78
*Queen Victoria*, S.S., 74
Queenston Heights, battle of, 33
Queen's University, 191
Quiet Revolution, 204, 231

racial prejudice, 106, 148, 170–71, 196, 217
radicalism, 94–95, 156, 159, 171, 180, 247–48, 254
radio, 176–77, 181, 183, 204, 218, 223; influence of, 171–72, 185
Radisson, Pierre, 20, 63
railways, 10, 12, 45, 47–48, 60, 71, 78, 81, 87–89, 122–23, 128–30, 137, 144, 155, 162–63, 165, 169, 179, 215–16, 224, 262
Railways, Minister of, 130
Ralston, J. L., 198, 199, 201–2
Rand Formula, 208, 209
Rasminsky, Louis, 210
Rat Portage, 104
rationing, 196, 209
*Readers' Digest*, 238
Reagan, Ronald, 242, 270, 279
rearmament, 191, 212–13, 215, 220
Rebellion Losses Bill, 46
Rebellions of 1837, 27–28, 44, 59
recessions, 223, 226–28, 234, 279–81
Reciprocity Agreement, 1854, 46, 60, 71, 77, 89, 110; 1911, 142–43; 1935, 185, 191
Reconstruction, Department of, 208
Reconstruction Party, 184–85
recruiting, First World War,

146–49, 151; Second World War, 192, 199
Red Army, 205
Red Cross, Canadian, 146
Redpath, Joseph, 46
Red River colony, 65–66, 68–69, 71, 85, 86, 109; conflict, 81–84
re-establishment bonus, 158
referenda, on prohibition, 1898, 134; Quebec, 1980, 275, 277
Reform Bill, 1830, 37
reform, Canadian, 133, 158, 184, 204–6, 240–41, 257
Reformers, Upper Canadian, 37, 38, 39, 43, 50, 72, 80; United Provinces, 58–59; Nova Scotia, 59–60; Canadian, 72, 80, 103
refugees, 190–91, 210
Regina, 98, 100, 101, 182, 184; manifesto, 182
Regional Economic Expansion, Department of, 256
regionalism, 52–53, 165, 273, 275
Regulation 17, 144, 149
relief, 174, 176, 178, 184
religion, 14, 17–18, 45, 49, 78, 181, 271; conflict, 57, 76, 90, 97, 108, 114–16
"Rep by Pop," 49, 72, 76
reserves, Indian, 62, 84–85, 96–97
responsible government, 41, 42, 45, 59–60
revenue, federal, 195, 263
Richelieu River, 28, 47
Richler, Mordecai, 242
Riddell, W. A., 190
Rideau Canal, 43
Riel, Louis, 82–84, 85, 88, 107, 108, 111–12, 128, 171, 186; and 1885 rebellion, 98–101, 103
riots, 40, 46, 135, 207, 242, 253, 265, 276
Robarts, John, 236–37, 245, 268
Robinson, John Beverley, 34, 37
Roblin, Sir Rodmond, 135
Rocky Mountains, 10, 61, 84, 96, 123, 168
Rolland, J. D., 139
Rolph, Dr. John, 38
Romanow, Roy, 276–77
Rome, 108, 113
Roosevelt, Franklin Delano, 183, 186, 191, 194, 195, 200, 207, 230
Roosevelt, Theodore, 127–28
Ross, J. G., 29
Ross rifle, 145, 150

rouges, 46, 47, 48, 49, 50, 80, 85, 86, 100, 102, 103, 120
Rowell, Newton W., 153
Rowell-Sirois Report, 195, 205
Royal Air Force, 150, 197
Royal Canadian Air Force, 169, 191; and Second World War, 197, 199, 200
Royal Canadian Legion, 235
Royal Canadian Mounted Police, 180, 184, 196, 226, 255, 271
Royal Canadian Navy, 141–42, 151, 191; and Second World War, 197, 199–200
Royal Commissions: on Arts and Letters, 218; on Bilingualism and Biculturalism, 234, 244; on Broadcasting, 175–76; on Capital and Labour, 107; on Labour Relations, 162; on Status of Women, 244
Royal Institution, 25
Royal Engineers, 68
Royal Military College of Canada, 88
Royal Navy, 53, 56, 68, 141, 151
Royal Northwest Mounted Police, 180; see also North-West Mounted Police and Royal Canadian Mounted Police
Royal Society of Canada, 95
royal visits, 192, 242
"rummies," 59
Ruperts Land, 63, 65, 81
ruralism, 13, 137, 140, 166, 231, 241
Russell, Bob, 159
Russia, 67, 141, 145, 147, 152, 155, 157, 210–11, 190; see also Union of Soviet Socialist Republics
Ryan, Claude, 243, 254–56, 275–76
Ryerson, Egerton, 11, 45

Saguenay, Kingdom of the, 16
Saguenay River, 102
St. Alban's raid, 71
St. Catharines, 168
St. Croix River, 53
St. Dénis, 27–28
St. Eloi, battle of, 150
St. Eustache, 28
Saint-Jean Baptiste day, 253; Society, 243
Saint John (N.B.), 12, 14, 55, 56, 57, 59, 60, 74, 98; fire in, 90
St. John River, 53–55
St. John's (Nfld.), 52, 56, 57, 76, 214, 215

St. Laurent, Louis, 205, 212–13; as Prime Minister, 213–14, 218–19, 221–23, 224, 226, 230, 244–45
St. Lawrence River, 9, 10, 17, 19, 22, 26, 43, 52, 162, 240
St. Lawrence Seaway, 176, 215, 240
St. Mâlo, 16
St. Paul (Minn.), 69, 93
St. Pierre and Miquelon, 54
Salaberry, Col. Charles de, 34
Sandwich (Ont.), 34
San Francisco, 84, 210
San Juan Island, 67
Sapiro, Aaron, 173
Sarnia, 9, 10, 48, 88, 208
Saskatchewan, 138, 163, 166, 170, 179, 182, 204, 222, 230, 236, 258, 260, 276; creation of, 139
Saskatoon, 123
Sault Ste. Marie, 130
Saunders, Charles, 122
Sauvé, Paul, 231
Sayer, Guillaume, 69
scandals, political, 113, 140, 167
Scarborough (Ont.), 232
Scheldt estuary, battle for, 203
Schreyer, Edward, 258, 276
Scottish Canadians, 35, 64
Scugog, 94
Seafarers' International Union, 258
Secord, Laura, 34, 39
Section 98, 180
seigneurial system, 18–19, 20, 23, 24, 26, 27
Selkirk, Lord, 57, 65–66; Selkirk settlers, 65–66, 69
Selkirk Range, 93
Senate, Canadian, 75, 120, 144, 167, 276; American, 176
separatism, Quebec, 111, 242–43, 245, 247, 258; western, 281
Serbia, 145
settlers, 22, 66, 121–23; see also immigration
Seven Oaks, battle of, 66
Seward, W. H., 50
Shaughnessy, Lord, 162
Shawnee Indians, 33
Shelburne (N.S.), 54
Shell Committee, 147
shipbuilding, 56–57, 59, 147, 194
shipping, 43–44, 57–58, 89–90, 94, 168
Sicily, 201
Sifton, Sir Clifford, 115, 117, 120–22, 133, 138, 142, 170, 217, 253

Simcoe, John Graves, 31–32, 35
Simpson, Sir George, 66–67
Sinclair, Gordon, 177
Singapore, 197
Skelton, O. D., 165, 189
Skookum Jim, 119
slavery issue, 50, 72
Smallwood, Joseph, 214, 261
Smith, Adam, 44
Smith, Albert J., 76–78
Smith, Donald A. (Lord Strathcona), 82, 83, 88, 93, 106, 126
Smith, Goldwin, 110
Smith, Ralph, 136
Smith, William, 30–31, 72
Smythe, Conn, 202
Social Credit, 166, 180–81, 182, 184–85, 194, 207, 215, 223–24, 231, 239, 258; see also Créditistes
socialism, 136, 137, 140, 163, 181, 182, 207
Socialist Party of Canada, 136
social welfare, 11, 178, 205, 249
soldier voters, 155, 207
Sorbonne, 242
Soulanges rapids, 45
South Africa, 119, 125–27, 128, 228
South Saskatchewan River, 96, 99; dam, 224
sovereignty-association, 243, 275
Spain, 21, 67, 190
Speed River, 30
sports, 172, 177, 271, 280
Stalin, J. V., 181, 210, 211
Stanfield, Robert, 244–45, 252, 258, 261–63, 264, 267, 273
starvation, 52, 57, 178–79
Statute of Westminster, 170, 175, 176, 189
Steel Company of Canada, 133
steel industry, 163, 209
Stevens, H. H., 167, 183, 184, 185
Stoney Creek, battle of, 34
Stowe, Emily, 95, 135
Stowe-Gullen, Amelia, 135
Strachan, Archdeacon John, 34, 36, 45
Straits of San Juan de Fuca, 67
Stratford Festival, 218
Strathcona, Lord, see Smith, Donald A.
strikes, 136, 163, 178, 180, 187, 206, 209, 226, 240, 261
submarines, 151, 152, 156, 194. 199
Sudan crisis, 124
Sudbury, 106, 168

Suez Affair, 221, 227–28
suffrage, women's, 135, 153
Sullivan mine, 123
Superior, Wisconsin, 215
Sutton, John Manners, 73
Sweden, 33
Switzerland, 33, 66, 282
Sydenham, Lord, 43
Syncrude, 269

Taché, Sir Etienne-Pascal, 73
Taft, William, 142
Tagish Charlie, 119
Talon, Jean, 19, 20, 24
tar sands, 261, 269, 280
Tardivel, Jules-Paul, 126, 140
tariffs, 90–91, 106, 117, 121, 124, 135, 137, 142, 143, 165, 175, 176, 179, 184, 228, 254
Tarte, J. Israel, 101, 113, 116, 120, 126
Taschereau, Alexandre, 170, 265
Taschereau, Archbishop Elzear, 90
taxes, 31, 74, 208–9, 225, 257, 259, 278; rental agreements, 208, 226; reform, 257, 259, 278–79
Taylor, E. P., 195–96
technology, 208, 269, 281–82
Tecumseh, 32–34
Tel Aviv, 273
television, 215, 218, 223, 245, 276
Temiskaming and Northern Ontario Railway, 130
temperance, 134
Territorial Grain Growers Association, 129, 137
terrorism, 247, 254–55
Thatcher, Margaret, 270
Thatcher, Ross, 258
Théâtre du Nouveau Monde, 218
Thirteen Colonies, 10, 21, 23, 53
Thom, Adam, 27
Thompson, David, 65, 67
Thompson, Sir John, 94, 97, 114–15
Thornton, Sir Henry, 168
Ticonderoga, 22
Tilley, Sir Leonard, 59, 73, 76–78, 80, 92, 97
timber industry, 24, 44–45, 46, 56–57, 89–90, 146, 174
Time, 238, 251
Tories, 37–38, 44, 47, 137; see also Conservatives
Toronto, 9, 12, 13, 14, 37, 38, 43, 45, 49, 75, 85, 94, 95, 97, 101, 107, 110, 131, 132–33, 135, 137, 142, 145,

151, 163, 181, 198, 226, 227, 236, 271, 280
Trade and Commerce, Minister of, 183
Trades and Labour Congress, 136, 137, 151, 159, 160, 181–82, 193
Trail (B.C.), 123
Trans-Canada Airlines, 185, 208
Trans-Canada Highway, 215
transcontinental railway, 84, 85, 87–89, 92–93
treaties, Indian, 62, 84–85, 168, 241
Treaty of Utrecht, 53
Treaty of Versailles, 189–90
Treaty of Washington, 86
Tremblay, Arthur, 273
Trois-Rivières, 20
Trudeau, Margaret, 212, 268
Trudeau, Pierre Elliott, 198, 216, 239, 241, 245, 248–49, 253, 255, 257, 258, 259, 260–63, 268, 273; background, 240–41, 245–46, 249, 267, 272; and economy, 264–65, 280; foreign policy, 250, 275; and West, 257, 260–61; and Quebec, 241–42, 252, 254–55, 259, 268, 275; and federalism, 241–43, 255–56, 276–77; Trudeaumania, 251
Tupper, Sir Charles, 76, 78, 80, 94, 97, 115, 120, 127, 130; as Prime Minister, 116–17
Turner, John, 263, 264, 274
Turner Valley, 215
two-party system, 164–65, 167, 184–85

Ukrainian Canadians, 139, 190
Underground Railroad, 50
unemployment, 89–90, 144, 149, 158, 174, 176, 185, 192, 199, 204, 228, 259, 263, 269, 279; statistics, 11, 13, 177
unemployment insurance, 177, 184, 205, 256–57, 259
Uniacke, James, 60
unilateral disarmament, 282
Unionist government, 153–58
unions, labour, 57, 133, 135–37, 140, 156, 177, 186, 205–6, 217, 228, 256, 264; membership, 136, 158–59
Union Métisse de St-Joseph, 99
Union Nationale, 186, 207, 224, 231, 234, 240–41, 253, 254, 266
Union of Soviet Socialist Republics, 174, 197, 205, 210,

211–12, 213, 235, 278, 279; and wheat, 279
United Church of Canada, 171, 180, 218
United Farmers of Ontario, 163, 166
United Grain Growers, 161
United Nations, 210, 212, 213
United Provinces of the Canadas, 41, 44–45, 72–73; government, 46–47, 51
United States, 26, 27, 32, 39, 44, 46, 55, 67–68, 136, 152, 161, 162, 174, 185–86, 191, 196–97, 207–11, 213, 221, 228, 232, 235, 243; and Canada, 50, 71, 84, 94, 99–100, 110–12, 119, 147, 172, 176, 194, 211, 215, 218, 242–43, 247–48, 251, 271, 278–79, 282; immigration from, 217
universities, 147, 217, 218, 219, 236–37, 248, 256, 281; grants to, 228
University of Montreal, 171
University of Ottawa, 144
University of Toronto, 69, 180, 182, 248
unrestricted reciprocity, 110, 115
Upper Canada, 24–26, 29, 31, 35, 37, 41, 59, 65, 123, 135; rebellion in, 35–39
uranium, 215
urbanization, 95, 172, 178, 217, 220

Valcartier, 146
Valleyfield, 94
Vancouver, 106, 123, 136, 159, 178, 217
Vancouver, George, 67
Vancouver Island, 67–68
"Vandoos" (Royal Twenty-second Regiment), 149
Van Horne, William, 93, 111, 142
Vanier, Georges, 241
Vaudreuil, Pierre de Rigaud de, 22
Verchères, Madeleine de, 17
Vermont, 28, 71, 78
Verville, Alphonse, 137
veterans, 146, 161, 163, 169; and bonus, 158; post-1945 benefits, 209
Victoria, 68, 106, 150, 217, 256
Victoria Bridge, 10, 12
Victoria Charter, 256, 276
Victoria *Colonist*, 84
Victoria, Queen, 40, 95, 115, 124
Victory Bonds, 227; Loans, 146

Vietnam War, 238, 242, 250–51, 259
"Vieux Brûlot," 28, 46
Vikings, 16
Vimy Ridge, battle of, 150–52
Voltaire, François Arouet, 22
*Voltigeurs*, 34
*voyageurs*, 19, 64

wages, 13, 15, 177, 196, 263; and controls, 261–62, 264
Wagner, Claude, 253, 268
Walker, Sir Edmund, 142
Wall Street crash, 173
*Wall Street Journal*, 250
Wallace, N. Clarke, 114, 115, 117
War, French–Indian, 17–19; French–English, 20–22; with Americans, 23–24, 25–26, 33–35, 119; First World War, 145–57, 191, 195, 197; Second World War, 187, 189–203, 209; Korean, 213, 215, 221, 238
War of 1812, 25–26, 33–35, 43, 50, 57, 67, 73
Wartime Elections Act, 154
Wartime Labour Relations Order, 206
Wartime Prices and Trade Board, 193, 195, 264
Washington, 71, 77, 89, 157, 165, 183, 185, 196, 197, 210, 211, 212–13, 221, 225, 230, 234, 237, 257, 268
Washington, George, 21
Waterloo, battle of, 34
Watkins, Melville, 244, 251
Welland Canal, 36
West, Canadian, 81–85, 96, 128–29, 135, 153, 159–61, 178–79, 253, 280; grievance, 137–39, 245, 257, 260–61, 278; politics, 164–66, 224, 225, 232–33, 239, 259
Western Federation of Miners, 137
Western Labour Conference, 1919, 159; 1932, 181
West Indies, 56, 168; immigrants from, 281
Westminster Palace Hotel Conference, 78
Westmount, 133
Whalen, Eugene, 259
wheat, 11, 24, 25, 26, 30, 36. 44–45, 46, 56, 89, 96, 106, 119, 121–23, 128–29, 137–38, 142, 147, 160–61, 165, 173–75, 176, 178–79, 209–10, 225, 228, 235, 257, 279
Wheat Board, 160, 161, 173,

225, 235, 257
Wheat Pool, 173–74, 176
Whigs (British), 27, 37, 40, 44
Whitehorse, 197
White, Sir Thomas, 143, 146–47, 156, 161, 164
Whitney, Sir James, 144
Wilson, Woodrow, 161
Wiman, Erastus, 110
Windsor, 48, 168, 209
Winnipeg, 89, 93, 96, 129, 133, 135, 148, 164, 175; general strike, 159–60
Winnipeg *Free Press*, 111, 145, 180, 191
Winnipeg Grain Exchange, 137–38, 160, 173
Winters, Robert, 244
Wisconsin, 215
Wolfe, James, 22, 29
Wolseley expedition, 83
women, 13, 95, 111, 134–35, 178, 247–48; and work, 135, 146, 196, 198, 217, 247; and politics, 95, 134, 153–55, 275, 277
Women's Christian Temperance Union, 134
Women's Institutes, 134
Wood, Henry Wise, 166, 265
Woodsworth, J. S., 164–65, 170, 177, 180–81, 185, 196; and CCF, 181–82, 183
work camps, 178
workers, 13, 57, 90, 106–7, 173, 209, 270
Workers Unity League, 160, 178
World Bank, 210
World Wars, First, 145–57, 191, 195, 197; finance in, 146–47; production in, 147; and French Canada, 147–49; manpower in, 146–49, 151–56; consequences of, 150–57; Second, 187, 189–203, 209; production during, 194–95; and United States, 196–97; manpower in, 192–93, 197–98, 201–3; active service in, 199–203; impact of, 204–7

XY Company, 64

Yellowhead Pass, 93
Yonge Street, 31
York, 31, 36, 38; *see also* Toronto
York South, 262
youth, 247, 248, 250, 272
Ypres, battle of, 149–50
Yukon, 119, 121, 128, 273

"zombies," 199, 203